THE EMERGENCE OF WORD-MEANING IN EARLY CHINA

SUNY series in Chinese Philosophy and Culture

Roger T. Ames, editor

THE EMERGENCE OF WORD-MEANING IN EARLY CHINA

NORMATIVE MODELS FOR WORDS

JANE GEANEY

SUNY PRESS

Credit: Qiu Ying 仇英 (Chinese, 1494–1552), Zhao Mengfu Writing the Heart (Hridaya) Sutra in Exchange for Tea (1542–43). Detail. Handscroll, ink and light color on paper. Cleveland Museum of Art, John L. Severance Fund 1963.102.

Published by State University of New York Press, Albany

© 2022 State University of New York

All rights reserved

No part of this book may be used or reproduced in any manner whatsoever without written permission. No part of this book may be stored in a retrieval system or transmitted in any form or by any means including electronic, electrostatic, magnetic tape, mechanical, photocopying, recording, or otherwise without the prior permission in writing of the publisher.

For information, contact State University of New York Press, Albany, NY
www.sunypress.edu

Library of Congress Cataloging-in-Publication Data

Names: Geaney, Jane, author.
Title: The emergence of word-meaning in early China : normative models for words / Jane Geaney.
Description: Albany : State University of New York Press, [2022] | Series: SUNY series in Chinese philosophy and culture | Includes bibliographical references and index.
Identifiers: LCCN 2022003485 (print) | LCCN 2022003486 (ebook) | ISBN 9781438488936 (hardcover : alk. paper) | ISBN 9781438488950 (ebook) | ISBN 9781438488943 (pbk. : alk. paper)
Subjects: LCSH: Chinese language—Semantics, Historical.
Classification: LCC PL1291 .G43 2022 (print) | LCC PL1291 (ebook) | DDC 495.12—dc23/eng/20220202
LC record available at https://lccn.loc.gov/2022003485
LC ebook record available at https://lccn.loc.gov/2022003486

10 9 8 7 6 5 4 3 2 1

Contents

Acknowledgments		vii
Introduction: General Context		1

Part One
Key Metalinguistic Terms and Yi 義 as External

Chapter 1	The Metalinguistic Implications of Words versus Names	21
Chapter 2	Speech (*Yan* 言) from Within and Names (*Ming* 名) from Without	33
Chapter 3	*Yi* 意 and the Heartmind's Activities	47
Chapter 4	The Externality of *Yi* 義	69
Chapter 5	The Resilience of the Externality of *Yi* 義	83

Part Two
Yi 義 as Model

Chapter 6	*Yi* 義 as Model: Stable, Accessible Standards	105
Chapter 7	*Yi* 義 as Model in Diagrams, Genres, Figurative Language, and Names	121
Chapter 8	A Framework Preceding the *Shuowen*'s Metalinguistic Choices	137
Chapter 9	*Yi* 義 Justifying with Models	161
Chapter 10	*Yi* 義 in the *Shuowen Jiezi*	181

Conclusion		195
Appendix A	Why Translate *Yi* 義 as "Model"?	199
Appendix B	*Yi* 義's Externality in Dispute: The *Mengzi* and the *Mo Bian*	207
Appendix C	Glossary of Terms with Aural or Visual Associations	219
Bibliography		243
Index		267

Acknowledgments

I wish to express my gratitude to the staff at SUNY Press, who guided me through many years and stages in completing this companion volume to *Language as Bodily Practice: A Chinese Grammatology* (SUNY 2018): the late Nancy Ellegate, Christopher Ahn, Chelsea Miller, Andrew Kenyon, James Peltz, Ryan Morris, Eileen Nizer, Brian Kuhl, and Michael Campochiaro.

A National Endowment for the Humanities Summer Fellowship in 2012 helped me begin the project. The University of Richmond consistently provided summer research support, and in 2019, Patrice Rankine, Dean of the School of Arts & Sciences at the University of Richmond, granted funding for preparation of the manuscript for publication.

I am deeply thankful to Lynn Rhoads for providing insightful commentary along with her excellent editing style. Her observations frequently prompted me to rethink and improve my ideas. I am delighted that Pierke Bosschieter has agreed to undertake the task of indexing the book.

Many friends and colleagues offered critical comments and useful suggestions that inspired me. Special thanks go to Alan Chan, who most graciously shared his expertise by contributing to the quality of my translations. I am indebted to Dan Robins and Jessica Chan for supplying crucial early reactions.

I am grateful for conversations with colleagues at several academic conferences. I benefitted from feedback at a graduate workshop organized by Martin Kern, Mercedes Valmisa, and Sara Vantournhout at Princeton University in 2014. At the invitation of Wolfgang Behr, Polina Lukicheva, and Rafael Suter, I was able to hone my arguments at the University of Zurich in 2016. I am thankful for reactions from colleagues at a conference organized by Shengqing Wu and Huang Xuelei at the University of Edinburg in 2018. I especially appreciate the generous comments from Wolfgang Berh and support from Carine Defoort. Early in the writing process, suggestions from Michael Nylan helped set me on the right track. At a workshop in the Department of Religious Studies at the University of Richmond, I received valuable responses from my colleagues: Stephanie Cobb, Scott Davis, Frank Eakin, Mimi Hanaoka, Miranda Shaw, and Doug Winiarski.

I dedicate this book to my mother, Julia S. Geaney.

Introduction

General Context

As presently used in Modern Standard Chinese, the key normative term, *yi* 義, can be translated as "word-meaning." *Yi* 義 is not, however, employed to signify "word-meaning" in the wide range of texts from Early China that form the sources for this book, even in the first-century *Shuowen Jiezi*, arguably the first "dictionary" to appear in China. My task in *The Emergence of Word-Meaning in Early China* is not to posit a date when *yi* 義 crossed some imaginary line—when it "emerged," if you will—to assume the particular remit of lexical meaning but, rather, to ascertain what groundwork was laid and what conditions were met that allowed *yi* 義, at some unspecified time after the first century CE, to accrete that particular usage.[1] What was it about *yi* 義 that, in retrospect, we can identify as predisposing it to be a likely, or perhaps even the apparent, candidate to function as a word's "meaning"?

Meaning, Sense, or Significance

It is easy to be misled by vocabulary related to meaning. In common English-language parlance, "mean" implies a muddle of different ideas, including: to indicate, inform, suggest, refer, show, reveal, warn, entail, require, prove, imply, be sincere, etc. Hence, as Jeffrey Stout notes, discussions of meaning are confused and confusing.[2] Meanings are things that float in a linguistic orbit, and it is a matter of

---

1. Exact dates are not available, but *yi* 義 was being used for lexical meaning as early as the third century. According to Hsu Wen, "The first systematic use of fanqie to notate the sounds is generally attributed to the book *Erya Yinyi* 爾雅音義 [*Pronunciation and Meaning in the* Erya]. This commentary on *Erya*, a thesaurus compiled before 100 B.C., was written by Sun Yan 孫炎 who lived around A.D. 220, near the end of the Eastern Han Dynasty." Hsu, "First Step toward Phonological Analysis," 142.
2. Stout, "What Is the Meaning of a Text?" 1–12. For the rise and fall of the heyday of meanings, see Hacking, *Why Does Language Matter to Philosophy?*

debate whether "meanings of words" are individual entities at all.³ The ontological status of "meanings" thus complicates the task of historicizing the adoption of *yi* 義 for semantic use.

The terms *yi* 義 (as used in early Chinese texts) and "meaning" resemble each other in their breadth of scope: just as *yi* 義 has semantic as well as normative applications, so too "meaning" has semantic and ethical uses.⁴ Historical links between "meaning" and "sense," however, reveal an important difference from *yi* 義. In ancient Greek, there was no overlap in terms used for "to signify" (*semainein*) and those used for sense perception.⁵ But later Latin applications of a word related to "meaning" extended to uses for perception. That is, the church fathers translated the Greek word *nous* into Latin as *sensus*—a translation made possible by the understanding of sense as both physical and linguistic. In other words, as a consequence of the Latin translation of *nous*, the term *sens* also meant inner sense or "moral sense."⁶ By contrast, early Chinese texts employ no specific term linking perceptual processing with introspective linguistic or moral cogitation.⁷ The term often translated as "the senses" (*guan* 官) is a metaphor for the important bodily officers, rather than a term used to mean "to sense."⁸ Absent a term functioning like *sensus*, there is no reason to expect similarities between usage of "sense" or "meaning" and early Chinese uses of *yi* 義.

---

3. Stampe, "Toward a Grammar of Meaning," 153–154.

4. Meaning-bearing items include things like utterances, gestures, names, marks, clothing, expressions, dances, plays, films, events, and lives.

5. Simon et al., "Sense/Meaning," 949. Retrieved from https://muse-jhu-edu.newman.richmond.edu/chapter/1449331/pdf.

6. In French, *sens* is also used for direction, as in a current of water, as well as in "the right direction" and "common sense" (which is also used to mean the "right sense.") So "*le bon sens*" is used to mean "common sense," but also "the right direction" or the "right way." Simon et al., 949.

7. In other words, early Chinese texts evince no overarching term like "to sense," notwithstanding standard translations of *guan* 官. I expand my argument on this point in "Aural and Visual Hierarchies in Texts from Early China," (forthcoming). For a similar observation, see Mahaut de Barros, *Translation and Metalanguage in Laozi*, 184.

8. Some sensory terminological overlap occurs for "to hear" and "to smell" (*wen* 聞), and for "to see" and "to be apparent" in sound and sight (*jian* 見).

The most detailed discussion of "sensing" in texts from Early China, the *Xunzi's* "Zhengming" chapter, uses *gan* 感 (another modern term for "to sense") but only once as "stimulus," and in the context of glossing *xing* 性 (latent natural dispositions). On *xing* 性 and *qing* 情, see Plaks, "Before the Emergence of Desire," 324–331.

Dictionaries, Translation, and the Idea of Linguistic Abstractions

Along with unfamiliar approaches to meaning, texts from Early China offer no evidence of study of grammatical constructs, no clear term for "word," and no explicit discussion of the ontology of semantic objects or abstract objects (such as propositions, properties, and numbers). We cannot even take for granted that early Chinese texts feature a single "folk theory of language."[9] The monumental nature of the *Shuowen Jiezi*, the first-century "dictionary of graphic etymology" compiled by Xu Shen, tempts us to mistake it for an accurate reflection of "early Chinese thought." But it is unlikely that the *Shuowen* embodies or reflects ideas about language belonging to inhabitants the Yellow River valley for the prior half millennium. Despite the rich ethnic diversity and probable presence of bilingualism in Early China, texts that have been taken to predate the first millennium make few references to oral interpretation and scarcely any to translation—activities that might foster new thinking about language. Subsequently, conceptions of language surely changed with increasing textualization and the rising prestige of "writing," as well as reports of (sketchily understood) alphabetic scripts.

A term for "word-meaning" depends, of course, on a concept of "word." As a semantic or grammatical feature of language, a "word" is a unit (or value) in a larger system. The system of language is often pictured as a structure or web with no direct connection to events and objects in the world "outside it."[10] Not so with *ming* 名, a "name," which paradigmatically points at something visible, say an object or event in the world. One might say a name has a "referent" or a "reference." Its function differs, then, from that of a "word," and so the presence of the term *ming* 名 in early Chinese texts does not constitute evidence of a concept of "word."[11] Moreover, even the use of *zi* 字 as the standard term for a minimal unit of writing is insufficient proof of the existence of a concept of "word." Before the *Shuowen*

---

9. The dates for specific passages in early texts are generally uncertain. As Martin Kern puts it, "When looking at a text that is traditionally dated to pre-imperial times, it is impossible to separate its original core from the shape and organization it was given by its Han editors. To some extent, all received pre-imperial texts are Han texts." Kern, "Kongzi as Author in the Han," 270.

For Chad Hansen's contrast between a "Chinese folk theory of language" and a "Western folk theory of language," see Hansen, "Chinese Ideographs and Western Ideas," 373–399. In a later publication, Hansen clarifies that by "Chinese folk theory" he means framing disputes "around a shared view." Hansen, "Why Chinese Thought Is Not Individualistic," 82.

10. See section on "Concepts of Word" (below).

11. The explicit arguments that uses of *ming* 名 in early Chinese texts are not evidence of a concept of word are rare (Moeller, "Chinese Theory of Forms and Names," and Geaney, "Grounding 'Language' in the Senses").

Jiezi (first century), it remains debatable whether *zi* 字 was understood to mean "word." But by taking note of graphs' pronunciations, the *Shuowen* signals that *zi* 字 was understood to mean more than *simply a unit of writing*.¹²

In general, a dictionary facilitates conceptualizing speech as segmented into invariant words whose definitions are their meanings. Typically, a dictionary entails the existence of concepts of "word" and "word-meaning." A dictionary's one-to-one word equations are fundamentally decontextualized. But there is nothing inevitable about the decontextualized approach to linguistic thinking that dictionaries facilitate. When we listen to people speaking, we automatically hear what they say, but we have to be trained to "hear away" from them in order to segment speech into words and trained even further to construe those segments as invariant.¹³ Conceptualizing meaning as something that can be abstracted from words involves a kind of mind/body dualism, wherein the sound of the language is its "body" and the meaning is its disembodied soul. As post-phenomenologist Don Ihde puts it, "meanings float above and beyond the embodiment" that presents itself to us.¹⁴

As early as the second millennium BCE, dictionary-making was well entrenched in Mesopotamia, with bilingual word-lists equating terminology in Sumerian and Akkadian. Bilingual lists seem to have fostered the translational habit of matching words as if they were invariant objects rather than embedded within a situational context and directed toward an intended audience.¹⁵ In due course, the Sumer/Akkad word for "lexeme" became conflated with the Platonic "logos," which functioned

---

12. Of the various interpretations of the *Shuowen*'s title, Françoise Bottéro's is particularly compelling. She contends that that for Xu Shen, "*Wen* are graphs and *zi* are graphic representations of spoken words." Bottéro, "Revisiting the *wen* 文 and the *zi* 字," 23. The distinction is subtle but important: "the focus of *wen* is on graphology and physical shape of characters" (26). By contrast, *zi* are simply written words. When Xu Shen uses the term *zi*, he is not emphasizing their shape, as he does with the term *wen*. As Bottéro notes, the *Shuowen* describes *wen* in terms of kinds, likeness, and forms (類象形), which point to the patterns of writing, whereas it describes *zi* in terms of sound and form added (形聲相益), which approximates the idea of "word." She writes, "Adding *sheng* 聲 to *xing* 形 in Xu Shen's genealogy of writing means assigning pronunciations to graphs" (23).

See chapter 1 for examples pointing to the late standardization of the terminology for "word."

13. Ihde, *Listening and Voice*, 153.

14. Ihde, 153. My point here is not that early Chinese thinking about "language" is not "abstract" in the sense of noticing shared traits among many perceptual experiences. Rather, I am saying that its approach to "language" does not strip bits of speech and writing of their individual characteristics to posit ideal entities. See below for discussion of immersed views of language.

15. Andre LeFevere describes these conclusions from Hans Vermeer in LeFevere, "Chinese and Western Thinking on Translation," 16–24. Vermeer, *Skizzen Zu Einer Geschichte Der Translation*, 1992.

as both grammatical "word" and as "reason," "principle," etc. Thus, Mesopotamian developments in lexicography and translation fostered a distinctly abstract framework for conceptualizing speech.

In Chinese history, however, dictionaries were slow to appear (the *Shuowen Jiezi* arguably being the first) and a strong oral component characterized the early history of translation. Earlier "word-books" show that oral practice strongly affected the history of translation. The *Erya* 爾雅, of uncertain date, is often referred to as a dictionary, but a more apt description is "synonymicon."[16] The *Erya* provides lists of synonyms for certain terms in classical texts. Its taxonomy is organized not phonetically or by "semantic classifiers" but by categories such as plants, fish, and domesticated animals.[17] Its entries gloss terms rather than defining them.[18] For instance, the *Erya* arranges half a dozen terms from classical texts in a row to which is appended a single gloss in the form "X 也"—a formula that implies something like: the members of this list share some semantic connection to this gloss.[19] The formula varies along these lines: "This is called X" or "That which is X, we call Y." The vocal practice of "calling" (*wei* 謂) implies the use of "names," not "words"; hence, the items glossed in the *Erya* were likely to have been understood as "names" for things, not as a technical concept of "words." The *Erya* does not resemble a dictionary insofar as its entries pertain to a particular context (items from a limited set of classics) and glosses names (which *refer* to things) rather than defining words (which have meanings).[20]

The *Fangyan* 方言 of Yang Xiong (53 BCE–18 CE) has also been called a dictionary, but it too is best understood as something else. As with the *Erya*, the *Fangyan* arranges entries according to non-lexical categories, and it speaks of "calling" things, which again suggests reference rather than word-meaning. Its entries

---

16. While some scholars date the *Erya* 爾雅 to the third century BCE, Michael Nylan places it after Han Wudi (141–87 BCE), noting, among other factors, that "*erya*" was also used to mean elegant lyrical style. See Nylan, *Yang Xiong*, 120.

17. As William Boltz points out, "semantic classifiers" are not "radicals," as they are often called, because they are graphic accretions, not graphic roots. Boltz, *Origin and Early Development*, 67–68.

18. As Roy Andrew Miller puts it, "word x is somehow equivalent to word y." Miller, "*Shih Ming*," 425.

19. For a more technical explanation of the formula, see Michel Teboul's application of "linguistic enumeration theory" to the text's first three sections. Teboul describes the text itself as "a compilation of Chinese characters" that "aims to elucidate them through contrast with other characters which the various commentaries to the Classics show to have related meanings." Teboul, "Enumeration Structure," 267. See also Coblin, "Erh ya 爾雅," 94–99; and Von Rosthorn, "Erh-ya and Other Synonymicons," 137–145.

20. Early Chinese texts often note an obligation to name things properly, but it does not account for the development of *yi* 義 as a metalinguistic term, because the minimal units to which metalinguistic uses of *yi* 義 apply are not names (*ming* 名). See chapter 1.

consist of terms from different regions and different eras. The *Fangyan* collects regional speech and, given its inclusion of archaic scripts and obsolete phrases, it is arguably a preliminary foundation for philological study.[21] Like the *Erya*, it manages to gloss terms without employing anything like a term for "meaning" and, thus, does not appear to be a dictionary.

Nor did word-for-word translations foster an idea of word-meaning. References to translation are extremely rare in Chinese texts dating before the first millennium[22] and allusions to oral interpretation of mutually unintelligible speech scant.[23] For instance, some early Chinese texts mention minor functionaries, sometimes called "tongue people," orally interpreting foreign speech ("reverse tongues") for the purposes of conveying the ruler's policies and accepting tribute.[24] Although no transcript of such oral interpretations exist, they were probably not "word for word." Even when efforts were launched to translate Buddhist texts in the second century, those translations were not likely to have been word for word either since the mode of their transmission was oral.[25] Not until the fifth century, it appears, did translators of Buddhist texts even attempt to grasp the concept of a "word" in inflected alphabetic languages.[26]

---

21. Nylan places Yang's somewhat puzzling twenty-seven-year commitment to collecting regional speech in the *Fangyan* within the *haogu* (loving antiquity) movement to reform language, which also included his expansion of the *Cang Jie* 倉頡 word list. She notes that the *Fangyan* contains archaic as well as regional terms, and she suggests that Yang might have hoped collecting regional speech would contribute to language reforms, if he believed that it contained clues to more pristine forms of the early language. Nylan, *Yang Xiong*, 123–124.

22. Joseph R. Allen observes, "There is not one mention of 'translation' (at least in terms now recognized) in the standard Pre-Han classics (*Shijing*, *Shujing*, *Yijing*) or the early Confucian canon (*Chunqiu*, *Lunyu*, *Mengzi*, *Xunzi*), nor is there any mention in the core Daoist texts (*Zhuangzi*, *Laozi*)." As he points out, the earliest record of translational activity (in the *Shiji*) discusses "translation activity," does not mention translators, barely mentions translations or interpretations, and treats the matter as of no particular importance. Allen, "Babel Fallacy," 122, 124.

23. Rejecting the term "dialect," Victor Mair proposes "topolect" for *fangyan* (方言), regional speech that is not mutually intelligible. Mair "What Is a Chinese 'Dialect/Topolect'?," 7.

24. The *Liji*'s mention of a group of translators called *xiang* 象 (a term whose uses often imply visual associations), however, might seem to suggest writing rather than voice. But it might be a transcription of a foreign word, as Joseph Allen suggests, following Wolfgang Behr's approach to a related term. In that case, as Allen puts it, "the standard Chinese word 'to translate' (*yi*) itself may be a calque of a northern non-Chinese word." Allen, "The Babel Fallacy," 127, and Wolfgang Behr, " 'To Translate' Is 'To Exchange,' " 173–209.

25. According to Daniel Boucher, these translations were fundamentally oral/aural. The texts being translated had often been committed to memory. Moreover, records indicate that, even with the scripture at hand, the process entailed oral delivery. Boucher, "Gāndhārī," 475.

26. Sengyou 僧祐 (445–518). Link, "Earliest Chinese Account," 282n187.

Concepts of Word, Linguistic Media, and "Sociological Word"

Alphabetic writing contributes to an impression of identity of items across aural and visual linguistic media, which is conducive to the development of a metalinguistic concept of a word-type. Texts from Early China that depict the origin of writing, however, do not suggest any dependence on sound or speech even in the face of the obvious value of script to record speech.[27] Instead, writing is traced back to visible things. Writing was assumed to be "non-glottic" in the way that charts, diagrams, or mathematical notation are.[28] For example, when the *Laozi* advocates a return to knotting cords, it suggests "writing" not as recorded speech but as something quite different. Early mythology traces the inspiration for writing to visible tracks of birds and animals, rather than (as might seem equally plausible) records of heaven's commands (*tianming* 天命). This writing—with its mnemonic functions assisting in counting, and its mantic functions suggested by hexagrams—began as something irreducible to a transcript of speech. In this conception, it is the (standardized) graph rather than an invariant word-type that resolves speech ambiguity.[29]

Yuan Ren Chao has introduced a term into the scholarly discourse that is quite useful for my discussion here: the *sociological word*. As Chao explains it, a "word" in this construct is understood as a unit that "the general nonlinguistic public is conscious of, talks about, has an everyday term for, and is practically concerned with in various ways. It is the kind of thing . . . which a writer is paid for so much per thousand . . . the kind of thing one makes slips of the tongue on, and for the right or wrong use of which one is praised or blamed."[30] A variety of terms in early Chinese texts meet the specifications that Chao sets forth. For instance, *yan* 言 (speech) and *ming* 名 exhibit some of the practical features of a

---

27. This is noteworthy in light of what scholars have called the threat of "pure phoneticization" that Chinese writing encountered in the late Warring States. William Boltz suggests that, for scholars of the third century BCE, trends that were natural "in a strictly evolutionary sense" would have threatened to collapse the perceived "natural order" toward balancing "graph-sound-sense" (*Origin and Early Development*, 176–177). In my view, the early Chinese habit of framing the world in aural-visual polarities (graph-sound, in this case) might plausibly have posed resistance to desemanticization (loss of semantic properties involved in creating a syllabary or alphabet). Indeed, the prestige of non-glottic writing seems to have functioned as a counter to the importance of speech. But the third item Boltz mentions here, linguistic "sense," was not evident in the third century BCE. See Geaney, "Grounding 'Language' in the Senses," 267–270.

28. Roy Harris uses the term "non-glottic writing" in *Origin of Writing* and in *Signs of Writing*.

29. For a detailed description of the process of using graphs to resolve ambiguity, see Allen, "I Will Speak," 189–206.

30. Chao raises this point in connection with arguing that a graph is a sociolinguistic word in modern China. Chao, *Grammar of Spoken Chinese*, 136.

sociological word. In early Chinese texts, the term *yan* 言 functions as meaning speech or utterance, not an abstraction that connects written and spoken tokens. Consider, if you will, the texts' repeated metaphors of *yan* coming out of the mouth, being emitted, being heard, and being listened to, often as explicitly contrasted to writing. As Chinese texts began to pay more attention to the differences between speech and writing, their increasingly frequent contrasts between *yan* and writing continued to depict *yan* as sound-based.[31] As a term of measurement, "one *yan*" (*yi yan* 一言) is a unit of speech, varying in size from what we might call a "word" to what we might call a "phrase." Prior to the uniform use of *zi* to mean "graph," *yan* was also a means for counting textual units.[32] Early Chinese texts often refer to texts as speaking and being heard, which does not counter the understanding of

---

31. These are a few examples from the first-century *Fayan*.

> 故言、心聲也，書、心畫也。
> Thus, *yan* 言 (speech) is the heartmind's sound, writing is the heartmind's drawing.
> *Fayan* 法言 問神卷第五

> 吾見諸子之小禮樂也，不見聖人之小禮樂也。
> 孰有書不由筆，言不由舌？
> I have seen the various masters slight the rites and the music, but I have not seen a sage slight the rites and the music.
> Who has writings that are not produced by a brush? Or *yan* 言 (speech) that is not produced by a tongue?

For other examples, see the *yan* 言 section of appendix C. All citations to early Chinese texts are to the *CHinese ANcient Texts* (CHANT) 漢達文庫 database unless otherwise noted.

I will supply a tentative date range on first mention of traditional texts, but readers should be aware that the early Chinese texts I examine in this book are "composite texts." Rather than circulating as standardized editions, most were forged fluidly from a range of multiple preexisting documents and oral traditions. Even when there is little doubt that a given text contains early material, assigning a date for when specific parts were written or redacted is generally a matter of debate.

32. The *Shiji* and the *Hanshu* often refer to texts in terms of thousands of *yan*. But when the *Lunheng* distinguishes *yan* from *wen*, the *yan* is spoken.

> 文吏不通（一）經一文，不調師一言；諸生能說百萬章句，非才知百萬人乎？
> Scribal officials are not in accord on single *wen* 文 of one Canon, and are not attuned to one bit of *yan* 言 from a teacher. Students, however, are able to explain hundreds of thousands of sections and phrases; is not their talent and knowledge equal to ten thousand people?
> *Lunheng* 論衡 《效力篇》

yan 言 as speech but rather reflects that the texts were understood to be recorded sayings that were recited.³³

Ming 名 also correspond to sociological words insofar as they, along with *yan*, are the focus of lexicons like the *Erya* and the *Fangyan*. Moreover, the *Shiming* 釋名, a lexicon of sound glosses written about 200 CE, focuses on *ming* rather than *zi*, at a time when *zi* had already become the uniform term for "word." The second-century commentator Zheng Xuan (127–200) was misinformed, however, when he surmised that *ming* 名 was formerly used to mean what readers of his own time meant by *zi*. There are only two cases in which uses of *ming* 名 also refer to graphs, and they seem to be brief experiments at the end of the Warring States period, when interest in standardizing the writing system may have encouraged people to seek a single term for a unit of writing.³⁴

Nothing about early Chinese uses of *ming* or *yan*, despite their sharing features of a sociological word, suggest that they were taken to imply the idea of a word as detached or disembodied.

"Immersed" versus "Abstract" Views of Language

For my purposes, two models are especially constructive in helping us identify significant differences in cultural practices and historical shifts in conceptions of language: "immersed" versus "abstract."³⁵ The immersed model focuses on linguistic

---

33. The distinction continues when the *Wenxin Diaolong* (fifth or sixth century) treats what is emitted from the mouth as *yan* 言, whereas what belongs to the brush is literature:

> 發口為言, 屬筆曰翰.
> That which is emitted from the mouth is deemed speech, and what is entrusted to the brush is called literary writing.
> *Wenxin Diaolong* 總術第四十四 《《文心雕龍》》《《卷九》》《《總術》》

34. *Ming* 名 seems to have that role in the *Guanzi* (Ch. 10.5 君臣上) and in the *Yili* (Ch. 8 聘禮).

Zheng Xuan's (鄭玄) influential interpretation of *ming* 名 is as follows. Commenting on the *Zhouli* "Chun guan" (春官), he wrote, "In the past they said *ming*, now we say *zi*." (古曰名, 今曰字 。). Discussing the *Yili*, he wrote, "*Ming* are written graphs. Now we call them *zi*." (名, 書文也。今謂之字。) Buttressing his interpretation of the *Lunyu*'s use of *zhengming* 正名 to mean rectification of *written words*, he cited the passage from the *Yili* (mistaking it for the *Liji*) in which he takes *ming* to be 'graph,' noting, "Of old they said *ming*. These days we say *zi*." (古者曰名, 今世曰字). Liu Baonan, *Lunyu zhengyi*, vol. 3, 82. For a refutation of Zheng Xuan's interpretation, see Geaney, "Grounding 'Language' in the Senses," 279–280.

35. The titles I give these models are not particularly important. I could, for instance, call the immersed model "engaged," "embedded," or "participatory," as others have done. For similar categories, see Hanks, *Language and Communicative Practices*, and Kristeva, *Language* (esp. 50).

practice embedded in its surroundings, thereby foregrounding the relation of language to the world. By contrast, detached conceptions of language emphasize its structure, systematicity, and/or constancy.

An immersed model, in which language is receptive to its environment, pays special attention to the materiality of linguistic activity, viewing it as moved by situational factors and continuous with bodily expression and gestures. Indeed, it treats language itself as a totality of linguistic practices. In an immersed model, there is no clear gap between, on the one hand, the ontological status of speech and names and, on the other, what is spoken about and named. Different versions of immersed models might highlight the bodily processes of speaking and listening or focus on the intersubjectivity of utterances. "Languaging" might be linked to what it talks about and, thus, what speakers believe about the world might be taken to be reflected in phonic similarities.[36] Such models might emphasize the rhythm and tone of communication or present naming as a force with physical consequences that are powerful enough to require taboos. From this perspective, in the absence of abstractions like word-types, basic similarities in sounds or signs might seem sufficient to account for communication, but communication failures might attract as much attention as its successes. In sum, language would be rooted within ongoing discourse and occasions of utterance.

An abstract, or detached, conception of language accentuates its formal elements. Examples of this approach might identify and theorize about certain standardized linguistic units that constitute it, such as nouns, verbs, particles, subjects and predicates, meanings, words, sentences, formal definitions, or the distinction between types and tokens. Those elements might be taken to be "obviously natural linguistic kind[s]."[37] Moreover, a detached conception of language might posit rules regarding combining units of language or assert the requirements that linguistic communication entails in addition to terms and referents, such as signifieds, concepts, ideas, or word-meanings. An abstract conception might involve viewing language as a differential system or a web in which elements have "values."[38] In other words,

---

36. Hence I entitled my volume on concepts of language in Early China *Language as Bodily Practice in Early China*. Julie Tetel Andresen's use of the term "languaging" in *Linguistics and Evolution* is a striking image of language as practice.

37. The phrase is Chad Hansen's, and he uses it to cast doubt on A. C. Graham's view that the Neo-Mohists discovered the sentence. Hansen, *Daoist Theory*, 239; Graham, *Later Mohist Logic*, 8.

38. For example, in Ferdinand de Saussure's distinction between *langue* and *parole*, *langue* is the relatively permanent synchronic aspects of language as a formal system of signs with definitions. He describes it as "speech less speaking" or the whole set of an individual's linguistic habits that exist within a community of speakers. Saussure, *Course in General Linguistics*, 77.

the meaning of every element would be determined through the negation of the meaning of every other element. Such models might conceptualize language not as utterances but as a stable entity whose alterations can be bracketed to produce a more useful long-range perspective.

The distinction between immersed and detached models also applies to views of linguistic meaning. Approached from an abstract or detached perspective, words seem to possess determinate meanings in isolation from their use in any specific utterance.[39] Rather than emphasizing that words are employed to mean things in individual moments of language use (the immersed model), the contrary approach might contend that words possess, encode, or transmit meanings (the abstract model). Immersed theories tend to stress the material contexts that produce the meanings of utterances in specific, contingent acts of use. Such relational approaches to meaning attend to the manner in which individual speakers construct linguistic meaning by borrowing social norms—in variable ways—to express their intentions in response to immediate situations.[40] Instead of positing meanings as abstractions that belong to words or sentences (entities that are themselves abstract), immersive approaches identify the meanings of utterances in relation to relevant situational factors, including intentions and motives.[41]

To apply the distinctions I have outlined above to Early China, I maintain that conceptions of language insofar as they are evident in early Chinese texts are not abstract or detached.[42] Instead, early Chinese texts' statements about *yan* 言

---

39. I do not mean to suggest that abstract models do not recognize the effects of social norms on semantic meaning. Both types of linguistic models do that.

40. See, for example, Hanks, *Language and Communicative Practices*, and Volosinov, *Marxism and the Philosophy of Language*.

41. As Dennis Stampe puts it, "the concept of intention, unlike the concepts of an idea, a concept, semantic marker, semantic regularity, and so forth, at least does not swim in the same orbit of conceptual space as does 'meaning' itself." Stampe, "Toward a Grammar of Meaning," 296.

42. My position on this point is slightly different from that of Christoph Harbsmeier, although he also maintains that the early Chinese interest in language was mainly social, noting that "the Chinese did not have a distinct abstract notion of language as opposed to speech, talk, words, no division between *dialektos* 'language' versus *logos* 'word, speech.'" Our views diverge in that Harbsmeier posits that certain texts, such as the Mohist Canons (*Mo Bian*) and the *Xunzi*, employ terms for linguistic abstractions like "sentence" and "proposition" and that the Later Mohists had a concept of meaning but did not show interest in it as a philosophical topic. Harbsmeier, *Language and Logic*, 46–47, 329n4.

Although different from my presentation on most details, Bao Zhiming also makes a case that language and the world are inseparable and interdependent in what he calls "the classical conception of language" in ancient China. Bao, "Language and World View," 195, 216.

(speech) and *ming* 名 (names) would lead a reader to assume that they reflect an immersed view of linguistic practices.[43]

For the investigation I set forth in the remainder of this book, one key attribute of the immersed model is especially pertinent: the interpenetration of language and non-language or, to put it another way, the fluidity of the boundaries between them. To the extent that abstract conceptions stress language's invariant, organizational structure, language is likely to appear as isolated from the rest of the world, particularly if the world is seen to be fluctuating or evolving. The expression "language and reality" seems to imply that language is not part of the world in the way that other things are. "Language and the world" has the same exteriorizing effect.[44] If language is the external counterpart of the world or reality, then language is a massive entity. The implications of a phrase like "language and the world" are more evident if we consider why we are so much less likely to say "speech and the world" or "names and the world." That is, juxtaposing language to either reality or the world renders it constitutive of one entire pole of human experience. Early Chinese texts, by contrast, discuss not language but speech, names, and writing. Nothing so monumental as the polar opposite of reality or the world is at issue.

Early Chinese Immersed Views of Language

Early Chinese depictions of names and speech feature some obviously "immersed" characteristics. For one, the texts do not advance grammatical terms or discuss grammar.[45] They also clearly focus on names (*ming* 名), which paradigmatically link

---

43. To be clear, I am not claiming that the Chinese language was incapable of formulating abstractions or that there were no discussions of abstract ideas in Early China. My point is merely that linguistic speculation in Early China did not favor thinking about language as an abstract entity.

44. To some it seems that the phrase "language and reality" need not imply that language is not itself a thing or that it is not involved in the constitution of things. For instance, Vincent Descombes argues that the idea of outside of language is not "reality plain and simple" but is "the outside reality of the sequence of language under consideration." Descombes, "Quandaries of the Referent," 55–56.

45. Arguably the *Erya* and the *Shuowen Jiezi* use terms that suggest a recognition of the difference between grammatical terms and ordinary words. For instance, Lin Yushan notes that the *Shuowen* glosses words like *jie* 皆 and *ge* 各 by means of terms like *yu* 語 and *ci* 辭, which implies that these are terms about speech. Lin, *Hanyu Yufa Xueshi*, 27. Nevertheless, the texts do not discuss them as such.

The first use of the grammatical terms "empty" and "full" dates to around the eleventh century, and grammar was not an object of study in China until the late nineteenth century. Peyraube, "Recent Issues in Chinese Historical Syntax," 164.

to actions or things (*shi* 實) and are not characterized by the (imaginary) fixity of dictionary entries as formal definitions free of context.⁴⁶ Texts from Early China do not theorize about what makes a bit of speech complete enough to constitute a unit like a "sentence."⁴⁷ They show little interest in establishing a uniform scope for the terms that refer to different linguistic elements. For instance, terms like *ming*, *yan*, and *ci* 辭 have no standard sizes nor any rules governing what constitutes a single unit of each.⁴⁸ Furthermore, Pre-Qin texts rarely make generalized claims about large-scale diachronic linguistic changes.⁴⁹ As is often observed, early Chinese concerns about language primarily involved its practical political consequences.⁵⁰

An immersed model helps us understand a variety of early Chinese linguistic practices that might otherwise remain largely obscure. Consider, in no particular order, the following. Texts from Early China commonly use puns to explain the meaning of two apparently different terms (e.g., *de* 德 "potency" and *de* 得 "obtain"; *zheng* 政 "govern" and *zheng* 正 "straight," etc.). Speech is concretely depicted as "breath-energy" (*qi* 氣) in the mouth, which is produced by sound and taste.⁵¹

---

46. See the discussion of dictionaries above.

47. The Neo-Mohists did not recognize or invent a linguistic construct like "sentence," as opposed to a deliberately composed utterance. As Dan Robins argues, Graham provides no compelling reason to view the *Mo Bian*'s use of *ci*—in what Graham calls "Names and Objects" 10, 11, and 12—as a departure from ordinary usage. Robins, "Later Mohists and Logic," 247–285; Graham, *Later Mohist Logic*, 207.

Christoph Harbsmeier rightly notes that the use of certain particles makes it clear that early Chinese texts recognize the boundaries of a bit of speech, but to my mind, that recognition is not sufficient to establish what Harbsmeier calls an "operative concept of a sentence." We may be defining "sentence" differently. I take the word "sentence" to involve something with a grammatical structure—something more than just a string of speech that ends. Thus, in contexts where, as Harbsmeier notes, "formulation" would do just as well for translating *ci* 辭, I would recommend retaining "formulation." Harbsmeier, *Language and Logic*, 175, 182–183.

48. See note 34 and chapter 1.

49. Wolfgang Behr notes, "comparison of different diachronic levels of speech" was a marginal concern in the Pre-Qin period. Behr, "Language Change," 21.

50. My point approximates Harbsmeier's: "The Chinese see sentences as deeply embedded in personal and social reality. The meaning of sentences was not for them a grammatical and lexical question. It was a historical question. Sentences are only messengers (*shih* 使) for meaning, they are not taken to articulate meaning literally." Harbsmeier, *Language and Logic*, 185–186. For my alternative interpretation of the line about phrases and names serving as messengers in the "Zhengming" chapter of the *Xunzi*, see my *Language as Bodily Practice*, 104–105.

51. See chapter 2 and *Language as Bodily Practice*, 188–189.

Taboos apply to speaking names, especially in the context of death.[52] Also, knowing the names of ghosts and animals gives one power over them.[53] The prospect of "straightening" names (rectifying names) is credited with extraordinary potential benefits, including producing order, eliminating confusion, and eradicating falsehood. The "Zhengming" chapter of the *Xunzi* suggests that something beyond mere convention connects names to things when it both claims that names are

---

52. The *Zuozhuan* lists these naming taboos:

> 不以國，不以官，不以山川，不以隱疾，不以畜牲，不以器幣。周人以諱事神，名，終將諱之。故以國則廢名，以官則廢職，以山川則廢主，以畜牲則廢祀，以器幣則廢禮。
>
> One does not use the name of a domain; one does not use the name of an office, of a mountain or a river, of a malady or illness, of domestic animals or of utensils and precious ceremonial objects. The Zhou leaders used a system of respectful concealment in serving spirits, and when one passed away, his name was avoided as respectful concealment. Therefore, using a domain name would do away with that name. Using the name of an office would do away with that official duty. Using the name of a mountain or a river would do away with the spirit master of that place. Using the name of a domestic animal would do away with a sacrifice. Using the name of a ceremonial vessel or a ceremonial gift would do away with a rite.
> *Zuozhuan* 春秋左傳 桓公 B2.6 《桓公六年傳》 Durrant, Li, and Schaberg trans., *Zuo Tradition*, 1:101.

David Schaberg discusses the challenge of dating the *Zuozhuan*, which might have been completed ca. 300 BCE. See Schaberg, *Patterned Past*, 315–324.

The naming taboos are often explicitly a matter of speaking, as in this case:

> 二名不偏諱，夫子之母名徵在；言在不稱徵，言徵不稱在。
>
> With a double name, they [the two names] were not both avoided together. The Master's mother's name was Zheng-zai. When he said (*yan* 言) "Zai," he did not call (*cheng* 稱) "Zheng." When he said "Zheng," he did not call "Zai."
> *Liji* 禮記 〈檀弓下〉

The "Qu Li Xia" chapter of the *Liji* notes several name-avoidance rules. For example,

> 天子不言出，諸侯不生名。
>
> The son of Heaven should not be spoken of as "going out" (of his state). A feudal prince should not be called by his name, while alive.
> *Liji* 禮記 〈曲禮下〉 2.17 Legge, *Li Ki*, 113.

Even if, as Dennis Grafflin argues, the naming taboos in the *Liji* represent private reverence and serve to enforce respectful conversation, the text still treats naming as a force that needs to be accommodated. Grafflin, "Onomastics," 385.

53. For the notion of masters of naming prodigies, see Lewis, *Writing and Authority*, 34–35; Sterckx, *Animal and the Daemon*, 219–221; and Harper, "Chinese Demonography," 94–95.

conventional and asserts that names have "certain goodness" (*yougushan* 有固善).⁵⁴ The *Mengzi*'s description of Mengzi's ability to "know speech" treats *yan* as utterances—not an abstraction—that unwittingly reveal things about the speaker.⁵⁵ Puns involving *ming* 鳴 and *ming* 名 for both human and non-human animal sounds, as well as non-human animals having the ability to speak (*yan*), also reflect an immersed approach to "language."⁵⁶

The terminology for linguistic activity in early Chinese texts defies the stasis one might expect if they had conceived of language as abstract, standardized, and constant. Speech and names exhibit flux, as well as deviation that needs to be made straight (*zheng* 正). While speech and names should coincide (*dang* 當) with entities spatially and temporally, they often fail to do so by passing (*guo* 過) or not coming up to a limit (*jin* 盡). The texts find fault with names for being distant from that to which they refer, as if they keep slipping away from where they are supposed to be. Bad names are slanted (*yi* 倚), and speech has no closure because both speech (*yan*) and phrases (*ci*) can be "split" (*zhe* 折). It is difficult to imagine a systematic approach to language emerging from this variability and movement among names and phrases.

Method and Interpretive Theory

Donald Munro long ago observed that textual inconsistencies are an unavoidable feature of early Chinese texts, which are, quite simply, not as troubled by those inconsistencies as we are.⁵⁷ Recent discoveries about the nature of textual formation help explain why. As William Boltz describes it, early Chinese texts are composed of "moveable units" and "paragraph-size textual building blocks."⁵⁸ Therefore, no non-circular way for adjudicating which parts of texts should be interpretively privileged

---

54. The *Xunzi* is attributed to Xun Kuang 荀況 (third century BCE) but scholars posit that its chapters have been rearranged. Knoblock, *Xunzi*, 1:105–128.

55. Arguing for a similar interpretation of the *Mengzi* 2A2, Jiuan Heng points out, "it is unlikely that one could count on knowing a man by 'knowing doctrines' as such." Heng, "Understanding Words and Knowing Men," 155.

56. The *Liji* mentions that the parrot and ape can speak (*yan*; chapter 1.6 曲禮上). The *Shanhai Jing* asserts that some "apes know human naming" (狌狌知人名, *Shanhai Jing*, chapter 10, "Hai Nei Nan Jing"). The *Zhouli* 5.24 and 5.26 also mention that barbarians are able to speak with birds and other animals.

57. Munro, *Concept of Man*, xxi.

58. Boltz, "Composite Nature of Early Chinese Texts," 61–62. On the concept of authorship see chapter 8, note 12.

at the expense of others seems to be available.⁵⁹ In light of these observations, my interpretations do not aim to impose a particular perspective—or "school" of thought, or retrospective heuristic—on a text. In pre-imperial texts compiled before the emergence of the idea of a school or an "author," layers of texts, multiple editors, and graphic instability undermine the likelihood of coherent arguments stretching across large portions of text. Hence, when a text does not include part of a passage that is commonly present elsewhere, I do not assume that the omission expresses disagreement with the norm. Even when passages invoke ideas recognizable as belonging to contemporaneous texts, I take it as possible that the texts are talking past each other. There might have been "disputes," as A. C. Graham famously argued, but the materials we possess are refracted intentions in compilations of fragments disputing fragments, not samples showing authors engaging in what we might now call reasoned debate. At best, we can look for coherence in the largest apparent textual unit while also recognizing that the multiple compilers reworking a text might have included a line or word or a whole passage for any number of reasons.

As a work of cross-cultural metalinguistics, *The Emergence of Word-Meaning in Early China* contributes an account of sociolinguistic concepts in ancient sources.⁶⁰ My task requires that ideas implicit in a broad range of texts be attended to, in part because early Chinese scholarly communities shared habits of word-use and repurposed bits of texts. My approach employs literary methods (word-pattern analysis) to construct and confirm a historically situated argument about a linguistic concept. By performing myriad searches in the Chinese University of Hong Kong's comprehensive online "Chinese Ancient Texts" (CHANT) database, I analyze metalinguistic terms and references to speech and writing in a wide variety of sources, which include works of medicine, mathematics, literature, politics, and ritual as well as glossaries and transcripts of excavated texts. I take note of patterns of word use, parallel structures, repeated metaphors, binary oppositions, and rhetorical circumscription, and I interpret these references in light of one another.⁶¹ Insofar as dates for the

---

59. Chad Hansen defends applying the principle of humanity, which was coined by R. E. Grandy. Grandy, "Reference, Meaning and Belief," 439–452. For the principle of charity, see Donald Davidson, "On the Very Idea of a Conceptual Scheme," 5–20. Hansen and David Wong discuss these principles in Xiao and Yong, *Moral Relativism and Chinese Philosophy: David Wong and His Critics*.

60. I think of this as part of the "linguistic turn" with a post-humanist slant. As Magnus Course argues in a study of the rural Mapuche of South America, when post-humanists have criticized the linguistic turn, they have done so by means of "Western language ideology" and, therefore, missed the ways in which *language as actant* is not strictly human and language is not about human agency. Course, "Birth of the Word," esp. 20–21.

61. My method does not include an etymological study of *yi* 義, for which, see Jia and Kwok, "Clan Manners," 33–42.

"Rhetorical circumscription" is my term for the way early Chinese texts sometimes circumscribe an entity by referring to what is above, below, outside, inside, near, and far from it.

texts are available, I aim to detect not only broad patterns in usage but also changes over time that suggest new ways of thinking about language.

Instead of reconstructing philosophical arguments from early Chinese texts, I look for insight into their underlying assumptions about human situations (language, meaning, bodies, and the world). Some scholars have called stylistic patterns like those analyzed here the products of a "discourse machine" in which words simply assemble themselves in relentlessly predictable ways.[62] I, too, think of these repeating linguistic arrangements and their variations as having a momentum of their own. And I hope this book's account of that momentum might encourage us to attend to possible new interpretations of early Chinese texts—undermining the obviousness of our own habits of thinking and facilitating a recognition of unfamiliar ideas.

Texts from Early China construct a way of conceptualizing semantic meaning derived in part from their historical and material conditions, including their writing system, the geographic situation (relative isolation from other writing systems), increases in "textualization," and first encounters with a radically different system of writing.[63] The materiality of this language in its geographical context set conditions for a way of thinking about a normative continuum that spanned from ethical action to the normativity of certain sayings, texts, earthly configurations, and heavenly shapes and movements. My book is not a conventional historical study. The "actants" in this book are habits and customs, as well as styles of the mouth when uttering, the ears when listening, the hands when writing, and the eyes when looking.[64] My description of the way in which yi 義 evolved from normative and ethical uses that highlighted visual materiality—that is, that were perceptible to the eyes in particular—to become a semantic term that, at some later time, came to signal a disembodied concept like "word-meaning" is new and unorthodox, based squarely as it is in an immersive model of language.[65] The novelty of my thesis should not be surprising, however, for it proceeds directly from the ability to subject an entire corpus of texts to data-driven systematic scrutiny, thus yielding fresh insights into a world vastly distant from the present. In what follows, I am attempting to understand that world of Early China, by "living within" its language.

---

62. Owen, "Liu Xie and the Discourse Machine," 175. Other scholars depict the patterns as reflections of reasonable rules, attention to which should yield coherent interpretations. For instance, Rudolf Wagner, who calls this "interlocking parallel style" (IPS), sees it as that kind of rational faculty that should forestall Orientalist translations. For Wagner, IPS draws attention to argument and limits "attributing the seeming lack of coherence in Chinese philosophical arguments to inconsistent thinking by the Chinese authors." Wagner, *Craft of a Chinese Commentator*, 56.

63. Emphasizing the importance of ritual pattern related to writing, Michael Nylan introduces this term as part of her argument that the prestige of "writing" in the Han did not necessarily entail increases in literacy. Nylan, "Textual Authority," 229.

64. I am adapting "actant" from Bruno Latour's sense of "acting agents" or "interveners" or what he glosses as "any entity that modifies another entity in a trial." Latour, *Politics of Nature*, 75, 237.

65. See appendix A for a discussion of the puzzle of connecting ethical to semantic uses of yi 義.

PART ONE

Key Metalinguistic Terms and Yi 義 as External

CHAPTER ONE

The Metalinguistic Implications of Words versus Names

What precisely constitutes the difference between "names" and "words"—not to mention the nature of their respective relations to propositions, sentences, symbols, signs, and the like—is a central question for scholars of language. According to one definition, "names" can be discriminated from "words" insofar as "names" lack "word-meaning," a distinction that is especially useful to any effort to identify the origins of that abstract linguistic concept. The task is complicated in the case of early Chinese texts, however, because early sources do not always use terms consistently; moreover, the use of terms in excavated texts sometimes raises suspicions that multiple editors have shaped and altered transmitted editions. Hence, at best we are able to identify patterns of term usage, not offer definitive explanations. An additional complication is encountered when modern translations of pre-second-century Chinese received texts interchangeably render *ming* 名 as "word" and "name." Carefully examining patterns in how *ming* 名—and related terms that help delimit its functions—operate within early Chinese texts will help us clarify their usage and, in turn, aid in the larger exploration of the origins of "word-meaning."[1] But first, a more thorough introduction into how modern linguists distinguish between "word" and "name" is in order.

"Name" and "Word" in Modern Scholarship on Language

The difference between "name" and "word," on one theory, is that names originate in an ostensive gesture that bestows an identification on some specific thing. This

---

1. I offered a preliminary examination of the question of an early Chinese concept of "word" in Geaney, "Grounding 'Language' in the Senses," 251–293.

bestowal model implies that a name points at a single particular thing (presumably one that actually exists) and says, in effect, "This single thing is X."[2] A "word," by contrast to a "name," does not involve that characteristic pointing.

A semantic way of differentiating words from names maintains that names "denote" things outside of language, as distinct from words, which "connote" other words or concepts. Names typically do not appear in dictionaries because they do not have lexical meanings, whereas words do.[3] On those grounds, one might claim that names do not "mean" or, less strictly, names do not "mean" in any significant sense.[4] This general approach to pinpointing the difference between names and words sometimes emphasizes that words function as "values" within a signifying system, but names do not. That is, words relate to concepts or other words within a system of intralinguistic relations.[5] By contrast, names characteristically apply to things in the non-linguistic world. A variant of the semantic distinction between the two terms posits that, unlike words, names have no grammatical function. It then follows that paradigmatic words are "function words" (such as "the" and "not"). The extreme formulation of this contrast is thus: names have referents but no function; words have functions but not referents.

A loosely allied theory treats words, as distinct from names, as units or subdivisions of a larger entity. As in semantic approaches to the idea of a word, the unit view of "word" implies that, in contrast to names, words are relatively detached from things in the non-linguistic environment. Because a word's identity arises primarily from its position within language as a whole (whether as unit or through relations with other words), words appear not to be directly dependent on things. Names, on the other hand, are attached to things. Names are rooted in contexts and situations, making them seem less like units of a larger linguistic whole.

Because the continuous flow of speech is not easily segmented, the notion of a "word" as a separate unit of a larger whole is often attributed to the rise of literacy. According to this view, through the practice of reading, people learned to conceptualize speech as a series of written units, the spaces between which serve as boundaries that differentiate the sound of one word from the sounds of those

---

2. Debates in the philosophical literature related to this approach center on whether a name refers to a singular particular or, instead, can generalize over groups of things, which often hinges on an established distinction between proper and common nouns.

3. One might also argue that names have lexical meanings only indirectly as a result of their reference to objects.

4. Jon Wheatley argues against any firm distinction between names and words (especially common nouns), but he notes, "If we are going to talk about names in the context of meaning, then the obvious difference which seems to obtain between names and other words is that names do not importantly mean anything while ordinary words do." Wheatley, "Names," 84.

5. I explore this idea in *Language as Bodily Practice*, 54–62.

surrounding it.⁶ Literacy and the homogenization of writing practices are not easy to date with any precision, but some degree of both seems prerequisite for the recognition of a "word," insofar as it is understood as a standardized unit.⁷

"Word" and "Name" in Early Chinese Texts

For these reasons, it is clear that to translate *ming* indiscriminately as both "name" and "word" conceals the technical distinctions by means of which scholars differentiate the two terms. When applied to early Chinese texts, such inexact translation practices have cascading implications, as will become increasingly obvious. To introduce a necessary precision into my discussion, then, I stipulate the following definitions.⁸ By "name," I mean something that designates things. Thus, when I say that the term *ming* is like "name" rather than "word," I mean that *ming* refers to something (like an event, action, object, or person), in contrast to a linguistic term that gains its identity through relations among elements in a language system. A name, in the sense that I mean it here, also has certain features of an indexical (that is, something that serves as a pointer or indicator, like "here" and "this") because of its connection to things. Like indexicals, names are grounded in some material context. By "word," I mean something that is fundamentally understood as a unit (or a value) in a larger linguistic structure or system.

<u>Ming 名 in Early Chinese Texts in Relation to Particulars vs. Groups.</u>—A distinction between "name" and "word" as they refer to generalizing over groups has no counterpart in early Chinese texts. The *Mo Bian* 墨辯 (*Mohist Canons*) A78 presents three forms of referencing pertaining to *ming*: reaching (*da* 達; extending widely), grouping (*lei* 類), and personalizing (*si* 私).⁹ The examples it offers are not parallel:

---

6. I discuss the same idea in the introduction to *Language as Bodily Practice*, xvii–xxviii.

7. R. M. W. Dixon and Alexandra Y. Aikhenvald write, "in Old English the primary meaning of *word* was (a) for referring to speech, as contrasted with act or thought. There was a second sense, which may then just have been emerging: (b) what occurs between spaces in written language." Dixon and Aikhenvald specify that languages with "an established (non-ideographic) orthographic tradition" are likely to have a word for "word." Moreover, "the idea of 'word' as a unit of language was developed for the familiar languages of Europe which by-and-large have a synthetic structure. Indeed . . . some of the criteria for 'word' are only fully applicable for languages of this type." Dixon and Aikhenvald, *Word*, 1–3.

8. I am not endorsing any of these various definitions of names and words. Instead, I use them to help clarify how early Chinese texts use the term *ming* 名.

9. The *Mo Bian* 墨辯 (*Mohist Canons*, books 40–45 of the *Mozi*) is a set of concise, technical sayings and their explanations written by followers of Mozi (late fifth to the early fourth centuries BCE), probably dating to the first half of the third century BCE, according to Chris Fraser ("Mohism"). They cover a range of topics including mechanics, geometry, optics, economics, epistemology, science, and "logic." The *Mo Bian*'s obscurity and textual corruptions pose serious interpretive challenges. For a discussion of *yi* 義 and externality in the *Mo Bian*, see appendix B.

for reaching, the name "thing" (*wu* 物); for grouping, naming something "horse" (命之馬); and for personalizing, the proper name "Cang" (臧).¹⁰ A discussion is in order because these three levels of referencing might seem to suggest that the first and/or second are "words," whereas the third are "names." In other words, the *Mo Bian* A78 might seem to mean *leiming* and/or *daming* are something like an idea of "common nouns." But we should keep in mind that, in the absence of grammatical distinctions like noun, verb, etc., a distinction between singular and general *ming* does not imply that between proper and common noun.¹¹ In sum, *Mo Bian* A78 does not—by means of (*si* 私), (*da* 達), and (*lei* 類)—present a division between "names" and "words."¹²

Ming 名 in Early Chinese Texts in Relation to Lexical Terms, Function Words, and Grammar.—The absence of function words serving as examples of *ming* provides additional evidence that early Chinese texts do not use *ming* to mean "word." When passages self-consciously examine *ming*, they do not cite examples of *ming* that resemble "words" (terms defined by their intralinguistic relations).¹³ Their instances of *ming* are not, in other words, terms with roles as abstract intralinguistic relations: modal particles (such as *hu* 乎), auxiliary words (such as *zhi* 之), or similar words—like "not" (*fei* 非) or "thus" (*gu* 故). Instead, the *ming* they use as examples encompass "thing," "white," "stone," "horse," "rich merchant," "Cang" (a person's name), "birds-and-beasts," "dog," "black," and "Yao's dutifulness," as well as names of less delimited entities like "knowing" (*zhi* 知) and "situations" (*shi* 事).¹⁴

---

10. The activity in the second example—naming a horse—directs attention to naming rather than names per se, which informs my translation.

11. Furthermore, because the *Mo Bian* A78 distinguishes grouping (*lei* 類) *ming* from the obscure "reaching" (*da* 達) *ming*, it does not propose a simple binary such as proper versus common. Something else is at issue with *da* 達, although it is not clear what it is. Its usage here might merely mean names "reaching" far, but not so far as to include everything. The Explanation of the Canon begins with "thing" (*wu* 物) and apparently glosses it as "reaching." Then it adds that if there is a *shi* 實, it must take this *ming* (物, 達也。有實必待文 (多) [名]也). (For emending *wen* 文 to *zhi* 之, see Graham, *Later Mohist Logic*, 235.) In other words, the Canon's Explanation, having glossed "thing" as "reaching" (物, 達也), adds that any *shi* 實 is included under the term "thing." But "reaching" need not suggest encompassing everything. The condition specified in A78 is the presence of a *shi* 實, but a *ming* is not a *shi* 實. (See Geaney, "What is Míng?" 15–32, esp. 25). In fact, the term "thing" (*wu* 物) might not encompass *ming*, because *wu* 物 sometimes refer specifically to visible things. See appendix C entry on *wu* 物.

12. See also Fraser, "Language and Ontology," 438–439.

13. I make a similar argument in "Míng (名) as 'Names,'" 140.

14. "Yao's dutifulness" need not imply an invisible abstraction. As I argue in chapter 6, *yi* 義 is visible because it refers to actions. In light of Yao being long dead, those who saw his actions would also be dead, but later generations might hear about (but not see) his (formerly visible) actions. Whether terms like "duty" are understood as immaterial abstractions depends on the ontology in question. For a discussion of general terms, singular terms denoting kinds, and nominalism in early Chinese texts, see Fraser, "Language and Ontology," 420–456.

Some of the examples are long *ming* that include functional words within them, but function words are not what the texts take to be *ming*.

In the ancient Greek tradition, "name" and "noun" (ὄνομα) are effectively the same word.[15] In the grammatical theory that ensued, a noun became a type or category of word used to name a person, place, or thing. There is no indication, however, that early Chinese texts posit a word class "noun" (much less a vocabulary for labeling grammatical parts of speech). A *ming* often, but not always, serves as what we would call a noun in early Chinese texts. Consider this example, which occurs in a *Huainanzi* passage wherein the use of "*ming*" is not thus restricted. The fragment says that when someone is shaking, whether due to cold or fear, we use the *ming* "shake," although the fruit/effect is different. The line reads:

> 故寒者顫, 懼者亦顫, 此同名而異實。
> Those who are cold shake; those who are frightened also shake. The *ming* is the same, the *shi* (act, fruit, filling out) is not.[16]
> *Huainanzi* 淮南子 說山訓

Alternate readings:

> Being cold is shaking; being frightened is also shaking. The *ming* is the same, the *shi* (act, fruit, filling out) is not.

> The cold shake. The frightened shake. The *ming* (shake) is the same. The *shi* (action) is not.

> Cold [people] shake. Frightened [people] shake. The *ming* ["shake"] is the same. The *shi* (action) is not.

If we were to rephrase the above in grammatical terms, we might say: the *ming* names a verb ("to shake" or "is shaking"), which is the same whether the feeling is cold or fright. The *shi* names another verb ("to act" or "to fill out like

---

15. See the introduction to *Language as Bodily Practice* for a similar discussion pertaining to nouns. A. C. Graham seems to decide that *ming* is used to mean "word" because it is used for terms that are not nouns, and he cannot identify any other term that corresponds to what he means by a "word." But his conclusion is unjustified because "word" is notoriously difficult to define and not universal to all cultures. Graham, *Later Mohist Logic*, 197.

16. John Major et al. contend that most of the *Huainanzi* was written between 157–41 BCE, but they describe the sayings in the chapter in which this passage occurs as fitting a time "between when the *Hanfeizi* and *Shuoyuan* collections were compiled." Queen and Major, *Huainanzi*, 3, 622; and 617–624.

a fruit") which differs depending on whether the feeling is cold or fear.[17] Shaking from fear is not "the same as" shaking from cold, but they are both called shaking. While it is possible to turn an action (to shake) into a gerund to make a noun (the shaking), nothing in the line compels that interpretation. Thus, in contrast to Aristotle's conception of names as "non-temporal," early Chinese texts imply that *ming* can involve a process. Even when *ming* appears to be a noun, it is not particularly separable from activity. *Ming* is "naming" as well as "name," and it refers paradigmatically to actions (*shi* 實, as in "fulfilling," and *xing* 行, as in "walking"). Hence thinking of *ming* as nouns obstructs our understanding of early Chinese concepts of time as well as of *ming*.

Early Chinese Texts and "Words" as Units

The idea of a linguistic unit being a "word" seems to presuppose standardized units. Early Chinese texts did not, however, segment speech and writing into uniform constituents with standardized terminology, as is evident in the treatment of terms like *zi* 字, *wen* 文, *yan* 言, *ci* 辭, and *ming* 名.

Zi 字 was used for a countable unit of writing before it was explicitly associated with speech (evident when the *Shuowen Jiezi* associated pronunciations with graphs). But even as late as the first century CE, *zi* 字 was not the only term used for counting writing.[18] Other terms in texts from the first century CE serve this function as well. The biography of Yang Xiong (53 BCE–18 CE) in the *Hanshu* asserts that Yang wrote the *Taixuan Jing* in five thousand *wen* 文, not *zi* 字. As the biography notes,

作《太玄》五千文。
[He] created the *Taixuan Jing* in five thousand *wen*.[19]
Hanshu 漢書 傳《揚雄傳第五十七下》

---

17. The term *shi* 實 can be used to mean "fruit" but not "effect," as in cause-effect. Fruition is not about pinpointing a single cause as in causality.

18. The two rare cases where *ming* fulfills that role, which might date to the Western Han, seem to have been doomed to fail. See Geaney, "Grounding 'Language' in the Senses," 275–278.
   Later Chinese metalinguistic theories confirm that, since early Chinese texts used *ming* to refer to audible "names" and "fame," *ming* was never a serious candidate for being adopted to mean a written "word." See, for example, the *Chu sanzangji* (出三藏記集) of Sengyou (僧祐, 445–518), translated by Arthur E. Link in "Earliest Chinese Account," 281–299. See also Dai Tong's (戴侗) thirteenth-century *Liushugu* (六書故) in Hopkins, *Six Scripts*, 27–28.

19. The *Hanshu* is attributed mainly to Ban Gu 班固 (32–92), but was completed by his sister, Ban Zhao (ca. 48–ca. 114) and Ma Hsu (fl. first half of second century). Wilkinson, *Chinese History*, 711.

Consider as well two more examples from the first-century *Lunheng*.[20] The second occurrence in the passage below refers to a single graph as a *wenzi* 文字.

> 孝明 之時, 讀《蘇武傳》, 見武官名曰《栘中監》, 以問百官, 百官莫知。夫《倉頡》之章, 小學之書, 文字備具, 至於無能對聖國之問者, 是皆 美命隨牒之人多在官也。"木"旁"多"文字且不能知, 其欲及若董仲舒之知重常, 劉子政之知貳負, 難哉!
>
> When Emperor Xiao Ming was reading the biography of Su Wu, he saw a military office name called 栘中監 (Yi Zhong Jin). He asked all his officers about it, but none of them knew (*zhi* 知). In terms of the sections of the *Cang Jie* and the texts of elementary learning, their *wenzi* (文字) were fully prepared, but since they were unable to reply to His Imperial Holiness's questions, the officials turned out to be mostly just lucky commission appointments. Since they were unable to know the "*mu* 木" on the side of "*duo* 多" *wenzi* (文字) [*referring to the two parts of the graph yi 栘*], it would be difficult indeed if one wanted them to have something like Dong Zhongshu's knowledge (*zhi* 知) of "*zhong chang* 重常" or Liu Zi Zheng's knowledge (*zhi* 知) of "*er fu* 貳負"![21]
>
> *Lunheng* 論衡《別通篇》

Here, *yi* 栘, a single graph (composed of *mu* 木 on one side and *duo* 多 on the other), seems to count as a *wenzi*.[22] At the same time, the *Lunheng* also reveals non-standard measurements for *ci* 辭, a term commonly used for "well-formulated phrasing." It uses "one *ci*" in a way that resembles what we might call one graph or even one word:

> 故「毋」、「必」二辭, 聖人審之。
>
> Thus, as for "not" and "must," these two *ci* 辭, the sage examines them.[23]
>
> *Lunheng* 論衡 Qian Gao《譴告篇》

Ci is more often used in the context of speech than of writing in texts from Early China, and so a well-formed phrase might apply to both. This use of *ci*, as

---

20. The *Lunheng* is attributed to Wang Chung 王充 (27–100). Wilkinson, 717.

21. Forke translation modified, *Lun-Heng*, 2:106–107.

22. Interestingly, the passage also gives the impression that the question of whether the *wenzi* 文字 is "known" (recognized) takes priority over the "meaning" of the *wenzi*.

23. It might seem like the *Xunzi*'s "Zhengming" chapter and the *Mo Bian* treat *ci* as an amount of language that falls between a *ming* and *bianshuo* 辨說, but see below for my argument that those passages concern *ming*, *ci*, and *bianshuo* as parts of *arguments*, so while *ci* might be longer than *ming* and not as long as *bianshuo*, the point of the passages is not to provide the defining characteristic of *ming*, *ci*, and *bianshuo* as bits of language in general.

perhaps a single word or graph, shows that linguistic measurement was not yet standardized.

Early Chinese texts sometimes refer to "a bit of speech" as "one *yan*." A bit of speech is implied in such phrases as "May I have a word with you?" or "And now, a word from our sponsor." In this sense, "word" is a spoken unit of unspecified length. While *yan* (speech, speaking, or utterance) in such instances include *ming*, that is, names of things, the constituent units of *yan* are not called *ming*.[24] Texts from the beginning of the first millennium that analyze graphs and pronunciations show increased specificity in metalinguistic terminology, but they do not measure *yan* by means of *ming*. "One *yan*," rather than "one *ming*," is the minimal unit of "*yan*." In other words, one *ming* is one *ming*, not one *yan*.

One unit of *yan* can be as small as what we would call one word and yet still be called "one *yan*" rather than "one *ming*." When Kongzi is asked for "a single *yan*" by which to live,[25] his response is

> 子貢問曰:「有一言而可以終身行之者乎?」子曰:「其恕乎! 己所不欲, 勿施於人。」
>
> Zigong asked saying, "Is there one *yan* that can be used to act one's whole life?" Kongzi said, "Perhaps reciprocity. That which you do not desire, do not apply to others."
>
> *Lunyu* 論語 〈衛靈公〉第十五

Assuming that the elaboration on *shu* 恕 (reciprocity) is not part of the "one *yan*" discussed, the implied concept of one *yan* is compatible with certain technical definitions of "word." However, when Kongzi provides an example of one *yan* that sums up (or exemplifies) the *Shijing*, his one *yan* seems to contain three words.

> 子曰:「《詩》三百, 一言以蔽之, 曰:『思無邪。』」
>
> Kongzi said, "In the *Shi*, there are three hundred [songs]. One *yan* covers them, saying: Think without deviating."[26]
>
> *Lunyu* 論語 〈為政〉第二

---

24. See the introduction to my *Language as Bodily Practice*. Chad Hansen most clearly articulates the contrary view. He writes, "The smallest units of guiding discourse are *ming*. We string *ming* together in progressively larger units." Thus, for instance, because Hansen takes *ming* to be characters, he contends that correctly ordered *ming*/characters are the building blocks of a *ci*: "Correctly ordered strings of characters constitute the *ci*." Hansen, *Daoist Theory*, 3, 45.

25. The date of composition of the *Lunyu* is highly debated. A variety of recent perspectives are collected in Hunter and Kern, *Confucius and the Analects Revisited*.

26. My translation might exaggerate the spoken features of *yue* 曰, but I do so because its presence reinforces that this is uttered.

In the *Shiji*, when someone requests "one *yan*" before dying, what follows expands well beyond a word or two.[27] Overall, then, a *yan* seems a rather imprecise measure, stretching as it does from a single word to an extended paragraph, thereby reinforcing the assumption that linguistic units were not yet standardized.

Even in texts with more complex metalinguistic terminology, like the first-century *Baihu tong*, *ming* still do not serve as constituent units of *yan*.[28]

> 諡或一言，或兩言何？
> 文者以一言為諡，質者以兩言為諡。
> [Question] Posthumous titles: Why are some one *yan* and some two *yan*?
> [Answer] Those who emphasize the form use one *yan* for posthumous titles; those who emphasize the substance use two *yan* for posthumous titles.
> *Baihu tong* 白虎通 諡

Again, *yan* is treated as a bit of speech. A posthumous title is a type of name, yet the question does not ask whether a posthumous title consists of one or two *ming*.[29] Nor is this question about "one *yan*" and "two *yan*" referring to graphs because the *Baihu tong* was composed late enough that it uses *zi* 字 for "graph." Instead, insofar as posthumous titles are things that people say (in lieu of saying the person's name while living), in this case "one *yan*" refers to the number of sounds involved in uttering someone's posthumous title. The title is measured as either one or two sounds or utterances; hence, this passage seems to take what we would call a single meaningful vocalized sound to be a single *yan*.

Additional evidence for understanding a single *yan* as a variable measurement of speech can be found in the *Chunqiu Fanlu*. Its often-cited lines propose a two-part etymology for the term *yi* 義 (duty): sounding like the graph 宜, and including the component 我. The concluding line invokes "saying 'duty'" (*yan yi* 言義).

---

27. The request uses "one *yan*," which, as with "one word" in such colloquial uses, might be more like a last utterance.

> 曰：「願一言而死。」
> He said, "I would like one *yan* 言 before dying."
> *Shiji* 史記 傳《季布欒布列傳第四十》

Endymion Wilkinson describes the *Shiji* as completed in 91 BCE. Wilkinson, *Chinese History*, 704.

28. The *Baihu tong* is attributed to Ban Gu (32–92), who was charged with summarizing a conference in the White Tiger Hall in 79. According to Michael Nylan, doubts have been raised about the text, but as a whole it is authentic. Nylan, "Baihu tong," 23–24.

29. In early Chinese texts even personal names—surnames, style names, nicknames, etc.—are not necessarily monosyllabic.

何可謂義？義者、謂宜在我者。
宜在我者，而後可以稱義。故言義者，合我與宜，以為一言。
What is referred to by *yi* 義 (duty)? It refers to appropriateness (*yi* 宜) in me (*wo* 我).
Because appropriateness is in me, thus it can be termed "duty."
Hence, when saying (*yan* 言) "duty" (*yi* 義), we unite "I" (*wo* 我) and "appropriate" (*yi* 宜) to be a single utterance (*yan* 言).[30]
Chunqiu Fanlu 春秋繁露 春秋繁露卷八《〈仁義法第二十九〉》

While the foregoing analysis of *yi* 義 addresses both visual and audible features of the graph, the concluding phrase refers to "one utterance," not one graph. Uttering "*yi*" unites "I" and "appropriate" as a single *yan*, but writing the single graph "*yi*" does not. A single *yan* is, in other words, one bit of speech, not one bit of text.

A passage in the *Lunheng* adds a further layer of complexity to the way in which *yan* operates within differing contexts. In this passage, *yan* is the "measure word" (classifier) for bits of discursive sound.[31] The passage, which discusses posthumous titles as graphs (*zi* 字), uses different measure words for different "textual" forms, including the abbreviated "genre" of posthumous titles (謚 *shi*), as well as the more familiar genre of *lun* 論 (sorting discourses) and *song* 頌 (hymns of praise).

夫一字之謚，尚猶明主，況千言之論，萬文之頌哉？
If even a single *zi* 字 of posthumous titles (*shi* 謚) should still illustrate its subject,
how much more so should sorting discourses (*lun* 論) of thousands of *yan* 言,
or hymns of praise (*song* 頌) of many thousands of *wen* 文!
Lunheng 論衡 《〈須頌篇〉》

Each textual form takes a different measure word: *zi* 字 for posthumous titles (謚 *shi*), *yan* 言 for sorting discourses (*lun* 論), and *wen* 文 for hymns of praise (*song* 頌). As the text's size increases, the units switch from one graph to thousands of utterances, to many thousands of praise-filled memorials. Because measure words pertain to the nature of the thing being measured (not the quantity), genre determines the unit of measure. Because *yan* 言 is paradigmatically spoken, the use of *yan* 言 might imply that sorting discourses (*lun* 論) were originally spoken.[32] But in any case, *ming* is

---

30. Sarah Queen and John Major ascribe this chapter to Dong Zhongshu's immediate circle ca. 130–100 BCE. Queen and Major, *Luxuriant Gems*, 27–28.

31. Measure words in English include things like a *flock* of sheep or a *drink* of water. The choice of measure word pertains to the nature of the item being measured.

32. See appendix C entry on *yan* 言 for its associations with speech. The relation of *zi* 字 and *wen* 文 to writing is well known.

not invoked to refer to a bit of speech of any size, which indicates that variously sized bits of *yan* were still called *yan*.

Another term that occasionally appears in early Chinese texts in ways that seem to suggest "word" is "*ci* 辭."[33] In the passage discussed above, the *Lunheng* uses "one *ci*" as one might use "one word":

故「毋」、「必」二辭, 聖人審之。
Thus, as for "not" and "must," these two *ci* 辭, the sage examines them.[34]
Lunheng 論衡 《〈譴告篇〉》

In this departure from the use of *ci* as "well-formulated phrasing," we see yet another sign of unstandardized terminology for linguistic terms.

Thus, early Chinese texts exhibit variability in units for measuring speech and writing. One *ci* 辭 is sometimes a single word, but is also sometimes a phrase. One *yan* 言 might be a single word, a few words, many words, or even a measure word specific to a genre. In sum, early Chinese texts do not consider unit-hood to be a defining characteristic of a "word."

Conclusion

With its addition of pronunciation to each graph, the *Shuowen Jiezi*, China's first-century "dictionary of graphic etymology," is the first source that indisputably standardizes the use of *zi* to mean "word." While that standardization process may well have been occurring across many centuries, tracing its historical progress is complicated by the layered composition of early Chinese texts, the fact that they do not segment language into uniform constituents, the ever-present complexity of defining "word," and the difficulty of determining precisely what standardization entails.

---

33. I treat the term *ci* (辭 phrasing) and *yan* as similar because early Chinese texts describe phrases as simply a particular kind of speech. (See appendix C entry on *ci*.)

The term *yu* 語 seems to be used a bit differently. Uses of *yu* involve speaking *to* someone. Western Han texts might sometimes use it to mean "dialect" (in a non-technical sense). Here "one *yu*" seems like one conversation's worth of advice.

明主之道, 臣不得兩諫, 必任其一語;
The dao of the bright ruler is that he does not obtain two different counsels from
his ministers, but he definitely holds them responsible for one consultation.
Hanfeizi 韓非子 八經第四十八

The *Hanfeizi* is generally accepted as an authentic text written by Hanfei (ca. 280–233 BCE). For questions raised about specific sections, see Jean Levi, "Han fei tzu," 116–117.

34. On *ci* 辭, see note 23 above.

What we can say at this point, however, is that the second-century commentator Zheng Xuan (127–200 CE) was wrong in asserting that "graph" is an optional reading of *ming* in pre-Qin texts—a claim that presumes *ming* (like *zi*) meant "word."[35] Before there was a term for "word," *ming* was not taken to be the equivalent of "word." M*ing* are not semantic, grammatical, or function terms. They refer to things, not concepts or other *ming*. Thus *ming* are "names." While *ming* and *yan* are related, their relation reflects that both are paradigmatically spoken.[36] In light of modern scholarship on metalinguistic terminology, we should not interpret "*ming*" as found in early Chinese texts to be a synonym for the concept "word."[37]

---

35. See introduction, note 34.

36. Naming implies calling by name in the ubiquitous expression *ming zhi yue* 名之曰. Moreover, one performs the act of *ming* by means of speaking. An explicit example articulates as much.

> 故言而名之曰「宙合」。
> Therefore he speaks and names it "All embracing Unity."
> *Guanzi* 管子 管子卷第四 宙合第十一

Here and elsewhere in this volume I follow W. Allyn Rickett's dating of the *Guanzi*, for which see his accompanying headnotes to each chapter. Rickett dates this chapter to the early second century BCE. Rickett, *Guanzi*, 1:204.

Yan 言 often takes the place of *ming* in being paired with *shi* 實 (the term for reference, with which *ming* is most often paired), which implies that *yan* and *ming* overlap to some degree (speech contains names). By contrast, no term used to mean something like "writing" performs that function of replacing *ming* in being paired with *shi* 實. In other words, while there is "*ming* and *shi*," there is no "*zi* 字 and *shi* 實." Moreover, there is no "*shu* 書 and *shi* 實." In the only cases of "*wen* 文 and *shi* 實," *wen* 文 seems to mean something other than writing: the *Liji* 33.9, *Xunzi* chapter 5, and the *Qianhanji* 前漢紀 chapter 29—a second-century text in which speech and writing are juxtaposed to action and *shi* 實. There is a related usage that could potentially constitute an exception in the *Gongyangzhuan*. In reference to ritual texts, the repeated phrase asserts that something is acceptable in practice (*shi* 實) but not for being put into writing: 實與、而文不與. (According to David Schaberg, the *Gongyangzhuan* was "transmitted orally for some time before being committed to writing in the Western Han." Schaberg, "Classics," 178.)

37. In "Grounding 'Language' in the Senses," I examine the implications of this conclusion for allegations of Chinese "logocentrism."

CHAPTER TWO

Speech (*Yan* 言) from Within and Names (*Ming* 名) from Without

As I have previously argued in *Language as Bodily Practice in Early China*, language during this period was not conceived of as an abstraction, and therefore must be appreciated as bodily phenomena—utterances that are emitted from the mouth and received through the ears. A term's relation to the body is determinative. Paradigmatically, *yan* 言 (speech) comes out from the mouth, while *ming* 名 (names) enter the ears. A signal distinction between *yan* 言 and *ming* 名 hinges on *yi* 意. People's *yi* 意 express their internal states through *yan* but not *ming*.[1] The standard usage is that *ming* 名, which are used to pick or raise things up, originate from outside and are experienced as external.[2] Speech (*yan* 言) uses names that refer outside, but speech emerges from inside the speaker. It can proclaim and dredge up what is on the mind, giving voice to an internal aspect of the self. *Ming* 名, on the other hand, have no expressive function.

Trajectories of *Ming* 名 and Speech

In early Chinese texts, there are "exemplary situations" in which *ming* tend to be discussed.[3] For example, a ruler assigns *ming* to people upon observing what they reveal about themselves. Consider this case from the *Lüshi Chunqiu*:

---

1. In the context of early Chinese ideas about the boundaries of a person, internal and external are not entirely distinct spheres but shade into one another by a matter of degrees.

2. See *Language as Bodily Practice*, 94–109.

3. The philosopher Annemarie Mol argues for the usefulness of thinking about "exemplary situations" in which philosophical theories are embedded. Mol, "I Eat an Apple," 28–37.

人主出聲應容，不可不審。凡主有識，言不欲先。人唱我和，人先我隨。以其出為之入，以其言為之名，取其實以責其名，則說者不敢妄言，而人主之所執其要矣。

With a ruler, the sounds he produces and the responses on his face cannot but be examined. Whenever a ruler has an insight, in his speaking he will not want to go first. "Others sing and I harmonize. Others first and I follow." What is put into something should be based on what it puts out: the *ming* should be based on the speaking. Pick their fruits to hold them responsible for their *ming*. Then the "explainers" (*shuo zhe*) will not dare to derange speaking and the ruler will control the essential.[4]

Lüshi Chunqiu 呂氏春秋 審應覽第六 《審應》

By strategically withholding his own comments and bodily expression, the ruler compels officials to speak and, thus, to divulge what is within themselves in ways that help determine the *ming* they deserve. The ruler listens to the speaking that comes out (*chu*) and, on that basis, decides which *ming* he should "enter in" (*ru*, presumably into their ears).

The *Hanfeizi* similarly describes the listening that precedes the apportioning of shares and titles.

凡聽之道，以其所出，反以為之入。故審名以定位，明分以辯類。

Now, the dao of listening is to use what comes out in order to, in turn, enter something into it. Therefore examine *ming* 名 (titles) to assign positions, clarifying shares and distinguishing kinds.[5]

Hanfeizi 韓非子 揚權第八

The ruler's *ming* is the input that enters the officials as a response to their output in the form of speaking and acting. From the perspective of the officials, the ruler's *ming* are external in the sense that they are the commanded titles that the ruler imposes on them from without. By contrast, the officials' speaking is internal insofar as it is something they bring out of themselves. In other words, the ruler's *ming* in the exemplary context is not simply a more specific or narrow form of *yan*; in a certain sense, it actually contrasts with it.

The Physiological Trajectory of Speaking

The early Chinese understanding of the physiology of speech, as gleaned from the era's texts, also supports the argument that, during that period, "*ming*" cannot be

---

4. The *Lüshi Chunqiu* is a third century text probably completed in outline by the time of Lü Buwei's death in 235 BCE, according to Knoblock (*Annals of Lü Buwei*, 32).

5. Here, as in the *Xunzi*'s "Zhengming," distinguishing and clarifying are both consequences of naming.

equated with the concept "word." While *ming* and *yan* are usually audible (and typically) human utterances, they differ in a significant way: *yan* emerges from the heartmind (*xin* 心), whereas *ming* does not.[6]

What I call "quasi-physiological" passages address the arrival of speech before mentioning the existence of *ming*. Speech precedes *ming* and speech exhibits a function that includes improving the condition of *ming*. An example from the *Guoyu* depicts how qi forms in the mouth and becomes speech.[7] After speaking occurs, it makes *ming* trustworthy.

口內味而耳內聲, 聲味生氣。氣在口為言, 在目為明。言以信名, 明以時動。名以成政, 動以殖生。政成生殖, 樂之至也。
若視聽不和, 而有震眩, 則味入不精, 不精則氣佚, 氣佚則不和。於是乎有狂悖之言, 有眩惑之明, 有轉易之名, 有過慝之度。

When the mouth contains flavors and the ears contain sounds, the sounds and flavors produce qi. Qi in the mouth becomes *yan*. In the eyes it becomes clear-sightedness (or clarity or brightness). *Yan* is that which makes *ming* trustworthy. Clear-sightedness is that which makes movement timely. *Ming* is that which completes governing. Action is that which produces growth. Completed governing and produced growth are the ultimate joy.

If what is seen and heard is not harmonious, if there is thunder and dazzling light, then flavors enter, but are not *jing* (vital); if they (the flavors) are not vital then the qi is dissipated; if the qi is dissipated, then there is no harmony. Thereupon, we have crazy *yan*, blinded and confused (clear)-sightedness, revolving transforming *ming*, and an excess wickedness past the point of measure.[8]

Guoyu 國語 周語 《單穆公諫景王鑄大鍾》

In this extended explanation, speaking and *ming* are distinct from one another, with markedly different roles. The role of speaking is to influence *ming*: harmonious qi produces speaking, which in turn makes *ming* trustworthy. Inharmonious or slanted qi produces crazy speaking, which renders *ming* topsy-turvy. The role of *ming* is to affect governing. Rather than being comprehended as constituent elements of speech in early Chinese texts, *ming* come after speaking and are transformed by it.

---

6. As a translation of *xin* 心, I use the awkward but useful term "heartmind" to signal that the faculty of reason and emotion are not separate.

7. The *Guoyu* might have been composed as early as the fifth century BCE. On the difficulty of dating the *Guoyu*—from a changing and developing oral transmission, through its transcription, commenting, and editing—see Schaberg, *Patterned Past*, 315–324.

8. Chang I-jen, William Boltz, and Michael Loewe date this section of the text to fifth century BCE in "Kuo yü," 264.

Similar physiological sequences whereby qi produces speech in some relation to the mouth's tastes, subsequently followed by *ming* 名, appear in some form in other early Chinese texts.

> 味以行氣，氣以實志，志以定言，言以出令。
> The tastes are used to move the qi. The qi is used to solidify the aims. The aims are used to settle the *yan* (speech). The *yan* is used to give out orders (*ling* 令).[9]
> *Zuozhuan* 春秋左傳 昭公 B10.9 《昭公九年傳》

This particular representation of the origin of speech uses *ling* 令 (command), rather than the related *ming* 名/命 (name or command), when identifying what comes after speech: in this case, commands. The suggestion that *ming* are commands that can be ordained once tastes and qi give rise to speech undermines the notion that *ming* 名 could ever be the building blocks of *yan*.

A *Dadai Liji* passage also gives precedence to speaking, which in turn fixes (*ding* 定) *ming*. The passage responds to a question about the value of salary (or, more literally, groceries).

> 食為味，味為氣，[氣]為志，發志為言，發言定名，名以出信。
> 信載義而行之，祿不可後也。
> Food makes flavor, flavor makes qi, qi makes aims/aspiration (*zhi* 志), expressing aims makes *yan*, expressing speaking (*yan*) settles *ming*, *ming* are that by which trust emerges. Trust bears duty and enacts it. Groceries (emolument) cannot be put last.[10]
> *Da Dai Liji* 大戴禮記 大戴禮記卷第九 《四代第六十九》

In short, rulers are obligated to provide the salary that will set in motion the string of physiological transformations—a salary furnishes the means to buy food; food produces flavor in the mouth; flavor generates qi, which yields aspirations that are expressed as *yan*—that are required to settle or "fix" (*ding* 定) *ming*, which, if all goes well, instill trust. We are not given insight into how *ming* develop or precisely how they come to be fixed, but their fixity is the external product of a series of

---

9. Compare the translation by James Legge, *Ch'un Ts'ew*, 626, and the translation of Durrant, Li, and Schaberg, *Zuo Tradition*, 3:1451.

10. The *Dadai Liji* is traditionally considered to be from the second century BCE, but as a collection, it might be no earlier than the beginning of the second century CE. Riegel, "Ta Tai Li Chi 大戴禮記," 456–459.

Alan Chan raises the interesting possibility of translating *zhi* 志 as "aspiration," given aspiration's sense as "breathing." Chan, "Harmony as a Contested Metaphor," 58.

events.[11] In effect, the *Da Dai Liji* passage says that people's utterances come from what they eat, but it does not say that about names. *Yan*, then, derives not from accumulated *ming* but from expressed aims, which are composed from qi, which is made of the flavors of food. In short, *ming* decidedly do not function as words, individual components that, when strung together, constitute speech.

Even though it is an excavated text of uncertain authenticity, we may also take note that the "Heng Xian," too, distinguishes between the origins of speaking and *ming*. The reference to *xing* 性 resembles passages that describe a quasi-physiological development.[12] The "Heng Xian" says,

> 意出於性，言出於意，名出於言，事出於名。
> *Yi* (what is on the mind)[13] emerges from spontaneous dispositions, *yan* emerges from *yi*,[14] *ming* emerge from *yan*, situations emerge from *ming*.[15]
> "Heng Xian" 楚竹書十二 《恒先》四

Speaking proceeds from *yi* 意, which in turn produces, or allows for the "emergence" (*chu* 出) of *ming*. Each step of the physiological process is discrete: *yan* is not *yi*, *ming* is not *yan*, *shi* 事 (situation) is not *ming*. In other words, although *yan* gives rise to *ming*, it is not itself composed of *ming*.

Take, on the other hand, titles and names. With the exception of nicknames, people do not typically name themselves or assign themselves titles in early Chinese texts.[16] A person's fame (*ming*) is dependent on the speech of others and is beyond one's control. In other words, the term "*ming*" as title or fame is imposed from without by the speech of others, not from within, as is one's own *yan*.

---

11. In short, it would not make sense to interpret these passages as saying that once there is a group of words then something can be done about the problem of words.

12. I am uncertain about the best translation of *xing* 性, but it might be something like an unmanifest spontaneous character or disposition.

13. I translate *yi* 意 as "what is on the mind" because it evokes the breadth of uses of *yi* but also to allude to the physical trajectory from inside to outside that early Chinese texts emphasize in discussing speech, but not *ming*, in relation to *yi*.

14. This is close to the *Dadai Liji* passage that moves from food to flavor to qi, but here the passage speaks of *yi* 意, rather than *zhi* 志 (aims).

15. The date assigned to the *Heng Xian* is ca. 300 BCE, but it is "unprovenanced" (i.e., brought to the market as a result of tomb robbing) and thus may be unreliable. See Goldin, "*Heng Xian* and the Problem of Studying Looted Artifacts," 155.

16. Several passages from Western Han texts make this explicit by noting that names are dependent on other people, which makes them external in that sense. See *Kongzijiayu*, chapter 22, "Kun Shi," and *Yi Zhou Shu*, chapter 1.54, "Shi Fa Jie."

Readers may be wondering how this description of *ming* as externally imposed fits with the relation of *ming* and *yan* in the well-known *Lunyu* 13.3 description of *zhengming* ("rectifying names"). In the physiological passages discussed above, *yan* and *ming* have different moments of origin, with *ming* appearing later. By contrast, in *Lunyu* 13.3, *ming* come first and influence speaking by making it compliant or smooth.[17] Names and speech are somewhat independent phenomena, no matter whether one is seen to have priority or to be acting on the other. If we consider both the *Lunyu* 13.3 prioritization of *ming* and the physiological prioritization of speaking, depending on the perspective (speaker or listener), one or the other will come first. But insofar as *ming* can be acted on by speech, it is unlikely that speech would be seen as being composed of a succession of *ming*.

Speech as an Expression of the Heartmind's *Yi* 意

So far, I have established that speech gives voice to internality, but that process can be described more precisely. Speaking expresses the interior in terms of the *yi* 意 of the heartmind (*xin* 心). The passage that, arguably, most famously discusses the relation of *yi* 意 to speaking is found in the "*Xici*."

> 書不盡言，言不盡意。
> Writing does not exhaust *yan* (speaking). *Yan* does not exhaust *yi* (what is on the mind).[18]
> "Xici Shang" *Zhouyi* 周易 《繫辭上》

The line implies that, just as writing comes from speaking, so too speaking comes from *yi*. The *Guanzi* describes the derivation of speech with a sequence that begins in the heartmind.[19]

---

17. The line reads:

> 13.3 名不正，則言不順；言不順，則事不成 . . .
> If *ming* are not *zheng* (straight, rectified), then speech will not comply, if speech does not comply, then tasks/service will not complete themselves . . .
> *Lunyu* 論語 〈子路〉第十三

18. Edward Shaughnessy proposes that the *Xici* contains different strata. Regarding this line, he notes, "the author of this second stratum of the *Xici* was participating in a debate . . . [that] seems to have emerged within a decade or so of 300 BCE and then became quite ubiquitous by the middle of the following century." Shaughnessy, "Writing of the *Xici Zhuan*," 209.

19. In a related passage in *Guanzi* 16, the following line asserts that after shapes, there is speech. Thereupon, after speech, there is *shi* 使 (control). The sequence terminates in achieving order.

Speech (*Yan* 言) from Within and Names (*Ming* 名) from Without / 39

心之中又有心。意以先言，意然後刑，刑然后思，思然后知。
Within the *xin* (heartmind) there is another *xin*. The *yi* comes before *yan*. After *yi*, there are shapes. After shapes, there is thinking. After thinking, there is knowing.[20]
Guanzi 管子 管子卷第十三 心術下第三十七

The fishnet analogy from the *Zhuangzi* grounds the motivation of speech in *yi*.[21]

言者所以在意，荃者所以在魚
The purpose of *yan* lies in *yi*. The purpose of the net lies in the fish.[22]
Zhuangzi 莊子 外物第二十六

The *Lüshi Chunqiu* also draws a direct line between speaking and *yi*:

言者，以諭意也。言意相離，凶也。
Yan is for proclaiming *yi*. When *yan* and *yi* are distant, there is disaster.
Lüshi Chunqiu 呂氏春秋 審應覽第六 《《離謂》》

To be sure, well-formed phrasing (*ci* 辭), and indeed all forms of speaking, is external because it constitutes the externalization of personal feeling, aiming, and desiring. As the *Lüshi Chunqiu* puts it,

夫辭者，意之表也。
Ci (phrasing): the surface (*biao* 表) of *yi* (what is on the mind).
Lüshi Chunqiu 呂氏春秋 審應覽第六 《《離謂》》

Biao suggests the outer layer of something or that which it displays. So speaking and phrasing are in their origins rooted in the interior, but in their functions, as they express what is inside, they are exterior.

Counterargument: *Ming* 名 with *Yi* 意

In order to substantiate my argument about the relationship between *yi* 意 and *yan* 言, I must consider any instances that deviate from the pattern I have described.

---

20. Rickett assigns this chapter to the second century BCE. Rickett, *Guanzi*, 2:56.
21. I discuss the *Zhuangzi* fishnet passage at length in *Language as Bodily Practice*, 113–121.
22. The *Zhuangzi* is a multilayered text containing material dated to the fourth to second century BCE. See Roth, "*Chuang tzu*," 56–57; and Klein, "Were There 'Inner Chapters,'" 299–369.

Among those rare instances in which *ming* appear in close proximity to *yi* 意 (what is on the mind), one seems to involve "the *yi* 意 of a *ming*."²³ The passage, which is from the *Jiayi Xinshu*, concerns a prescriptive discourse that is meant to inspire nobles to take responsibility for their people, the *min meng* 民萌, or the masses.

> 是故君明而吏賢，吏賢而民治矣。故苟上好之，其下必化之，此道之政也。夫民之為言也暝也，萌之為言也（肓）[盲]也，故惟上之所扶而以之，民無不化也。故曰：「民萌。」民萌哉! 直言其意而為之名也。
>
> Thus, if the lord is bright, then the officer is virtuous; if the officer is virtuous, then the people are ordered. Hence, if those above are fond of something, those below will necessarily transform. This is the dao of governing. Now, as spoken, "masses" (民 *mi[ŋ]) is "dark" (暝 *mêŋ). As spoken, "sprout" (萌 *mrâŋ) is "blind" (*mˤaŋ). Therefore, in the absence of those above supporting them, none of the people would transform (i.e., improve). Hence, we say "*min meng.*" *Min meng*, indeed! [We] are directly (*zhi* 直) speaking its *yi* 意 while giving to it a name. [Alternative reading: "while naming it" 而為之名也.]²⁴
>
> *Jiayi Xinshu* 新書 賈誼新書卷九 《大政下》

Employing the common strategy of punning, the exhortation encourages nobles to recognize that when they utter the name "masses" (*min meng* 民萌, which sounds like "dark" and "blind"), they proclaim a concern and commitment to help the blind masses improve.

The crucial feature to note about this example is that, while it seems to say that a certain *ming* 名 have *yi* 意, the passage explicitly describes the *yi* in terms of *speaking ming*. This association of *yi* 意 with *ming* 名 is anomalous, but it is intriguing. The passage suggests that the sounds of *ming* connect them with other similar-sounding *ming* such that the heartmind expresses similar *yi* 意 by uttering similar sounds. More precisely, the passage makes its point by emphasizing the idea of an utterance more so than sound per se. Twice it refers to speaking. First, it is "as spoken" (之為言也) that "*min*" is "*ming*." Second, the *yi* is directly (*zhi* 直) spoken.

---

23. I examine Chad Hansen's theory about preserving the sage's original intentions (*yi* 意) when coining names in *Language as Bodily Practice*, 45–56. Hansen contends that the *Mo Bian* passage on what I call the "tripartite division of argument" (see below) implies that subsequent uses of a *ming* do not have an *yi* 意 because, once the name is instituted, information about how to use the name derives from the world, not from the sages' intentions. That theory interprets only a *Mo Bian* understanding of why *ming* do not appear with *yi*. It does not address the related passage in the *Xunzi*'s "Zhengming" chapter or the widespread evidence that speech expresses *yi* 意.

24. The *Xinshu* is traditionally attributed to Jia Yi (200–168 BCE), but its authenticity has often been questioned. Nylan, "Hsin shu," 166–167.

That is, the *yi* 意 is not directly named but directly spoken. Whereas one might be tempted to say that the name's meaning is implied in the name's sound (i.e., proper pronunciation), the passage says something different. It says that whatever the heartmind intends, wishes, or plans about the name is invoked within the process of uttering it. In other words, the passage does not say, "You should treat the people as blind masses because the name itself implies it." The difference is slight, but it says instead, "You should treat the people as blind masses because *speaking* the name itself implies it." It is only in uttering them that *ming* are accompanied by *yi* 意. To that extent, it is still the speaking, not the name, that expresses what is on the mind. Thus *ming* differ from *yan* in that they cannot express the heartmind except through the vehicle of uttering or, in other words, through *yan*.

The "Zhengming" chapter of the *Xunzi* offers another example of a potential association between *yi* 意 and *ming* that we should not overlook. Regarding the speech of the *junzi* (noble person), the "Zhengming" line seems to be open to two interpretations. Either, as it has been commonly understood, it posits that the *junzi*'s names and phrases are the messengers of their thoughts, or it declares that the *junzi*'s names and phrases are messengers whose aim is focused on duty (*zhiyi* 志義).[25] The line is as follows:

> 彼正其名、當其辭以務白其志義者也。彼名辭也者、志義之使也，足以相通則舍之矣；苟之，姦也。故名之足以指實，辭足以見極，則舍之矣。。。 彼誘其名，眩其辭，而無深於其志義者也。
>
> They [the *junzi*] correct their names and make their phrases coincide in order to strive to clarify their *zhiyi* 志義. Their names and phrases are *shi* 使 (officers, messengers) of the *zhiyi*. They should be sufficient for mutual *tong* 通 (non-obstruction), and that is all. Carelessness with them is heinous. Therefore the name should be sufficient to point to the *shi* (action/thing). The phrase should be sufficient to make visible extremes, and that is all. . . . [Ignorant people] entice with names and confuse with phrases, and they have no depth to their *zhiyi*.
>
> *Xunzi* 荀子 正名篇第二十二

Note the *yi* 義 in *zhiyi* 志義. *Zhi* 志 is an ethical term used to mean aim or intent. As an ethical term, *yi* 義 means something like "duty." As a compound in texts of the period, *zhiyi* 志義 can refer to an official with moral purpose, one whose aim is focused on duty. For example, the *Liji* speaks of ministers who are characterized as *zhiyi*:

---

25. For another discussion of this term, see *Language as Bodily Practice*, 104–105.

君子聽琴瑟之聲則思志義之臣。

When the *junzi* listens to the sound of the *qin* and *se* (stringed instruments), he yearns for ministers who are *zhiyi*.[26]

Liji 禮記 〈樂記〉 19.25

The *Lunheng* uses the term *zhiyi* to describe a flaw in the character of Guanzhong, chancellor of Qi.

管仲分財取多，無廉讓之節，貧乏不足，志義廢也。

Guanzhong, when dividing money, picked the larger portion for himself. He had no measure of incorruptibility; his finances were insufficient and his *zhiyi* was abandoned.

Lunheng 論衡 《〈定賢篇〉》

Interpreted in light of the foregoing cases of *zhiyi*, the line in the "Zhengming" seems to suggest that the *junzi*'s names and phrases are his officers. They proceed from the *speaker's mouth* as messengers intent on duty. As such, they do not press on once they have accomplished their mission. In sum, the passage declares, the *junzi* make names correct in order to clarify not their thoughts in general but their moral purpose. The names and phrases they utter are ambassadors of that moral purpose. In contrast to a *junzi*'s deep-seated and unwavering concentration on duty, ignorant people's approach to duty is shallow, which coincides with dubious uses of rhetoric. My reading of the names and phrases in this passage, then, does not concern meaning; rather, it centers on the normative objective of speech and its effect on curtailing verbosity.

The customary interpretation of the passage *does*, however, focus on semantic meaning. That reading turns, in part, on a substitution of *yi* 意 for *yi* 義 to evoke the compound *zhiyi* 志意 (aims and intentions). The conflation of the two terms seems historically unlikely, though, since *yi* 意 and *yi* 義 do not appear to have been pronounced similarly at the time.[27] Nevertheless, for the sake of argument,

---

26. The line also appears in the *Shiji* and the *Shuoyuan*. Desiring to employ an officer who is *zhiyi* (欲使志義之士) also occurs in the Later Han text the *Qianfu Lun* (潛夫論 《〈本政第九〉》), and the term continues to appear in Wei and Jin texts.

The sections of the *Liji* probably did not originate together and its date and origin are controversial. See Riegel, "Li chi 禮記," 293–295. According to Liu Yucai and Luke Habberstad, the compilation of the *Liji* belongs to the "institutional context of the study and transmission of ritual learning during the Western Han and Eastern Han." Liu and Habberstad, "Life of a Text," 296.

27. In William Baxter and Laurent Sagart's phonetic reconstruction, *yi* 意 is pronounced OC *ʔ(r)ək-s > MC *'iH, whereas *yi* 義 is pronounced OC *ŋ(r)aj-s > MC *ngjeH. Baxter and Sagart, *Old Chinese: A New Reconstruction*. http://ocbaxtersagart.lsait.lsa.umich.edu/BaxterSagartOCby-MandarinMC2014-09-20.pdf, 136.

let's consider the interpretation on its own terms. As such, it appears to suggest that names alone (without phrases) are the direct messengers of what is on a person's mind, evidence that *yi* 意 accompany names. Even if we grant that we should read *zhiyi* 志義 as *zhiyi* 志意, however, the passage does not assert that names, on their own, convey *yi* 意. The line from the "Zhengming" under discussion, unlike other parts of the chapter, employs two compounds, *mingci* 名辭 and *zhiyi*. We should approach these compounds as a specialized vocabulary not only because their use is unique in the context of this chapter but also because *mingci* 名辭 appears only one other time in pre-Han and Han texts, and in a context not about language.[28] If this line in the "Zhengming" concerns a messenger of thoughts and intentions at all, apparently it can fulfill its function only in the presence of *ci* (phrasing). Hence, even granting that *yi* 義 here replaces *yi* 意, by tethering *ming* 名 to *ci* 辭 the "Zhengming" confirms that *ming* 名 alone are not messengers of *yi* 意.

The strongest challenge to my contention that *yan* (speech) and *ming* are different in kind not just in quantity (that is, that *yan* is not simply a string of *ming*) occurs in what I call the "tripartite division of argument" passages in the *Xunzi*'s "Zhengming" and the *Mo Bian*.[29] The line could be interpreted incorrectly as follows: insofar as phrases express *yi* 意, they do so by conjoining *ming* that express *yi*. The passage reads,

> 名也者、所以期累實也。辭也者、兼異實之名以（論）[諭]一意也。辨說也者, 不異實名以喻動靜之道也。
>
> *Ming* (names or naming) is that by which one arranges [?][30] accumulated[31] *shi* (actions/things).
>
> With *ci* (phrases or phrasing): Compound the names of different *shi* (actions/things) in order to proclaim one *yi*.
>
> With *bianshuo* (distinguishing explanations): Do not [?][32] differentiate *shi* (actions/things) from names in order to elucidate the dao of movement and stillness.
>
> *Xunzi* 荀子 正名篇第二十二

The passage is problematic. First, "sequencing" is an uncharacteristic description of the function of *ming*, and the translation of the word preceding *shi* is uncertain.

---

28. *Shuoyuan* 說苑 尊賢 8.23.
29. On the "tripartite division of argument," see also *Language as Bodily Practice*, 53–55, 105–108.
30. This term is used frequently and obscurely in the chapter.
31. It is possible that this graph should be *yi* 異, meaning "different things/actions," hence the translation is tentative.
32. The graph for "not" here is arguably extraneous.

Second, the presence of "not" (*bu* 不) in the description of distinguishing explanations is also perplexing. However, if we set those enigmas aside, we may still glean an understanding from an apparently uncorrupted portion of the passage: "Phrasing: Compound the names of different *shi* in order to proclaim one *yi* 意." Two common, misguided interpretations go something like this: "Phrases proclaim what is on the mind (*yi* 意) by compounding *ming*"; and "Phrasing is bringing together several *ming* to proclaim a single thing on the mind." The inference might follow that *ci* 辭 are strings of names that permit the expression of *yi* 意 by virtue of their length and/or structure. Individual *ming* do not suffice; a succession of them does. In such a reading, *ci* 辭 could be taken to be a midsized linguistic category that is more expansive than *ming*, on the one hand, but not as general as speaking, on the other. The above passage, then, is an important source for the linguistic view that *yan* and *ci* are abstractions that, when divided into their constituent components, consist of *ming*; therefore, the difference between *ming* and *yan* is ultimately a matter of number.

The passage's context is vital and must be considered when assessing the persuasiveness of the interpretation outlined above. That context does not concern itself with categories of language but with elements of an argument.

The "Zhengming" chapter implies that arguments have three segments, and the third segment—on *bianshuo* "distinguishing explanations"—signals the thrust of the passage. Because it is about an argument, it is called "distinguishing explanations." If these were categories of language, the names of the segments would indicate as much. Not only does the final segment *not* refer to speech per se (which we would expect it to do if it were making a point about language), but the concluding reference to the dao of movement and stillness also makes it unlikely that the description of phrasing could be extended to an assertion about *yan* in general. The dao of movement and stillness assuredly does not pertain to speech or utterances but may plausibly pertain to techniques for argumentation. In my interpretation, the passage states that arguments include segments called phrasings, which can be used to proclaim something on the mind by combining names of different things. My next point is a bit more complex. The passage states that *ci* 辭 (phrasing) involves compounding the *ming* of different *shi* (actions/things) in order to proclaim one issue that is on the mind. Thus the terms are, on the one hand, the *ming* of different *shi* (actions/things) and, on the other, a single *yi* (a single issue on the mind).[33] The passage refers not to "multiple *ming*" or even "different *ming*" (as it might if it were discussing segments of language) but to the names of different *shi*

---

33. This could presuppose the goal of having any different action/thing have a different *ming* (使異實者莫不異名也). But this goal need not be interpreted as saying that a single action/thing should have no more than one name. It does not say that different things/actions should have one name or a single name. See also my *Language as Bodily Practice*, xxxi, n68.

(actions/things). There would be no reason for it to mention the "*ming* of different things" (as opposed to "multiple *ming*" or "different *ming*") if this were a description of language. Debaters making an argument, however, must raise a variety of points (different things) in order to be persuasive, that is, to offer "distinguishing explanations." When debaters seek to proclaim a single thing on their minds—in this case, the argument they want to propound—they use phrasing; they do so because the functions of phrasing include pulling together the names of multiple things to proclaim one thing that is on the mind (*yi* 意).

A comparison to a similar segment of the *Mo Bian* supports my line of reasoning.[34] The comparison draws attention to the "Zhengming" chapter's use of "that by which" (*suoyi* 所以) to describe *ming*, a formula it does not apply to phrasing and distinguishing explanations. "That by which" could be read as inclusive, as a quality true of all *ming*, a form of linguistic definition (i.e., "a *ming* is that by which . . ."). But the *suo* 所 is absent in the "Zhengming" characterizations of phrasing and distinguishing explanations. It simply notes something that can be done by means of these things, which implies that the characterizations are not linguistic definitions. The *Mo Bian* is more explicit than the *Xunzi* in presenting all three terms—*ming*, phrasing, and explanations[35]—in relation to their functions rather than their definitions.

> 以名舉實，以辭抒意，以說出故。
> With *ming* (names or naming), pick *shi* (actions/things).
> With *ci* (phrases or phrasing), dredge up *yi*.
> With *shuo* (explaining), issue forth the *gu* (basis).
> *Mozi* 墨子 墨子卷十一 11.2 《小取第四十五》

Phrasing expresses what is on the mind, but the passage makes no mention of *ming* in this regard. Here, too, the passage builds toward its ultimate focus, explaining—not speaking.[36] I think we are on safe ground, then, if we conclude that the corresponding passages from the "Zhengming" and the *Mo Bian* refer not to linguistics but to argumentation. Therefore, the passages lend no support to the claim that speech consists of a string of names or that names in sufficient quantity express what is in the heartmind in more or less the same way that combined words express complex thoughts. *Ming* do not "issue out" (*fa* 發), "proclaim" (*yu* 諭), or "dredge out" (*shu* 抒), as speech and phrases do.

---

34. The passages are different and there may be important reasons for those differences, but in this case their similarities are revealing.

35. The *bian* (distinguishing) is absent.

36. It might say that debaters can use explaining to draw out causes or reasons for arguments.

Conclusion

Texts from Early China do not describe *ming* as arising from the heartmind or as the outer layer of the heartmind's *yi* 意, at least directly. Moreover, *ming* are generally depicted as being heard rather than as issuing from one's own mouth.[37] *Yan*, on the other hand, does characteristically emerge from the mouth. *Yan* is the product of a person's physical cultivation, even to the point of being traceable to ingested food. No such claims apply to *ming*. How then could *yan* or *ci* consist of the sum of *ming*? If a *ming*, as an act of naming, points outward, and *ming*, as title or fame, does not come from the interior, then why would more *ming* linked together be credited with the ability to express the interior of a person? The directional vector from within to without distinguishes both speaking (*yan*) and phrasing (*ci*) and definitively differentiates both from *ming*. Speech comes out from the inside and expresses the heartmind. Names point outward, do not come from the heartmind, and do not express it except insofar as names are parts of utterances.

---

37. I explore this difference between *ming* 命/名 and *yan* 言 in *Language as Bodily Practice*, 185–193.

CHAPTER THREE

Yi 意 and the Heartmind's Activities

In any consideration of the ways in which human beings communicate with one another via language, "meaning" might seem to be an inevitable part of the inquiry. But what, exactly, people intend when they invoke "word-meaning" is rarely obvious. In everyday speech in Modern Standard Mandarin, the term *yisi* 意思 is used to ask "What does this word mean?"[1] Thus, the compound *yisi* (and similar compounds) might contribute to the impression that early Chinese texts used *yi* 意 to denote the meanings of words in a dictionary.[2] Moreover, by the Tang dynasty (618–907) if not earlier, *yi* 意 came to suggest, especially in aesthetics and literary criticism, creative inspiration in the imaginative process.[3] Like the term "idea," this association of *yi* 意 with creativity might seem to derive from a conception of ideas as pictures or shapes in the mind that are in turn attached to the meanings

---

1. I discuss the anachronism of *yiyi* 意義 for Early China in chapter 8.
2. Translating *yi* 意 as "propositions," Bao Zhiming makes a brief argument that *ming* 名 include both "sense" and "sign." Bao, "Abstraction," 434.

Focusing on the potential of a different term, *zhi* 指, for use as "word-meaning," A. C. Graham rightly contends that the "opposition *ming/shi* 'name/object' is very unlike the Saussurian signifier/signified. . . . A name is used to 'point out' *chih* [指] an object. . . . Nominalized *chih* is sometimes conveniently translated by 'meaning,'" he writes, but "there is consequently no tendency for the *chih* of names to turn like 'meanings' or the 'signified,' into third entities on the same level as the objects and the sounds of names." Graham, *Disputers*, 228.

3. Cai Zongqi sketches some of the history of *yi* 意 in relation to "refined feelings." Observing that Lu Ji (261–303) and Liu Xie (fifth century) generally used *yi* 意 straightforwardly as "intended meaning," Cai describes the "*Lun Wen Yi*" of Wang Changling (ca. 698–756) as the earliest literary critical work that gives *yi* 意 "full paradigmatic significance." Cai, "Toward an Innovative Poetics," 182.

of words.⁴ In my survey of early Chinese texts from across a range of disciplines, however, I have found that uses of yi 意 do not suggest mental pictures. Yi 意 instead signals intent, attitude, wish, opinion, plan, suppose, and conjecture. Yi 意 is expressive, intentional (directed toward something), and mobile. It was not used to mean mental images serving as semantic meaning in Early China. To make my case, I will explore in this chapter where yi 意 was believed to originate, how it was accessed, how it was perceived, and how it functioned in early Chinese texts.

Reaching Internal Yi 意

The nature of yi 意 is evident, in part, in the process of trying to discern an yi 意. Early Chinese texts commonly describe requests to speak about yi 意 being met by answers involving intentions, plans, aims, etc. No textual clues allow us to say that yi 意 in those responses is anything more technical than intentions, wishes, or speculations.

But several passages in the *Xunzi*'s "Zhengming" chapter and the *Mo Bian* associate yi 意 with something specific: ci 辭 (phrases). Let's return to an example I presented in the previous chapter as the "tripartite division of argument."

> 名也者、所以期累實也。辭也者、兼異實之名以（論）[諭]一意也。辨說也者，不異實名以喻動靜之道也。
>
> *Ming* (names or naming) is that by which one arranges [?] accumulated *shi* (actions/things).
>
> With *ci* (phrases or phrasing): Compound the names of different *shi* (actions/things) in order to *proclaim* one yi.
>
> With *bianshuo* (distinguishing explanations): Do not [?] differentiate *shi* (actions/things) from names in order to elucidate the dao of movement and stillness.
>
> *Xunzi* 荀子 正名篇第二十二

---

4. Michael Syrotinski's note on "idea" in the *Dictionary of Untranslatables* reads: "The word 'idea' comes from the philosophical Latin idea (from *videre*, 'to see'), used notably by Seneca (*Letters* 58.18) in translating Plato's Greek idea [ἰδέα] (from *idein* [ἰδεῖν], the aorist of *horaô* [ὁράω], 'to see'), which—in a running set of exchanges and cross-references with the closely related term *eidos* [εἶδος]—means 'visible form, aspect,' and later 'distinctive form, essence.' . . . In Aesthetics, of particular importance is the relationship between the surface or image, and the underlying reality or model." Syrotinski, "Idea," 477.

Yi 意 can seem to be part of an internal language of "Mentalese," into which language is translated in order to be understood. Chad Hansen argues convincingly against this view in general and particularly as a way of interpreting concepts of thinking in early Chinese texts. Hansen, "Language in the Heart-mind," 75–124.

What is this *yi* 意 in the gloss about phrasing? With minor variations, a section in the *Mo Bian* also associates *yi* 意 with phrasing.

> 以名舉實，以辭抒意，以說出故。
> With *ming* (names or naming), pick *shi* (actions/things).
> With *ci* (phrases or phrasing), dredge up (*shu* 抒) *yi*.
> With *shuo* (explaining), issue forth the *gu* (basis).
> *Mozi* 墨子 墨子卷十一 11.2 《〈小取第四十五〉》

The action that the "Zhengming" tripartite division attributes to phrases makes what one does with *ci* appear to be an internally guided process, because the term is usually emended from "sorting" (*lun* 論) to "proclaiming" (*yu* 諭). The emendation seems justified because it does not make sense to "sort" *yi* 意, whereas early Chinese texts often describe sound as "proclaiming."[5] Whether proclaiming or dredging up, then, the action the two passages attribute to *ci* appears to be occurring or emanating from within a person.

In the *Mo Bian* passage, the term *shu* 抒, as in dredging up the *yi* 意's activity, is even more clearly focused on expressing one's interior.[6] The effort involved in dredging is evident in an occurrence of *shu* in the *Huainanzi*, where it pertains to cleaning a pigsty.

> 以絜白為污辱，譬猶沐浴而抒溷，薰燧而負豕。
> Deeming cleanliness and honesty to be humiliating and shameful is like bathing and yet dredging (*shu*) a pigsty, burning sweet grass, and yet carrying swine.[7]
> *Huainanzi* 淮南子 說山訓

An example from the *Shouyuan* describes speech dredging the chest (*xiong* 胸) and expressing the *qing* 情.

---

5. Other early Chinese texts refer to "proclaiming" as an act of pulling something from within oneself. In the *Huainanzi*, for example, the sound of weeping is said to "proclaim" the heart. *Huainanzi*, "Surviving Obscurities" (淮南子 覽冥訓). See the section on *tongyi* 通意 in *Language as Bodily Practice*, 125–138. Although it does not employ *yi* 意, a revealing passage in the *Lüshi Chunqiu* compares the sincere *qi* 氣 and *zhi* 志 (aims) that horses and geese utter (*yu* 諭) to the way in which human speech proclaims the sincerity of the heartmind. *Lüshi Chunqiu*, "The Comportment of the Scholar Knight" 〈士容論〉第六—. See Knoblock and Riegel, *Annals of Lü Buwei*, 645.

6. While *shu* 舒 might be an alternative reading in the *Mo Bian* (perhaps with an implication that it involves pouring out the heartmind), the repeated use of *shu* 抒 in other related metaphors suggests that it is the more likely of the two options.

7. For the date of this *Huainanzi* chapter, see chapter 1, note 16.

> 夫言者，所以抒其胸而發其情者也。
> Speech is that which *shu*-es one's chest and issues one's *qing* 情.[8]
> *Shuoyuan* 說苑 尊賢

In another *Huainanzi* passage, phrases (*ci* 辭) assist in the task of *shu* 抒 (dredging) the depths of the dao.[9] The passage justifies its own lengthy discussion by asserting that the dao's depth requires an ample amount of phrases to effectively dredge it up.

> 夫道論至深，故多為之辭以（杼）[抒]其情。
> The dao discussions are extremely deep. Therefore much was the phrasing (*ci* 辭) applied to it in order to *shu* its *qing* 情.[10]
> *Huainanzi* 淮南子 要略

The *Heguanzi* describes dredging the heartmind and improving the *yi* 意, with the mouth replacing phrases as the instrument that dredges.

> 口者、所以抒心誠意也。
> The mouth is that by which one *shu*-es the heartmind and makes the *yi* sincere.[11]
> *Heguanzi* 鶡冠子 能天第十八

The *Mo Bian* states that "phrases dredge *yi* 意," which, following the example from the *Heguanzi*, we might usefully expand to read "phrases dredge the heartmind's *yi* 意." As with dredging the dao and a pigsty, dredging one's heartmind is difficult. An utterance might be categorized as dredging the mind's *yi* 意 if that particular utterance struggles to articulate what is occupying the mind. In debate, in the case of the "Zhengming" and the *Mo Bian*, but also in writing (as I discuss in chapter 8), finding the right phrases to express what one intends can be a painstaking process of ladling out what is on the mind. Still, insofar as it can be dredged and proclaimed, an *yi* 意 is discernible.

---

8. I leave *qing* 情 untranslated, but my understanding of the term is informed by Andrew Plaks' analysis of *qing* 情 emerging from *xing* 性. Plaks, "Before the Emergence of Desire," 317–326. The *Shuoyuan* is attributed to Liu Xiang (ca. 77–ca. 6 BCE). Wilkinson, *Chinese History*, 698.

9. The relevant similarity between the heart and the dao here is that the heart represents the depths of the person and apparently the dao also has *qing* 情.

10. See also the translation by Sarah A. Queen and Judson Murray, in Major et al., *Huainanzi*, 861.

11. Possible dates for the *Heguanzi* range from the third to the second century BCE. For a discussion, see Defoort, *The Pheasant Cap Master*, 21–30.

Perceptible Yi 意

Once they emerge from the heartmind as expressions, yi 意 are observable. Some early Chinese texts present yi 意 as reliably evident. The *Mo Bian* A70 is certain that it recognizes yi 意 when it implicitly compares yi 意 to a compass, although the passage is otherwise unclear. If we read yi as "speculation" (a use I argue for below), the passage might be read as follows:

> 10.1.42 法、所若而然也。
> 10.3.67 法。意、規、員，三也，俱可以為法。
> *Fa* (standard): That which is like, is thus so.
> *Fa*: An yi 意; a measuring device [a compass?]; and a circle, are three [steps]. Together [they] can be deemed a *fa*.[12]

While the *Mo Bian* A70 offers little context, the presence of a measuring device with yi 意 should at least forestall interpreting it as something immaterial. Moreover, in relation to the earlier Mohist tradition, the idea that yi 意 is comparable to a device like a compass could refer to heaven's aim, *tianzhi* 天志, which, according to the text, Mozi employs as his compass and square.[13]

> 子墨子言曰: 我有天志，譬若輪人之有規，匠人之有矩。
> Mozi spoke, saying, "I have heaven's aim (*zhi* 志), like the way a wheelwright has a compass and a carpenter has a square."
> *Mozi* 墨子 墨子卷七 7.1 《天志上第二十六》

An aim (*zhi* 志) might be more readily evident than an yi 意, but the *Mozi* reference may have inspired later Mohists to regard yi 意 as an appropriate stand-in for *zhi* 志

---

12. This gloss of *fa* 法 starts with a puzzling list (意、規、員，三也): an yi (whatever it is), a measuring device, and a circle, as three things. Even if we replace "measuring device" with a compass, and presume the yi is that of a circle, why would such a list terminate with a circle? "Method" is a common translation of *fa*, which Martin Powers extends to "procedure." Here, if we try "procedure," then the term *fa* 法 is being glossed by stages in a method's process. In the first step, one speculates (yi 意) about the shape of something. Next, one measures it. If that measurement indicates a circle (or if one compares the speculation and the compass' result to a circle)—that is, when one has all three—then one has a particular method (*fa* 法). Powers, *Pattern and Person*, 55–57. An alternative translation by Chris Fraser reads: "A70: (法) 。意規員三也，俱可以為法。 (Models). Thought, compass, circle are three. All can be used as models." Fraser, "Language and Ontology," 439.

13. This passage occurs in the "ten triads" of the *Mozi* which are, according to Fraser, of varied date and origin. See "Significance and Chronology of the Triads" supplement to Fraser, "Mohism." Yi 意 and *zhi* 志 frequently occur together and are interchangeable. See chapter 7 for the *Zuozhuan* B9.25 passage about speech expressing aims.

in the circle and measuring-device analogy. In any case, many hundreds of years later, the *Lunheng* still makes the point that *yi* 意 are things that can be sensed.¹⁴ If some *yi* 意 remain obscure, perhaps it is because, as the chapter on divination explains, we need to see people face-to-face to know their *yi*:

相問, 不自對見其人, 親問其意, 意不可知。
In mutual inquiries, unless we see people face-to-face, and personally ask about their *yi* 意, their *yi* 意 cannot be known.¹⁵
Lunheng 論衡 《卜筮篇》

In other words, *yi* 意 *are* discernible in simple face-to-face communication, which makes them seem rather ordinary and not at all unknowable. All we need do is ask. Or look. Both seeing (*jian* 見) and asking (*wen* 問) are present in the passage, so eyes may also be involved in perceiving *yi* 意. In any case, *yi* 意 are knowable through the body. In such contexts, *yi* 意 seem accessible.

Yi 意, *Si* 思, and *Lü* 慮

In early Chinese texts, three terms appear most frequently as functions of *xin* 心 (the heartmind)—*yi* 意, *si* 思, and *lü* 慮—and *yi* 意 occurs most often, making *yi* 意 an important activity of the heartmind. *Si* 思 and *lü* 慮 both have a variety of uses that do not accord nicely with an activity like "thinking," but for the purposes of argument, I will highlight the instances in which the two terms are associated with cogitation.¹⁶ In other words, I will show that they involve hard work and, not unrelatedly, contribute to knowing, which is *not* the case with *yi* 意.

---

14. The "Zhishi" chapter sounds less confident about knowing heaven's intentions.

天意難知, 故卜而合兆, 兆決心定, 乃以從事。
Heaven's *yi* 意 are difficult to know, therefore [the Duke of Zhou] divined and united the omens. When omens were decided, his heartmind was settled, and he acted accordingly.
Lunheng 論衡 《知實篇》

15. A different *Lunheng* chapter, the "Chu bing" (初稟), argues that heaven and earth do not possess a human body. For a discussion of the passage, see chapter 7.

16. *Si* 思 also serves to mean "longing" or "yearning," especially in association with *you* 憂. For example, we see this when the *Liji* prescribes mourning:

思其居處, 思其笑語, 思其志意, 思其所樂, 思其所嗜。
The mourner thinks of (*si* 思) his departed, how and where they sat, how they smiled and spoke, what were their aims and views, what they delighted in, and what things they desired and enjoyed.
Liji 25.2 禮記 《祭義》. (Legge, *Li Ki*, 211.)

Textual searches in early Chinese writings that focus on the activities of the heartmind in conjunction with those of the senses and/or the limbs reveal a difference between, on the one hand, *si* 思 and *lü* 慮, and on the other, *yi* 意.[17] Some of these occurrences indicate that *si* 思 and *lü* 慮 entail effort, such as focusing or deliberating.[18] Just as overuse can lead to eye strain, according to early Chinese texts, the ears may be strained as well. So, too, the heartmind's *si* 思 and *lü* 慮 wear it out. The *Mengzi* speaks of the sages exercising their eyes, their ears, and their heartmind's *si* 思.[19] The *Huainanzi* describes laboring in reference to the strain on the eyes to see and ears to hear as well as the embittering of the heartmind in employing knowing (*zhi* 知) and *lü* 慮 to bring order to governance.[20] The "hard work" applies to the heartmind as well as the body. The *Mozi* speaks of ministers

---

Uses of *lü* 慮 also suggest anxiety.

> A *Shiji* line illustrates a relation of *si* 思 to *yi* 意 as "aims."
> 寡人思念先君之意，常痛於心。
> When I think (*lü* 慮) and remember the *yi* 意 of ancient lords, it often pains my heartmind.
> *Shiji* 史記 紀 《〈秦本紀第五〉》

17. I have argued that analogies of the *xin* 心 to the senses are a contributor to the impression that the *xin* 心 is not *radically* or *qualitatively* different from the other senses. Geaney, *Epistemology of the Senses*, 84, 108. But as I now see it, we should not take for granted that any term in early Chinese texts (including *guan* 官) is equivalent to "the senses." Geaney, "Aural and Visual Hierarchies," forthcoming.

18. *Lü* 慮 often functions as something like "deliberate" or "consider." Kwong-Loi Shun points out that Arthur Waley probably rightly uses "focusing attention" as the main translation equivalent of *si* 思. Shun, *Mencius and Early Chinese Thought*, 150.

19. The *Mengzi* says:

> 聖人既竭目力焉，繼之以規矩準繩 . . . 既竭耳力焉，繼之以六律正五音 . . . 既竭心思焉，繼之以不忍人之政 . . .
> When the sages exhausted the strength of their eyes, they relied on the aid of the compass, the square, the level, and the line. . . . When they exhausted the strength of their hearing, they called in the pitch-tubes to correct the five notes. . . . When they exhausted the *si* 思 of their heartminds, they called in a government that could not endure to witness the sufferings of others.
> *Mengzi* 孟子 《〈離婁上〉》 7.1

Wilkinson describes the *Mengzi* as a Warring States text. Wilkinson, *Chinese History*, 697.

20. The *Huainanzi* says:

> 夫任耳目以聽視者，勞形而不明；以知慮為治者，苦心而無功。
> Now when we rely on the ears and eyes to hear and see, we labor their forms but do not get clearer. When we use the knowing and *lü* 慮 to make order, we embitter our *xin* but without success.
> *Huainanzi* 淮南子 原道訓

exhausting their limbs' strength and the *silü* 思慮 of their knowing.²¹ The *Shiji* parallels troubling the *xin* with *lü* 慮 to stressing the body until the flesh is calloused and the skin lacks hair.²² The *Zhuangzi* observes that those who spend night and day in *silü* 慮 neglect the needs of their bodies.²³ The *Mozi* advocates borrowing other people's eyes, ears, mouths, and limbs and using their heartminds to assist in *silü* 思慮.²⁴ *Si* 思 and *lü* 慮, then, toil endlessly in the service of *xin* but in the process drain and deplete it.

---

21. The *Mozi* implies that the strain of *silü* 思慮 is like exerting the limbs.

> 今也卿大夫之所以竭股肱之力，殫其思慮之知 . . .
> Now, the ministers and secretaries exhaust the strength in their limbs and stretch the knowing of their *silü* 思慮 . . .
> *Mozi* 墨子 墨子卷九 9.5 《〈非命下第三十七〉》

This chapter from the *Mozi* is part of the "ten triads" section. See note 13.

22. The *Shiji* says:

> 心煩於慮而身親其勞，躬胝無胈，膚不生毛。
> His heartmind was perturbed with *lü* 慮, and his body/person closely labored, so his legs and calves lacked flesh and stopped growing hair.
> *Shiji* 史記 傳 《〈司馬相如列傳第五十七〉》

23. The *Zhuangzi* points out:

> 夫貴者，夜以繼日，思慮善否，其為形也亦疏矣。
> Night and day, respected people *silü* 思慮 about whether or not they are good. And their treatment of their bodies is also negligent.
> *Zhuangzi* 莊子 至樂第十八

Not surprisingly, the *Zhuangzi* advocates not engaging in *silü* 思慮 at all:

> 不思慮，不豫謀 . . .
> Do not *si* 思 and *lü* 慮, do not prepare and plan . . .
> *Zhuangzi* 莊子 刻意第十五

24. Explaining the astounding faculties of a sovereign, the *Mozi* says:

> 夫唯能使人之耳目助己視聽，使人之吻助己言談，
> 使人之心助己思慮，使人之股肱助己動作。
> It is only that they are able to make the ears and eyes of the people assist their own looking and listening; make the lips of the people assist their own speaking

The *Mengzi* describes the labor of *si* 思 and *lü* 慮 as a struggle to manage the attractions and repulsions of things. The world exerts a pull on the ears and eyes; so the "office" of the *xin*, with its activity of *si* 思, is to inhibit that tugging.²⁵

> 耳目之官不思, 而蔽於物。物交物, 則引之而已矣。
> 心之官則思, 思則得之, 不思則不得也。
>
> The offices of the ears and eyes do not *si* 思 and they are occluded by things (*wu* 物). Things interact with things and exert a pull (*yin* 引) on them and that's all. The office of the heartmind, then, is thinking. When there is *si* 思, then there is getting. When there is no *si* 思, then there is no getting.
> *Mengzi* 孟子 《告子上》

As the "Zhengming" chapter of the *Xunzi* explains, the heartmind engages in *lü* about certain feelings, which enables it to act on them with deliberation. The chapter also observes that *lü* 慮 moderates the activity of seeking what is desired,

---

and talking, make the heartminds of the people assist their own *silü* 思慮, and make the limbs of people assist in their own movements and operations.
Mozi 墨子 墨子卷三 3.2 《尚同中第十二》

For the date of this passage from the *Mozi*'s "ten triads," see note 13. The *Guanzi* also associates *lü* 慮 with utilizing the effort of other people's heartminds, along with using their eyes to look and their ears to listen:

> 以天下之目視則無不見也, 以天下之耳聽則無不聞也,
> 以天下之心慮則無不知也。
>
> If you used the whole world's eyes to look, there would be nothing not seen.
> If you used the whole world's ears to listen, there would be nothing not heard.
> If you used the whole world's heartminds to *lü* 慮, then nothing would not be known.
> *Guanzi* 管子 管子卷第十八 九守第五十五 (Rickett dates the chapter to the third century BCE. *Guanzi*, 2:232.)

25. The *Zhuangzi* confirms this standard conception of each part's role by recommending a life in which the limbs remain strong, the eyes and ears remain clear, the *silü* 思慮 is far reaching, and the *xin* is not labored. It says:

> 邀於此者, 四肢彊, 思慮恂達, 耳目聰明, 其用心不勞, 其應物无方。
>
> For those who engage this, their four limbs are strong, their *silü* is unimpeded and far-reaching, their ears and eyes are perspicacious and clear, their use of the *xin* is not laborious, and their responsiveness to things is not limited by location.
> *Zhuangzi* 莊子 知北遊第二十二

and *lü* 慮 sets the stage for knowing in the service of getting what one wants. In short, the "pull of things" amounts to the activation of desires and preferences that must be managed by *si* 思 or *lü* 慮.²⁶

Yi 意 in the Absence of Knowing

In cases wherein *yi* 意 is associated with the heartmind in analogies concerning the senses or the body, I have found only one instance of hard work.²⁷ And unlike the organized, persistent mental activity of *si* 思 and *lü* 慮, the mental process of *yi* 意 appears haphazard and impromptu. An examination of the contexts in which *yi* 意 accompanies *xin* 心 (the heartmind) will help differentiate it from *si* 思 or *lü* 慮.

A passage in the *Zhuangzi* attempts to clarify the obscure operations of the *yi* 意. One point is clear: *yi* 意 moves within a more subtle or thin (empty?) environment than does speech.

---

26. The "Zhengming" chapter of the *Xunzi* indicates that *lü* has the role of figuring out what is possible to accomplish in the face of desires and aversions.

> 性之好、惡、喜、怒、哀、樂謂之情。
> 情然而心為之擇謂之慮。
> What is called *qing* 情: the *xing*'s 性 likes, aversions, happiness, anger, sorrow and joy.
> What is called *lü* 慮: the *qing* 情 being so, the heartmind, on its behalf, selecting.
> *Xunzi* 荀子 正名篇第二十二

The *Guanzi* calls these *bian* 變. See chapter 5. Furthermore, *lü* provides moderation in seeking what is desired.

> . . . 所求不得, 慮者欲節求也
> . . . if that which is sought cannot be obtained, the *lüzhe* (the pondering, or the one who ponders) desires to regulate the seeking.
> *Xunzi* 荀子 正名篇第二十

27. The only potential exception I found is this case where the *xin* is anxious and something "labors" or "troubles" (*lao* 勞) the *yi* 意:

> 不能為君者, 傷形費神, 愁心勞意,
> Those unable to rule, harm their forms,
> exhaust their spirits (*shen* 神), tax their *xin* and labor their *yi* 意.
> *Mozi* 墨子 墨子卷一 1.3《所染第三》

Fraser assigns an approximate date of the first half of the third century BCE to this early section of the *Mozi*. Fraser, "Mohism."

可以言論者，物之粗也；可以意致者，物之精也；言之所不能論，意之所不能察致者，不期精粗焉。

What can be sorted (arranged) in speech is the thickness of things; what can be reached in *yi* 意 is the subtlety of things. What speech cannot sort out, and *yi* 意 cannot examine and arrive at, is not [even] at the phase of thick or subtle.
Zhuangzi 莊子 秋水第十七

Relative to speaking, here the activity of *yi* 意 is to *zhi* 致 (send, convey, extend to, or reach) and also to examine (*cha* 察). Or it may examine *in order to* reach something tenuous. The most tenuous of things are those that are incipient.[28] *Yi* 意 exists on a spectrum between the thick (*cu* 粗) things that speech can arrange in some way and the subtlest of all things. Insofar as *yi* 意 acts on things that have some degree of thickness, it does not operate in the realm of completely immaterial entities. Still, it must be noted, *yi* 意 does not interact with the ordinary, perceivable "thicknesses" of the external world.

Whereas the *Zhuangzi* passage quoted above seems to commend *yi* 意 for its ability to operate within a tenuous environment, other texts present *yi* 意 in a pejorative fashion, arguably on the same basis. For example, the *Lunyu* congratulates Kongzi for a series of behaviors, first of which is his rejection of *yi*.

子絕四：毋意，毋必，毋固，毋我。

There were four things that Kongzi cut off: he did not *yi*, he did not necessitate, he did not act inflexible, he did not privilege himself.
Lunyu 論語 〈子罕〉第九

This list implies that people are inclined to *yi* 意, just as we are inclined to privilege ourselves and to be insistent. *Yi* seems to function at a level that is difficult to control: easy to do and hard to stop. A proverb cited in the *Shuoyuan* disparagingly portrays *yi* 意 as a trait mastered by "small" people:

---

28. Some kind of attenuated consciousness seems at play in the *Huainanzi* description that depicts a blind (talented) musician either releasing or abandoning *yi* 意:

瞽師之放意相物，寫神愈舞，而形乎絃者，兄不能以喻弟。

For a blind musician to banish (or set loose) *yi* 意 upon encountering things, to release the spirit (*shen* 神), to further the dance, and to sculpt with the strings, is something an elder brother cannot elucidate to a younger.
Huainanzi 淮南子 齊俗訓 (See also, Andrew Meyer's translation in Major et al., *Huainanzi*, 416.)

君子善謀, 小人善意。
Rulers are good at planning. Little people are good at *yi*.
Shuoyuan 說苑 權謀

Thinking or intending do not seem like activities that Kongzi would want to curtail or at which trivial people would excel. "Guess" or "conjecture," although not generally preferred, has been proposed by some scholars as an equivalent for *yi* in such contexts.[29]

A passage that appears in multiple early Chinese texts is illustrative.[30] A commoner, at some remove, observes his ruler having a conversation with another individual. Using his senses, especially his ears and eyes, the commoner correctly assumes that the interlocutors are planning an attack on another state. Given his ability to draw the right inference from afar, the ruler heralds the commoner as a sage, that is, one who can sense things even at a distance.[31] But with a modesty appropriate to his station, the commoner describes his assessment as *yi* 意—just a

---

29. Scholarship in early Chinese philosophy does not typically favor "speculation" as a translation equivalent of *yi* 意, but the usage is well known. Anthony Cua translates it as "conjecture" in "Virtues of *Junzi*," 20; Donald Harper uses "guess," in "Communication by Design," 172; John Knoblock and Jeffrey Reigel translate it as "guess" in *Annals of Lü Buwei*, 251, 543; Zong-qi Cai assumes the possibility of the use of *yi* 意 as "speculate" *yixiang* 臆想 in "Richness of Ambiguity," 266; and Roger Ames and David Hall translate it as "conjecture" in *Focusing the Familiar*, 152.

Among the many uses of *yi* 意 in early Chinese texts (again, including intent, attitude, wish, opinion, and plan), when it appears as "conjecture," it is occasionally, but not always, written with a flesh classifier (as in *yi ce* 臆測). According to Baxter and Sagart's reconstruction, the lexical root is the same: 臆 yì 'ik ('- + -ik D) *?(r)ək and 意 yì 'iH ('- + -i C) *?(r)ək-s. Baxter and Sagart, *Old Chinese*.

30. Different versions of this story appear in the *Lüshi Chunqiu* 呂氏春秋 審應覽第六 《重言》, the *Shuoyuan* 說苑 權謀13.5, and the *Lunheng* 論衡 《知實篇》.

31. The commoner reveals that he based his inference on subtle visual clues, but the passage credits him with "hearing without sound." Technically, in some contexts, there are two kinds of exceptionally intelligent people: "knowers" (*zhizhe* 知者, 智者), with extraordinary powers of sight, and sages or "audient ones" (*sheng* 聖人), with extraordinary powers of hearing. The two types see and hear into the minute, into the distance, and into the far past and future. The *Wenzi* says:

聖人知天道吉凶, 故知禍福所生; 智者先見成形, 故知禍福之門。聞未生聖也, 先 見成形智也。

"Audient ones" know the dao of heaven, and good and bad prognostications, therefore they know where fortune and misfortune come from. Knowers see in advance what takes form, therefore they know the gate of fortune and misfortune.
Hearing that which has not yet been born is "audient." Seeing that which has not yet taken form is knowing.
Wenzi 文子 道德

(According to Andre Fech, the *Wenzi* was likely to have been composed during at the beginning of the Eastern Han. Fech, "Auditory Perception and Cultivation," 208.)

guess—as opposed to knowledge. Indeed the passage includes the disparaging proverb about small people excelling at *yi* 意—a reminder that, sagely or not, conjecturing (*yi* 意) might be obligatory for commoners.

Another revealing case of *yi* 意 as "conjecture" occurs in a tale of a man who wrongly suspects his neighbor's son of stealing his ax. The passage deploys *yi* to describe the man's unjustified initial assessment of his neighbor's son.

> 人有亡鈇者, 意其鄰之子, 視其行步竊鈇也, 顏色竊鈇也, 言語竊鈇也, 動作態度無為而不竊鈇也。
>
> A man's ax was lost. He *yi*-ed his neighbor's son. Looking at his pace, he was an ax thief; from the expression on his face, he was an ax thief; from his speech and conversation, he was an ax thief. In his movements and attitude, there was nothing that was not ax thief.
>
> *Lüshi Chunqiu* 呂氏春秋 有始覽第一 《去尤》

The presence of *yi* 意 is the first clue that the man's sensory inclinations are colored by his suspicions. Here *yi* 意 is tantamount to "assuming." In contrast to the commoner's celebrated visual acuity, the ax owner's justifications for *yi* 意 go unmentioned, leaving the impression that he has none. Ultimately, the story emphasizes that nothing about the neighbor's son changed, but the man eventually received information that altered his unfounded supposition.

A line from the *Chuci* associates *yi* 意 with prediction by means of divination. Beginning with a series of paradoxes, it sets the stage for another concerning whether the diviner (or the shells or stalks) is able to know the matter about which Qu Yuan has posed questions:

> 夫尺有所短, 寸有所長, 物有所不足, 智有所不明, 數有所不逮, 神有所不通。
> 用君之心, 行君之意, 龜策誠不能知事。
>
> [Even] a "foot" has that which is small; an "inch" has that which is long; things have that which is incomplete; knowledge has that which is not clear; calculation has that which cannot be captured; and *shen* 神 (spirits) have that with which they cannot commune.
> Even using my Lord's heartmind and acting on his *yi* 意, the tortoises and stalks truly cannot know the events.[32]
>
> *Chuci* 楚辭 卜居

There is no apt translation for the use of *zhi* 知 or *zhi* 智 in *zhizhe* (知者, 智者). It is important to recognize its visual aspect, but it is also important to keep in mind that *zhi* 知 is the same term used in the ordinary sense of "to know," which is obscured if we translate it with some other knowledge-related term like "insight" or "wisdom." I discuss these paired aural and visual talents at length in Geaney, "Aural and Visual Hierarchies," forthcoming.

32. The "Bu Ju" chapter of the *Chuci* was likely composed in the Han. Hawkes, *Songs*, 203.

An alternative translation of this last line would instruct Qu Yuan to go with his heart and act on his supposition (*yi* 意) because divination will not yield the knowledge he seeks. On either reading, in contrast to what we have seen in cases with *si* 思 and *lü* 慮, knowing is not a product of *yi* 意.

The *Lunheng* says that listening to sounds has a *shu* 術 (skill, technique) and examining colors ("visuals") has a *shu* 數 (count, calculation). When they are combined in the presence of *yi* 意, they appear to have a spirit-like foreknowledge.

> 據術任數, 相合其意,
> 不達視、[洞]聽、遙見、流目以察之也。
> 夫聽聲有術, 則察色有數矣。推用術數, 若先聞見, 眾人不知, 則謂神聖。
> They [certain sages] depended on a technique and relied on a calculation. If those two estimates (*yi* 意) are combined, one does not have to extend looking, connect listening, see in the distance, or wander the eyes to discern it.
> For hearing sounds there is a technique,
> and for discerning colors there is a calculation.
> Using these methods is like foreseeing (*xian wenjian* 先聞見). The masses do not know this, so they call them spiritual beings and sages (*shen sheng* 神聖).
> *Lunheng* 論衡 《實知篇》

Yi 意 in this instance are estimates that result from the ears' techniques and the eyes' calculations, which—in combination—prevent the senses from being overtaxed, a process that strikes the masses as uncanny.

These various instances indicate that sometimes *yi* 意 is what the heartmind does in the absence of full contact with the world. In its most common uses in early Chinese texts, *yi* 意 seeks to make the world conform to the person's desires, intentions, etc. By contrast, these less familiar uses of *yi* 意 as speculation reverse the direction: the person strives to understand (not alter) circumstances in the world.

Yi 意 with *Xiang* 象

In light of the prevalence of less flattering uses of *yi* 意, as explained above, we would do well to consider a famous passage from the *Hanfeizi* often interpreted in

---

33. Examples of interpreting *yi* 意 in the "Explaining Laozi" passage as "imagination" include Rudolf Wagner's translation: "Thus people call that by which they imagine something in their minds an elephant *xiang* 象 [= an image] . . ." Wagner, *Language*, 119. Richard John Lynn translates the same line as "when anyone imagines something, this is always called a *xiang* (image)."

relation to Tang dynasty and later poetic and artistic tributes to the imagination.³³ The passage, from the "Explaining Laozi" chapter, explicates the phrase "shape without shape, *xiang* 象 without thing," which involves an etymology of *xiang* 象, a term used to mean "elephant" as well as something like "emblem."³⁴ In this etymology, *xiang* 想—some sort of mental process I will translate neutrally as "think"—gives rise to the term *xiang* 象, or "emblem." After explaining that people *xiang* 想 about *xiang* 象, the "Explaining *Laozi*" chapter then pairs *yi* 意 with *xiang* 想.

人希見生象也, 而得死象之骨, 案其圖以想其生也,
故諸人之所以意想者皆謂之「象」也。
今道雖不可得聞見, 聖人執其見功以處見其形,
故曰:「無狀之狀, 無物之象。」

People rarely see living elephants (*xiang* 象), but if they obtain the bones of dead elephants, then according to the diagram (of their bones), they *xiang* 想 its life.

Thus, whatever people use to *yi* 意 and *xiang* 想 is called *xiang* 象.

Now, although the dao cannot be gotten to hear or see (*wenjian* 聞見), the sages grasp its visible (*jian* 見) accomplishments by locating and seeing (*jian* 見) its shape. Therefore [the *Laozi*] says, "Shape without shape, *xiang* 象 without thing."
Hanfeizi 韓非子 解老第二十

Lynn, "Truth and Imagination," 16. Zong-qi Cai takes *yixiang* 意想 in the *Hanfeizi* passage to mean "imagine." Moreover, he translates the *Laozi*'s line, 無狀之狀, 無物之象, as "The shape without shape, the image without image." See Cai, "Toward an Innovative Poetics," 189 (*Laozi*) and 204n19 (*Hanfeizi*). A. C. Graham translates both *xiang* 想 and *xiang* 象 as "image": "Men seldom see a live elephant, but when they find a dead elephant's bones they resort to its picture to imagine it alive. Therefore everything which men use to form an idea or image is called a *hsiang* (elephant/image)." Graham, *Later Mohist Logic*, 213.

Interestingly, Graham acknowledges that the Mohists are "preoccupied" with "the danger" of *yi* 意 being "confused" by *ci* 辭. He points to the use of *shu* 抒 as "dredge," and cites a *Hanshu* use of *yi* 意 to "dredge out once and for all my foolish idea." But instead of seeing this as a negative attitude toward *yi* 意, he takes the Mohist preoccupation to reflect a desire to "detach ideas from all confusing accretions and present them in their pure state." *Later Mohist Logic*, 211–212.

34. *Xiang* 象 proceeds from similarity, so something like resemblance seems right, but "resemblance" suggests appearance/reality distinctions. Common translations of *xiang* 象 include figure, image, sign, symbol, and manifestation, among others. Roger Ames, who uses "image," refers readers to Willard Peterson's argument for "figure." But both "figure" and "image" perhaps emphasize visual perception too much. I say more below about the mistake of restricting *xiang* to the visual realm. Ames, "Meaning as Imaging, 229; Peterson, "Making Connections," esp. 80–81.

The reading I propose is unorthodox but is consistent with how *yi* 意 is used across a range of early Chinese texts. Thus: The bones of an elephant lead to speculation (because we rarely see elephants), and the means by which people speculate (such as the bones of an elephant) are called emblems: things that resemble something else but are not necessarily any less valuable than what they resemble.

> <u>Line 1</u>: 人希見生象也, 而得死象之骨, 案其圖以**想其**生也。
> People rarely see living elephants (*xiang* 象), but if they obtain the bones of dead elephants, then according to the diagram (of their bones), they *xiang* 想 its life.

The two graphs in bold, 想 and 其 ("*xiang* its") rarely appear together in texts as early as the *Hanfeizi*.[35] Since there is no object after *sheng* 生 (life)—such as its living "form" or "shape"—people apparently *xiang* (think about) the elephants' lives (or living elephants), not about their bodies per se. If we remove bodies from our reading of the line, then, it becomes less concerned with visual features.

> <u>Line 2</u>: 故諸人之所以意想者皆謂之「象」也。
> Whatever people use to *yi* 意 and *xiang* 想 is called *xiang* 象.

Similarly, as above, the graphical pair 意想 (*yixiang*) is not found elsewhere in early Chinese texts, which undermines the likelihood that they are a binome (two words combined to form a stable compound).[36] In the second line of the passage, *yi* 意 earns inclusion in addition to *xiang* 想, thereby suggesting that its meaning is different from that of *xiang* 想. In fact, there is a textual example that places *xiang* in close proximity to *yi* while treating them as separate terms—related but presumably different.

> 故有道之主, 因而不為, 責而不詔, 去想去意, 靜虛以待 。
> Thus, a ruler who has the dao depends and does not act, gives responsibility and does not inform, dismisses *xiang* 想 and dismisses *yi* 意, and waits in quiet emptiness.
> *Lüshi Chunqiu* 呂氏春秋 審分覽第五 《〈知度〉》

Here *xiang* and *yi* are to be avoided by a ruler who "has the dao." Both appear to be unnecessary mental activities incompatible with the ruler's quiescence.[37] Hence,

---

35. *Xiangqi* 想其 occurs, however, a few times in later texts from Early China—the *Lingshu* section of the *Huangdi Neijing* and the *Lienu Zhuan*, both thought to be composed in the first century BCE.
36. A. C. Graham treats *yixiang* 意相 as a related binome. See *Later Mohist Logic*, 213. His claim is not supported by database searches.
37. See Knoblock and Reigel, *Annals of Lü Buwei*, 425. The passage also appears in the *Huainanzi*.

even if *xiang* 想 is taken to mean "imagining," there is no reason to assume that *yi* 意 means the same.

Many interpretations of the *Hanfeizi* passage treat *xiang* 想, *yi* 意, and *xiang* 象 as vision related, all three terms working together to assert the relationship between "image" and "imagining." In effect, the bones of an elephant spark mental pictures (imagining), and that which prompts the sparking (like the bones of an elephant) is called an image. The presence of the generalizing "all" (*zhu* 諸, which I translate as "whatever") in line 2, however, suggests that its focus is more expansive. Furthermore, the line's incorporation of *yi* 意 extends the action discussed from *xiang* 想 ("call to mind" or even "imagine)" to something different, that is, speculating (according to my line of reasoning as sketched out above). And speculating does not necessarily involve visualization.

More important, although the term *xiang* 象 is often framed in visual terms, it applies to sound as well. The *Liji* says,

> 樂者, 心之動也; 聲者, 樂之象也。文采節奏, 聲之飾也。
> Music (or joy) is the movement of the heartmind;
> sounds are the *xiang* 象 of music; patterns, colors, and segments are the ornaments of sounds.
> *Liji* 禮記 〈樂記〉 19.16 (Also *Shiji* and *Shuoyuan*)

In Han omenology, the *xiang* are celestial and terrestrial portents that include calling things by similar-sounding names. The *Lunheng* says,

> 名布為侯, 示射無道諸侯也。
> 夫畫布為熊麋之象, 名布為侯, 禮貴意象, 示義取名也。
> Name a piece of cloth a target (*hou*) to illustrate shooting princes (*zhu hou*) who are lacking in regard to the dao.
> Paint a piece of cloth with the *xiang* 象 of bears and elks, and name the cloth a target (*hou*).
> The rites value conjuring (*yi* 意)[38] the *xiang* 象, and [they] illustrate the *yi* 義 by picking the name.
> *Lunheng* 論衡 〈〈亂龍篇〉〉

Although the first *xiang* 象 connects directly to the painted bears and elks, the second—in the culminating comment about the value of *yi*-ing (*yi* 意) the *xiang* 象—seems to refer to the overall activity described in the passage. The rites value the *xiang* not just as painted bears and elks but as an amalgamation involving sound semblance ("target" [*hou*] and "princes" [*zhu hou*]) as well as visual elements.

---

38. I translate *yi* 意 as a verb here because *yi* 意 and *xiang* 象 only appear two other times directly next to each other in early Chinese texts, with neither case seeming to be a binome.

Explaining the powerful effects of resonances, the *Xunzi* says that harmonious sounds have responses, and good and bad (responses) have mutual resemblances (*xiang* 象).

> 唱和有應, 善惡相象, 故君子慎其所去就也。
> Harmonious sounds have responses. Good and bad have mutual *xiang* 象.
> Therefore, the *junzi* are careful about goings and completions.
> *Xunzi* 荀子 樂論篇第二十

Whereas the *Xunzi* makes its point in two phrases (唱和有應, 善惡相象), the *Hanshu*'s treatise on pitchpipes, "Lüli Zhi," says, simply, that harmonious sounds have *xiang* (唱和有象). 漢書 志 《《律曆志第一》》. An association of *xiang* 象 with sound also occurs in the *Lunheng*, which contends that "worthies" have merit equal to that of "sages."

> 見兆聞象, 圖畫禍福, 賢聖共之;
> 見怪名物, 無所疑惑, 賢聖共之。
> For seeing omens and hearing *xiang* (聞象), as well for diagramming sketches of disaster or fortune, worthies and sages are equal.
> For seeing anomalies and naming things, with no suspicions or doubts, the worthies and sages are equal.
> *Lunheng* 論衡 《《實知篇》》

Perhaps the *Lunheng* mentions *hearing xiang* 象 because the aural-visual pattern (seeing and hearing, seeing and naming, and, more debatable, worthies and sages)[39] calls for something audible, or perhaps the emblems (*xiang* 象) for speculating on the unknown do not exclude strange sounds. In sum, although *xiang* 象 are often visible, insofar as early Chinese texts also record instances in which *xiang* 象 is a sound, translating *xiang* 象 as a visual term alone is misleading.

We are now better equipped to return to the *Hanfeizi* and examine its concluding line.

> Line 3: 今道雖不可得聞見, 聖人執其見功以處見其形 . . .
> Now, although the dao cannot be obtained through hearing or seeing (*wenjian* 聞見), the sages grasp its visible (*jian* 見) accomplishments by locating and seeing (*jian* 見) its shape.

I noted above that the use of "all" (*zhu* 諸) in line 2 points to the need for a capacious translation of *xiang*. Here too, in line 3, a broad scope is implied in the

---

39. In the excavated Guodian "Wuxing" 《《五行》》 (ca. 300 BCE), those who know based on seeing are "worthies" (*xianren* 賢人), who contrast with those who know by hearing (*shengren* 聖人).

mention of the dao being neither heard nor seen (聞見). The emphasis on sight (the repetition of *jian* 見) in this line cannot be overlooked. Still, since hearing is alluded to specifically, we cannot easily discount its relevance to the *yi* 意, *xiang* 想, and/or *xiang* 象 in the previous line. Moreover, as I have argued elsewhere, early Chinese texts often describe people asking to *hear* one another's *yi* 意.[40] Coming from the heartmind, *yi* 意 is generally expressed in speech.

In addition to its etymological argument, the *Hanfeizi* passage seems to concern the sages' ability to make manifest (*jian* 見) that which is barely sensed. As I argued above, *si* 思 and *lü* 慮 are activities of the heartmind that work to manage desires of the ears, eyes, etc., whereas opportunities for hearing and seeing are often restricted when *yi* 意 is invoked. In the context of rarely seen elephants and the dao, people might be obliged to *yi* 意 instead of engaging in *si* 思 or *lü* 慮. But sages and dao-possessing rulers have greater perceptual powers than common folk. They can see and predict at a distance, discerning what ordinary people can only *yi* or *xiang*. If we want to get from elephant bones to a living elephant, then, conjecture would be no less relevant than imagination.

Yi 意 versus Knowing

In accord with the use of *yi* 意 to mean "conjecture," early Chinese texts explicitly contrast *yi* 意 to knowing. By describing something as "not *yi* 意," for example, the *Liji* affirms that it must be knowledge.

> 故聖人耐以天下為一家, 以中國為一人者, 非意之也, 必知其情 . . .
> Thus the sage is someone who takes on the whole world as a single family, and treats the central state as one person. [His doing so] is not *yi*-ing (意) it. He definitely knows their *qing* 情.
> *Liji* 禮記 〈禮運〉 9.22

Similarly, the *Lüshichunqiu* characterizes knowledge as based in sources (or information), whereas *yi* 意 is not.

> 聖人上知千歲, 下知千歲, 非意之也, 蓋有自云也。
> The sage knows what happened a thousand years before him and what will happen a thousand years after him. [This is not] *yi*-ing (意) it, because he has sources.[41]
> *Lüshi Chunqiu* 呂氏春秋 恃君覽第八 〈《觀表》〉

---

40. See *Language as Bodily Practice*, esp. 94–99.
41. Knoblock and Reigel, *Annals of Lü Buwei*, 543.

The passage forestalls any potential doubts about the sage's extensive knowledge by declaring that, since it is based in sources, he has no need of *yi* 意. *Yi* 意 again seems to involve speculation, an activity that thrives in the absence of sufficient information.

The unfortunately obscure *Mo Bian* twice contrasts *yi* 意 to knowing. One line simply asserts that *yi* 意 differs from *zhi* 智 (some form of knowing).⁴²

智與意異。
Knowing and *yi* 意 are different.⁴³
Mozi 墨子 墨子卷十一 11.1 《〈大取第四十四〉》

The context, as is typical of the *Mo Bian*, is unclear, as it is in *Mo Bian* B58 (10.2.37), where *yi* 意 is called not knowable: 推之意未可知. Much about the line is uncertain, including where it begins and the identity of the first graph, but it asserts the unknowability of an *yi* 意.⁴⁴

---

42. Graham translates this as "Knowing is different from having a pictorial idea" (NO3), a translation that supports another claim he makes about mental images and "a priori" knowledge. *Later Mohist Logic*, 471. It is worth noting that creativity, as in poetry where *yi* 意 serves this function, is not likely to interest the authors of the *Mo Bian*.
43. Graham rearranges the text, moving a section addressing various types of sameness (*tong* 同) and difference (*yi* 異), so in his rearrangement, the next line uses *yi* 意 in relation to jade discs, pillars, fingers, and other things that he takes to be stock examples of pictorial ideas. My interpretation would read:

意楹，非意木也，意是楹之木也。意指之人也，非意人也。意獲也，乃意禽也。
Speculating about a pillar is not speculating about wood. It is speculating about this pillar's wood. Speculating a finger's person is not speculating about a person. Speculating about a catch is speculating about a bird.
Mozi 11.1 《〈大取第四十四〉》

Graham claims this section contributes to the Later Mohists' eventual arrival at of the concept of a logical proposition. "The recognition that mental pictures are variously interpretable is perhaps the Mohist's crucial step in his discovery of the proposition." Graham, *Later Mohist Logic*, 473. For an evaluative response to Graham's reconstruction of the *Mo Bian*, see Geaney, "Critique," 1–11.
44. Graham, *Later Mohist Logic*, 429. In his reconstruction of the text, Graham produces this translation: "The idea of a hammer is not knowable a priori." (Graham emends *tui* 推 "pull, adduce, or extrapolate" to *chui* 椎 "hammer.") Treating this as "a priori" is not justified. Even if graph was *xian* 先, Graham would be positing a technical term for something that is generally just used to mean "know ahead of time." My interpretation (assuming the line is not too corrupt to interpret) is that the unknowable thing might be *yi* 意, the *yi* 意 of something, or the results of pulling on (extrapolating from?) something's *yi* 意.

When modern readers encounter terms related to the heartmind, such as *yi* 意, in technical discussions of knowledge, they might assume that an *yi* 意 is a mental idea. The concept of mental pictures is a common way of conceptualizing what we do when we think, especially in the context of understanding meanings of words and sentences. But the various uses of *yi* 意 as "conjecture" that I discuss above provide a more plausible interpretation of these *Mo Bian* cases. A term that contrasts to "knowing" is not likely to be employed to mean mental operations that lead to knowing. *Yi* 意 needs to be "cut off" (*jue* 絕) because it comes from the heartmind rather than the world, suggesting it is what we do when we lack the sensory access that would lead to knowledge.

Conclusion

Although speech is the predominant means of expressing the heartmind, the use of *yi* 意 with speech and phrases does not suggest that it acquired a technical metalinguistic use. Even in the context of speech communication, *yi* 意 does not appear to be strictly attached to the form or content, as distinct from the intent, of an utterance. As with the graph *zhi* 志 ("aim"), with which *yi* 意 frequently appears, an *yi* 意 may be focused, but it rarely toils with the *xin*. Instead, *yi* 意 often seems unrelated to the task of knowing, not to mention generating mental pictures. The association of *yi* 意 with speculating accounts for its use in relation to prediction and emblems (*xiang* 象) in the "Explaining *Laozi*" chapter of the *Hanfeizi*.

As I explain in chapter 8, early Chinese ideas about meaning should not be interpreted through the compound *yiyi* 意義, which occurs in Modern Standard Chinese and related languages. The modern compound masks the nature of the relationship between the two graphs in early Chinese texts. In texts from before the first century, I will now argue, the terms *yi* 意 and *yi* 義 represent two locations for ideas related to meaning that are, if not opposed, then at least in tension. This chapter has shown the connection of *yi* 意 to the heartmind and its activities. *Yi* 意 comes from "inside" a person, albeit in a framework wherein the inside-outside interface is always in a mutually constituting state of flux. By contrast, I will now argue, early Chinese texts associate *yi* 義 with things that are external or even "public." In a multipart argument extending over several chapters, I will show that early Chinese ideas about *yi* 義 align it with things external to the person. And yet like *yi* 意, in early Chinese texts, the term *yi* 義—the successfully emergent term for dictionary "word-meaning—is not an abstract entity.

CHAPTER FOUR

The Externality of *Yi* 義

The earliest evidence of semantic metalinguistic usage in Early China is embodied in two terms, *yi* 意 and *yi* 義. Having introduced the interior origin of *yi* 意 in the prior chapter, I now want to turn to the other *yi*, *yi* 義. In the texts that form the evidentiary basis for my arguments in this book, *yi* 義 is a key normative term, readily identifiable as something like duty, righteousness, impartiality, or appropriateness.[1] In general, early Chinese texts associate *yi* 義 with locations that are external.[2] The exteriority of *yi* 義, in contrast to the interiority of *yi* 意, contributes to my explanation of how *yi* 義 emerged as the formal term for word-meaning.

Readers of early Chinese philosophy are likely to recognize the saying, "*Ren* (kindness) is inside, *yi* (duty) is outside."[3] In delineating the parameters of *yi* 義, early

---

1. *Yi* 義 and *yi* 宜 (appropriate, suitable) are related insofar as 義 is pronounced similarly to *yi* 宜, interchanges with *yi* 宜 in oracle-bone inscriptions and excavated texts, and is frequently glossed with *yi* 宜 (appropriate, suitable). See appendix A.

Translating *yi* 義 simply as "morality" is, however, problematic because, as Dan Robins notes, *ren* 仁 is included in morality and the two should be "genuinely co-ordinate." See Robins, "Debate over Human Nature," 278.

2. Important objections to this conventional view occur in the *Mengzi* and the *Mo Bian*, which I treat in depth in appendix B.

When translating passages where *yi* appears alone or in contrast to *ren*, I usually leave both terms untranslated because my point is to highlight the externality of *yi*, not to argue for its best translation in any particular case. In passages where *yi* appears without *ren*, if the gloss is uncontroversial, I supply a typically accepted gloss in parentheses.

3. Although the saying is best known in relation to the figure of Gaozi from the *Mengzi*, scholars might exercise more caution about crediting it mainly to Gaozi. He was probably only one among many people in Early China who held that view. As Alan Chan observes, "There is . . . reason to believe that this [the idea of *yi* being external] was a well-established if not the dominant position in early China, to which some Confucians also subscribed." Chan, "Harmony as a Contested Metaphor," 52. For the association with Gaozi, see Graham, "Background of the Mencian Theory of Human Nature," 227; Rickett, *Guanzi*, 1:379; Goldin, "Xunzi," 139.

Chinese texts often contrast it in this way to related and complementary virtues.[4] Although the straightforward statement that "yi 義 is external" is not particularly revealing or informative, the range of its implications is suggestive: the externality of yi pertains not only to space but also to outsiders and to the public sphere. The exteriority of yi allows it to function as a standard regarding those who are at a distance. Moreover, as a behavioral standard, yi is discriminating, as distinct from, for example, the comparatively less discriminating, tolerant intimacy that is associated with ren 仁 and the family.[5]

In the first section below, I muster a variety of examples of the exteriority of yi 義. I do so for two reasons: first, to dissuade readers convinced by a claim in the Mengzi (the topic of appendix B) that both ren 仁 and yi 義 are internal; second, to counter theories about the use of yi 義 drawn from etymological speculation on the graph's components.[6] In texts from Early China, affirmations of yi's exteriority are the norm, not the exception.[7] (Readers who already accept that claim may want to skip this section, unless they are interested in the evidence I select and how I present it.)

The Pervasive Externality of Yi 義

With few exceptions, I do not examine the examples I catalog below because my goal is simply to demonstrate the pervasiveness of yi's externality. I present my illustrations in a sequence that moves from expansive to intimate: territory, neighborhood, family, the "inner family," and the body. The categories I have constructed are just one way to organize the examples; other methods might do equally well.

---

4. Some contrasts concerning the externality of yi involve virtues related to ren, including kindliness (en 恩), love, and trust.

5. In a different, but not incompatible approach, Alan Chan offers an ethics-related explanation of the widespread evidence for the externality of yi. He notes, "As duties associated with social roles or stations, yi may be said to be 'external' (wai 外) to oneself. A person is born into certain roles in society, with particular obligations and responsibilities." Chan, "Harmony as a Contested Metaphor," 51.

6. I follow William Baxter and Laurent Sagart's phonetic reconstruction, in which the wo 我 (we, I) element of yi 義 (OC *ŋ(r)aj-s) is the phonetic component. Baxter and Sagart, Old Chinese, 136.

7. My approach concurs with that of Jinhua Jia and Kwok Pang-Fei insofar as they adopt "awe-inspiring manners" to gloss yi 義. I depart from their position, however, when—citing Peter Boodberg's theory and possible variant forms of yi 義—they argue that yi 義 is specifically for one's "we-group," or kinship group. To the contrary, I show in this chapter and the next that in standard usage yi 義 is etiquette to be used with anyone who is in some sense outside, although "outsiders" may at times include even certain family members. Jia and Kwok, "Clan Manners," 33, 39. Boodberg, "Semasiology," 330–331. For Boodberg's claim, see appendix A.

In other words, readers should not be distracted by my process but should attend, instead, to the frequency with which *yi*'s externality is repeated across a range of texts. Early Chinese texts characteristically conceptualize interiority and exteriority relationally. From the breadth of a territory to the intimacy of the body, however, *yi* is consistently external. In other words—and this is my main point—although the circumstances outlined in the illustrations below may vary, the externality of *yi* does not.

<u>Inside and Outside Territory.</u>—Insofar as a state's boundaries demarcate inner from outer, *yi* falls outside. In these examples, early Chinese texts contrast it not with the term *ren*, but with a term associated with "soft" cultural power (as opposed to official power). In the following instance, *yi* involves military force against groups beyond the state's boundaries.

> 凡建國君民,內事文而和,外事武而義。
> As a rule, those who establish a state and rule as lords over the people, within their state, engage in civil affairs and harmonizing, and on the outside, engage in military affairs and *yi* 義 (dutifulness).[8]
> *Yi Zhou Shu* 逸周書 《武紀解》

Inside the state, the ruler employs regulations, but outside he uses patterns and *yi* 義.

> 明主內行其法度,外行其理義。
> The illustrious ruler will, internally, act according to rules and regulations and, externally, act according to patterns and *yi* (dutifulness).[9]
> *Guanzi* 管子 管子卷第二十 形勢解第六十四

When a ruler takes military action against an outside state, he should do so on the basis of *yi*. And inside the state, the government must be cultivated lest its *yi* be assessed negatively beyond its borders.

> 臣聞內政之不脩,外舉義不信。
> I have heard that when, internally, government has not been cultivated, the promotion of *yi* (dutifulness) abroad will not be trusted.[10]
> *Guanzi* 管子 管子卷第七 大匡第十八

---

8. Robin McNeal's translation slight modified. McNeal tentatively dates the "Wuji" chapter to the end of the second half of the fourth century BCE. McNeal, *Conquer and Govern*, 165.

9. Rickett says the "Xing shi jie" cannot be assigned a date before the first century BCE. *Guanzi*, 1:62.

10. Rickett assigns the chapter to the third century BCE. *Guanzi*, 1:285.

Yi is what the *junzi* uses to create order on the outside.

> 君子敬以直內，義以方外。
> The *junzi* uses respect to align the inside, and *yi* (dutifulness) to square the outside.
> "Wenyan" 文言 *Zhouyi* 周易《坤第二》

One can demonstrate things to those who are nearby via loyalty and trustworthiness, but those in the distance require *li* 禮 (ritual action) and *yi*.

> 近者示之以忠信，遠者示之以禮義。
> Those who are close should be shown things by means of loyalty and trust. Those who are far should be shown things by means of ritual action and *yi* (duty).[11]
> *Guanzi* 管子 管子卷第九 霸形第二十二

Treating people as outsiders entails *yi*, whereas insiders merit a gentler approach.

> 賓者接人以義者也，故坐於西北。主人者，接人以德厚者也，故坐於東南。
> As for guests, they engage with others according to *yi* (dutifulness), and therefore the guest sits in the northwest. As for hosts, they engage with others according to *de* (virtue/potency) and generosity, and therefore the host sits in the southeast.
> *Liji* 禮記《鄉飲酒義》

The people who "return to *yi*" are distinguished from those on the inside who are at peace with their governance.

> 百姓內安其政，外歸其義：可謂安矣。
> When the hundred surnames, on the inside, are at peace with the government,
> and when, on the outside, there is a return to its *yi*: this can be called peace.[12]
> *Yanzi Chunqiu* 晏子春秋 內篇問下
> 《景公問國何如則謂安晏子對以內安政外歸義》

---

11. This chapter is likely to be from the Early Han according to Rickett. *Guanzi*, 1:350.

12. Stephen Durrant describes disagreement about ascribing a date to the *Yanzi Chunqiu*, ranging from after 400 BCE to late Warring States. Durrant, "Yen tzu ch'un ch'iu," 486–487.

Inside the state, virtuous ministers remonstrate with their rulers. Outside, they die for *yi*.

> 故忠臣廉士，內之則諫其君之過也，外之則死人臣之義。
> Therefore loyal ministers and honest scholar-knights, internally [at court], remonstrate about their ruler's failings, and externally [on missions], die for the sake of their *yi* (duty) as minister.
> *Lüshi Chunqiu* 呂氏春秋 恃君覽第八《恃君》

In a *Yuejue Shu* passage featuring *yi* 義, however, one goes outside the state *in lieu* of dying.[13] Thus, it is location, rather than a particular behavior, that makes something *yi* 義. *Yi*, no matter its context, pertains to the outside.

<u>Dwelling and Traveling</u>.—Texts from Early China also identify *yi* 義 as specifically useful when leaving home, as against virtues resembling *ren* that concern where one dwells. Associated with the heartmind, *ren* generally involves caring for others, with particular attention to the sphere of the personal and the familial. Thus *yi*, insofar as it is posed against *ren*, contrasts with intimacy and closeness.

Sometimes the distinction between residing and traveling is subtle. For instance, the excavated text "Yucong Yi" only barely, perhaps arguably, makes a point about traveling.[14]

> (22) 仁生於人，義生於道。
> (23) 或生於內，或生於外。
> *Ren* is born from a person. *Yi* is born from the dao.
> The one is born on the inside. The other is born on the outside.
> "Yucong Yi" 郭店楚簡十五《語叢一》

Here we might read "dao" in the physical sense of being "on the road," although the primary justification for doing so derives from the fact that many examples contrasting *yi* to *ren* suggest travel.

In different formulations using the graph *lu* 路 rather than *dao*, the *Mengzi* describes *yi* as a road, which is plainly distinguished from a dwelling. First,

> 仁、人之安宅也，義、人之正路也。
> *Ren* is a place where one peacefully abides, *yi* is the correct road.
> *Mengzi* 孟子《離婁上》

---

13. See chapter 5.

14. "Dao" here can also be read as "the way," but this seems less plausible because it would mean a contrast between "in people" and "in the way."

Moreover,

> 居惡在？仁是也；路惡在？義是也。居仁由義，大人之事備矣。
> Where should one dwell? *Ren* is it. What should be one's road? *Yi* is it. Dwelling in *ren* and going out from *yi*—this is the whole task of the great person.
> Mengzi 孟子 《盡心上》

Regarding the *junzi* of old, we are told, *ren* is their dwelling and *yi* is their walking:

> 惟仁之處，惟義之行。
> [The *junzi* of the past] would abide in *ren* and walk in *yi*.[15]
> Yantie Lun 鹽鐵論 鹽鐵論卷四 《地廣第十六》

In the *Chunqiu Guliangzhuan*, instructions about a formal meeting with foreigners assigns different virtues to the ruler's assistants according to their role in the diplomatic process. The assistant who embodies *yi* walks or travels with his lord, while the assistant who embodies *ren* stays home and guards the state.

> 知者慮，義者行，仁者守。
> One who knows deliberates, one who is *yi* travels, and one who is *ren* protects.[16]
> Guliangzhuan 1.2 春秋穀梁傳 隱公 《隱公二年》

Ren is the village, whereas *yi* is the gate to the outside. Thus *yi* is the means by which one moves away from the internal community.

> 仁、愛也，故親。義、理也，故行。禮、節也，故成。仁有里，義有門。
> *Ren* is love, therefore there is closeness. *Yi* is pattern, therefore there is walking.
> *Li* is regulated, therefore there is completion. With *ren*, there is a neighborhood.
> With *yi*, there is a gate.
> Xunzi 荀子 大略篇第二十七

A similar contrast in the *Liji* and the excavated "Liude" uses *en* 恩 (kindliness) in the place that *ren* normally occupies, as it describes what occurs inside the gates

---

15. The *Yantie Lun* (Discourse on salt and iron) concerns a court debate in 81 BCE.

16. According to David Schaberg, after being transmitted orally, the *Guliangzhuan* was written down in the Western Han. Schaberg, *Classics*, 177.

of the home. The passage concerns rules for mourning, which differ according to whether they are being performed within the home or outside of it.

> 門內之治, 恩揜義; 門外之治, 義斷恩。
> In terms of ruling within the gates [of the family], kindliness overshadows *yi*. In terms of ruling beyond the gates, *yi* cuts short kindliness.[17]
> *Liji* 禮記 〈喪服四制〉 50.4

The *Zhuangzi*, a contrarian text, expresses the difference between *ren* and *yi* as a paradox. First, it contradicts the usual sense of *yi* as "distant" by referring to it as a necessary dwelling. Then it prescribes that *ren*, which typically does not extend beyond interior borders, be broadened.

> 遠而不可不居者, 義也; 親而不可不廣者, 仁也。
> Distant, and yet necessary to dwell in. Such is *yi*. Intimate, and yet necessary to spread. Such is *ren*.
> *Zhuangzi* 莊子 在宥第十一

Despite the text's paradoxical qualities, however, *yi* remains on the outside.

<u>Family Intimacy.</u>—Although intimacy (*qin* 親) is often synonymous with familial relations in early Chinese texts, within the family *yi* and *ren* can mark certain distinctions. According to the "Liude," *ren* applies exclusively to the members of the family who are related by blood. It says,

> 仁, 內也。義, 外也。禮樂, 共也。內立父、子、夫也; 外立君、臣, 婦也。
> *Ren* is inside. *Yi* is outside. *Li* 禮 (rites) and music are common to both. The inner establishes the father, son, and husband. The outer establishes the ruler, minister, and wife.[18]
> "Liude" 《六德》三

Presumably, *ren* excludes the wife because she is in essence an outsider who enters the family by means of marriage.[19] A similar statement occurs in the *Xinyu*.

---

17. The "Liude" version is almost identical but has *zhan* 斬 "chop" where the *Liji* has *duan* "break." The version in *Kongzi Jiayu* 26.2 uses *yan* 揜 "cover over" in both parts of the saying.

18. The Guodian "Liude" 《六德》 is dated to ca. 300 BCE.

19. A passage from the "Tianlun" chapter of the *Xunzi* indicates a slightly different distinction wherein *yi* applies to the ruler and minister; *qin* 親 (closeness, intimacy) to the husband and child; and *bie* 別 (separation) to the husband and wife.

骨肉以仁親, 夫婦以義合, 朋友以義信, 君臣以義序, 百官以義承。
Those of the same flesh and bones are intimate via ren. A husband and wife are connected via yi. Friends have trust via yi. The ruler and ministers have sequence via yi. The hundred officers line up via yi.[20]
Xinyu 新語 《道基第一》

Yi may also signal potentially fraught familial relationships, as when the Xunzi asserts that liyi 禮義 is required to avoid struggles between younger and elder brothers.[21]

A few passages illustrate the inherent tension between ren and yi by posing intimacy against reverence. For instance, the "Yucong Yi" presents intimacy and reverence as a polarity:

[厚於仁, 薄] 於義, 親而不尊。
厚於義, 薄 於仁, 尊而不親。
[If one emphasizes humanheartedness and one deemphasizes] rectitude, then one will be affectionate but not reverent; if one emphasizes rectitude and one deemphasizes humanheartedness, then one will be reverent but not affectionate. [slip 77, slip 79, and slip 82].[22]
"Yucong Yi" 郭店楚簡十五 《語叢一》

A similar dynamic plays out in the "Tang Yu Zhi Dao," which implies that an overarching love of one's relatives will cause the individual to disregard standards while, on the other hand, a too narrow concern for standards will damage one's relationship with family members.

愛親忘賢, 仁而未義也; 尊賢遺親, 義而未仁也。
Loving relatives and forgetting worthiness, that is ren but not yi.
Esteeming worthiness and abandoning relatives, that is yi but not ren.
"Tang Yu Zhi Dao" 《唐虞之道》四

The Guliangzhuan also implies that yi involves standards in contrast to the less discriminating familial love characteristic of ren. In criticizing the unauthorized conferral of one's property on one's descendants, the text declares that such an act might accord with ren, but it is not yi.[23]

---

20. The Xinyu is attributed to the Western Han scholar, Lu Jia.

21. Xunzi, "Xing E.'"

22. This slip arrangement and translation are from Christoph Harbsmeier, "Reading of the Guōdiàn 郭店 Manuscript Yǔcóng 語叢," 39.

23. For the Guliangzhuan, it would be another matter if the descendent were actually the rightful heir. Interestingly, the line adds that ren should not win out over dao (also "road"), which it implicitly associates with yi.

雖通其仁, 以義而不與也。故曰: 仁不勝道。
Even if it is in accord with *ren*, with regard to *yi*, it is not given (presented by the text). As it is said: *ren* does not take precedence over *dao*.
Guliangzhuan 春秋穀梁傳 僖公 《僖公二年》

The tension between *ren* and *yi* is expressed in these conflicting demands. With regard to the outside in general, one must employ standards of interpersonal behavior and ritual norms. Within the family, *yi* pertains to those familial relationships that seem to require standards.

In a later illustration, the *Baihu tong* disputes a claim that a son may act as minister to his father because the capable should not be ignored:

子得為父臣者, 不遺善之義也。
A son should be able to serve as minister for his father, on the *yi* 義 that to do otherwise would neglect the worthiness [of the son].

The *Baihu tong* appeals to a different model:

《傳》曰:「子不得為父臣者, 閨門尚和, 朝廷尚敬。人不能無過失, 為恩傷義也。」
The *Zhuan* says, "A son may not act as a minister to his father, for within the women's gates there must be peace, and at court there must be reverence. [Such] people are unable to avoid slipping and committing errors, violating *yi* 義 by kindliness (*en* 恩)."
Baihu tong 白虎通 王者不臣

Here *en* 恩, a soft virtue, is in tension with *yi* 義. The passage also introduces the virtue of harmony (*he* 和) for inside and respect (*jing* 敬) for the court.[24] The "Yiwenzhi," in explaining relations among different traditions of thought, similarly positions *ren* and *yi* as complementary opposites.

其言雖殊, 辟猶水火, 相滅亦相生也。仁之與義, 敬之與和, 相反而皆相成也。
Although there were differences in their speech, which attacked like fire and water, they were mutually destroying but also mutually generating. [Like] the relation of *ren* 仁 to *yi* 義, and the relation of respect (*jing* 敬) to harmony (*he* 和), they were in opposition but all mutually completing each other.
Hanshu 漢書 志 《藝文志第十》

---

24. These are not necessary correlations. For example, when *yi* 義 itself is the contrasting term, *jing* 敬 can be a virtue for the internal sphere. See "Wenyan" example above.

One must be careful not to let kindness get in the way of *yi* 義 (implicitly referring to harmony in the women's quarters and reverence at court).²⁵

To have standards is to prioritize *yi*. To relax them in favor of one's family is to prioritize *ren*. Thus, the tension between *yi* and *ren* highlights the association of *yi* with standards.

External Standards versus Internal Equalizing

Early Chinese texts treat things associated with internality as local and familiar, with the heartmind (*xin* 心) being the bodily site that is most near and intimate. Rarely is *yi* explicitly contrasted to the heartmind, but the "Mu He" commentary on the *Zhouyi* is one such case.

> 夫古之君子, 其思舉錯 (措) 也, 內得於心, 外度於義。
>
> As to the *junzi* of old, their thoughts raised up and articulated—internally, obtaining in the heartmind, and, externally, measuring up to *yi*.²⁶
>
> "Mu He" 繆和, *Zhouyi* 周易

The heartmind, the passage implies, is that place within a person that most directly contrasts to *yi*. Likewise in the military classic the *Simafa*.

> 凡民以仁救, 以義戰。。。
> 故心中仁, 行中義。
>
> Now as for the masses, rescue by means of *ren*, and battle by means of *yi*. . . .
>
> Thus, the heartmind centers on *ren*, and actions (walking) center on *yi*.
>
> *Simafa* 司馬法 4 〈嚴位〉

The heartmind is not where *yi* 義 belongs; it belongs with "walking," which is to say acting in the world outside the gates.²⁷

Nevertheless, even though *yi* 義 is separate from the heartmind, it is not disassociated from feelings.²⁸ Nothing about *yi*, in other words, suggests that love or hatred cannot motivate it. Take, for example, a passage from the *Heguanzi*.

---

25. While this example provides little to go on except the contrast of respect (*jing* 敬) to harmony (*he* 和), I discuss *yi* 義 in such *yin-yang* pairings more in chapter 5.

26. See Shaughnessy translation in *I Ching*, 254–255. The "Mu He" is from a Mawangdui tomb (sealed in 168 BCE).

27. Readers might recognize the direct conflict with the claim in the *Mengzi* that *yi* is rooted in the heartmind. I discuss that section of the *Mengzi* in appendix B.

28. The idea that entities "outside" are sites of disinterestedness and emotional detachment—rather than, for instance, incitements to desire—is distinctly modern; it does not apply in Early

所謂仁者、同好者也，所謂義者、同惡者也。
That which is called *ren* is shared fondness. That which is called *yi* is shared hatred.
Heguanzi 鶡冠子 學問第十五

The *Gongyangzhuan* aligns *yi* with intolerance and *ren* with mercy.

故君子以其不受為義，以其不殺為仁。
Therefore the *junzi* deems his not tolerating to be *yi*, and his not killing to be *ren*.[29]
Chunqiu Gongyangzhuan 春秋公羊傳 襄公 《襄公二十九年》

Killing, then, is incompatible with *ren* but not with *yi* (as can be inferred from its military applications). Moreover, to be tolerant of something that is unacceptable is incompatible with being *yi* but is compatible with (or acceptable for) *ren*.

It is also not uncommon for early Chinese texts to present *yi* and *ren* as sharing the same feeling. Still, they act on that feeling differently relative to the distance between them and their target. The target of the heartmind is so close that it lacks distinctions; thus, in this sense, it is less discriminating. The target of *yi* is sufficiently distant to allow a comprehensive view from which distinctions and patterns are visible and standards emerge. An example from the *Xunzi* focused on killing argues that warfare can involve both *ren* and *yi*. Xunzi is reported to have said:

仁者愛人，愛人，故惡人之害之也；
義者循理，循理，故惡人之亂之也。
Ren is loving people. If you love people, then you hate people harming them. *Yi* is following patterning. If you follow patterning, then you hate people disordering it.
Xunzi 荀子 議兵篇第十五

Hating what is not *ren* is close to *yi*.

惡類三，惡不仁為近義。
Hatreds fall into three categories. Hating what is not *ren* is near to *yi*.[30]
"Xing Zi Ming Chu" 《性自命出》 五

China. For a history of objectivity, see Lorraine Daston and Peter Galison's study, which traces the development of the scientific idea of objectivity through a study of changing styles in illustrations (drawings, photographs, etc.) produced for science texts, especially atlases, from the eighteenth to the twentieth centuries. Daston and Galison, *Objectivity*.

29. The *Gongyangzhuan* was orally transmitted before its written composition in the Western Han. Schaberg, *Classics*, 178.

30. The "Xing Zi Ming Chu" is a Guodian text (ca. 300 BCE).

Although early Chinese texts differ on the subject of whether killing is compatible with *ren*, feelings' involvement in *yi* is never in question. Rather, its target is different from that of *ren*. Hating chaos characterizes *yi*, whereas hating the idea of people being harmed characterizes *ren*. Chaos can be perceived only from a distance, where disruptions to a pattern can be observed, while empathy for the harm being done to others depends upon a certain closeness.

Yi's association with patterning and abhorrence of chaos serve to enhance regulation.

愛由情出謂之仁，節愛理宜謂之義。
Loving that emerges from *qing* 情[31] is what we call *ren*.
Regulated loving and patterned appropriateness is what we call *yi*.[32]
Hanshi waizhuan 韓詩外傳 卷第四

Ren, then, is less regulated, whereas *yi*'s association with pattern marks it as more regulated and controlled. That *yi* corresponds to something more mature than the *qing* is an idea that emerges in another text.

道始於情，情生於性。
始者近情，終者近義。
The *dao* begins in *qing*. *Qing* are born from *xing* 性.
Beginnings are near to *qing*. Endings are near to *yi*.
"Xing Zi Ming Chu" 《性自命出》 一

Thus, regulated love applies to *yi*, and regulated love derives its patterned appropriateness from responding to something other than *qing*. Perhaps external encounters foster the patterned love and appropriateness that characterize *yi*.

Conclusion

As the number of examples above indicate, *yi* is associated with externality, an externality that pertains to space, territory, and human relationships. *Yi*'s externality allows it to function as a standard for relating to those who are distant. As such, *yi*

---

31. The *qing* 情 are difficult to identify, but bodily functions other than the heartmind have *qing*. For instance, the *Mozi* speaks of the *qing* of the ears and eyes: 耳目之情 (*Mozi* 9.4 非命中36). (The passage is from is the "ten triads" section of the *Mozi*. See chapter 3, note 13.) Since identifying *qing* is not crucial for this particular argument, I leave it untranslated here.

32. The *Hanshi waizhuan* is attributed to Han Ying (fl. 150 BCE).

is discriminating and contrasts with the intimacy and immediacy of *ren* (and similar terms). In short, the contrasts between *yi* and *ren*-like virtues concern distance-based patterning versus proximity so near as to preclude differentiation.

Why do I not just assert the meaning of the externality of *yi* 義? In the next chapter, as I explore the flexibility and resilience of *yi*'s association with externality, I will posit that pinning it down to a single significance would be ill-advised. In fact, *yi*'s externality, with its contrasting/balancing internal complement, functions more like a way of thinking than a particular idea. I will conclude with an exploration of *yi*'s role in yin-yang pairings, from which we learn more about this term that eventually comes to serve as "word-meaning."

CHAPTER FIVE

The Resilience of the Externality of Yi 義

Having considered the externality of *yi* 義 from the distance of an outlying territory to the proximity of a person's feelings, I would now like to explore the persistence, extraordinary adaptability, and usefulness of that idea. The implications of *yi*'s externality appear in its role in discussions of self-cultivation and politics, as well its occurrence in yin-yang constellations, the patterns of binary thinking so prevalent in early Chinese texts. (I do not refer to these relations as a totalizing "yin-yang cosmology" because the correlations in these binaries are still too sporadic and unstable at this historical juncture to justify use of the term.) In a basic sense, as I will show, inside versus outside is a rubric for arranging things in their places, with *yi* being external within a structural order of classification. Within the context of yin-yang constellations, *yi* is not only an external standard for making discriminations in interactions with outsiders but also a form that is accessible to the eyes and likely to be employed in rites.

The Externality of Yi 義 in Self-Cultivation and Politics

A comparison of two rather different uses of the phrase "*yi* from outside" (義從外) demonstrates both how context neutral and how resilient *yi*'s association with externality can be.

Passage 1.—The passage I wish to discuss from the *Guanzi* pertains to the human body. The passage's abrupt alterations in topic and style serve as frequent reminders that, like most texts from Early China, it was likely composed of different units stitched together into a single piece.

The speaker, Guan Zhong, offers advice to Duke Huan of Qi. Guan Zhong notes that *ren* emerges from within a person, whereas *yi* acts from (or on) the outside. The single line concerning the locations of *ren* and *yi*, which appears after a prescriptive portrait of contrasts regarding the sage's body, situates them with mouths, colors, and sounds. The key part of the passage that treats "cultivating life" (*yangsheng* 養生) occurs amid a series of questions and responses that presumably elaborate on a single topic, the value of former kings' seasonal, spatial tours of inspection.

滋味動靜，生之養也；
好惡、喜怒、哀樂，生之變也；
聰明當物，生之德也。
是故聖人齊滋味而時動靜，御正六氣之變，禁止聲色之淫，邪行亡乎體，違言不存口，靜然定生，聖也。
仁從中出，義從外作。
仁故不以天下為利，義故不以天下為名。
仁故不代王，義故七十而致政。

Taste and flavor, activity and rest, these are the nourishment of life.
Likes and aversions, happiness and anger, sorrow and joy, these are the changes of life.[1]
Keen hearing and brightness's matching things, these are the *de* (virtues/potencies) of life.
Therefore the sage evens out tastes and flavors, and makes timely his actions and repose. He manages and aligns the changes of the six *qi*. He prohibits enticement (leakage) from sounds and colors. He absents illicit behaviors from his body. Violent speech does not remain in his mouth. Peacefully he settles his life. Such is *sheng* 聖 (sageliness).
Ren *comes out from inside.* Yi *operates from outside.*
[He is] *ren*, therefore he does not use the empire for profit. [He is] *yi*, therefore he does not use the empire for fame. [He is] *ren*, therefore he does not [try to] replace the king. [He is] *yi*, therefore he delivers over the government at the age of seventy.[2] (Emphasis added.)
Guanzi 管子 管子卷第十 戒第二十六

The reference to the externality of *yi* appears to be a non sequitur, but considering it within a holistic interpretation of the entire passage seems to yield a coherent reading. The comments that precede the line about the internality of *ren* and the externality of *yi* describe a method of bodily cultivation. Among other undertakings, the sage regularizes his tastes, manages the timing of his actions, arranges his

---

1. The *Xunzi*'s "Zhengming" chapter identifies the same list as *qing*: 性之好、惡、喜、怒、哀、樂謂之情。*Xunzi* 荀子 正名篇第二十二.

2. Rickett dates this passage to traditional material from the late fourth or early third centuries BCE. Rickett, *Guanzi*, 1:380.

feelings, and avoids sensory enticement. Given that ordering, one might assume that acquiring the virtues of *ren* and *yi* is a consequence of bodily cultivation. That is, *ren* and *yi* become operative only once the sage has gone through the process of smoothing out his tastes, aligning the qi, etc. In this reading, the passage does not seem particularly concerned with staking a claim about the initial location of *ren* and *yi* (as in the *Mengzi* debates discussed in appendix B). The inner-outer contrast is not about origins, and indeed in that regard, there is no contrast: both are grounded in bodily cultivation, after which *ren* comes from inside and *yi* works on (or from) the outside.

But the passage's *ren-yi* contrasts relate not just to the body but to the sphere of interpersonal relations as well. *Ren*'s internality and *yi*'s externality correspond to some of the tendencies of the various binaries described in the previous chapter. Being *ren*, the *junzi* does not try to replace the king, which in this context would probably entail violence (or even regicide).³ Being *yi*, the *junzi* makes tempered distinctions; hence, he carefully calculates the proper time to turn the government over to the state.

If we interpret the chapter's larger dialogue as a discussion sharing a common thread with this passage, we can posit what the assertion of *yi*'s externality implies for its relation to the human body. In lines preceding the passage under discussion, Guan Zhong offers advice about the former kings' tours of inspection, which had deeply impressed Duke Huan. Guan Zhong then adds a cryptic statement:

無翼而飛者，聲也；
無根而固者，情也；
無（方）[立]而（富）[貴]者，生也。

---

3. The *Gongyangzhuan* specifically mentions not killing as a characteristic of *ren*. We might also associate *ren* with an avoidance of violence from the fact that *ren* is usually discussed in terms of intimacy and love, whereas *yi* is often associated with war and death. *Gongyangzhuan* 襄公二十九年9.29.8. The *Baihu tong* associates the *xing* 性 ("nature") of *yi* with willingness to die under certain circumstances. The other virtues have their own *xing*, but *yi* 義 in particular entails risking one's life:

(伯) [陷]諫者、義也，惻隱發於中，直言國之害，勵志忘生，為君不避喪身，義之性也。
Brave remonstrance is *yi* 義. With feelings of hidden compassion expressed from the center, and direct speech about danger to the state, inciting one's aims to the point of forgetting one's own life, and, for the sake of one's lord, not shunning death, such is the *xing* 性 of *yi* 義.
Baihu tong 白虎通 諫諍

Ceyin 惻隱 is the *Mengzi*'s gloss of *ren* 仁 (孟子《告子上》), so this arguably starts with *ren* and terminates with *yi* 義. See the *ren* and *yi* pattern in chapter 4.

公亦固情謹聲，以嚴尊生，此謂道之榮。
What has no wings yet flies is one's reputation.
What has no roots yet remains firm is one's *qing*.
What has no orientation and yet enriches is life.
Your lordship should be firm about your *qing* and cautious about your reputation, and honor life by being scrupulous. This is the way of flourishing.[4]
Guanzi 管子卷第十 戒第二十六

The statement, like all that follow, is about life (*sheng* 生), which, Guan Zhong asserts, consists of two somewhat contrasting elements of concern: reputation (sound 聲), which flies in areas exterior to the person; and *qing* 情, which is associated with change. In light of the wings-roots contrast in the first two lines, the changes of *qing* are firmly located within the body in a way that does not permit them to fly off (become detached). Life requires that one attend to both reputation and *qing*, and the rest of the passage explains how one might do so.

In response to a request for clarification, Guan Zhong proceeds to elaborate on his advice about reputation and *qing*, noting that the body is important and the mouth potentially dangerous.

任之重者莫如身，塗之畏者莫如口，期而遠者莫如年。
以重任行畏塗，至遠期，唯君子乃能矣。
No responsibility is more important than the body/person.
No street is more fearful than a mouth.
Of things that are appointed/scheduled but distant, nothing is like the years.
To be serious about responsibility and walk the fearful street to the far appointment: only the *junzi* can do that.
Guanzi 管子卷第十 戒第二十六

Herein the order of the initial comments about reputation and *qing* are reversed and its metaphors mixed, making the mouth a street. Yet the two poles remain the same: on the one hand, what is heard or what comes from the mouth; and, on the other, the body (*shen*) to which the *qing* are prescribed to be firm.

Following the vague "explanation" above, another request for clarification ensues. It is at this point that Guan Zhong begins talking about self-cultivation (tasting, repose, etc.), concluding with the assertion that *ren* and *yi* are, respectively, internal and external. Read from this perspective, Guan Zhong's comments on the passage at hand extend his focus on life, which he describes in relation to its nurturing, changes, and potencies. He reintroduces the body/mouth binary. On the one

---

4. See Rickett, *Guanzi*, 1:380.

hand, one should make one's actions timely; on the other, one should equalize the tastes of one's mouth. The binary reappears two lines later: one should remove bad actions from the body; one should eliminate bad speech from the mouth. Again, the advice relates to the conduct of life. Presumably, life is also at the heart of the injunctions not to seek profit over *ren* (replacing the king) and not to put fame over *yi* (retaining power beyond its appropriate endpoint).

If we are willing to accept, at least for argument's sake, that a coherent thread runs through Guan Zhong's answers in this series of exchanges, his contention about *ren* appears to pertain to the part of life that is close to the body/person—like the changes of *qing* and the material comforts of profit. This aspect of life is internal and not violent.[5] *Yi*, conversely, is associated with that sector of life, like reputation, that leaves the internal, travels forth, functions on the outside, and must be in sync with time (the seasons). In that case, assuming that the passage follows a single train of thought, the *Guanzi*'s statement about the externality of *yi* responds to a question about a ruler's seasonal tour of inspection by discussing the importance of cultivating life by attending to its inner and outer domains.[6]

Passage 2.—The phrase "*yi* from outside" (義從外) also appears in the *Yuejue Shu*, but in that text it has an entirely different significance than it does in the passage from the *Guanzi*. In the *Yuejue Shu*, leaving the state for ethical reasons is what counts as *yi*. At issue is whether Fan Li (范蠡), a minister of Yue who has departed his state, is as virtuous as Wuzixu (伍子胥), a minister who instead chose to die. In the course of its defense of Fan Li, the *Yuejue Shu* blurs the distinction between *ren* and *yi*, but it makes a clear connection between *yi* and "going" or "leaving." It cites several examples in which departure constitutes *yi*, including that Kongzi left (*qu* 去) the state of Lu because he walked (*xing* 行) away from it, so to speak. It is in this context that the *Yuejue Shu* contrasts *yi* 義 to trustworthiness. Despite the use of "trustworthiness" instead of *ren* 仁, the line closely resembles the phrase from the *Guanzi*. It says,

信從中出，義從外出。
Trustworthiness emerges from the inside. *Yi* emerges from the outside.[7]
Yuejue Shu 越絕篇敘外傳記第十九

Here the externality of *yi* pertains to Fan Li leaving the state instead of killing himself as Wuzixu did. By contrast, in the *Guanzi* passage discussed above, "*yi* from

---

5. See below for the tension between *li* (profit) and the virtue of *yi*.

6. Of the two yin-yang constellations that I describe below, this is closer to the first since *yi* aligns with sound, but the passage does not contain enough of the usual paired terms to justify identifying it as either one.

7. See Milburn, *Glory of Yue*, 387.

outside" is a virtue emerging from self-cultivation that allows one to manage the flight of one's reputations and walk the street to the far appointment. The *Yuejue Shu* dates to sometime around the first century.[8] And so, assuming the *Guanzi* passage dates to the Warring States period, this shows the persistence of the externality of *yi*—not because it serves a specific role in any given argument (in fact, it is used quite differently in the two texts) but because, as a slogan of sorts, it helps make sense of the world.[9] Thus, claims about *yi* being external to the body, the country, the village, the family, and the inner family fall into the category of a general habit, a loosely held body of contrasts. The whole weight of tradition, then, impels a judgment that *yi* is external.

Constellations of Binaries

The external-internal contrasts I have been discussing are related to the large-scale patterns of binary thinking now known as yin-yang cosmology. As I suggested above, I call them "constellations" when they occur in early Chinese texts because not every element or pairing is always present and the patterns are not systematized. *Ren* and *yi* often appear within broad, contrasting correlations, including yin-yang and heaven-earth.[10] We can learn something about *ren-yi* from the way the polarity functions within larger groups of pairings.

The pair *ren-yi* sometimes appears in two main constellations that, based on available sources, seem to have been still coalescing in Early China. In the first constellation, *yi* aligns with heaven. That alignment, I contend, might have been decisive in determining the rest of the group, including yang and hardness (or military strength). In the second constellation, *yi* aligns with earth. What seems to follow from that second alignment is often some combination of yin, ritual action, externality, and the sense of vision.

The presence of two overarching constellations in early Chinese texts suggests that disagreement (or at least different ways of thinking) preceded yin-yang

---

8. Alex Schuessler and Michael Loewe note that the *Yuejue Shu* could have originated in the work of unknown writers or compilers in the Later Han period, and point out that scholars have tended to agree there would be no conflict with dating the text to the mid-first century. Schuessler and Loewe, "*Yueh Jueh Shu*," 491. More recently, Olivia Milburn identifies it as dating to the very beginning of the Eastern Han. Milburn, *Glory of Yue*, 37.

9. Allyn Rickett suggests this section of the chapter dates to the late fourth or early third century BCE. Rickett, *Guanzi*, 1:379.

10. Of course, they also appear in other categorizations that are not binary. At times the categories make a three-part division of heaven, earth, and human or a five-part division of different virtues. When the division is tripartite or five-part, sometimes the elements have to be split in different ways to fit the pattern.

cosmology. Indeed, even in texts possibly dating to the early Han, yang's alignment with heaven is not yet firmly established.[11] Compromises would be required to incorporate seemingly incompatible pairings into a single constellation. Perhaps conflicts over the compromises account for the two different constellations. The implications for the alignment of *yi* are significant: some passages present it as a yang-type virtue, while others treat it as yin. In what follows, I take stock of the opposing approaches to locating *yi* on one side or the other of the yin-yang binary. In short, aligning *yi* with hardness implies a further alignment with heaven and yang. On the other hand, the omission of any hard-soft contrast seems to open up the possibility of casting *yi* as earth-related and visual in a way that generally suggests yin. In addition, the inclusion of an inner-outer binary might demand an identification of *yi* with earth.

Constellation One: *Ren-Yi* as Soft-Hard.—In what I am calling the first constellation, *yi* is yang. This constellation is never clearly formulated in the extant texts from Early China, but bits of it appear, primarily in excavated texts. The Mawangdui "Yi Zhi Yi" commentary on the *Zhouyi*, for example, sets up three binary contrasts that align yin, softness, and *ren* in opposition to yang, hardness, and *yi*.[12]

---

11. This is evident in the Yinqueshan "Master Cao's Yin and Yang," as Lisa Raphals notes in *Sharing the Light*, 157–158. The relevant line presents heaven as yin and earth as yang because of their relationship to movement and activity.

天无為也。主靜行陰事。
地生物有動行陽事。

Heaven is non-active (*wuwei* 无為). It is in charge of quiescence and performing (*xing* 行) yin (-type) activities. Earth gives birth to things that move (*you dong* 有動) and performs yang (-type) activities.
Yates, "Yin-Yang Texts," 97.

According to Yates, the Yin-Yang texts from Yinqueshan are among the earliest Yin-Yang texts in existence and they provide insight into thinking from the late Warring States through early Han. Yates, "Yin-Yang Texts," 78.

The *Zuozhuan* also provides evidence of early disagreements about the alignment of such binary categories insofar as it describes women in terms of yang.

女、陽物而晦時, 淫則生內熱惑蠱之疾。
Women being a thing of the yang but of the dark time,
in excess she generates the diseases of inward heat and deluding poisons.
Zuozhuan 春秋左傳 昭公 B10.1 《昭公元年傳》

A. C. Graham's translation modified. Graham, *Yin-Yang*, 71.

12. The "Shuo Gua" 說卦 commentary on the *Zhouyi* also contains the three-part claim that yin-yang pertains to heaven as soft-hard pertains to earth and as *ren-yi* pertains to humans. But the additional claim that heaven is hard while earth is soft does not appear in the "Shuo Gua."

是故位（立）天之道曰陰與陽，
位（立）地之道曰柔與剛，
位（立）人之道曰仁與義。

This is why establishing heaven's way is called yin and yang,
establishing earth's way is called the soft and the hard,
and establishing the human way is called *ren* and *yi*.[13]
"Yi Zhi Yi" 易之義 commentary, *Zhouyi* 周易

The pattern is, however, more inferred than stated. But the implication can be given additional credence with reference to other texts where, because *ren* 仁 is soft, *yi* must be hard. For instance, the *Fayan* asserts,

曰：「君子於仁也柔，於義也剛。」

[Yangxiong] said, "In the case of *ren*, the *junzi* is soft. In the case of *yi*, he is firm.[14]
Fayan 法言 君子卷第十二

Moreover, the Mawangdui "Wuxing" identifies *yi* as hard and *ren* as soft.

簡，義之方也。匿，仁之方也。 剛，義之方殹[15]（也）。柔，仁之方也。

Simplicity is the orientation (or "position")[16] of *yi*. Being hidden is the orientation of *ren*. Hardness is the orientation of *yi*. Softness is the orientation of *ren*.[17]
Mawangdui "Wuxing" 五行

We may also surmise from this passage that *yi* is yang. The connection of hardness to yang is sufficiently stable to justify the assumption that in any binary in which *yi* is hard, it is thereby also yang.

Whereas the passage above treats yin-yang as features of heaven and hard-soft as features of earth, another passage in the "Yi Zhi Yi" aligns heaven and earth with hard and soft, respectively. As the text elaborates its system, heaven includes both yin and yang, but hardness is characteristic of heaven.

---

13. Shaughnessy translation modified, *I Ching*, 218–219.

14. The *Fayan* is a work by Yang Xiong (53 BCE–18 CE).

15. This graph seems extraneous here.

16. The word is used to mean square, but we might take it to mean a direction from whence things "square up."

17. Martin Kern dates the composition of the Mawangdui "Wuxing" manuscript as likely to be no later than 195 BCE. Kern, "Early Chinese Poetics," 38.

天之義剛建(健)僮 (動) 。。。
地之義柔弱沈靜不僮 (動) 。。。
The yi 義 of heaven is to be hard and vigorous and to move (dong 動) . . .
The yi 義 of earth is to be soft and weak and to be tranquil without moving (bu dong 不動). . . .[18]
"Yi Zhi Yi" 易之義

Here yi 義 is neutral with regard to a heaven-earth orientation. But insofar as yi 義 is hard in other passages, it aligns with yang, which aligns with heaven. Thus yi 義's primary alignment with heaven remains implicit in the pattern.[19] In sum, the constellation is spotty. Still, even though it is incomplete, the constellation gathers together yi 義, hardness, yang, and perhaps heaven.

The compromises involved in constellation building can be extrapolated from the fact that none of the contrasts in the foregoing passages refer to yi 義 being external. Many texts, as we have seen, rather automatically cast ren-yi as an internal-external contrast. Moreover, they often present the internal-external feature of ren-yi as connected to something like soft versus hard, although they employ other terms like peaceful versus warrior-like or military, loving versus esteeming, not killing versus intolerance, and love versus pattern.[20] And so, because the first constellation includes ren-yi, we might reasonably expect it to reference internal-external as well.

In fact, an yi-related hard-soft contrast appears simultaneously with an inner-outer contrast only once in the CHANT Pre-Han and Han database, and, significantly, that passage does not extend its binaries to include either yin-yang or heaven-earth.[21] The heartmind is the most internal aspect of a person, and feelings associated with ren derive from the heartmind. But the Xunzi calls the heartmind the "heavenly ruler" (tianjun 天君). Might it not seem inappropriate to suggest that

---

18. Shaughnessy translation modified, I Ching, 221.

19. Evidence from the Wuxing is even less explicit and less clear. It does not address the relation of ren-yi to heaven-earth or yin-yang, but insofar as it associates heaven with hardness the implications would be the same.

However, this is complicated by the fact that Mawangdui "Wuxing" also mentions ren (along with peacefulness) as heaven's dao: 仁而能安，天道也。

20. Esteem (zun 尊) and respect (jing 敬) seem very close, but in the Zhouyi "Wenyan" Commentary's remark on kun 坤, jing 敬 applies to the internal, so it depends on the items being contrasted. Zhouyi 周易 《坤第二》. See chapter 4.

21. The Yi Zhou Shu passage—which substitutes he 和 (peace) for ren—makes an implicit soft-hard contrast by means of a military-culture contrast. Yi pertains to foreign military affairs, whereas culture obtains within the state. (See chapter 4 discussion of Yi Zhou Shu 逸周書 chapter 68, 武紀 in the section on "Inside and Outside Territory.")

heaven is external to the "heavenly ruler," while earth is internal to it?²² The idea of the *xin* being an "earthly ruler" (*diguan* 地官) would be a slight to both heaven and the *xin*.²³ It appears that the internal-external distinction conflicted with other more important binaries, and thus it never found its place within the first constellation.

In sum, as we saw in the prior chapter, *yi* is hard. And if hardness is part of a yin-yang constellation, then *yi* will align with the hardness side. Heaven is likely to be hard because hardness seems superior to softness.²⁴ So *yi* is hard and heaven is hard, while *ren* is soft (weak) and so is earth. If, however, internal-external is added to that grouping, then heaven would seem to end up being placed outside of the heartmind. To avoid such potential tensions, then, the constellation must either 1) not align *yi* with heaven or 2) simply exclude the internal-external binary. In other words, in texts before the second century, because *yi* is hard, an internal-external contrast of *ren-yi* would have seemed incompatible with a hard-soft contrast (which only occurs when internal-external is absent). To be sure, other factors might be involved in why the first constellation was never fully elaborated, but they are beyond the scope of my current project.

<u>Constellation Two: *Ren-Yi* as Sound-Vision.</u>—The second constellation evident in texts from Early China is wholly distinct: it does not include parts of the first, and it deploys other pairs. Specifically, the second constellation does not employ hard-soft (or warrior-peaceful). This omission is evidence of a compromise, because hard-soft—and variations thereon—is an important binary in early Chinese texts. Nevertheless, it seems the hard-soft pairing must ultimately be abandoned so that *yi* can align with earth without heaven being cast as soft in relation to earth.

---

22. As the *Xunzi* "Tian Lun" chapter puts it, the heartmind resides in emptiness in order to govern the five *guan*, and it is called the heavenly ruler: 心居中虛，以治五官，夫是之謂天君。*Xunzi* 天論篇第十七.

23. The *Zhengming* chapter of the *Xunzi* does not present this as part of a contrast between heaven and earth. If there is any contrast being made in the passages, it is the distinction between the "heavenly ruler" and the "heavenly officers." (*Xunzi* 正名篇第二十二)

24. Certainly, if there is any reason for resisting the alignment of *yi* with yang and outside, subsequent developments indicate that it does not lie with aligning yin to inside. When gender became a feature of yin-yang pairing in the oldest commentary to the *Zhouyi*, the "Tuan," women were assigned to the inside and men to the outside. For example,

《象》曰:《家人》, 女正位乎內, 男正位乎外。男女正, 天地之大義也。
The "Tuan" says: "Within the family," women are correctly established on the inside and men are correctly established on the outside. This is the great *yi* of heaven and earth.
"Tuan," *Zhouyi* 周易《家人第三十七》

The second constellation does not explicitly incorporate internal-external, but it aligns *yi* with *li* 禮 (ritual action), *xing* 行 (action or walking), form, and vision, all of which are presented as external in other contexts. The second constellation is particularly evident in the *Liji*, in which multiple *ren-yi* associations point in a direction opposite from those in the first constellation. The *Liji* says:

> 天高地下, 萬物散殊, 而禮制行矣。流而不息, 合同而化, 而樂興焉。春作夏長, 仁也; 秋斂冬藏, 義也。仁近於樂, 義近於禮。樂者敦和, 率神而從天, 禮者別宜, 居鬼而從地。故聖人作樂以應天, 制禮以配地。
>
> Heaven is above and earth below. The ten thousand things scatter apart, and ritual regulations move (*xing* 行) them.
> In flow without ceasing, there is uniting and transforming, and music arises within it. In the spring there is creation and in the summer there is growth. This is *ren*. In the autumn there is holding back and in winter there is storing. This is *yi*. *Ren is close to music. Yi is close to ritual action.* Music is kindly and harmonious. It leads spirit-souls and follows heaven. Ritual action is differentiating and appropriate. It stores ghost-souls and follows the earth. Therefore the sage creates music in response to heaven, and establishes rites in accompaniment with earth. *Liji* 禮記 〈樂記〉

On one side is heaven above, where there is music, warm seasons, yang-souls (*shen*), flowing, growth, leading, kindliness, and *ren*. On the other, there is earth, where there is ritual action, cold seasons, yin-souls (*gui*), scattering, storing, following, differentiating, and *yi*. In this way, the *Liji* aligns *yi* with earth and yin. At the same time, the passage introduces the notion that *yi* corresponds to visual things in contrast to *ren*, which is associated with music. The visual aspects include the movements (*xing* 行) of ritual action and scattered, divisible things (*wu* 物).[25] They are aligned with autumn and winter because, by virtue of their divisible forms, they resemble items that are stored in these seasons. Scattered visible items contrast to the blended flowing, uniting, easy transformations (because less divisible) that characterize music, which, in effect, flows with the airs of the heavens. Such movements are like spring because they have not yet matured into their final form. The eyes perceive discernible things, which makes them like the earth, while the ears perceive in a less differentiated way, which associates them with the heavens. This contrast illuminates *ren* and *yi*, aligned with music and rites respectively, because *ren* is the sort of thing that equalizes, unites, and does not strive to differentiate.

---

25. The argument that *xing* 行 is something that is seen is based on contrasts with things that are heard. See appendix C.

By contrast *yi*, like vision, involves making stable distinctions and establishing standards. Thus, *ren* is spring-like, heavenly, and characterized by sound, whereas *yi* is autumn-like, earthly, and characterized by vision. In sum, the second constellation expands the category of *yi* to include a number of additional features that are external in some sense: most obviously ritual action but also scattered and differentiated things that can be discerned and stored.

Another passage in the *Liji* clarifies the assertion that music and sound are yang, and it illuminates the association of *ren-yi* with spring-autumn.

凡飲, 養陽氣也; 凡食, 養陰氣也。故春禘而秋嘗; 春饗孤子, 秋食耆老, 其義一也。而食嘗無樂。飲, 養陽氣也, 故有樂; 食, 養陰氣也, 故無聲。凡聲, 陽也。
All drinking nourishes yang qi; all eating nourishes yin qi. Therefore, there were the spring sacrifices and autumnal sacrifices. Feasting the orphaned young in spring and feeding the aged in autumn have a single *yi* 義. But in the feeding and at the autumnal sacrifice, there was no music. Drinking nourishes yang qi and therefore it occurs with music. Eating nourishes yin qi, and therefore it does not occur with sound. All sound is yang.
Liji 禮記〈郊特牲〉

In a striking simile, young orphans are equated with the spring insofar as they are still fluid (not, in contrast to the elderly, fully formed); thus, they are like sound rather than vision.[26] Like sounds, liquids are tenuous and dispersed, which echoes the distinction between *ren* and *yi*, wherein *ren* is nondiscriminating and equalizing, that is, fluid. By contrast, the eyes perceive things that are formed and individuated. What the eyes see, like solid foods, have shape. In this sense, sight is associated with *yi*, which makes discriminations that are regularized and patterned. It is particularly worth noting that, in its schematic presentation of the second constellation, the *Liji* does not extend its solid-fluid opposition to include hard-soft, as binaries in the first constellation would suggest. In the *Liji*'s elaborate formula, turgidity, visibility, and individuation place *yi* decidedly on the yin side of the yin-yang polarity.

---

26. This passage is a reminder of the polysemy of music and joy (*le/yue* 樂), which augments the association of music and spring to *ren*, in light of *ren* being used in connection with closeness, intimacy, and presumably happiness. But one must be cautious in speculating about the cause of happiness: for instance here, because yang and sound are joyous, music is prohibited for weddings, which are sad occasions.

昏禮不用樂, 幽陰之義也。樂, 陽氣也。昏禮不賀, 人之序也。
The marriage ritual does not use music. Its *yi* 義 is dark yin. Music is yang qi.
In marriage rituals one does not congratulate. It is the generational succession.
Liji 禮記〈郊特牲〉

The second-century-BCE *Xinyu* specifically associates *ren-yi* with the yin-yang polarity. It declares,

陽氣以仁生，陰節以義降。
Yang qi is produced by *ren*. Yin regularities descend via *yi*.[27]
Xinyu 新語 《道基第一》

The *Guanzi* couples *yi* 義 with earth and *ren* with heaven.

正形攝德，天仁地義，則淫然而自至 。
If you align the shape and assimilate the *de* (virtue/potencies), heavenly *ren* and earthly *yi* will then flow forth and spontaneously arrive.[28]
Guanzi 管子卷第十六 內業四十九

---

27. Mei-kao Ku translation modified, *Chinese Mirror*, 176.
   The *Xinyu* might also make the connection of *yi* to ritual action and *ren* to music, in a passage that discusses the titles of texts as they pertain to *ren* and *yi*, but this requires emending the text.

   《鹿鳴》以仁求其群，《關雎》以義鳴其雄，《春秋》以仁義貶絕，《詩》以仁義存亡，《乾》、《坤》以仁和合，《八卦》以義相承，《書》以仁敘九族，君臣以義制忠，《禮》以仁盡節，樂以禮升降。
   In the "Lu Ming" [deer] seek their herd via *ren*. In the "Guan Ju" [ospreys] seek their females via *yi*. The *Spring and Autumn Annals* use *ren* and *yi* to condemn or to cut off. The *Odes* preserves or loses according to *ren* and *yi*. *Qian* and *Kun* are united and harmonized via *ren*. The *Ba Gua* is mutually arranged via *yi*. The *Shu* arrays the nine families via *ren*. The ruler and minister establish sincerity via *yi*. Rites complete regularities via *ren*, and music ascends and descends via rites.
   Xinyu 新語 《道基第一》

Mei-kao Ku cites Yu Yue 俞樾 (1821–1907), who contends that the last line is corrupt on the basis of the *Liji* alignment of *yi* with *li* and *ren* with music. (Ku, *Chinese Mirror*, 176.) But the corruption is actually evident within the terms of the passage itself. The final phrase does not fit the pattern. Moreover, the last line contradicts an earlier one: whereas the earlier line treats music as both *ren* and yang, in contrast to yin regularities (*jie*節), this line treats ritual action as *ren* and associates regularities with *ren* instead of *yi* (with which it regularly appears in other contexts). It is unclear how the line could become this garbled, but a matching line would read:

   《禮》[陰節]以[義降]，《樂》[陽氣]以[仁] 升。
   Li are yin regularities that descend with *yi*. Music is *yangqi* that is produced by *ren*.

28. Describing the material in the chapter as "quite early," Rickett dates it to no later than the fourth century BCE. *Guanzi*, 2:37.

The alignment of *yi* with earth as opposed to heaven takes various forms in a number of early Chinese texts. Extolling *li* 禮 (ritual action), the *Zuozhuan* distinguishes the earth's *yi* 義 from the "warp" (*jing* 經) of heaven.

> 夫禮、天之經也, 地之義也, 民之行也
> Now ritual action is the warp of heaven, the *yi* 義 of earth, and the action of the people.
> *Zuozhuan* 春秋左傳 昭公 B10.25 《昭公二十五年傳》

The *Xiaojing*'s subject is *xiao* 孝 (filiality), but it too juxtaposes the *yi* of earth and the warp of heaven.

> 夫孝、天之經也, 地之義也, 民之行也。
> Now filiality is the warp of heaven, the *yi* of earth, and the action of the people.[29]
> *Xiaojing* 孝經 7 〈三才章〉

The *Yi Zhou Shu* distinguishes the *yi* of earth from the auspiciousness of heaven.

> 地有五行, 不通曰惡。天有四時, 不時曰凶。天道曰祥, 地道曰義, 人道曰禮。
> Earth has five actions (*xing*). If they are obstructed, it is called bad. Heaven has four seasons, if they are not seasonal, it is called disaster. Heaven's dao is auspiciousness, Earth's dao is *yi*. Humanity's dao is ritual action.[30]
> *Yi Zhou Shu* 逸周書 《武順解》

Despite differences in wording and focus, then, a number of early Chinese texts, when taken together, demonstrate a second constellation that differentiates earthly *yi* from heaven and furthermore, either explicitly or implicitly, yin from yang.

The expansion of the second constellation's set of binaries to include hearing and vision is also broadly evidenced in early Chinese texts. One example from the *Guoyu* foregrounds *yi* 義 as something to be seen insofar as *yi* is what the eyes should focus on.

> 夫目以處義, 足以踐德, 口以庇信, 耳以聽名者也。
> Now the eyes are for dwelling in *yi*. The feet are for treading virtue.

---

29. Traditionally ascribed to Kongzi or his disciple Zengzi 曾子 (Zeng Shen 曾參), the *Xiaojing*'s date is uncertain, but William Boltz notes that it complements certain sections of the *Liji*, being similar in content and style. Boltz, "Hsiao Ching 孝經," 141.

30. According to McNeal, the "Wushun" chapter may have been composed during the last few decades of the second century BCE.

The mouth is for guarding trustworthiness. The ears are for listening to (obeying) *ming* 名 (commands/titles).³¹
Guoyu 國語 周語 《單襄公論晉將有亂》

The association of *yi* 義 with vision strongly correlates with its connection to ritual action (*li* 禮), which stands in contrast to music. Indeed, the alliance of *yi* and ritual action is in time formalized as a compound (*liyi* 禮義) that becomes increasingly common in texts from Early China.³² The *Hanfeizi* explains the relationship of *yi* 義 to ritual action as if *yi* consists of things that rites collect and decoratively arrange.

> 禮者, 所以貌情也, 群義之文章也。
> Ritual action is that which gives appearance to the *qing*;
> it is the adornment of collected *yi*.
> *Hanfeizi* 韓非子 解老第二十

The alignment of *liyi* 禮義 (rites and *yi*) with vision contrasts it to hearing. For example, the brightness of *liyi* is juxtaposed to the thick (condensed?) sound of *de* (virtue/potencies).

> 故厚德音以先之, 明禮義以道之。
> Therefore, you should condense virtuous sounds and treat them as your precedent; you should brighten *liyi* and treat it as your way.
> *Xunzi* 荀子 王霸篇第十一

Explaining that visible things have form, the *Heguanzi* contrasts *yi* to *ren*, with its focus on formless things like taste and sound.

> 和也者、無形而有味者也,
> 同和者、仁也,
> 相容者、義也。
> Harmony has no form but it has taste.
> Similarity in harmony is *ren*.

---

31. This also appears in *Jiayi Xinshu* 卷十 10.2 禮容語下
32. The *Xunzi* in particular emphasizes this compound, for example, in this visual description of *yi*:

> 在天者莫明於日月, 在地者莫明於水火, 在物者莫明於珠玉, 在人者莫明於禮義。
> In the heavens, nothing is brighter than the sun and moon. On the earth, nothing is brighter than water and fire. Among things, nothing is brighter than pearls and jade. Among humans, nothing is brighter than *liyi*.
> *Xunzi* 荀子 天論篇第十七

Likeness in visual appearance (countenance) is *yi*.³³
Heguanzi 鶡冠子 泰鴻第十

The perceptual functions of the ears and nose coincide in the word for harmony, *he* 和, and also in the ordinary term for hear-smell (*wen* 聞). In the *Heguanzi*'s description, then, *he* 和 serves to highlight the pairing of *yi* 義 with visible forms insofar as *he* 和 participates in the harmonious formlessness associated with *ren*. In short, the passages referring to *yi* 義 affirm that it is something sensed by the eyes, as distinct from something the ears hear (or the nose smells).³⁴

A differentiation between heaven-oriented sages with auditory talent and "knowers" with visual skills is evident in some received and excavated texts.³⁵ As the Mawangdui "Wuxing" says, heaven is the specialty of the sage, who is expert in hearing, whereas the "knowers" are expert in seeing.³⁶ Although the *Wenzi* does not directly align it with the opposition *ren-yi*, this later text usefully enlarges upon the various processes entailed in hearing-seeing.³⁷

聞而知之, 聖也, 見而知之, 智也。故聖人常聞禍福所生而擇其道, 智者常見禍福成形而擇其行, 聖人知天道吉凶, 故知禍福所生; 智者先見成形, 故知禍福之門。聞未生聖也, 先見成形智也。

Those who hear and know (*zhi* 知) something are the "audient ones."
Those who see and know something are the "knowers."
"Audient ones" have the constancy of [being able to] hear wherein fortune and misfortune is born, and select their dao accordingly. Knowers

---

33. The passage concludes by stating that the pleasure that unites *ren* and *yi* also has no form, but the first line still makes a clear association of taste with formlessness, harmony, and *ren*.

34. A later example from the *Hanshu* connects *yi* 義 with implicitly hard military movements in contrast to kindly (implicitly soft) sounds of *ren*:

昭光振燿, 龥呰如神, 仁聲惠於北狄, 武義動於南鄰。
Bright brilliance rising radiantly, quick and godlike,
ren sounds benefit the northern Di,
while military *yi* 義 moves (*dong* 動) among southern neighbors.
Hanshu 漢書 傳 3.58 〈揚雄傳〉第五十七上

35. See chapter 3, note 32 and Geaney, "Aural and Visual Hierarchies," forthcoming.

36. In the Mawangdui "Wuxing," heaven is contrasted to "human" rather than the earth.

The observation that sages and "knowers" are keen of hearing and clear sighted, respectively, also appears in the *Shuoyuan* "Jing Shen" (敬慎) chapter and in the "Zhong Yong" chapter of the *Liji*.

37. Andre Fech suggests a date of composition in the early decades of the Han. Fech, "Auditory Perception," 208.

have the constancy of [being able to] see wherein fortune and misfortune take shape, and select their walking (or "actions," *xing* 行) accordingly. "Audient ones" know the dao of heaven, and good and bad prognostications, therefore they know where fortune and misfortune come from. Knowers see in advance what takes form, therefore they know the gate of fortune and misfortune.
Hearing that which has not yet been born is "audient." Seeing that which has not yet taken form is knowing.
Wenzi 文子 道德

What is seen is something that has taken form, but what is heard is amorphous.[38] The things that are heard are merely born or generated somewhere (*suosheng* 所生). The "knowers" know at the "gate" of happiness and disaster, which is only after their "birth." Thus, the "audient ones" are a step ahead. Things that are heard are more inchoate, in contrast to more mature, formed things.

Other passages confirm the connection between the "audient ones," "knowers," heaven, and earth. In the *Zhoubi Suanjing* (周髀算經), an astronomical text, the "audient ones" are aligned with roundness, as distinct from the squareness of earth and "knowers."

> 方屬地, 圓屬天, 天圓地方。。。 是故知地者智, 知天者聖。
> Square is affiliated with earth. Round is affiliated with heaven. . . . Heaven is round and earth is square. One who knows the earth is called the "knower." One who knows heaven is called the "audient one."[39]
> *Zhoubi Suanjing* 周髀算經 《周髀算經》卷上 《勾股圓方圖》

The *Yantie Lun* does the same, but adds an explicit hierarchy on the distinctions it describes:

> 故聖人因天時, 智者因地財, 上士取諸人, 中士勞其形。
> Therefore the "audient one" accords with the time of the heavens. The "knower" accords with the resources of the earth. The higher official picks from the people. The middling official labors his body.
> *Yantie Lun* 鹽鐵論卷一 《力耕第二》

---

38. In other texts from Early China, there are references to *xing* 形 in relation to sound, but there is also some reluctance about it, as evident in examples like this one.

39. The date of the composition of the *Zhou bi suan jing* 周髀算經 is in question, but Christopher Cullen suggests it achieved its final form sometime between 50 BCE and 100 CE. Cullen, "*Chou pi suan ching*," 34.

As the analogy to the higher and middling officials suggests, the hierarchy between hearing and seeing favors the "audient ones," which conforms to the hierarchy of heaven over earth.[40]

And so we have the second constellation. When it is fully articulated, *yi*, earth, yin, winter, death, knowing, ritual action, vision, square, food, and discrete things form one half of the equation; *ren*, heaven, yang, summer, growth, sagacity, music, sound, roundness, fluids, and tenuous things form the other. Only the *Liji* systematically lays out this second constellation in all its binary fullness. But passages from other texts reinforce elements of its binaries, in essence asserting that *yi* is affiliated with earth and perceived by the eyes.

Conclusion

In myriad ways, early Chinese texts express the idea that *yi* 義 is external. From its role in self-cultivation to its appearance in a political context, little remains the

---

40. For example, the *Guanzi* says,

> 神聖者王，仁智者君，武勇者長，此天之道，人之情也。
> It is in the way of heaven and the *qing* 情 of humans that the divine and "audient ones" (*sheng* 聖) become kings, the benevolent and knowing ones (*zhi* 智) become princes, and the warlike and brave ones become military leaders.
> *Guanzi* 管子 管子卷第十一 君臣下第三十一

Rickett translation slightly modified. Rickett assigns the date of the chapter as the middle of the third century BCE. Rickett, *Guanzi*, 1:414, 419.

In the *Hanfeizi* (chapter 3, "Nan Yan"), the sage is the ruler in contrast to the minister and the traits characterize specific figures.

> 上古有湯，至聖也；伊尹，至智也。
> In remote antiquity, Tang was the most "audient," and Yi Yin was the most knowing.
> *Hanfeizi* 韓非子 難言第三

The hierarchy is less obvious in this *Shangjun Shu* passage, but the "audient one" is associated with teaching (presumably oral/aural), while the knower is associated with governing.

> 臣聞之，聖人不易民而教，智者不變法而治。
> I have heard a *shengren* 聖人 teaches without changing the people,
> and a *zhizhe* 智者 achieves order without altering the laws.
> *Shangjun Shu* 商君書 更法

Wilkinson describes the *Shangjun Shu* as a mid-third-century-BCE text. Wilkinson, *Chinese History*, 285. Regarding the complexity of assigning a date to the *Shangjun Shu*, see Yuri Pines, "Dating of a Pre-Imperial Text," esp. 178.

The Resilience of the Externality of Yi 義 / 101

same except for the notion that "*yi* is outside," whether it invokes the position of *yi* in external space or in its interactions with outsiders. In exterior relations, *yi* references the need for a standard that involves distance, timely movement, and discrimination, and that is what *yi* provides. Thus, in its externality, *yi* is an organizing model. It sorts by means of its position within a constellation of binaries that helps structure the world. In addition, it creates order by managing difficult interactions involving outsiders. Internal-external is a way of regulating the world, and *yi* is part of that crucial dynamic. Hence, contra the *Mengzi* and the *Mo Bian* (discussed in appendix B), the general understanding, as evident in a wide range of early Chinese texts, is that *yi* has nothing to do with internality, a view that may reflect certain rhetorical habits and world-ordering conceptions rather than any reasoned argument per se. The main goal of my analysis of *yi*'s externality is to give readers sufficient background to follow my train of thought as I begin to examine the emergence of *yi* as a metalinguistic term. In short, the fact that *yi* is external helps clarify why it becomes aligned with ritual action, vision, form, solids, etc.

PART TWO

Y<small>I</small> 義 <small>AS</small> M<small>ODEL</small>

CHAPTER SIX

Yi 義 as Model

Stable, Accessible Standards

Having focused in part 1 of my study on the dominant, pervasive, and persistent characteristic of yi 義, its externality, I would now like to pursue these questions more by considering uses of yi 義 not as explicitly linked to ethical behavior. As we have seen, yi 義 is a key normative term, often coordinate with ren 仁, a caring, affectionate virtue of the intimate domain. By contrast, yi 義, which is proper to the external sphere, is reserved, discerning, and publicly available, there for all to see. The question that will occupy us throughout part 2, then, is: How do yi 義's externality and its normative value relate to the emergence of word-meaning in Early China?

Yi 義 is involved in maintaining stable, accessible standards, and it is this characteristic that I will investigate further. As a way into that task, I want to focus on a common formula found in early Chinese texts, "the yi of X" (X 之義). In texts from Early China, the formula appears in relation to actions, social roles, objects, and even life and death. In situations directly related to ethics, "the yi of X" can be roughly understood to mean "the duty of X," but at times its occurrence is detached from normative concerns. Common translations of yi 義 in this formula include "appropriateness," "advice," "principle," "importance," "property," "norm," "reason," "meaning," "sense," "significance," "dogma," "objective," or "purpose," to name a few. Resorting to the customary translations is not sufficient, however, if the goal is to account for these particular uses in total and to fold them into a comprehensive understanding of the evolving role of yi 義 in early Chinese texts.

A Sampling of Perplexing Uses of *Yi* 義 as a Way into a Solution

In a statement like the following from the *Xunzi*, we readily assume that *yi* 義 is functioning in a normative capacity because the *yi* 義 pertains to an educational endeavor.[1]

> 學惡乎始? 惡乎終? 曰: 其數則始乎誦經, 終乎讀禮; 其義則始乎為士, 終乎為聖人。
> Where does learning start? Where does it end? It is said, "Its sequence is to begin with reciting the *Shi* and to end with reading aloud the *Li*. Its *yi* 義 is to begin with the scholar and to end with the sage."
> *Xunzi* 荀子 勸學篇第一

In the following case from a Mawangdui commentary to the *Zhouyi*, however, the *yi* of X is baffling. The "Yi Zhi Yi" states:

> 歲之義, 始于東北, 成于西南。
> The *yi* of the year begins in the northeast and is completed in the southwest.[2]
> "Yi Zhi Yi" 易之義 *Zhouyi* 周易

Such a statement does not appear to be normative; it does not appear to be speaking to the "duty," "propriety," "meaning," or even the "(moral) rightness" of the year.

Let's try to unravel the puzzle. The opening line of the "Yi Zhi Yi"—"The *yi* 義 of the *Yi* 易 is yin and yang"—is mystifying as well, until we notice that both it and the *yi* of the year involve that which can be seen. If the *yi* 義 of a year is to begin "in the northeast" and be completed in the southwest," the *yi* 義 appears to be a trajectory of movement, a visible pattern.[3]

A passage in the *Huainanzi* draws attention to the *yi* 義 in the *Zhouyi*.

> 溫惠柔良者,《詩》之風也, 淳厖敦厚者,《書》之教也; 清明條達者,《易》之義也; 恭儉尊讓者, 禮之為也; 寬裕簡易者, 樂之化也; 刺幾辯義者,《春秋》之靡也。

---

1. Knoblock translates it as "real purpose." Knoblock, *Xunzi*, 1:139. Watson uses "objective." Watson, *Hsün-Tzu*, 19.

2. I use the transcription that Edward Shaughnessy provides of the Mawangdui text.

3. The drawback of "properties," which is Shaughnessy's translation, is that properties are often considered to be abstracta. Moreover, early Chinese philosophy does not distinguish properties from substances. Yin and yang are "relations," suggesting an ontology that does not feature substances with properties. Shaughnessy, *I Ching*, 214–233.

Warmth, kindness, gentleness and goodness are the influences (winds) of the *Shijing*.
Purity, grandeur, nobility, and generosity are the teachings of the *Shujing*.
Clarity and brightness, orderliness and reaching are the yi 義 of the *Zhouyi*.
Deference, thrift, respect and humility are the actions of the *Rites*.
Broadmindedness, magnanimity, simplicity, and easiness are the transforming qualities of the *Music*.
Reprimands, critiques, disputation, and yi 義 are the meticulousness of the *Chunqiu*.[4]
Huainanzi 淮南子 泰族訓

In these exemplars of six different genres, yi 義 links to more than one text: the *Chunqiu*, well known for its normative judgements, and the *Zhouyi* divination manual. In my discussion of the *Guliangzhuan* (chapter 9), I will show that yi 義 is a feature of the *Chunqiu*'s ethical judgments and, as such, fits well among reprimands, critiques, and disputation. The depiction of the yi 義 of the *Zhouyi*—emphasizing clarity, brightness, orderliness, and reaching—is more pertinent for my purposes in this chapter. In what sense is the yi 義 of the *Zhouyi* comparable to the transformations that constitute the *Book of Music*, the actions that constitute the *Book of Rites*, and the teachings that constitute the *Book of Documents*? The passage, which goes no further than to characterize the yi 義 of the *Zhouyi* as visually clear, orderly, and able to reach its aim, is not particularly informative. The six different textual categories suggest, however, that the distinctively visual yi 義 of the *Zhouyi* manual might be either its trigram configurations or its divinatory determinations or both. Hence, this passage may be saying that the visual figures of the *Zhouyi* are clear, bright, orderly, and reach their aim in scope. At the very least, because it says that its yi 義 are clear and bright, we can conclude that the yi of the *Zhouyi* has something to do with its visible appearance.

The visual nature of yi is also apparent in this line from the *Zhuangzi*, spoken in the voice of the stock character, Laozi. The *Zhuangzi* describes an individual's shape as being "yi-like" (*yiran* 義然):

---

4. It is possible that not all six are texts. My translation is indebted to that of Sarah Queen and John Major in Major et al., *Huainanzi*, 808.

The correlations of virtues with texts varies in different cases. The *Baihu tong* aligns yi 義 with the *Shujing*:

《五經》經所以有五何? 經, 常也。有五常之道, 故曰《五經》:《樂》仁、《書》義、《禮》禮、《易》智、《詩》信也。
Regarding the "five classics," why are there five classics? [Answer] *Jing* (warp) is constant. It has the dao of five constancies. Thus it is said "Five Classics" are *Yue* 樂 (Music) for *ren* 仁, *Shu* 書 (Writings) for yi 義, *Li* 禮 (Rites) for ritual action, *Yi* 易 (Changes) for knowing, and *Shi* 詩 (Odes) for trusting.
Baihu tong 白虎通 五經

老子曰：「而容崖然，而目衝然，而顙頯然，而口闞然，而狀義然，似繫馬而止也。」

Laozi said, "Your face is arrogant-seeming; your eyes are insulting-seeming; your forehead is protruding-seeming; your mouth is growling-seeming; your shape is *yi*-seeming (義然); and you are like a tethered horse being held back."

Zhuangzi 莊子 天道第十三

Whatever the specific insult implied (perhaps stern or imposing), if the likeness in *yi* 義 is a question of visual demeanor, then *yi* 義 is characteristically visible.

"How do you hit the mark in archery?" a passage in the *Baihu tong* asks. The *yi* 義 in the answer does not take the form of a "duty," a "reason," a "purpose," or a "meaning."

射（主）[正]何為乎？
曰：射義非一也。
夫射者、執弓堅固，心平體正，然後中也。

In archery, how does one hit the mark?
[Answer] The *yi* 義 of archery is not just one.
[But] in archery in general, grasp the bow hard and tight. The heart-mind should be calm and the body should be straight. Then, you will hit the center.

Baihu tong 白虎通 鄉射

In light of the examples above, let us return to the *yi* 義 of the year in the "Yi Zhi Yi" passage and relate it to similar comments about the trajectories of yin-qi and yang-qi in the *Huainanzi* and the trajectory of the qi of heaven and earth in the *Liji*.[5] In those instances, the geographic locations of beginnings and endings refer to the patterns of seasons or winds. Therefore, the comment about the *yi* 義 of the year

---

5. See *Huainanzi* 14 詮言訓 and *Liji* 46 鄉飲酒義.

In the *Liji*, another trajectory for the *yi* 義 of yin-yang is seeking a person's souls where they return: above and below. It links the *yi* 義 to yin-yang when describing their development in the Yin and the Zhou periods.

魂氣歸于天，形魄歸于地。故祭，求諸陰陽之義也。
殷人先求諸陽，周人先求諸陰。

The *hunqi* 魂氣 returns to heaven, the *xingpo* 形魄 returns to earth.
Hence, the sacrificial rite is the *yi* 義 of seeking them (the souls) in yin and yang. The Yin (殷) people first sought them in yang. The Zhou people first sought them in yin.

Liji 禮記 〈郊特牲〉 11.27

might refer to what we see in the sky as the year follows the course in which it is disposed to move. These unusual uses of *yi* 義, then, suggest something like patterns.

I would like to go a step further and introduce the concept of "model." "Model," I believe, captures the way in which *yi* 義 functions in "the *yi* of X." Some noteworthy aspects of the word "model" from the *Oxford English Dictionary* (third edition) definition of its noun form may be useful.

I. A **representation** of structure, and related senses.

   1. a. A set of **designs** (plans, elevations, sections, etc.) for a projected building or other structure; a similar set of drawings made to scale and representing the proportions and arrangement of an existing building. Also (occasionally): a plan of a town, garden, etc. Also **figurative**. *Obsolete*.

      b. A description of structure. *Obsolete. Rare.*

      c. **A summary, epitome, abstract; the argument of a literary work.** *Obsolete.*

   2. a. Something which accurately resembles or represents something else, esp. on a small scale; a person or thing that is the likeness of another.

      b. An archetypal image or pattern. *Rare.*

   3. A small portrait, as on a medal; (hence also) a medal. *Obsolete.*

   4. **a.** A three-dimensional representation, esp. on a small scale, of a person or thing or of a projected or existing structure; *esp.* one showing the component parts in accurate proportion and relative disposition.

      b. *Art.* An object or figure made in clay, wax, etc., as an aid to the execution of the final form of a sculpture or other work of art; a maquette. Formerly (also): †a sketch or study made for a painting (*obsolete*).

   5. = mould. *Obsolete. Rare.*

II. An **object** of **imitation**.

III. A type or design.

In the remainder of the chapter, I would like to explore the appropriateness of my hypothesis that in Early China *yi* came to be used to mean "model."

Yi 義 and Yi 儀 as Ordinary Material "Model"

The interchanges between *yi* 義 and *yi* 儀 in early Chinese texts involve their externality. As I argued in chapter 4, its familiar contrast with *ren* 仁 stresses that *yi* 義 is an external, publicly available standard. The related term, *yi* 儀 (with the addition of the semantic classifier 亻), is used to mean things like ceremony, proper conduct, demeanor, visible norm, and gnomon. Taken together then, the interchanges of *yi* 義 with *yi* 儀 suggest a shared exemplar that is both visible and accessible—a model, if you will.

By "model," I mean something physical that can serve as a form of measurement or a guide.[6] Readily visible, it is a thing to be emulated rather than an abstraction to be performed. That is, it is not a fixed or ideal entity—as, for example, the term "type" is sometimes understood to be—that is repeatedly instantiated in other things or actions. In Early China, model emulation refers to an early Confucian method of learning that involved imitating the speech and behaviors of exemplary people; it does not involve performing a unique act of virtue from a moment in a historical person's life (as if those circumstances could be re-created).[7] The relationship of the learner to the model is, thus, one of analogy rather than concretization or manifestation.[8] Similarly, as models, *yi* 義 and *yi* 儀 are material, temporal entities available for imitation, such as gnomons or sundials. (Therefore understanding *yi* 義 as "model" in its uses in early Chinese texts is preferable to "standard" because a model implies a standard but, in addition, stresses its accessibility.)[9]

The interchangeability of *yi* 義 and *yi* 儀 is sometimes evident in compounds. For instance, *fayi* 法儀 is, in theory, the "correct" way to write that compound, but in more than a third of the cases in which it appears in early Chinese texts, it is actually written *fayi* 法義 instead.[10] Perhaps in some cases this is a scribal mistake or a loan graph (i.e., a homophonous or nearly homophonous word). The two terms overlap or interchange so often that there is little reason to deem it unorthodox when *yi* 義 appears instead of *yi* 儀.

---

6. Alfred Forke's occasional translation of *yi* 義 as "scheme" in *Lun-Heng: Philosophical Essays of Wang Ch'ung* is felicitous in suggesting a structure.

7. The term "model emulation" comes from Donald Munro, *Concept of Man*, esp. 102–103.

8. In the first half of *Language as Bodily Practice*, I argue against Chad Hansen's presentation of model emulation in early Chinese texts as a one/many dualism like model/performance or script/performance.

9. See appendix A.

10. In the received texts in the CHANT Pre-Han and Han database, it appears as 法儀 eleven times and 法義 six times.

In addition to its appearance in the compound *fayi* 法義, *yi* 義 also functions alone to mean "model."[11] *Yi* 儀 is often used to mean "gnomon" (sundial) or, less technically, "model," as in the famous passage on speech from the *Mozi* that equates models (*yi* 儀) with standards (*biao* 表):

> [言]必立儀，言而毋儀，譬猶運鈞之上而立朝夕者也，是非利害之辯，不可得而明知也，故言必有三表。
>
> For speech, we must establish an *yi* 儀. To have speech with no *yi* 儀 is like establishing [the directions of] sunrise and sunset on top of a revolving potter's wheel. The distinguishing of "this" and "not-this" and of benefit and harm cannot be clearly known. Therefore speech must have three standards.[12]
> *Mozi* 墨子 墨子卷九 9.3 《〈非命上第三十五〉》

Moreover, *yi* 義—and not just *yi* 儀—appears in this sort of usage. The association of *yi* 義 with visibility and the individuated, patterned components of earth (described in chapter 5) might explain why. As a standard shape, *yi* 義 is a square which is the shape of the earth. A dire description in the *Heguanzi* implies that *yi* 義 is a regular pattern against which things are gauged:

> 道與德館，而無以命也，
> 義不當格，而無以更也。
> 若是置之，雖安、非定也。
>
> Dao and *de* (virtues/potencies) were lodged, and yet there was no means to command.
> *Yi* 義 had not fit the standard (*ge* 格), and yet there was no means to change.

---

11. Similar substitutions also happen with *yi* 議 (used to mean "discussions"). For example, when the *Yantie Lun* mentions the *yi* 義 of salt and iron, reading *yi* 義 as a loan word for *yi* 議 seems required.

> 客曰：「余視鹽、鐵之義，觀乎公卿、文學、賢良之論，意指殊路，各有所出，或上仁義，或務權利。」
>
> The guest said, "I look at the *yi* 義 about salt and iron, observing that from the views of the high ministers, the scholars and the virtuous, their intentions (*yi* 意) point to different roads. Each has its own leave off point. Some elevate *ren* and *yi* (仁義). Others engage power and profit."
> *Yantie Lun* 鹽鐵論 鹽鐵論卷十 《〈雜論第六十〉》

12. For the date of the passage, which is part of the "ten triads" section of the *Mozi*, see chapter 3, note 13.

112 / The Emergence of Word-Meaning in Early China

If something is installed like this, even if it is secure, it is not settled.
Heguanzi 鶡冠子 著希 第二

Insofar as it functions to mean something like an exemplary pattern or instrument—gnomons, potter's wheels, and "hexagrams" (i.e., a stack of six broken and unbroken lines)—*yi* 義 can be understood, then, to be a model.

To fully comprehend the advantage of interpreting *yi* 義 as model, however, we should explore the use of "*yi* 義 for" in addition to its use as "*yi* 義 of."[13] Although it is true that *Yijing* references to hexagrams (the sixty-four six-line combinations of the *Zhouyi*) functioning as models are not always clear about what exactly is serving as the model for what—yin-yang as model for earth-heaven or vice versa—a hexagram is an object in the world that maps onto something else in the world. Moreover, hexagrams are not static; their value lies in their usage, during which they transform one into another.[14] Hence, if we define a model as a thing used instead of another for some purpose (such as measuring, imitating, justifying), there is no reason to ascribe to it any complex ontological status like that of a fictional or abstract entity.[15]

Yi 義 as Models: Heaven-Earth and Yin-Yang in Zhouyi Commentaries

Commentaries on the *Zhouyi*, which frequently mention the *yi* 義 (or 儀) of the *Zhouyi*, help illuminate the characteristics that support an understanding of *yi* 義 as model. With the Mawangdui commentaries on the *Zhouyi* (first published in English in 1993), we recognize similar applications of *yi* 儀 and *yi* 義 when we compare the assertion about the *yi* 儀 of the *Zhouyi* in the received text, the "Xici," and that about the *yi* 義 of the *Zhouyi* in the Mawangdui "Yi Zhi Yi." Taken together, the two statements might explain why the *Zhouyi* might be seen as being composed of clear and bright *yi* 義 (as in the *Huainanzi* passage above). The Mawangdui "Xici" says,

是故易有大恆，是生兩橫(儀)，兩橫(儀)生四馬(象)，四馬(象)生八卦，八卦生吉凶，吉凶生六(大)業。
是故法馬(象)莫大乎天地。變週(通)莫大乎四時。縣馬(象)著明莫大乎日月。

---

13. See appendix A for this notion of models, which I borrow from Clifford Geertz's classic depiction of the function of symbols. Geertz, *Interpretation of Cultures*, 93–94.

14. This is well described in Wonsuk Chang, "Reflections on Time," 216–229.

15. The ontological status of certain kinds of models as fictional objects, etc. is not a concern raised by *yi* 義 or *yi* 儀.

Thus, the Yi 易 (Changes) has great constancy. This gives birth to the two yi (儀).[16] The two yi give birth to the four emblems (xiang 象), the four emblems give birth to the eight trigrams, the eight trigrams give birth to fortune and misfortune, fortune and misfortune give birth to the great enterprise.

Therefore, of standards (fa 法) and emblems, none is greater than heaven and earth. Of the things that change and commune, none is greater than the four seasons. Of the emblems that hang clearly and brightly, none is greater than the sun and moon.[17]

"Xici" 繫辭 Zhouyi 周易

Note the succession of numbers in the passage: the Zhouyi gives birth to two (models yi 儀), which produces four, and finally eight. Next follows a sequence that parallels the prior one by, at least initially, repeating the numerical sequence of two (heaven and earth) and four (the four seasons). Whether we interpret the passage to mean that heaven and earth are models or that they are merely examples of models (of yin-yang, perhaps), in either case, yi 儀 are equated with heaven and earth. This is significant because the "Yi Zhi Yi" identifies the yi 義 of the Zhouyi as the yin-yang dyad, which, by the second century BCE, was regularly likened to the heaven-earth dyad. Moreover, the "Yi Zhi Yi" states explicitly that heaven is the great yang.[18] In short, we have two slightly different phrasings of seemingly identical claims. According to the "Xici," the yi 儀 of the Zhouyi is some unspecified pair of terms, probably heaven and earth. According to the "Yi Zhi Yi," the yi 義 of Zhouyi is the pair yin and yang. There is room to doubt that the two unspecified models (yi 儀) in the "Xici" are yin and yang, or that heaven and earth can be identified as yang and yin.[19]

---

16. For my purposes, the Mawangdui passage is not significantly different from that of the received text except that the Mawangdui version has a variant of yi 儀 with a "wood" semantic classifier.

17. Compare Shaughnessy translation, *I Ching*, 199–201.

18. Perhaps the alignment of heaven with yang as opposed to yin was not firm yet, as in "Mr. Cao's Yin and Yang" (see chapter 5, note 11), but it seems certain that they were aligned one way or the other. The "Yi Zhi Yi" says,

是謂大陽, 此天[之義也]。
This is called the great yang. This is heaven's yi (model).
"Yi Zhi Yi" 《易之義》 Zhouyi 周易
Compare Shaughnessy translation, *I Ching*, 215.

19. Yi 儀 should be read as "model" here, because it is often used that way and because the passage later correlates it to fa 法. (For a discussion of fa 法, see chapter 9 and appendix A.) A less plausible reading could take the "Xici" use of yi 儀 as meaning yi 義 in the sense that two "meanings" give birth to the four emblems. But in that case, it is not clear what the two meanings would be. The following line, which says heaven and earth are standards of the four emblems (seasons), also makes that option unlikely.

But if we recognize "the two" as heaven and earth and grant that by this point (by the second century BCE when the manuscript was copied) there is a strong equation between the heaven-earth and yin-yang pairs, then the "Yi Zhi Yi" use of *yi* 義 corresponds to the use of *yi* 儀 in the "Xici." Whether they are heaven-earth or yin-yang, they constitute the two models of the *Zhouyi*, which helps explain the *Huainanzi*'s statement that the *Zhouyi* is composed of *yi* 義, just as the *Shujing* is composed of teachings (*jiao* 教) and the *Shijing* is composed of "winds" or "influences" (*feng* 風). The *Zhouyi* is composed of *yi* 義 insofar as its combinations of solid and broken lines are models of heaven-earth and yin-yang dyads.

The "Yi Zhi Yi" notes as well that the ten-thousand things have an *yi* 義 involving hardness and movement—a use of *yi* 義 that can also be understood as a model.

> 萬物之義, 不剛則不能僮 (動), 不僮 (動) 則無功, 恒僮 (動) 而弗中則□, [此剛]之失也。
> The *yi* 義 of the ten-thousand things is that, if they are not hard, then they are not able to move, if they do not move, then they lack achievement, and if they constantly move and are not centered, then . . . ; [this is hardness's] loss.[20]
> "Yi Zhi Yi" 《易之義》 *Zhouyi* 周易

This statement is followed by a list of hexagrams that move constantly (exemplifying hardness's loss), which shifts the focus from the ten-thousand things to the hexagrams—or the ten-thousand things *as they are modeled* in the hexagrams. In commenting about the *yi* 義 of yin and yang, the "Yi Zhi Yi" also seems to be referring to hexagrams.

> 六剛無柔, 是謂大陽, 此天[之義也。]□□□□□□□□□□□方。六柔無剛, 此地之義也。
> Six hards with no soft. This is called great yang. This [is the *yi* 義 of] heaven.
> .. .. square. Six softs with no hard, this is the *yi* 義 of earth.[21]
> "Yi Zhi Yi" 《易之義》 *Zhouyi* 周易

It is difficult to read "six hards with no soft" as anything other than a description of the unbroken and broken lines of the hexagrams. But I found no evidence that

---

20. Shaughnessy translation slightly modified, *I Ching*, 219. The missing graphs and possible loan words are debated.

21. Shaughnessy translation slightly modified, 215.

yi is ever used to mean "hexagram" per se. So what, then, is composed of these six types of lines that is not the hexagram itself? The most likely answer is the hexagram *as* model or the model *for* the hexagram.

In such an interpretation, although *yi* 義 itself would not function as a normative term—it would not be, for instance, the year's duty or propriety—the context would not be entirely divorced from normative implications. If we interpret *yi* 義 as model, then the "Yi Zhi Yi" commentary would posit three models related to the *Zhouyi*: 1) yin and yang as the *Zhouyi*'s normative models that constitute the hexagrams; 2) a model for the progress of the year, according to which it should travel in a certain direction; and 3) the *Qian* and *Kun* hexagrams themselves as models of and for heaven-earth or yin-yang.

Yi 義 as Diagrammed in the Mawangdui *Zhouyi* Commentary "Mu He"

An unusual phrase about diagramming *yi* that is repeated in the "Mu He" 繆和 commentary illustrates the problem with translating *yi* 義 as "meaning" in texts prior to the second century. Let's consider a passage that falls after the introduction of the sage-king Tang. A less fragmented section of the story notes that the *Zhouyi* "diagrams its *yi*." We can infer that the *yi* 義 that has been diagrammed is the model of the fifth unbroken line of the *Bi* 比 hexagram because the claim about diagraming the *yi* 義 is followed by the line statement from the fifth line of the *Bi* 比 hexagram ䷇. The passage says,

> 諸侯聞之曰: 湯之德及禽獸魚鱉矣, 故共(供)皮敝(幣)以進者卌又(有)餘國。
> 《〈易〉》卦其義曰: 顯比, 王用三毆, 失前禽, 邑[人](原缺)不戒, 吉, 此之胃(謂)也。
>
> The many lords heard this and said: "Tang's virtue reached even the animals and fishes," and therefore there were more than forty states that sent in pelts and cloth to submit to him. When the Yi 易 diagrams (卦) its *yi* 義, and says (曰)—"Lustrously ally; the king herewith thrice drives the hunt, losing the front catch; the city men are not warned; auspicious,"—this is what it refers to (謂).[22]
>
> "Mu He" 繆和 *Zhouyi* 周易

The use of *gua* 卦 (hexagram) as a verb is unusual: *using* a hexagram (or "to hexagram"), which amounts to diagramming. To properly interpret the phrase "diagrams its *yi* 義," one must understand the act of diagramming. Diagramming is not a form

---

22. Shaughnessy translation slightly modified, 266–267.

of speaking, and so the line cannot be read as "diagrams its *yi* 義, **saying** . . ."; it must be read as "diagrams its *yi*, **and** says."[23] The phrase is not, in other words, a compound like *wen yue* 問曰 ("asked saying") or even *shu zhi yu ce yue* 書之於策曰 ("wrote it on bamboo saying").[24] The translation "diagrams its *yi*, and says . . ." thus rightly highlights that the *yi* 義 is not the verbal content of the quotation. A diagram is not the sort of entity that conveys verbal phrases, and semantic entities are not diagrammed; hence, *yi* 義 is not the "meaning" of the quotation. Instead, the *Yi* 易 draws the "model" of the fifth unbroken line of the *Bi* 比 hexagram, and says "Lustrously ally. . . ."

Again, the segment describes two distinct actions, diagramming and saying: "When the *Yi* 易 <u>diagrams</u> its *yi* 義, and <u>says</u>, 'Lustrously ally. . . .'" The diagram (*gua* 卦) occurs first. The judgment statement (*yue* 曰) follows. The act of referring (*wei* 謂, to call) belongs to speech. In the final line—"*This* is what *it* refers to" (*ci wei ye*)—"this" is the statement "Lustrously ally." The implied "it" that does the speaking/referring is the *Zhouyi*. The *Yi's statements* are matters of reference. Its *lines* are a matter of diagramming. Hence, "Lustrously ally" is not the *yi* 義 that has been diagrammed. Indeed, if we pull together what we have learned so far about *yi* 義 and the *Zhouyi*, it becomes clear that "to *gua* 卦 an *yi* 義," so to speak, requires the hand, not the mouth. The *yi* 義 of the *Zhouyi* is yin and yang. The *yi* 義 of heaven is great yang, which is six hardnesses. The *yi* 義 of the ten-thousand things is that they can only move if they are not entirely soft. The *yi* 義 of a year is to start in the northeast and end in the southwest. None of these *yi* 義 resembles a statement like "Lustrously ally; the king herewith thrice drives the hunt, losing the front catch; the city men are not warned; auspicious." In fact, they are not statements at all. The *yi* 義 that we have encountered so far are yin and yang, hard and soft, and directionals. They are models that are diagrammed in the *Zhouyi* through the hexagrams and their lines. What the "Mu He" commentary describes as having been diagrammed is something that actually lends itself to being diagrammed: a model as exemplified in the fifth unbroken line of the *Bi* hexagram.

Translating such uses of *yi* 義 in early Chinese texts as "model" is compelling because the texts also treat yin-yang—as well as heaven-earth—like models. Literally, heaven and earth are models "of" round and square and models "for" behavior. More subtly, yin and yang function as models, at least for sages who can perceive them. In any given instance, the model could be heaven, yang, and the *Qian* hexagram simultaneously.

---

23. Shaughnessy reads this as "diagrams its meaning, saying." Shaughnessy, 267.

24. The *gua* phrase should be read more like "danced and said" or "clapped and said."

Yi 義 "of" and "for" People in *Yi Jing* Literature

Some unusual occurrences of *yi* 義 in the "Zhao Li" (昭力) commentary to the *Zhouyi*—which have given rise to some translations that seem not quite right, too limited, or downright wrong—tend to sort themselves out if we think of *yi* 義 as model.

The "Zhao Li" consists of a series of questions and answers concerning whether the *Zhouyi* has an *yi* 義 for this or that person: ministers and officers, the lord of a state, etc. In the second half of the commentary, Zhao Li approaches his teacher with a question:

> 昭力問曰:《易》又(有)國君之義乎?
> Zhao Li asked saying, "Does the *Zhouyi* possess (*you* 有) an *yi* 義 for/of the lord of a state?"[25]
> "Zhao Li" 昭力 *Zhouyi* 周易

The affirmative answer indicates that it is possible to interpret *yi* 義 in this question and answer as *yi* <u>for</u> the lord of the state (in the sense of significance). This is the answer:

> 師之王三賜命, 與比之王三驅, 與桼之自邑告命者, 三者國君之義也。
> "The king thrice awards the command" of *Shi* ["The Troops" hexagram], and
> "The king thrice drives" of *Bi* ["Alliance" hexagram], and
> "From the city announce the mandate" of *Tai* ["Greatness" hexagram]—
> these three are *yi* 義 of/for the lord of a state.[26]
> "Zhao Li" 昭力 *Zhouyi* 周易

Below, I will return to the suitability of interpreting *yi* 義 as "significance" in other instances.[27] But first, note that this use of *yi* 義 does not seem like the "duties" of (or for) the lord of the state. What follows is a description of various social positions:[28]

---

25. Shaughnessy translation slightly modified, 275.

26. Shaughnessy translation slightly modified, 275, 343. According to Shaughnessy, these refer, in the Mawangdui text, to line Nine in the Second line of hexagram 37, Nine in the Fifth line of hexagram 19, and the Elevated Six line of hexagram 34.

27. For an extended defense of translating *yi* 義 as "model," see appendix A.

28. Instead of "social role," it is better to think of this as a social character or position, because for the purpose of understanding identity in early Chinese texts, the metaphor of "role" misleadingly suggests agents who are independent subjects detachable from parts that they play. See my *Language and Bodily Practice*, 213–214.

118 / The Emergence of Word-Meaning in Early China

□之潛斧, 商夫之義也;
無孟之卦, 邑途之義也;
不耕而稚 (穫), 戎夫之義也;
良月幾望, 處女之義也。

. . .'s submerged ax is the merchant's *yi* 義. *Wu Meng*, [the "Pestilence" hexagram] is the city urchin's *yi* 義. "Not planting and yet harvesting" is the belligerent fellow's *yi* 義. The fine moon almost being full is the virgin girl's *yi* 義.²⁹

"Zhao Li" 昭力 *Zhouyi* 周易

So how might we translate these various uses of *yi* 義—not just involving the lord of a state but also the merchant, the belligerent fellow, and the virgin? Let us begin by exploring three uses of "meaning": reference, sense/signification, and significance as interpretations of *yi* 義 in the passage: 師之王三賜命, 與比之王三驅, 與奈之自邑告命者, 三者國君之義也。

1. If we were to understand 三者國君之義也 as using *yi* 義 in the sense of <u>reference to a/the lord of a state</u>, it would follow that three different hexagram lines ("The king thrice awards the command"; "The king thrice drives"; "From the city announce the mandate") have a single *yi* 義, that is, they <u>point to</u> a/the lord of a state.

2. If we were to understand 三者國君之義也 as using *yi* 義 in the sense of <u>sense/signification of "lord of a state,"</u> it would follow that three different hexagram lines ("The king thrice awards the command"; "The king thrice drives"; "From the city announce the mandate") have a single *yi* 義: the <u>semantic concept</u> of the lord of a state.

3. If we were to understand 三者國君之義也 as using *yi* 義 in the sense of simply meaning "<u>significance</u>," then it would follow that the *Zhouyi* includes three lines ("The king thrice awards the command"; "The king thrice drives"; "From the city announce the mandate") that contain *yi* 義 that bear <u>significance</u> for the lord of the state (perhaps by revealing correspondences for prediction and guidance).

The first two options are not compelling. In other words, the passage does not say that the three hexagram statements ("The king thrice awards . . ." etc.) "mean"

---

29. Shaughnessy translation slightly modified, *I Ching*, 279, 343. Shaughnessy points out that the ax probably refers to Nine in the Fourth line of hexagram 52 of the Mawangdui text. He notes that "Not planting . . ." refers to Six in the Second line of the hexagram 7 and the final image probably refers to the Elevated Nine line of hexagram 58.

the lord of the state by pointing (reference) to a person or persons. Nor does the passage say that the three hexagram statements ("The king thrice awards . . ." etc.) "mean" the lord-of-the-state concept.

It is reasonable, however, to interpret the passage as saying that the hexagrams have significance, import, or a "life lesson" for people who occupy the stated positions. And yet it is not plausible that, of all possible lines, only three possess "significance" for the lord. Nor would it be likely that the text presents only a single hexagram or line with significance for belligerent fellows, virgin girls, merchants, etc. Presumably most (if not all) hexagrams and their lines would have significance for any user.

The specificity of the social positions involved suggests a better reading. Leaving behind the three uses of "meaning," let us consider again the concept of a "model." These particular hexagrams and lines are models of such people (or their social positions) as well as being models for them. Being a "model for" is much like meaning in the sense of "significance," and we have already seen that "significance" is a compelling, if incomplete, understanding of yi 義. Another, more convincing option presents itself with "model of." Yi 義 is a "model of" insofar as it "parallels" the structure of things. Again, to gua something's yi (卦其義) is to produce something akin to a diagram. This kind of model is visible but not necessarily based on visual likeness. By virtue of being a model of, an yi 義 is also a model for. In other words, by means of its form, an yi 義 normatively shapes social and psychological reality.

Conclusion

A pattern unfolds when we examine occurrences of yi 義 that are not easily interpreted as ethical uses. A material "model" is a translation of yi 義 that captures the pattern of usage described in this chapter. An yi 義 is not an ideal entity or an abstraction, in the sense that, for instance, the term "type" is sometimes understood. (See appendix A.) Understanding yi 義 as a material model sheds light on its interchanges of yi 儀, as well as the role of yi 義 in the Zhouyi as models of entities, (including heaven-earth and yin-yang). From these uses of yi 義, we can see that some lines and hexagrams are models that guide people in specific social positions, but they also map the structures of those positions in society. As with models of yin-yang and heaven-earth, they are both models of positions and models for emulation.

CHAPTER SEVEN

Yi 義 as Model in Diagrams, Genres, Figurative Language, and Names

Having explained that *yi* 義's visibility within heaven-earth and yin-yang polarities supports an interpretation that it serves as a model, to strengthen my case, I now turn to evocations of *yi* 義's visual features in other instances where semantic and ethics-related interpretations seem limited. That exploration draws us into the realm of writing and divination, as well as what I refer to as "figurative" language.

Non-glottal Writing and Yi 義

In the "Xici" commentary to the *Zhouyi* from the Mawangdui tombs, the visibility of *yi* 義 figures in the story of writing's origin.

> 古者包犧是 (氏) 之王天下也, (印) 仰則觀馬 (象) 於天, 付 (俯) 則觀法於地, 觀鳥獸之文與地之義 (宜), 近取者 (諸) 身, 遠取諸物, 於是始作八卦。。。
>
> In antiquity, when Pao Xi ruled all under heaven, looking up, he observed (*guan* 觀) the *xiang* 象 (emblems) in the heavens and looking down he observed (*guan* 觀) the *fa* 法 (patterns, models) in the earth. He observed (*guan* 觀) the markings (*wen* 文) of the birds and animals and **the *yi* 義 of the earth**. Near at hand, he picked them from his body; and at a distance, he picked them from things. Thereupon, he first made the eight trigrams . . .[1]
>
> "Xici" 繫辭 Zhouyi 周易

---

1. Edward L. Shaughnessy translation modified. I am using the transcription that Shaughnessy provides of the Mawangdui text. Shaughnessy, *I Ching*, 204–205.

I deliberately cite the Mawangdui "Xici" here because it differs from the received text, where yi 宜 ("appropriateness") is used instead of yi 義, which was pronounced similarly.² In the "Xici" narrative of writing's origin, however, yi 宜 seems not quite right: the emblems in the heavens, the patterns of the earth, and the markings of animals are all directly visible phenomena that Pao Xi observes (*guan* 觀), just as he does the yi 義 of the earth.³ Behavioral "appropriateness" does not seem to factor into such a sequence.

For my purposes, which version of the "Xici" was copied first or whether a "correct" ur-text ever even existed is irrelevant. What is important is that the Mawangdui lines are contextually coherent, so we need not treat this occurrence of yi 義 as a graphic mistake. Yi 義, the Mawangdui "Xici" suggests, were the visible models (yi 義)—especially those of the earth—that the ancients observed as they set about constructing writing.

Another graphic variation in the Mawangdui text of the "Xici" has the effect of praising the visibility of yi 義 and relating it to the *xiang* 象 (emblems) of hexagrams. The line evokes the idea that speech should be limited when expressing the heartmind, a common refrain that may date from the *Zuozhuan*'s attribution of this saying to Kongzi:⁴

> 『言以足志，文以足言。』不言，誰知其志? 言之無文，行而不遠。
> "Speech should be sufficient to the aim (*zhi* 志).⁵ The refinement (*wen* 文) should be sufficient to the speech." If you do not speak, who will know your aims (*zhi* 志)? If you say it without refinement, your actions will not go far.
> *Zuozhuan* 春秋左傳 襄公 B9.25 《襄公二十五年傳》

Although the passage merely affirms a constraint on speech (it "should be sufficient to the aim"), several later texts seem both to echo and to transform the assertion into a claim about speech's limitations.

Along these lines, the Mawangdui "Xici" declares that the hexagrams of the *Zhouyi* make the sages' yi 意 ("intentions") visible, whereas speech does not.

---

2. For a discussion of translations of yi 義 taking into account the connection to yi 宜, see appendix A.

3. See appendix C for discussions of *guan* 觀 and *wu* 物.

4. For a discussion of assigning dates to the speeches in the *Zuozhuan*, see Blakeley, "Authenticity and Nature," 218–267.

5. Because echoes in various texts exchange *zhi* 志 with yi 意, it is important to note the *Zuozhuan*'s *zhi* 志 in this use of 言以足志.

Presumably restating something like "言以足志, 文以足言," the "Xici" passage draws a distinction between the inaccessibility of *yi* 意 and the visibility of *yi* 義, about which I will have more to say in the next chapter.⁶ The passage is as follows:

子曰:『書不盡言, 言不盡意。』然則耶 (聖)人之意, 其義可見已乎?
耶 (聖)人立象以盡意。。。
Kongzi said, "Writing does not exhaust speech and speech does not exhaust *yi* 意." But as for the sages' *yi* 意, can its *yi* 義 not be seen? The sages established the *xiang* 象 in order to exhaustively express *yi* 意 . . .⁷
"Xici" 繫辭 *Zhouyi* 周易

Following the rhetorical question, the text affirms that the sages' *yi* 意 is visible through *yi* 義 ("models") because the sages established emblems (*xiang* 象). Recall that heaven's emblems and earth's models (*yi* 義) were Pao Xi's visual inspirations for the trigrams. Thus, *xiang* 象—here standing for the *yi* 義 of the *Zhouyi*—can reveal, in all its fullness, the sages' *yi* 意. According to this version of the "Xici," technically the *yi* 義 of the sages is visible in the *Zhouyi*, whereas the sages' *yi* 意 is somewhat hidden. We rely on the sages' *yi* 義 because speech and writing do not fully disclose the sages' *yi* 意 (intentions). Even if the Mawangdui is the only version of the "Xici" to makes this claim, its presence there supports my contention that *yi* 義 is particularly associated with visibility as well as myths about the origins of non-glottic writing.

---

6. The received text's version seems roundabout. It appears to revise the *Zuozhuan* assertion about writing, speech, and the heartmind's aims, then ask itself whether, if *yi* 意 is not fully expressible, the sages' *yi* 意 can be made visible, and finally proceeds to answer its own question by asserting that their *yi* 意 can be visible because the emblems of the *Zhouyi* exhaustively express their *yi* 意.

Thus *yi* 義 does not appear in the received text of the "Xici," so the Mawangdui line might seem like a mistake. This is Chen Guying's proposed revision of it:

然則聖人之意, 其不可見乎。 (Received text)
然則聖人之意, 其義可見已乎? (Mawangdui)
然則聖人之意言可見已乎。 (Chen Guying)

Chen Guying suggests the *qi* 其 should be *yan* 言 on the basis of the line that follows it: 聖人立象以盡意, 設卦以盡情偽, 繫辭以盡其言. (See Chen, *Zhouyi zhuyi*, 630.) As I argue in chapter 2, however, speech (*yan* 言) is not the kind of thing that could ever become visible (*jian* 見). Writing records speech, but in that case, the visible thing would be writing, not *yan* 言.

7. Shaughnessy, *I Ching*, 200–201.

The Six Writing Models (*Liu Yi* 六義)

"The six *yi* 義," a traditional expression in early Chinese texts, moves our understanding of *yi* 義 beyond mere suggestions about its capabilities as a visible model and squarely into the territory of writing. The *Mao Shi* "Great Preface" to the *Shijing* invokes the "six *yi*" in a manner that relates them to literary techniques and genres:

> 故《詩》有六義焉, 一曰風, 二曰賦, 三曰比, 四曰興, 五曰雅, 六曰頌。
> The *Shi* has six *yi* 義: the first is called airs, the second is called exposition, the third is called comparison, the fourth is called incitement, the fifth is called odes, and the sixth is called songs.[8]
> *Mao Shi* 毛詩〈國風. 周南〉〈關雎〉

In other words, the particular forms of the broad category of "writing" as described in the *Shijing* count as *yi* 義. Arguably, these genres and techniques which comprise the six *yi* 義 emerge as objects of study only when a text is analyzed in written form, which would make them products of the kind of thinking that writing makes possible; in that sense, *yi* 義 can be understood as features of writing. A more direct case where *yi* 義 is used to signify written models occurs in the *Shuijing Zhu*, possibly consisting of earlier material but attributed to Li Daoyuan 酈道元 (466–527). In that geography text, which relates the story of how Cangjie invented writing, the six *yi* 義 designate different kinds of scripts.

> 故文字有六義焉。自秦用篆書 . . .
> Therefore the graphs have six *yi* 義. From the Qin, they used the seal script . . .
> *Shuijing Zhu* 水經注 卷十六 16.1 穀水

As it evolved, then, *yi* 義 came to refer to models of writing in six different calligraphic styles.

If we combine the notions of *yi* 義 as calligraphic styles, hexagrams, and literary techniques/genres, *yi* 義 seems to be used to mean models for types of writing (in the broadest sense of that term). If "writing" of these sorts were understood as being *yi* 義, that state of affairs seems to foreshadow, as I will argue in chapter 10, the *Shouwen*'s adoption of *yi* 義 as a metalinguistic term and the eventual use of *yi* 義 as dictionary "word-meaning."

---

8. The Mao preface to the *Shijing* is attributed to Mao Heng of the third to second century BCE. Kern, "Early Chinese Literature," 21.

Figurative Language

Rather than appearing alongside a broad range of bits of language, as one might expect if *yi* 義 were to be understood as semantic meaning, the term *yi* 義 disproportionately occurs in early Chinese texts with what one might call figurative phrases. I choose the descriptor "figurative" for lack of a better term. With it, I intend to conjure the image of "figures" like hexagrams, which are not abstract and are no less real than any other visible phenomena, and to draw a distinction between figurative phrases and ordinary phrases, with neither possessing a lesser or greater ontological status. I hasten to add that my use of the descriptor "figurative" does not approximate any specific term from early Chinese texts. Nor does it entail a contrast to "literal," wherein "figurative" implies fictional or unreal. Finally, I want to be clear, not all phrases containing *yi* 義 are figurative; I am simply interested in highlighting those that are.

The occurrences of *yi* 義 in the "Zhao Li" (昭力) commentary to the *Zhouyi* that I referenced in the previous chapter include instances of figurative speech: a virgin girl as an almost full, fine moon; a belligerent fellow as harvesting without planting; and a city urchin as pestilence. As I argued there, the *yi* 義 serve as models of and for such people. Here I explore similar occurrences of *yi* 義 in the first-century *Lunheng* and the *Hanshu*. The *Lunheng*, which takes up the question of heaven's intervention in human affairs, makes the point that heaven lacks a body through which to decree its choice of a particular person to become ruler. Note the use of *yi* 義.

> 《書》方激勸康叔，勉使為善，故言文王行道，上聞於天，天乃大命之也。
> 《詩》曰：「乃眷西顧，此惟予度。」與此同義。
>
> According to the *Shujing*, Kang Shu is directly urged and incited, and the exhortation caused him to do good. Therefore it says that, when King Wen strode the dao, it was heard above in heaven, and heaven then commanded him with a great charge. When the *Shijing* says, "Thereupon, [it] looked kindly towards the west, and then gave a residence," this is the same *yi* (同義).
>
> *Lunheng* 論衡 《初稟篇》

The statement that immediately follows clarifies that heaven's bodily activity is what the *Lunheng* denies.[9]

---

9. It is tempting to call this a "simile" or a rejection of "literal meaning," but my starting point is the absence of such technical terminology.

天無頭面，眷顧如何？人有顧眄，以人倣天，事易見，故曰「眷顧」。「天乃大命文王」，眷顧之義，實天不命也。

Heaven has no head or face, how could it turn and look? Humans have the ability to look around. Heaven is shown as imitating humans. That is easy to see. Thus one says, "looked kindly." "Heaven then gave a great charge" has the *yi* 義 of "looked kindly." Indeed, heaven did not issue a charge.

Lunheng 論衡 《《初稟篇》》

Modern readers might assume that the "same *yi*" (*tongyi* 同義) of the phrases about heaven hearing, commanding, and looking is their shared semantic meaning. In other words, the statements "[Heaven] looked kindly" and "Heaven then gave a great charge" both possess the meaning: "Heaven performed [the activity] metaphorically." But a plausible semantic meaning must involve the specific elements of the phrases: in this case, looking kindly and giving a charge.

Indeed, "Heaven performed [the activity] metaphorically" is Wang Chung's *interpretation* of "[Heaven] looked kindly" and "Heaven then gave a great charge." Should *yi* 義, then, be understood as "interpretation" or as "significance for"? These are unlikely because, with this use of *yi* 義, Wang Chung spotlights flaws in phrases depicting heaven. His analysis builds to a logical conclusion: because heaven has no face to look kindly, it also has no voice to issue a charge. Heaven "look[ing] kindly" and heaven "[issuing] a great charge" have the same *yi* (*tongyi* 同義). Kang Shu was squarely urged and incited, but the incitement did not involve heaven's eyes or mouth. Heaven might have acted in any number of visible and audible ways—perhaps through movements of the stars or aberrations in the weather—but it did not do so through body parts such as those human beings possess. The sameness of *yi* (*tongyi* 同義) is the projection of human bodies, a kind of visual and concrete form of speech. Thus, heaven looking or giving a charge is figurative language, a type of linguistic model.

A similar instance of sameness of *yi* (*tongyi* 同義) pertaining to a material model occurs in the *Hanshu*'s comments about sayings from the *Shijing* and the *Zhouyi*. In support of an earlier claim that the *junzi*'s dao lasts a long time, whereas the small person's dao vanishes, the *Hanshu* comments on the *Tai* 泰 hexagram from the *Zhouyi*:

泰者，通而治也。《《詩》》又云「雨雪麃麃，見晛聿消」，與《《易》》同義。

Tai is that which communes and governs. The *Shijing* says, "The snow may have fallen abundantly, but when the sun appears, it vanishes." This has the same *yi* (同義) as the *Zhouyi*.

Hanshu 漢書 傳 《《楚元王傳第六》》

Again, *Tai*'s "communing and governing" does not have the same semantic meaning as the "snow may have fallen abundantly, but when the sun appears it vanishes." The *yi* 義 of the two statements do, however, share "the same" (or rather, a similar) spatio-temporal model. The shared *yi* 義 is not "the *Zhouyi*" itself but a specific part of it, the *Tai* hexagram. The cryptic *Tai* hexagram statement concerns "great coming and small going," which it deems auspicious. While it is unwarranted to say of these things that they have a similar meaning, we might allow that the hexagram statement is potentially evocative of the *Shijing*'s metaphor as well as the *Hanshu*'s initial assertion about the *junzi*'s dao lasting long. That is, "the sun making snow vanish" resembles "great [people] coming and small [people] going," and the latter bears some relation to the *junzi*'s dao being long-lived (in contrast to the dao of the small person). Again, "significance for" works to a certain extent, but not as well as "models for/of." The *yi* 義 that they share is that of a figurative model depicting the triumph of a noble minority.

In sum, related bits of figurative speech might be different in "meaning" and yet still have the same model, since a model does not require the specificity of semantic meaning. Furthermore, the relative rarity of these occurrences of *yi* 義 in early Chinese texts suggests that we understand them as something less pervasive than "meaning" or "significance." In these cases, *yi* 義 is a "figure" of speech, or a "model."

Binary Assessments: Same, Different, and "One"

In texts from Early China, binary options—like black-white, inside-outside, and above-below—are common. Modes of response often involve either-or answers that affirm or deny. So it is not surprising that when early Chinese texts compare *yi* 義, their frame of reference is restricted to a matter of sameness or difference. In other words, in relation to another *yi* 義, early Chinese texts do not indicate that a certain *yi* 義 is, for instance, more specific, apparent, well known, obscure, or important. When such passages evaluate relations among *yi* 義, they deem the *yi* 義 to be either the same or not. But some things that early Chinese texts describe as sharing an *yi* 義 do not seem to align along a same-different binary of either semantic meaning or ethical duty. Conceiving of *yi* 義 as models helps clarify their usage.

To assert that the *yi* 義 of multiple things is the same, the texts deploy formulas involving "same/similar" (*tong* 同) and "commune" (*tong* 通). To assert that the *yi* 義 is different, the texts either tag the *yi* as different (*yi* 異) or employ formulas that negate, such as the *yi* 義 "are opposed" (*xiangfan* 相反). In stating that *yi* 義 is "one" (*yi* 一), a passage might be suggesting that two different things share a singular *yi*

義. Stating that the *yi* 義 are two (*er* 二) signals that the things in question have different *yi* 義, which is often, but not always, presented as undesirable.¹⁰

In comparisons among *yi* 義 that are restricted to a binary judgment, those deemed "the same" merely bear some form of similarity to one another. They do not have the kind of shared identities that would count as sameness among "intensional" entities—i.e., those with no extensions, such as properties, propositions, or meanings. Moreover, when different things have a "single *yi* 義," the *yi* 義 seems to be a kind of complementary model, again not suggestive of an intensional object. These features of *yi* 義 support interpreting *yi* 義 as a material model.

Let us focus on the idea of an *yi* 義 being "one" or a "single *yi* 義." Consider intensional entities when interpreting this line in the *Huainanzi*: "When they accord [the ruler acts on] uprightness, when they are alternating, [the ruler acts on] expedience. The *yi* 義 is the same (義一)." The line is drawn from the "Ruler's Techniques" chapter, which outlines a series of contrasts and balances between the two major virtues, *ren* 仁 (kindliness) and *zhi* 智 (knowing or "wisdom").¹¹ It concludes:

> 故仁智[有時]錯, 有時合,
> 合者為正, 錯者為權, 其義一也。
> Thus kindliness (*ren* 仁) and wisdom (*zhi* 智) are sometimes alternating and are sometimes in accord.
> When they accord [the ruler acts on] uprightness.
> When they are alternating, [the ruler acts on] expedience.
> The *yi* 義 is one.¹²
> *Huainanzi* 淮南子 主術訓

The subject in question is the two phrases ("when they accord" and "when they are alternating") or the two actions (uprightness with accord, expedience with alternating).¹³

---

10. The *Zhouyi* and the *Chunqiu* are things that possess multiple *yi* 義 without it presenting a problem. Also, in this example, the *Lunheng* uses two *yi* 義 in a neutral way:

> 凡祭祀之義有二: 一曰報功, 二曰脩先。
> Generally, the *yi* 義 of/for sacrificial rites possesses duality: one is repaying merit; the second is cultivating [relations with] the ancestors.
> *Lunheng* 論衡《祭意篇》

Such examples might prompt translations like "duty," "significance," or even "reasons." For example, Forke translates it as "motives." Forke, *Lun-Heng*, 1:521. But "model" fits well here because the visible model of these ritual actions could simultaneously repay and cultivate the ancestors.

11. I typically avoid "wisdom" as a translation equivalent because it can sound fuzzy, but in this case, nothing else quite fits.

12. See Sarah Queen and John Major's translation, Major et al., *Huainanzi*, 337.

13. The entities that possesses the *yi* 義 are not kindliness and wisdom, which is evident from comparing this to the "single *yi* 義" patterns listed below.

Let's consider three possible ways of interpreting how the *yi* 義 is functioning in relation to them.

1. The phrases or the actions have a single meaning. But no paraphrase can encompass in a single proposition "When they accord [the ruler acts on] uprightness" with "When they are alternating, [the ruler acts on] expedience." Rather, the meaning in question is bifurcated into no fewer than two propositions.
2. The phrases or the actions have a single significance. The phrases might have a single significance *for* someone, and the actions might have a single significance *for* someone. However, because the actions are quite different, perhaps only the ruler would find it to be of similar significance whether he acted with regard to uprightness or expedience.
3. The phrases or the actions have a single material model. A single model could well be taken to characterize the ruler's actions of uprightness and expedience relative to the circumstances in which he is called to act.

In early Chinese literature, a single *yi* 義 may emphasize the difference between two different things even as it asserts that their *yi* 義 is one. Discussing the use of music for external aggression, on the one hand, and internal submission, on the other, the *Xunzi* says this:

故樂者、出所以征誅也，入所以揖讓也。
征誅、揖讓，其義一也。
Thus music is the method by which, on going out, one attacks and punishes, and on entering, one bows and declines.
Attacking and punishing. Bowing and declining. This is a single *yi* 義.
Xunzi 荀子 樂論篇第二十

Additional examples will illustrate the pervasiveness of this aspect of *yi* 義.

用下敬上, 謂之貴貴; 用上敬下, 謂之尊賢。貴貴尊賢, 其義一也。
Using those below to esteem superiors is called *guigui*. Using those above to respect inferiors is called *zunxian*. *Guigui zunxian* has a single *yi* 義.
Mengzi 孟子 《萬章下》

春饗孤子, 秋食耆老, 其義一也。而食嘗無樂。
Feasting the orphaned young in spring and feeding the aged in autumn have a single *yi* 義. But in the feeding and at the autumnal sacrifice, there was no music.
Liji 禮記 〈郊特牲〉

子得為父報讎者，臣子[之]於君父，其義一也。
A son taking vengeance on an enemy of his father and a minister [doing the same for] his ruler have a single *yi* 義.
Baihu tong 白虎通 誅伐

妻〔妾〕者、何謂〔也〕？
妻者、齊也，與夫齊體。自天子下至庶人，其義一也。
What do *qi* and *qie* refer to?
[Answer] *Qi* is uniform. With the husband, the wife is a uniform body. From the Son of Heaven down to the common man, the *yi* 義 is one.
Baihu tong 白虎通 嫁娶

故可以死，可以生，去、止，其義一也。
Thus possibly dying and possibly living, departing and stopping, have a single *yi* 義.
Yantie Lun 鹽鐵論 鹽鐵論卷五《殊路第二十一》

禮得其報則樂，樂得其反則安；禮之報，樂之反，其義一也。
When rites obtain their reward, there is music. When music obtains its return, there is peace.
The reward of the rites and the response of music have a single *yi* 義.[14]
Liji 禮記 〈樂記〉

At times, although the two things are clearly differentiated, their relation to one another is less obviously complementary.

臣聞主憂臣勞，主辱臣死，義一也。
I have heard: a ruler worrying about a minister laboring, and a ruler feeling ashamed of a minister dying is a single *yi*.[15]
Wu Yue Chunqiu 吳越春秋 勾踐伐吳外傳第十

An even more complex case follows:

婦人之制以棗栗（腶）[腶]脩者，
婦人無專制之義，御眾之任，交接辭讓之禮，

---

14. The complementary relation of rites and music is visual and aural, respectively. See my *Language as Bodily Practice*, 141–166.

15. For the dating of *Wu Yue Chunqiu*, see John Lagerwey, "Wu Yüeh ch'un ch'iu 吳越春秋," 474–475.

職在供養饋食之間。
其義一也。

Regarding the restriction on women to offering dates, chestnuts, and dried meat:
Women lack the *yi* 義 of controlling on their own, the responsibility (*ren* 任) of administering the multitudes, and the rite (*li* 禮) of entertaining, declining, and giving precedence. Their management lies between supplying nourishment and preparing food. This is a single *yi* 義.
Baihu tong 白虎通 文質

Even this extended passage exhibits complementarity: on the one hand, the long list of important official responsibilities that women cannot perform when giving ritual presents and, on the other, the short list of relatively trivial tasks women must accomplish. The pattern in which two different things share a "single *yi* 義" is, thus, a single complementary model. In light of this, the best solution for explaining such *yi* 義 does not invoke intensional features. In the case of the *Huainanzi* passage concerning the ruler and a single *yi*, we might at first assume the model is responsiveness to circumstances, but a more specific interpretation is possible. The model (*yi* 義) that is single (一也) is the spatio-temporal complementary relationship between the two different responses.

Models, understood as physical, space-time phenomena, are sufficiently capacious to accommodate a range of things that bear only a limited similarity to one another. Many things fit a compass or a square, and many things could be described as different from those models.

Human behavior when serving as a model also accommodates such binary categorizations. The life of a historical exemplar, for instance, invites emulation in many forms, and the generality of such a model produces results that are amenable to same/different evaluations. Different instances of emulation, while not precisely the same, might follow the same model. Similarly, a famous saying might constitute a model (not an abstraction but something once uttered) whereby various emulations of it would not be identical with one another but still fit the model. In comparison to abstract entities like meanings and significance, competing enactments of models are more plausibly judged as simply being at odds with or the same as. In short, the idea of a material model allows for broad assessments like being the same, being different, and being one.

The *Yi* 義 (Model) of Names in the *Zuozhuan* and the *Lunheng*

Though rare, *yi* 義 appears in relation to names in the *Zuozhuan* (fourth century BCE), and in slightly different form in two first-century texts, the *Lunheng* and the

Baihu tong. Word-meaning is not at issue. Moreover, translating the *yi* 義 of names as something like the "virtue of names" is not always possible. Again "model" is able to account for these cases of the *yi* 義 of names.

The *Zuozhuan*, which introduces the idea of an *yi* 義 of names, provides insufficient context for a reliable interpretation of how *yi* 義 is functioning. The relevant passage introduces five sources for names:

> 名有五, 有信, 有義, 有象, 有假, 有類。
> 以名生為信, 以德命為義, 以類命為象, 取於物為假, 取於父為類。
> Names have five [sources?]: trust, *yi* 義, *xiang* 象 (emblem, resemblance), borrowing, and kind.
> To name from birth is trust;[16]
> to name from *de* 德 (power/virtue) is *yi* 義;
> to name from kind (*lei* 類) is *xiang* 象 (emblem, resemblance);
> to pick [a name] from a thing is borrowing;
> to pick [a name] from the father is [of a] kind (*lei* 類).
> *Zuozhuan* 春秋左傳 桓公 B2.6 《〈桓公六年傳〉》

The passage does not go on to explain these five things that names "have." Assuming the "five" are the sources of names, the items on the list suggest the following questions. What does it mean to name on the basis of trust and why is that related to birth? What does it mean to name on the basis of *yi* 義, and why is that related to *de* 德 (power/virtue)? And what does it mean to name on the basis of resemblance, and what does that tell us about being "of a kind"? For the next two sources of names, one might wonder what is indicated by the switch in phrasing from naming on the basis (*yi* 以) of something to "picking" (*qu* 取) names from something or someone. If naming by resemblance involves being of a kind with something, why is picking from the father also characterized as relating to a kind? Does this not make the fifth source of naming redundant?

The "Jieshu" chapter of the *Lunheng* offers a context that addresses some of the questions above; those that remain might be unanswerable. The chapter evokes the *Zuozhuan* list, with slight changes, and elaborates with examples, although some are opaque.[17]

> 以生名為信, 若魯公子友生, 文在其手曰「友」也。
> 以德名為義, 若文王為昌, 武王為發也。
> 以類名為像, 若孔子名丘也。
> 取於物為假, 若宋公名杵臼也。

---

16. The *Lunheng* reverses 生 and 名 and since this pattern fits, my translation does the same.
17. For theories about some of the examples, see Forke, *Lun-Heng*, 2:414.

取於父為類, 有似類於父也。
其立字也, 展名取同義, 名賜字子貢, 名予字子我。

To name by birth is trust. Like You 友, Duke of Lu, who had writing on his hand that said "You."

To name by *de* 德 (power/virtue) is *yi* 義. Like Wen Wang being called Chang and Wu Wang being called Fa.

To name by kind (*lei* 類) is *xiang* 像 (emblem, resemblance). Like Kongzi being called Qiu.

Picking [a name] from a thing is borrowing. Like the Duke of Song being called Chujiu (Pestle and Mortar).

Picking [a name] from the father is of a kind (*lei* 類), there being likeness of kind (*si lei* 似類) to the father.

To establish a style-name, one expands on the name and picks something with the same *yi* (*tongyi* 同義). If the name is Ci 賜, the style is Zi Gong 子貢. If the name is Yu 予, the style is Zai Wo 子我.

Lunheng 論衡 《詰術篇》

The main thrust of this passage from the "Jieshu" chapter is to reject the notion that sound resemblance is one of the five sources of naming. In the course of its argument, it proposes clarifying examples.[18] Naming by trust, for instance, relates to birth insofar as infants might have writing on their hands.[19] The passage also introduces a new topic: the sources of style-names or (*zi* 字) bestowed in adulthood, as distinct from personal names. According to the "Jieshu," whereas personal names might derive from five sources (trust, *yi* 義, resemblance, borrowing, or kind), a style-name must have the same *yi* 義 as the name on which it builds.

Interpreting the *yi* 義 of names is particularly complicated because its two main terms—*yi* 義 and *de* 德—can be read in importantly different ways. The passage from the "Jieshu" seems to allow for an ethics-related reading of *yi* 義, insofar as naming based on *yi* 義 could mean naming based on "virtue" in a general sense

---

18. The *Baihu tong* mentions that hearing a name would suggest the style-name and vice versa, but the point does not seem to be that they *sound* the same.

或旁其名為之字者, 聞名即知其字, 聞字即知其名, 若名賜字子貢, 名鯉字伯魚。

Sometimes one tacks onto the name to make a style-name: one hears the name and then knows the style-name and hears the style-name and then knows the name. For example, if the name is Ci, then the style is Zi Gong. If the name is Li, then the style is Bo Yu.

Baihu tong 白虎通 姓名

The *Baihu tong* does not contain the Zai Wo (子我) example I discuss below.

19. Not that this explains what trust has to do with it!

(including an ethical trait or a potency). According to the "Jieshu," when a name is established on the basis of the infant's *de* 德, a term that can be interpreted to mean ethical virtue (although early Chinese texts do not always use *de* 德 as a normative term), that is naming by *yi* 義. The passage goes on to preclude translating *yi* 義, however, as a normative term. An example it introduces in its discussion of terms that possess the same or similar *yi* 義 (同義) presents a problem for an ethics-based reading of *yi* 義:

> 其立字也, 展名取同義, 名賜字子貢, 名予字子我。
> To establish a style-name, one expands on the name and picks something with the same *yi* 義. If the name is Ci 賜, the style is Zi Gong 子貢. If the name is Yu 予 the style is Zai Wo 子我.[20]
> *Lunheng* 論衡 《詰術篇》

The first example here offers no help for interpreting the shared *yi* 義 as based on *de* 德, but the choice in the second example of *yu* 予 and *wo* 我, both of which are used to mean "I," sheds some light.[21] Interpreting these terms for "I" as equivalent virtues is far-fetched. "I," of course, is not a "virtue," in that sense, at all.[22] In light of these terms used to mean "I," the reference to the same *yi* 義 seems to have little to do with ethical qualities.

We might thus be tempted to understand the *yi* 義 shared by the two terms for "I" as a metalinguistic term for word-meaning, even though that does not quite account for how the basis of *yi* 義 names would be *de* 德. We would have to say that the two names have *tongyi* (同義) insofar as *yu* 予 and *wo* 我 both "mean" the power of being a human subject (in whatever way the *Lunheng* understands words to mean).[23] The idea that the name "I" invokes the *de* 德 of individual agency is

---

20. The first examples in the passage arguably support both interpretations of *de* 德. The ancient King Wen was called Chang 昌, and King Wu was called Fa 發. We might take *chang* 昌 to mean "prosper" and *fa* 發 to mean "develop." If so, then at this point in the passage, naming as *yi* 義 could involve naming on the basis of either a normative quality or a potency.

21. On a normative reading, we could say that one develops the name Ci 賜, which is used to mean "to bestow," by adopting the style-name Gong 貢, which is used to mean "gift." Arguably, bestowing and giving have the same *yi* 義 insofar as they are similar virtues. On that reading, although interpreting *yi* 義 as semantic meaning is possible, it also could be understood to be an ethical term because this is establishing the name, "bestowing," on the basis of a virtue (*de* 德) and extending it to the style name, "giving," that is also a virtue.

22. It is not compelling to read this as saying that the name and style-name involve similar potencies either, but "I" is more likely to be a potency than a virtue.

23. As for early Chinese understandings of word-meaning, as I argue below, very little clear-cut evidence exists even in the *Shouwen Jiezi*, the editing of which was completed by the beginning of the second century. It is possible that the *Lunheng* treats *yi* 義 as a metalinguistic term much like the *Shouwen*, but as we will see in chapter 10, if we grant that the *Lunheng*'s use of *yi* 義 in relation to names resembles the *Shuowen*'s uses of *yi* 義, doing so requires treating *yi* as "model."

not particularly plausible, but interpreting *yi* 義 to mean word-meaning would at least pertain to both sets of examples in the passage.

Although other options are defensible, the best one, I believe, reflects the other cases of "same *yi* 義" that I have discussed above.[24] As we have seen, things that possess the same *yi* 義 do not always have the same semantic meaning. Moreover, having the same *yi* 義 seems to encompass an either/or judgment. Returning to the statement that "naming by *de* 德 (power/virtue) is *yi* 義," we can assume that *yu* 予 and *wo* 我 share the same model, and naming on the basis of *de* 德 pertains to models, rather than word-meaning. A conclusion that models possess *de* 德 is more compelling than that word-meanings do. A model, we must remember, is more capacious than a word-meaning—that is, more things are likely to have the "same" model than the same word-meaning. Because many things can follow a model, models are both normative and powerful.

Conclusion

As the examples above show, when a variety of early Chinese texts talk about the *yi* 義 of a text, a saying, or a name, translating *yi* 義 as "meaning" simply won't do. Moreover, the overuse of such a translation can convey the impression that *yi* 義 has no actual function at all. Indeed, because "meaning" by itself does not seem to say anything, occasionally translators simply omit a translation of *yi* 義 or add on properties like "of righteousness."

At the same time, *yi* 義 cannot be understood exclusively as an ethical term. As we have seen, the *yi* 義 of the belligerent fellow and the *yi* of the name "I" have no specific ethical valence. While the *Zhouyi* and *Chunqiu* literature rarely stray from ethical matters, reading *yi* as an ethical term does not apply in all instances in which it appears. In those cases that do not specifically involve ethics or semantics, "model" is the best translational equivalent for *yi* 義 because it capitalizes on the accessibility of *yi* 義 that is implied in its externality and visibility.

---

24. The less compelling options include that the names *yu* 予 and *wo* 我 might share the same "appropriateness" or the same "significance," in which case appropriateness or significance would have to be conceived as virtues or as potencies (*de* 德). The two terms for "I" would then share an appropriateness, and their names would be based on the virtue of appropriateness. Alternatively, the two terms for "I" would have the same significance, which would be naming based on significance's virtue or power.

CHAPTER EIGHT

A Framework Preceding the *Shuowen*'s Metalinguistic Choices

When Xu Shen (ca. 58–ca. 148) set out to compile the *Shuowen Jiezi* (first draft completed in 100 CE), he would have carefully considered terms available to him to express metalinguistic features when he glossed a graph. As a survey of slightly earlier and contemporaneous texts will show, *yi* 意 and *yi* 義 were both then in use to describe aspects of written texts. The obscure inaccessibility of *yi* 意 and the ready availability of *yi* 義, both well-established characteristics, were, I hope to demonstrate, central to how the two different terms were deployed in the *Shuowen*'s metalinguistic glosses. Writings have a body and bodies have *yi* 意, but *yi* 意 is often deeply concealed and at least partially inaccessible. By contrast, *yi* 義 is manifest.

Anachronism with *Yiyi* 意義

辭不達意。
Words do not fully express *yi* (意).
Chinese Proverb.

辭苟足以達, 義之至也。
If your phrasing is sufficient to arrive, that is reaching the *yi* (義).
Yili 儀禮 ("Rites of Courtesy" "Pin Li 聘禮")

With the well-known proverb above, I would like to leap forward to consider the assumption that *yi* 意 and *yi* 義 interchange.[1] The second quote, from the pre-Han

---

1. The proverb might be best known as the title of a 2006 song by Sandy Lam, *Ci Bu Da Yi*, (English translation, "Inaccurate Words") written by Nina Persson, Peter Svensson, and Xiaohan.

ritual text, the *Yili*, is often identified as the proverb's source in support of this view. In the *Yili*'s "Rites of Courtesy" chapter, however, the concern is not "language," but phrases pertaining to specific occasions—diplomatic etiquette for low-level aristocrats.² Moreover, mistaking the line from the "Rites of Courtesy" for the proverb's origin proceeds from incorrect parsing of *dayi* 達意.³

Notwithstanding the familiar compound *yiyi* 意義, rarely are *yi* 意 and *yi* 義 interchanged in texts composed before the Eastern Han (25–220 CE).⁴ They do not appear to have been pronounced similarly, and their uses are quite different even

---

2. As Wang Tingxian observes, in the "Pin Li" chapter, *cida* (辭達) refers to diplomatic rhetoric, not a theory of language or rhetoric in general. Wang, *Wenyan Xiuci Xinlun*, 44–46.

3. The *yi* 義 in the "Pin Li" line functions as an ethical term like "proper," and is not the object of the verb *da* 達. The *Gongyangzhuan*'s comment on the chapter affirms this.

> 聘禮，大夫受命不受辭。
> According to the "Pin Li," the grand officers accept instructions, but do not accept specific rhetoric/phrasing.
> *Chunqiu Gongyangzhuan* 春秋公羊傳 莊公 《〈莊公十九年〉》 13.19

The common formula, X *zhi* Y *ye* (X 之 Y 也), confirms the correct punctuation: *yi zhi zhi ye* 義之至也. Accordingly, the *Yili* line reads:

> 辭無常，孫而說。辭多則史，少則不達。辭苟足以達，義之至也。
> Rhetoric/phrasing lacks a constant, so just follow and speak. If your phrasing is excessive, then it will sound like a diviner/recorder (*shi* 史). If your phrasing is scanty, then it will not reach [the target]. If your phrasing is sufficient to arrive [at the target], that is reaching the *yi* 義.

4. For a discussion of a misinterpretation of a line from the *Xunzi*'s "Zhengming" that assumes *yi* 義 substitutes for *yi* 意 in the compound *zhiyi* 志義, see chapter 2.

One case of *yi* 意 substituting for *yi* 義 occurs in the *Taiping Jing*, an unusual text in nonstandard language, which Barbara Hendrichke judges to be a late second or early third century text based on its language. Hendrichke, "Dialogue Forms in the *Taiping Jing*," 720. The *Taiping Jing* restates a claim from the "ten triads" section of the *Mozi* (see chapter 3, note 13), replacing *yi* 義 with *yi* 意. The *Mozi*, when addressing why we should endorse the single *yi* 義 of conforming to superiors, describes the problem it would avoid:

> 若苟百姓為人，是一人一義，十人十義，百人百義，千人千義，逮至人之眾不可勝計也，則其所謂義者亦不可勝計。
> If we treat the hundred clans as people, then for one person [there would be] one *yi* 義; ten people, ten *yi* 義; a hundred people, a hundred *yi* 義; a thousand people, a thousand *yi* 義, until the point where it would be impossible to successfully count the people, and then what they call *yi* 義 also could not be successfully counted.
> *Mozi* 墨子 墨子卷三 3.3 《〈尚同下第十三〉》

If *yi* 義 is functioning as an ethical term here, it must be something neutral, like multiple different standards of norms. Thus, instead of "a hundred rightnesses," one finds translations like "a

when *yi* 義 does not function as an explicitly ethical term.[5] Consequently, *yiyi* 意義 does not provide a useful lens for understanding earlier stages in the development of the use of *yi* 義 as a metalinguistic term, but it is likely to reflect the *outcome* of those stages.

In the Pre-Han and Han corpus on the CHANT database, *yiyi* 意義 occurs but three times, and only one instance, from the *Guliangzhuan*, might predate the first century BCE.[6] With the in-depth explication of that difficult *Guliangzhuan* passage that follows, I hope to address anachronistic expectations about *yiyi* 意義 as well

---

hundred principles" (Johnston, *Mozi*, 119). (For a longer discussion of translating *yi* 義, see appendix A) "Hundreds of purposes," as in Y. P. Mei's translation, seems to assume *yi* 義 is the same as *yi* 意. (Mei, *Ethical and Political Works*, 71.) Such a rewriting of the passage also occurs in the *Taiping Jing*, which literally substitutes *yi* 意 for *yi* 義, resulting in a strikingly different understanding that culminates in a comment about the *xinyi* 心意 (heartmind's intent) of heaven.

> 「子之問也。是故百人百意,千人千意,萬人萬意,用策不同各殊異,故多不得天心意。」
> I have heard this. If there are a hundred people, then there are a hundred *yi* 意 (intentions, aims); if there are a thousand people, then there are a thousand *yi* 意; if there are ten thousand people, then there are ten thousand *yi* 意. The use of calculations cannot assimilate each separate difference, therefore most do not achieve heaven's heartmind's *yi* 意.
> *Taiping Jing* 太平經 太平經己部 《火氣正神道訣第一百三十五》

Something about the readership of the *Taiping Jing* might have rendered *yi* 意 a more compelling choice than *yi* 義. In any case, the outcome of this substitution supports my point, because *yi* 意, unlike *yi* 義, originates in the heartmind (*xin* 心). So once the two graphs are switched, it makes sense that the *Taiping Jing* introduces a *xin*.

5. See Baxter and Sagart's Old Chinese reconstruction, chapter 2, note 28.

The phrase *Chunqiu zhiyi* 春秋之義 occurs fifty-three times in texts before the second century, and although it is interesting that *Chunqiu zhiyi* 春秋之意 occurs at all, it only appears twice in the *Hanshu* and once in the *Shuoyuan*. By contrast, the phrase *Chunqiu zhidao* 春秋之道 occurs eight times, and *Chunqiu zhifa* 春秋之法 occurs eleven times. *Dao* 道, *fa* 法, and *yi* 義 seem related in certain uses. See appendix A and the *Baihu tong* "Sanjun" (白虎通 三軍) passage in chapter 9.

6. The compound appears once in an entry in the *Shuowen*, which I discuss in detail in chapter 10. In two occurrences (both circa second century), *yiyi* 意義 appears only once in each text. The contexts concern written texts but the passages supply no indications to tell us how their uses of *yiyi* 意義 were understood. The *Taiping Jing* passage says this.

> 故後世讀吾文書,從上到下,盡睹其要意義而行者,萬不失一也。
> Therefore later ages will read my writings, and from top to bottom, they will thoroughly see its crucial *yiyi* (意義) and put them into practice, and not one in ten thousand will be lost.
> *Taiping Jing* 太平經 太平經己部 《神司人守本陰祐訣第一百五十六》

The use in the *Qian Hanji* is in the chapter "Reign of Emperor Xuan 2" (孝宣皇帝紀二).

as highlight the complexity of translating yi 意 and yi 義 as semantic terms within an early Chinese context.

The *Guliangzhuan* passage comments on a typically terse statement from the *Chunqiu*, which says:

夏五月，公至自楚。
Summer. Fifth Month. The Duke arrived from Chu.
Chunqiu Zuozhuan 春秋左傳 襄公 A 9.29 《襄公二十九年經》

In hindsight, the *yiyi* 意義 that appears in the *Guliangzhuan*'s interpretive comment looks similar to certain later uses, that is, *yiyi* 意義 applied to something (as in X's 之意義). Thus, to readers familiar with that pattern, the *yiyi* 意義 in the *Guliangzhuan*'s comment might seem to function in the sense of something's meaning.

Explaining this line about the duke arriving from Chu, the *Guliangzhuan* says:

喜之也。致君者，殆其往，而喜其反，
此致君之意義也。
There is happiness in it. Regarding the lord being sent out (*zhijun* 致君), there is peril in his going but happiness on his return.
This (*ci* 此) is the *yiyi* 意義 of/about the lord being sent out (*zhijun*).
Guliangzhuan 春秋穀梁傳 襄公 《襄公二十九年》 9.29.2

Unfortunately, the referent of "this" (*ci* 此) is unclear. But the *Guliangzhuan* is associating something with "lord being sent out" (*zhijun* 致君) as its *yiyi* 意義. Adopting later semantic uses of *yiyi* 意義 might yield an interpretation that takes *zhijun* 致君 (lord being sent out) as a linguistic item—that is, as "lord being sent out." In that case, the *yiyi* 意義 of that phrase would be its "meaning," and its meaning would be "There is peril in his going but happiness on his return." Strictly speaking, however, the phrase "lord being sent out" seems to mean nothing more nor less than "lord being sent out." It might *portend* peril and happiness, but it does not *mean* it in any technical semantic sense. Thus, from this perspective, *yiyi* does not seem to be the meaning of a linguistic item.

If we take the context of the passage into account, however, we are able to narrow down explanatory possibilities by asking whose happiness is under discussion. It might be the lord's own happiness, or perhaps it is that of a minister whose lord has been sent away. The "lord" is unlikely to think of himself as "the lord," so it is probably the minister who is happy. Thus, we might posit that the passage says a perilous departure with a happy return has the significance (*yiyi* 意義) of the lord being sent out (*zhijun*). Reversing the elements, though, yields a clearer logic: it is the lord's being sent out that has the significance of "perilous departure but happy return." What, then, is the referent of "this" (*ci* 此)? Perhaps it refers even further back—not to anything in the *Guliangzhuan*'s statement but to the line from the *Chunqiu*, "The Duke arrived from Chu" (公至自楚). In that case, the phrase "the Duke arrived from Chu" means a lord being sent out (*zhijun*), but again it seems more reasonable that "the Duke arrived from Chu" means precisely what it appears to mean: the Duke arrived from Chu.

Alternatively, we might hypothesize that the Duke's arrival from Chu bears some significance for someone—a significance encapsulated in the idea of a lord being sent out. However, for the Duke himself, the concept of his arriving from Chu would probably not have the particular significance of a lord being sent out. And it is not clear why anyone else would take the Duke's arriving in Chu to have the significance of a lord having been sent out.

Any interpretation proffered for this passage must be underdetermined, but here are two brief, potential readings.

- First because, in Early China, one might reasonably impart ethical implications to a lord's departure and arrival, we might translate *yi* 義 as "duty." In that case, perilous going and happy return is the dutiful intent (or intent-on-duty) of a lord who is sent out.[7]

- Second, because (as I argue below) "beholding *yi* 意" and "reaching *yi* 義" are two important but different textual attainments, we might speculate that the compound *yiyi* 意義 in the *Guliangzhuan* reflects two such different attributes combined in a way that preserves what each contributes. On the basis of my argument that *yi* 義 is often best interpreted as a normative model, we might take the line to concern the model of a minister's responses to his lord's coming and going. That is, the *yi* 意 of *yiyi* 意義 here might refer to what should be on a minister's mind regarding his lord being sent out: happiness post-peril. So the *yi* 意 and the *yi* 義 of a sent-out lord (*zhijun* 致君) are, respectively, the minister's proper intentions about the situation (happiness on return after perilous going) and also the model that he emulates (again, happiness on return after perilous going).

Hidden Yi 意

In early Chinese texts, *yi* 意 (intentions) presented interpretive problems, in part because they are difficult to access. *Yi* 意 are not abstract entities. Like desires (*yu*

---

7. On this "intent-on-duty" reading, the use of *yiyi* 意義 would be similar to that of *zhiyi* 志義 as "aim for duty" in the "Zhengming" chapter of the *Xunzi*, for which see chapter 2.

欲), they can be manifest or hidden deep within the heartmind. Individuals might choose to conceal their yi 意 for strategic reasons. Rulers, for example, might find it useful to keep their counsel in order to better control their subjects. The *Hanfeizi* says,

> 君無見其所欲, 君見其所欲, 臣自將雕琢; 君無見其意, 君見其意, 臣將自表異。
> Rulers must not reveal their desires. If they reveal their desires, ministers will polish themselves accordingly.
> Rulers must not reveal their yi 意 (intentions). If they reveal their yi 意, ministers will alter their demeanor accordingly.[8]
> *Hanfeizi* 韓非子 主道第五

Quoting the *Laozi*, the *Huainanzi* says as much.

> 故人主之意欲見於外, 則為人臣之所制。故老子曰:「塞其兌, 閉其門, 終身不勤。」
> If the yi 意 (intentions) and desires of rulers are visible on the outside, then they will be controlled by their officials. This is why Laozi says, "Block up the holes, close the doors, and to the end of your life you will not labor."
> *Huainanzi* 淮南子 道應訓

The *Hanfeizi*'s and the *Huainanzi*'s advice to rulers suggests that it was not uncommon, nor unexpected, to keep intentions inaccessible.

In the case of texts, the obscurity of yi 意 can render them unreachable in the absence of guidance. As the *Lunheng* asserts (see chapter 3), in order to ascertain an individual's yi 意, one must directly ask him or her questions. With a text, however, the writer is not present, and so writing and reading necessarily involve complex interactions involving the yi 意 of both writers and readers. The *Lüshi Chunqiu* describes the process by which students learn to probe the yi 意 of writing.

> 凡學, 必務進業, 心則無營, 疾諷誦, 謹司聞, 觀驩愉, 問書意。
> When learning, you must strive to advance your work. Your xin 心 will thus lack perplexity. Hasten to recite and chant, carefully manage your hearing. Observe [your teacher's] gladness and joy, ask about the writing's yi 意.
> *Lüshi Chunqiu* 呂氏春秋 孟夏紀第四 《尊師》

---

8. The metaphor here is interesting because the heart is the ruler, the ruler is the heart, and the ruler hides his heart, which effectively means he hides himself.

In other words, students must be trained to fully comprehend the master's instruction. According to the *Shiji*, the potential for misdirection from students' own *yi* 意 motivated Zuo Qiuming to offer his commentary on the *Chunqiu*. The *Shiji* says,

七十子之徒口受其傳指，為有所刺譏襃諱挹損之文辭不可以書見也。
魯君子左丘明懼弟子人人異端，各安其意，失其真，故因孔子史記具論其語，成左氏春秋。

The seventy students orally received the transmitted points. Because they possessed patterned phrases that satirized, ridiculed, praised, concealed, and euphemized, these could not be shown by means of writing. The Lu gentleman, Zuo Qiuming, feared that the disciples, each with different starting points, would be content with their own guesses (*yi* 意) and lose what was genuine. Therefore, on the basis of Kongzi's scribal records, he sorted their conversations and formed *Master Zuo's Chunqiu*.
Shiji 史記 表《十二諸侯年表》

Whether *yi* 意 in this case refers to students' "opinions," "guesses," or "intentions," their intrusion into the interpretive act disrupts it. Correctly identifying the *yi* 意 of writing requires an authority. Making its point with a metaphor, the *Fayan* compares a column of writing to a lane in the market. In the absence of authoritative guidance, the *shuo* 說 (explanations) about the writings under consideration are as variable as the prices that buyers and sellers each intend (*yi* 意). In both cases, there must be a standard or there will be no end to the quarreling.

一閧之市，不勝異意焉；
一卷之書，不勝異說焉。
一閧之市，必立之平；一卷之書，必立之師。

On a single-lane market, one cannot restrain the different *yi* 意. For a text of a single roll, one cannot restrain the different explanations. On a single-lane market, one must establish a standard price; for a text of single roll, one must establish a teacher.
Fayan 法言 學行卷第一

The metaphor suggests that students bring their own *yi* 意 to writings as they strive to interpret them, but the teacher puts an end to all contention.

Despite this battling interpretation metaphor, the same writer, Yang Xiong, extols the interplay of depth, visibility, and hiddenness in the *yi* 意. A profoundly inaccessible *yi* 意 signals the value of his *Taixuan Jing* ("The Canon of Supreme Mystery" 太玄經). As the text's title implies, its very abstruseness is one sign of its quality. Speaking of its own heartmind, with its desires and *yi* 意, the *Taixuan Jing* adds:

不沈則其意不見。是故文以見乎質，辭以睹乎情，觀其施辭，則其心之所欲者見矣。

If [the *Taixuan Jing*] were not deep, then its *yi* 意 (intentions) would not manifest anything. Because of that, pattern is used to see into the simple; and phrasing to look into the *qing* 情. If we observe the phrases it lays out, then surely its heartmind's desires will become apparent.[9]

Taixuan Jing 太玄經 87 〈太玄瑩〉

Access to the deep *yi* 意 entails visual interpretative practices: seeing, looking, and observing (*jian* 見, *du* 睹, and *guan* 觀). Just as plainness (*zhi* 質) is rooted in pattern (*wen* 文), revelation is rooted in submergence (*chen* 沈). The value of the *yi* 意 of a text is predicated on hidden depths.

By the end of the first century, obscurity was a distinguishing feature of the *yi* 意 of texts. *Yi* are tenuous items that, while not entirely internal, at least originate in a person's heartmind, where they are easily hidden and often must be made visible. The *yi* 意 of texts are even more inaccessible, which is why teachers and scholars write commentaries. For some writers in the first century, knowledge of a text's *yi* 意 was prized in proportion to the degree to which it was abstruse and consequently hard to reach.

Hidden *Yi* 意 in the *Lunheng*'s "Chaoji" Chapter

Early Chinese writers valued the *yi* 義 of texts differently from their *yi* 意, as is evident in the "Chaoji" chapter of the *Lunheng*.[10] When the "Chaoji" defends the writings of certain scholars of its day, its primary criterion for assessing quality resembles that of the *Taixuan Jing*: it describes balanced polarities involving internal *yi* 意 and the strokes of the brush by which they are made apparent.

實誠在胸臆，文墨著竹帛，外內表裏，自相副稱。意奮而筆縱，故文見而實露也。

When there is full sincerity in the breast, then writing and ink appears on bamboo and silk. Outer and inner, surface and inside mutually balance. *Yi* 意 is exerted and the brush follows, thus writing appears and its fruits are exposed.[11]

Lunheng 論衡 〈〈超奇篇〉〉

---

9. Michael Nylan translation modified. *Canon of Supreme Mystery*, 436.

10. My interest in the chapter, which seeks to defend the quality of certain writings of its day, is not directly related to its aim.

11. The chapter plays with plant metaphors of writings as flowers, fruits, leaves, and kernels.

A Framework Preceding the *Shuowen*'s Metalinguistic Choices / 145

In this segment of the chapter's extended botanical metaphor, the heartmind's *yi* 意 produce the fruits of writing that are visible (*jian* 見) on the outside. The "Chaoji" credits Kongzi with writing that arises from the heartmind (presumably expressed through his *yi* 意 among other things). It also implies that aspects of the heartmind find their expression in writing and phrases.

> 心思為謀, 集絜為文, 情見於辭, 意驗於言。
> The heartmind's thoughts become plans; these are collected and bound into writing. [Its] *qing* 情 appear in phrases (*ci* 辭), and its *yi* 意 are examined through speech.
> *Lunheng* 論衡 《〈超奇篇〉》

That phrases reflect *qing* (情見於辭) is likewise found in the *Taixuan Jing* 87 (see above, 辭以睹乎情), and the two texts' overall arguments are similar: good texts balance that which comes from the inside (heart, thought, *qing* 情, and *yi* 意) with external manifestations.

The "Chaoji" also introduces another contrast to the external, concerning, in this case, the writing's subject matter. The "Chaoji" favorably contrasts writers who transmit *yi* 意 against those who, squarely focused on the external, merely "select and arrange the past and present, recording and making known actions and events" (抽列古今, 紀著行事).[12] As the chapter's imaginary opponent notes, such writing is "from without" (*wen you wai* 文由外).[13] The "Chaoji" explores the complicated case of two writers whose *yi* 意 come from within (*you yier chu* 由意而出), although their subject matter suggests that they are simply picking from without.

---

12. Transmitting *yi* 意 is not "authorial intention," in part because the *yi* 意 in a text can belong to the sage-rulers whose *yi* 意 is recovered. (See below where Kongzi's writing in the *Chunqiu* is valued not for his own *yi* 意 but for his presentation of the *yi* 意 of ancient rulers.)

Concerning Early China, we cannot even presume the existence of the concept of an "author" without defining the term. Responding to the idea that late Warring States texts presented Kongzi as the author of the *Chunqiu*, Martin Kern employs a limited Latin sense of the term in which "author" is one who augments or increases something. Kern, "Kongzi as Author," 269 n5. Another approach considers the first development of a "fully self-conscious author." Michael Nylan points out, borrowing Hiroshi Taniguchi's criteria for authorship, the concept would include the presence of a preface (or postface), chronologically arranging one's work as a writer, and self-presentation as writing for a living (not merely responding to events). Nylan, *Yang Xiong*, 59–60. See also Wai-yee Li, "Concepts of Authorship," 360–376; Hanmo Zhang, *Authorship and Textmaking*; Klein, *Reading Sima Qian*; and Schwermann and Steineck, *Wonderful Composite Called Author*. See appendix A for Mingdong Gu's interpretation of Wang Bi's (226–249) conception of authorial intention.

13. This writing is also associated with *yi* 意 that are shallow (*qianyi* 淺意).

> 若夫陸賈、董仲舒，論說世事，由意而出，不假取於外，然而淺露易見，觀讀之者，猶曰傳記。
>
> With those like Lu Jia and Dong Zhongshu, who sort and explain the affairs of the world, [their writings] come from their *yi* 意. They are not artificially picked from outside, but their manifest surface is easy to see, so their readers still say they are merely records.[14]
>
> *Lunheng* 論衡 《《超奇篇》》

In this example, the target of the two writers' interest is external—the "affairs of the world" (*shishi* 世事)—and so they may be wrongly accused of doing no more than recording. But the "Chaoji" defends them, emphasizing that although the surface (*qian* 淺) of their texts is exposed and easy to see (because they write about ordinary affairs), the writing is still superior insofar it emerges from their *yi* 意.

An additional version of this inside/outside contrast draws a distinction between writings that have an *yi* 意 and those that refer (*zhi* 指). As noted in chapter 2, the function of names is directed externally, whereas phrases and speech express the heartmind. Perhaps for that reason, the "Chaoji" chapter treats writing that refers (*zhi* 指) as having generally inferior implications by likening it to picking from outside and mere recording. Whereas Kongzi's writing has an element of the heartmind because it reveals rulers' *yi* 意, the writing of other scholars only allows readers to observe what lesser political figures refer or point to (*zhi* 指).

> 孔子作《《春秋》》，以示王意。然則孔子之《《春秋》》，素王之業也；諸子之《《傳書》》，素相之事也。觀《《春秋》》以見王意，讀諸子以睹相指。
>
> Kongzi wrote the *Chunqiu* in order to show the *yi* 意 of the rulers. That being the case, Kongzi's *Chunqiu* is the work of an uncrowned king. The masters' transmissions are matters of untitled ministers. Observe the *Chunqiu* to see the *yi* 意 of rulers. Read those scholars to view ministers' pointing.
>
> *Lunheng* 論衡 《《超奇篇》》

Although the passage does not directly criticize these masters who transmit, the passage clearly presents them as inferior to Kongzi. These masters not only align with lesser figures (ministers rather than rulers), whereas Kongzi is an uncrowned king, but they also only exhibit what is referred to externally, not what lies within.

---

14. The *Lunheng*'s assessment of these literary figures is generally positive, but not entirely consistent throughout the text. It faults Dong Zhongshu for his discussion of rain sacrifices and accuses Lu Jia of indirectness.

Hence, on multiple levels the "Chaoji" chapter establishes a distinction between writing that manifests yi 意 and writing that observes external things.

Still, the "Chaoji" chapter acknowledges, there are problems related to the yi 意 of texts. First, few writers have the talent to spread or develop (yan 衍) written yi 意.

> 衍傳書之意，出膏腴之辭，非俶儻之才，不能任也。
> Amplifying the yi 意 of transmitted writings and expressing phrases of glistening richness are things that one cannot undertake without unusual talent.
> *Lunheng* 論衡 《超奇篇》

Moreover, one of the chapter's oppositional interlocutors observes that not all yi 意 are worth the effort.

> 且淺意於華葉之言，無根核之深。
> Furthermore, [when there is] shallow yi 意 amid flowers of speech, there is no depth of roots or kernels.
> *Lunheng* 論衡 《超奇篇》

Not only might yi 意 be shallow, as other sections of the *Lunheng* acknowledge, even sages may fail to produce much with their yi 意. The fact that something is written by worthies, even those who employ their yi 意, does not guarantee positive results.

> 夫賢聖下筆造文，用意詳審，尚未可謂盡得實，況倉卒吐言，安能皆是？不能皆是，時人不知難；或是，而意沉難見，時人不知問。
> When worthies and sages took up the brush to write, using yi 意 and careful consideration, they still cannot be said to exhaustively bear fruits. All the more when they hurriedly emitted their speech—how can it all be right? It cannot all be right, but people of this era do not know about that difficulty. Or, it is right, but their yi 意 are profound and difficult to see, so people of this era do not know to ask about them.
> *Lunheng* 論衡 《問孔篇》

Sages who are in a hurry may express themselves poorly, but others might still record them, which dissuades posterity from challenging their writings. Or the sages' yi 意 may be buried deeply, and ordinary readers are not even aware that they should raise questions to gain a greater understanding of them. In sum, a number of problems beset the yi 意 of writing: they are difficult to transmit; they can be shallow; they might be hastily recorded; they might never be recorded; or they might be too deep for people to comprehend.

Accessible Yi 義 in the Lunheng

None of these difficulties affect the *yi* 義 of texts. Although the "Chaoji" is dismissive of "writing from the outside"—whether in the form of picking, recording, or referring—it speaks positively of the *yi* 義 of texts, despite *yi* 義's externality. To illustrate, let's consider a challenge that the "Xieduan" (謝短) chapter poses to imposters who pretend to understand important matters:

> 文吏自謂知官事，曉簿書。問之曰：「曉知其事，當能究達其義，通見其意否？」文吏必將罔然。
> Clerical workers claim to know official matters and understand books and registers. But if one were to ask them, "To understand these matters, must one not be able to masterfully reach (*da* 達) their *yi* 義 and unobstructedly behold (*tongjian* 通見) their *yi* 意?" the officials are certain to be befuddled.
> *Lunheng* 論衡 《謝短篇》

Beholding *yi* 意 and reaching *yi* 義 are the two interpretive tasks to be accomplished. For *yi* 意 to be observed, as we have seen, something deep within the heartmind must be brought to the surface. But what does it mean to "reach" (*da* 達) *yi* 義?

When one seeks to discern *yi* 意, one reaches inward, into the deep. Reaching across is different matter, and the terminology for measuring *yi* 義 suggests the latter. In early Chinese texts in general and in the *Lunheng* in particular, *yi* 義 is characterized in terms of its scope and size, not its depth. Its default for *yi* 義 is that it is large. A few passages in early Chinese texts mention alternative descriptors. For instance, a rare juxtaposition involves "public *yi*" (*gongyi* 公義) and "personal *yi*" (*siyi* 私義), the latter of which is damaging to the public good.[15] Slightly more common references to "small *yi* 義" appear in contrast to "great *yi* 義."[16]

In one case, the *Lunheng* references "small *yi* 義" in a context that is illuminating insofar as it indicates the improbability of a deep, hidden *yi* 義. The context

---

15. For examples of personal *yi* 義 among ministers, see *Hanfeizi* 〈飾邪〉 19 and *Zhanguo ce* 244 〈趙燕後胡服〉. (The *Zhanguo ce* was compiled in the first century BCE from materials by unknown Warring States authors. See Tsien, "Chan kuo ts'e 戰國策," 5.) For an example of personal *yi* 義 among the masses, see *Shangjunshu* 18 〈畫策〉.

16. There is a repeated comment that "Small/trivial *yi* damages the dao" This expression "小義破道" occurs in the *Dadai Liji* 11.1 〈小辨〉, the *Wenzi* 〈上仁〉, and the *Huainanzi* 20 〈泰族訓〉. There is a slightly different version of this in the Mawandui "Wuxing."

concerns the *Lunheng*'s objections to prohibiting burials on dates unpropitious for doing so. Unlucky dates do not exist, the passage asserts, because if they did, they would have been specified in the *Chunqiu*. It says,

> 周文之世, 法度備具, 孔子意密, 《春秋》義纖, 如廢吉得凶, 妄舉觸禍, 宜有微文小義, 貶譏之辭。今不見其義, 無葬歷法也。
>
> During the time of King Wen of Zhou, the rules and standards were complete. Kongzi closely [applied his] intentions (*yi* 意), hence the *yi* 義 (models) of the *Chunqiu* are minute. If abandoning luck would bring about misfortune, and acting rashly would bring contact with disaster, then it would have been fitting for [the *Chunqiu*] to have [at least] some tiny, fine, small *yi* 義 (model) [for it] and a word of disparagement and ridicule [on the subject]. Now, we do not see such an *yi* 義. [Thus] there were no standard burial times.
>
> *Lunheng* 論衡 《譏日篇》

The passage affirms that despite its default bulk, *yi* 義 can be quite tiny. Nonetheless, it implies that they are not the kind of thing that might be submerged in a text. Presumably, if *yi* 義 were something that could be hidden in the depths of a text, the argument would not work, because the reader would simply have to dig deeper in the *Chunqiu* to see the *yi* 義 about burial dates. Thus, *yi* 義 comes in quantities that are small and great and in ranges that are private and public, but it is not measured in terms of depth. As the *Liji* puts it,

> 仁有數,
> 義有長短小大。
>
> *Ren* 仁 has enumeration (*shu* 數).[17]
> *Yi* 義 has long, short, small, and big.
> *Liji* 禮記 《表記》 33.8

But small *yi* 義 is appropriate for youth. The *Shangshu Dazhuan* describes a developmental progression in schooling from little to big *yi* 義.

> 十五始入小學, 見小節, 踐小義; 十八入大學, 見大節, 踐大義。
>
> At age fifteen they entered small training and observed small disciplines and enacted small *yi* 義. At age twenty, they entered great (big) training and observed more great discipline and enacted great *yi* 義.
>
> *Shangshu Dazhuan* 尚書大傳 卷六 《略說上》

According to Griet Vankeerberghen, the *Shangzhu Dazhuan* is an "early imperial text." Vankeerberghen, "Rulership and Kinship," 5.

17. The *shu* 數 might also function as "several."

Whatever it means to associate *ren* with *shu*, *yi* 義 is gauged by size. In light of this understanding, "reaching *yi* 義" is likely to involve negotiating scale.

Its capacity for extension might help explain why the "Chaoji" pairs *yi* 義 with other terms that suggest externality without insinuating a troublesome lack of depth. The "Chaoji" uses *wenyi* (文義), for example, to indicate that good writing is patterned and stylized, even though the text negatively likens ornamentation (*wen* 文) to feathers. With the compounds *yizhi* (義指) and *yizhi* (義旨), the "Chaoji" implies that *yi* 義 is involved in pointing to something external.[18] And in tying *yi* 義 to *qian* 淺 (surface), the text deploys the compound as a compliment about Ban Biao's writing:

記事詳悉, 義淺理備。
[Ban Biao's writing] records events thoroughly and carefully, [its] *yi* 義 is light (*qian* 淺) and its pattern complete.
Lunheng 論衡 《《超奇篇》》

Whereas the chapter presents shallow intent (*qianyi* 淺意) as negative, *yi* 義 that is *qian* 淺 creates the impression of a flattering lightness. Thus, in the "Chaoji," although writings that exhibit *yi* 義 do not seem as worthy as those that reveal *yi* 意, depth is not the standard for evaluation of *yi* 義.

Returning to the two interpretive tasks set forth in the "Xieduan" (謝短)—beholding *yi* 意 and reaching *yi* 義—and the two textual faults explained in the "Chaoji"—lacking depth and lacking magnitude—we can surmise that reaching *yi* 義 is equivalent to achieving a comprehensive interpretation. When describing categories within texts, the *Lunheng* uses the "body" of the text to mean a large portion.

文字有意以立句, 句有數以連章, 章有體以成篇, 篇則章句之大者也。
Written graphs possess *yi* 意 to establish a line.[19] Lines possess quantity

---

18. There is not much evidence of these two compounds *yizhi* (義指) and *yizhi* (義旨) outside of the *Lunheng*, but *wenyi* 文義 is somewhat more common in Han texts. This *wenyi* example from the *Hanshu*, which occurs in Huan Tan's defense of Yang Xiong's writings, shows *yi* 義, preceded by *wen* 文, described in terms of depth. This is odd because neither element of *wenyi* 文義 is typically measured by surface/depth.

今揚子之書文義至深, 而論不詭於聖人。
Now in Yangzi's writings, the *wen* and *yi* 文義 are exceedingly deep, and [or but?] his treatises would not be strange to a sage.
Han Shu 漢書 傳 《《揚雄傳第五十七下》》

19. The stasis potentially suggested by "possess" (my translation of *you* 有) is difficult to reconcile with the transformation implied in the passage's verbs, especially "become" (*cheng* 成). In light of

to link into a section. Sections possess bodies (*ti* 體) to form a chapter.
A chapter is therefore the largest form of lines and sections.
Lunheng 論衡 《正說篇》

A text possesses a body when it is large enough.[20] Hence, in addition to advocating for textual commentaries that reveal the heartmind of a writer, the *Lunheng* also promotes those that account for a text's large frame.

The body's potential for manifesting itself provides a context for understanding a simile in the *Lunheng*'s preface, which bears the title "Self-Report Chapter" (*ziji pian* 自紀篇). As part of justifying the text's considerable length and plain style, the somewhat defensive preface (which speaks, alternately, in the first and third person) notes:[21]

---

the overall pattern, then, the first line asserts that an *yi* 意 is present only when enough graphs have accumulated to form a line (*ju* 句). ("Line" is a better translation than "sentence," because it sidesteps the notion of a grammatical entity.)

20. In the *Fayan*, the "body of a text" metaphor appears in a claim that speech does not reach (*da* 達, elsewhere "exhaust" 盡) intent and writing does not reach speech, where the implication is that speech is audible and writing is visible.

> 言不能達其心, 書不能達其言, 難矣哉! 惟聖人得言之解, 得書之體。
> Speech is unable to reach the heartmind. Texts are unable to reach speech. This is a problem! Only the sages achieve the unraveling (*jie* 解) of speech and achieve the embodiment (*ti* 體) of texts.
> *Fayan* 法言 問神卷第五

Shortly after, the passage discusses face-to-face speech and recording events by means of writing, followed by a description of speech as the heartmind's sounds and writing as its images. Thus the *jie* 解 of speech is audible and, the *ti* 體 of writing is visible.

21. On its shallow and easy style, it says:

> 何以為辯? 喻深以淺。何以為智? 喻難以易。
> How does one debate? By clarifying the deep with the shallow.
> How does one know? By clarifying the difficult with the easy.

On its voluminous length, it says:

> 韓非之書, 一條無異, 篇以十第, 文以萬數。
> 夫形大, 衣不得褊; 事眾, 文不得褊。. . . 書雖文重, 所論百種。
> Hanfeizi's writings are no different than a branch of a tree.
> His chapters are measured by tens, and the writings (graphs?) by tens of thousands. For a big body, the clothes cannot be narrow. So for a collection of subjects, the writing cannot be narrow. . . . Although this text is heavy on the writing, what it considers is in the hundreds.
> *Lunheng* 論衡 《自紀篇》

故口言以明志,言恐滅遺,故著之文字。
文字與言同趨,何為猶當隱閉指意?

Thus the mouth speaks to clarify aims, and [it] speaks from fear of them being neglected and lost. Hence we set forth [our aims] in writing.
Writing and speaking have a similar tendency, why ought [this text] conceal and hide its referent (*zhi* 指) and its *yi* 意?

After several more oral and visual parallels regarding writing and speaking, the preface goes on to compare the *yi* 義 of writing to an eye's pupil. Writers do not strive to be difficult any more than speakers try to be opaque, the *Lunheng* insists, before it introduces the perhaps facetious pupil analogy, hearkening to the *Mengzi*'s "Lilou Shang" (離婁上) chapter. The analogy subtly directs readers to look at this text's own *yi* 義.

夫筆著者,欲其易曉而難為,不貴難知而易造,
口論務解分而可聽,不務深迂而難睹。
孟子相賢,以眸子明瞭者;察文,以義可曉。

Writers want their texts to be easy to understand but challenging to make,
They do not value being difficult to understand and easy to compose.
Speakers strive to untangle parts and be comprehensible (*ting* 聽, listen-able),
They do not endeavor to be deep, abstruse, or difficult to understand (*du* 睹, see-able).
To physiognomize worthies, Mengzi used the brightness and clarity of their [eyes'] pupils.
To discern (*cha* 察) written texts, one can understand by means of their *yi* 義.

Writings have a body, the passage reminds us. And one method for interpreting a text's body corresponds to judging someone's character by observing their eyes. Because the comparison follows a series of comments on writing and speaking, and because the *Lunheng*'s preface itself concerns writing, its reference to inspecting pupils is significant. The preface reminds us that, although not large, the pupils are a key bodily site of human expression.[22] Keeping in mind that a text has both an *yi* 意

---

22. Interestingly, the preface does not mention *how* pupils manifest things about people, but we should be wary of the view that pupils are holes that penetrate, rather than light waves that resonate. It is worth noting (without implying necessary coherence to the *Lunheng* as a whole) that the "Ben Xin" (本性) chapter articulates what is to be ascertained from the pupils, but it misrepresents the *Mengzi*'s point and then proceeds to explain why it disagrees. The misinterpretation is that the *Mengzi* "Lilou Shang" passage concerns what cannot remain hidden in people (the moral state of the central chest, *xiongzhong* 胸中) when both *listening* to them talk and *looking*

and an yi 義, the preface directs readers to look at (cha 察) a text's yi 義.²³ Thus, instead of justifying itself by revealing its submerged yi 意, the preface tells readers to look at the body of its own text. Readers may see by means of a text's yi 義, just as physiognomists see by means of the pupils. If people can discern a person's value by observing the brightness of tiny pupils, the preface seems to say, then readers can fix their eyes on the yi 義 of this very long text in order to recognize its worth.

Other early Chinese texts note the textual virtue of possessing an yi 義 that is large in scope. Generally, a large or great yi (dayi 大義) is a political term (that is, when not functioning as an interpretive term), and in such cases it is used to mean something like "the great duty." In an example focused on writing, the Shiji praises the style of the "Li Sao," citing both its large referential range and the distance at which it can make yi 義 visible, which seems to suggest that it both possesses and manifests an impressively broad yi 義.

> 其稱文小而其指極大, 舉類邇而見義遠。
> Its style of writing is concise but its scope of reference (zhi 指) is huge.
> It adduces categories from the near, but it manifests yi 義 far.
> Shiji 史記 傳《屈原賈生列傳第二十四》

As later texts become more specific about methods of interpretation, they often place a text's yi 義 (or great yi 義) in opposition to a trend toward something akin to line-by-line analysis.²⁴ In other words, the great yi 義 is the big picture or model. If we consider the "Xieduan" chapter's reference to reaching yi 義 (daqiyi 達其義) within the context of an esteem for magnitude, those who do so

---

at the pupils of their eyes. But the Lunheng misinterprets the passage as a claim that the eye's pupils are bright or dull in spontaneous reflection of the current state of the xin 心 (heartmind), to which the Lunheng counters that the pupils' brightness level is not about the moment, but is instead already present at birth.

23. Cha 察 is mainly used in a visual sense. See appendix C.

24. Various comprehensive terms occur in contrast to the practice of zhangju (章句), including benzhi 本旨, which in later texts may describe getting a text's basic point. For instance, in the Zhonglang Ji of Cai Yong 蔡邕 (132/33–192), zhangju seems to involve using yi 意, probably one's own:

> 及前儒特為章句者, 皆用意傳, 非其本旨。
> Now former scholars were those in favor of zhangju, and they all used yi 意 as guidance, but this was not the [text's] main point (zhi 旨).
> Cai Zhonglang Ji 蔡中郎集 蔡中郎集卷十《月令問答》

In early translations of Buddhist texts, benzhi 本旨 is sometimes used in a different way: a plain translation in contrast to adorned language.

evidently reach an understanding of the coherence of a text's overall composition or architecture.²⁵

The ways in which yi 義 differs from yi 意 within the confines of textual interpretation can be summarized as follows. Yi 義 is not associated with depth. Although external, the outward aspect of yi 義 is not negative. In contrast to yi 意, yi 義 does not engage the heartmind or its qing 情, and it does not occur in compounds with the heartmind or derive from it. Instead, yi 義 appears in compounds with terms that point externally. All this confirms that yi 義 is characteristically external to the heartmind. Whereas the yi 意 of writings are at their best when they are deeply ensconced in the heartmind and therefore difficult to access, their yi 義 are always public and most significant when large. Thus, yi 義, as a textual feature, is not only different from yi 意 but also more accessible. Questions about the accessibility and visibility of yi 意 plague the issue of textual interpretation, but they do not affect yi 義. In the spirit of the "Chaoji" chapter's plant metaphor, to reach the yi 義 of a text, one must take in the entire forest and avoid fixating on any particular tree. By contrast, to reach the yi 意 of a text, one must dig up the roots and kernels of the heartmind.

---

25. When later texts contrast the "great yi" (dayi 大義) to "section and line" (zhangju 章句) commentary, the former achieves a grander perspective than the latter.

Sometimes zhangju seems compatible with getting the yili 義理 (a compound slightly different from yi 義). (See, for example, Hanshu 漢書 傳 《《楚元王傳第六》》). The Dongguan Hanji, however, commends "lifting up" the great yi 義 out of a text in this way:

不為章句，舉大義而已。
... not practicing zhangju and [instead] just pulling up the great yi.
Dongguan Hanji 東觀漢記 東觀漢記卷十六列傳十一 《《班固》》

Xu Gan's (171–218) Zhonglun uses a similar characterization. It criticizes zhangju readings on two counts. In terms of yi 義, they fail to comprehend the scope of the whole frame, and consequently, in terms of something more like yi 意, they fail to grasp the heartminds of former rulers.

。。。鄙儒之博學也，務於物名，詳於器械，矜於詁訓，摘其章句，而不能統其大義之所極以獲先王之心。
... the extensive studies of rustic scholars struggle over names of the things, provide fine detail about tools and instruments, esteem commentary and explanation, and opt for zhangju analysis. However, they are unable to marshall the extreme outlines of the great yi 義 to capture the heartminds of former rulers.
Zhonglun 中論 《《治學第一》》

The use and meaning of zhangju varies. The Lunheng is not always critical of it, and its preface mentions zhangju as part of the book's method. Zhangju is at odds with yi 義 in the Kongcongzi (孔叢子 卷七 《《連叢子下第二十三》》). It is also at odds with the dati 大體 (large body) in the Hou Hanshu (全上古三代秦漢三國六朝文 全後漢文卷三十一 楊終 《《上言宜令諸儒論考五經同異》》).

Buddhist Influence?

Although China had some contact with Indic languages during the first century of the Common Era, when the *Shuowen* was composed, Buddhist linguistic theory had not yet made a significant impact.[26] When the people of the Yellow River Valley region first encountered the alternate writing system manifest in Buddhist scriptures, they must have been startled to discover that they were not themselves the sole bearers of writing (*wen* 文), which is to say, culture. Buddhist scriptures spread slowly, though, and the specific implications of alphabetic writing were not immediately clear.[27] Thus, the *idea* of another writing system (Bhrami or Kharosthi) probably had more influence on the *Shuowen* than did any actual Buddhist texts or efforts to translate them.

What is known about the early translations of Buddhist texts does not inspire confidence that the source texts' metalinguistic nuances would have been easy to convey. The first translations were offered by non-native Buddhist monks who probably had little command of literary Chinese. Sometimes these monks recited texts from memory, but even when a physical text was present, they may have recited a text written in a local vernacular script, to which they would supply oral glosses and comments.[28] Oral explanations might have been necessary if the Chinese speakers whose job it was to translate were confused by the foreign monk's Central Asian pronunciation and their own lack of knowledge of Buddhist texts. In due course, a translation was written in literary Chinese. Commenting on the earliest Chinese translation of the *Saddharmapundarikasutra*, completed by Dharmaraksa in 286 CE, Daniel Boucher notes that some parts of the text appear to be attempts at word-for-word translations, while other renderings of the Sankrit "have the feel of paraphrases." Hence, he suggests, Dharmaraksa worked "in a piecemeal fashion,

---

26. As Jan Nattier puts it, "While a Buddhist presence had definitely been established in China at this time [during the first century of the Common Era], the form that it seems to have taken at this point was centered on ritual practices . . . and artistic objects . . . and not on scriptural texts. It would be nearly a century later before we encounter the first reliable accounts of the translation of Buddhist scriptures into Chinese." Nattier, *Guide to Early Chinese Buddhist Translations*, 37.

27. It appears that it was not until the fifth century (with Sengyou 僧祐, 445–518) that translators of Buddhist texts seriously attempted to grasp the concept of a "word" in inflected alphabetic languages. Link, "Earliest Chinese Account," 282.

28. Jan Nattier notes that the texts were probably not written in Sanskrit, because "classical Sanskrit had not yet become the dominant vehicle for Buddhist literary expression in India." Nattier, *Guide to Early Chinese Buddhist Translations*, 21. Daniel Boucher challenges the traditional assumption that the language of the original manuscripts was Gāndhārī, although he does not doubt that they may have been written in a *kharosthi* script and pronounced with Prakrit influence. Boucher, "Gāndhārī," 471–506.

glossing words and phrases while providing some additional exegesis of the overall import." Dharmaraksa's Chinese assistant would have "construct[ed] a coherent literary Chinese reading from such parts."²⁹ No doubt the aural/oral complications of this multilayered translation process hindered achieving philosophical clarity about the technical implications of metalinguistic terminology.

Nonetheless, even if that philosophical clarity had been achieved, the Buddhist sources seem unlikely to have pointed the translators in the direction of understanding word-meanings as abstract entities. *Artha*, the Sanskrit term Buddhist sources used for word-meanings, could be used to mean either an external object or a mental conception. According to Jonardon Ganeri, the Buddhist philosophers of early India generally used *artha* to speak of how symbols substitute for what they symbolize. Hence, the *artha* to which a linguistic symbol points would be an actual thing. Ganeri explains that the Indian theories of meaning at the time focused on examples of a specific type of noun (which they recognized as a grammatical category).³⁰ Thus, the philosophical tradition presumed a realist theory wherein *artha* means the external entities for which words or expressions are surrogates. Ganeri writes,

> The realist theory of meaning states that the meaning of an expression is the external object for which it stands. . . . In the Indian philosophical tradition, much speculation about the notion of meaning centered on, or better assumed, such a theory. This is particularly true of the early grammarians, Mīmāmsakas, Buddhists, and the Naiyāyikas, who belonged to the classical period of Indian philosophy, a period which ended in AD 900 or 1000.³¹

---

29. Boucher, "Gāndhārī," 500.

30. That is, Ganeri says they focused on what they called "general nominal terms," like cow. Ganeri, *Artha*, 9.

31. Ganeri, 9. Regarding early Indian grammarians, Ganeri's claim is not without controversy.

Ganeri cites Eivind Kahrs who agrees with P. Thieme's argument that "purpose" could serve "as a kind of logical semantic continuity" for translating *artha*. Kahrs argues that although *artha* can be used to mean something more abstract than simply referring to things meant, in indigenous discussions of grammar exemplified by the work of Patanjali (second century BCE), "questions of meaning are primarily questions of reference." Kahrs, *Indian Semantic Analysis*, 41, 47.

By contrast, Peter Scharf cites Subramania Iyer as saying that, for grammarians, *artha* means the thought caused by the word, not external reality. Scharf, "Early Indian Grammarians," 67.

Wang Youxuan's study of fourth to seventh century Chinese translations of Buddhist texts makes a qualified claim about the linguistic implications of uses of *nama* (*ming* 名) and *artha* (*yi* 義) in Indian Buddhist philosophy. Wang contends that ambiguity resulting from different uses of the term *artha* led to confusion between two fourth-century Indian authors. It is not always clear when *nama* is being used as name or word, and it is also not clear how *artha* is being used.

In sum, not only was *artha* a term that could be used to mean an external object, it was probably used in that way in the Buddhist sources.

The foundations for the *Shouwen*'s assumptions about meaning differed from those of the Buddhist texts, not least because the *Shuowen* did not presuppose the grammatical notion of nouns.[32] But, more important, given the realist theory of meaning underlying the Buddhist use of *artha*, even if Buddhist translations had influenced the *Shuowen*, the effect would not likely have been to encourage an understanding of word-meanings as mental concepts or abstract entities.

Yi 義 and Yi 意 in the *Shuowen*'s Myth about the Origin of Writing

Before I conclude, I would like to return to the *Shuowen*'s myth of the origin of writing, which occurs in its postface. The story, which also concerns hexagrams, concentrates on what heaven and earth reveal. It does not mention the *yi* 意 of Pao Xi, who first identified the lines of the hexagrams, or of Shen Nong, who began knotting cords, or even of Cang Jie, who was the founder of writing.[33]

Instead, we learn about the visual cues that inspired Cang Jie and the way in which the writing he created is linked to hexagrams. The postface's version of the well-known story is as follows:

> 黃帝史官倉頡，見鳥獸蹄迒之跡，知分理之可相別異也，初造書契。
> 百工以乂，萬品以察，蓋取諸夬。
>
> Cang Jie, the Yellow Emperor's scribal official, looked at the traces of the hooves and feet of birds and animals, and he knew that their divi-

---

Wang writes, "*Artha* can be the concept of a word/name since it is defined (by Sanghabhadra) as something that originates in an inner voice, and it can also mean the referent of a word/ name since it can be, according to Vashubhandu II, an individual being that is named." In sum, Sanghabhadra wants to sever the relation of word to referent and uses *artha* as originating in an inner voice in the process. Vasubhandu II seeks to separate the content of an articulation from the "means" of articulating it, and uses *artha* as a referent in the process. Thus, Wang concludes, they do not really disagree about the *relation* of a word to its meaning; they just use *artha* differently. Wang Youxuan, *Buddhism and Deconstruction*, 54.

For a broad approach to a related subject—Chinese Buddhist theories of language—see Douglas Berger's argument that the theories of language from the schools of Mahayana Buddhism that flourished in China were characterized by conventionalism or constructivism. Berger, "Did Buddhism Ever Go East?," 38–55.

32. Grammar was not an object of study in China until the late nineteenth century. The first use of the grammatical terms "empty" and "full" dates to around the eleventh century. Peyraube, "Recent Issues," 164.

33. Although *yi* 意 is prominent in statements about the limits of speech and writing in the "Xici," it does not occur in the narrative on the origin of writing per se. See discussion in chapter 7.

sions and patterns could separate different things. So he began to create writing and bindings (contracts?).

Then by this means, hundreds of workers were governed; and by this means, the ten-thousand items were examined, perhaps by picking from the hexagram, "Decide."

Shuowen "Postface" 說文解字敘

Not surprising for an account of the origin of writing, the myth's terminology emphasizes visibility: looking at (*jian* 見) traces and patterns and examining (*cha* 察) things with hexagrams. It relies on the ever-present obviousness of the cosmos's observable features, whose patterns the sages (whose own *yi* 意 is never mentioned) noted and copied when creating graphs. To put it differently, the visual inspiration for writing takes precedence over the intentions or aims (*yi* 意 or *zhi* 志) of the sages who invented it.

Although Xu Shen used an "archaizing" script for the *Shuowen*'s head characters (the terms it glosses), his choice need not have been motivated by a desire to recover the ancient inventors' intended meanings.[34] The postface asserts that when Kongzi and Zuo Qiuming wrote in the "old script" (*guwen* 古文), they did so precisely because its *yi* 意 could be elucidated.[35]

及宣王太史籀, 著大篆十五篇, 古文或異。
至孔子書六經, 左丘明述春秋傳, 皆以古文, 厥意可得而說也。

In the time of King Xuan, Grand Historian Zhou wrote the "Da Zhuan" in fifteen chapters. [With regard to] the old script, some were different. Coming down to the time when Kongzi wrote the six classics and Zuo Qiuming narrated the transmission of the *Chunqiu*, all this was in old script, because its *yi* 意 could be obtained and explained.

Shuowen "Postface" 說文解字敘

Some might argue on these grounds that Xu Shen chose an archaizing script in order to preserve the *yi* 意 for each graph from the heartminds of its inventors.[36]

---

34. I call these scripts "archaizing" and "current," because modern scholars refer to early Chinese scripts with a variety of different names that do not correspond to Xu Shen's terms (*zhuan* 篆文 "seal forms"; *gu* 古 "old"; and *Zhou* 籀).

Bottéro and Harbsmeier argue that Xu Shen used an archaizing script for the head characters because it clarified the structure of the graphs, not because he was concerned with how graphs were employed at any period. His goal, in their view, was an abstract analysis of the constituent elements of the graph. Bottéro and Harbsmeier, "*Shuowen Jiezi* Dictionary," 255–256.

35. For the contrary argument, see O'Neill, "Xu Shen's Scholarly Agenda," 413–440.

36. This is the argument in O'Neill, "Xu Shen's Scholarly Agenda," 425–427.

The passage merely indicates, however, that the old script yields yi 意. It does not specify whose yi 意 would be obtained. Humans are not the only sources of yi 意. We have seen that heaven has yi 意 and writings have yi 意. As the *Lunheng* points out, heaven has no face or head. Nevertheless, for heaven, the discourse of bodies persists, and a similar discourse also informs the terminology for writing and texts.[37] Because the *Shuowen* explores technical innovations for something like word-meaning, its uses of yi 意 as the gloss of the head character might be similarly metaphorical. Thus, it is reasonable to doubt that Xu Shen was trying to excavate each graphic yi 意 from the heartminds of sages, the very people whose yi 意 never occur in the *Shuowen*'s narrative of writing's origin.

Conceiving of yi 意 as plainly manifest in writing or any other body would be counterintuitive because significant yi 意 are generally understood to be difficult to access. Hence, in a text whose goal is to illustrate and explain, designating yi 意 as the standard semantic term for graphs almost certainly would have seemed counterproductive. Perhaps for this reason, the *Shuowen* resorted to yi 義 as a metalinguistic term in a small number of entries (an idea I explore further in chapter 10), a practice that may have pushed along the eventual emergence of yi 義 as word-meaning.

Conclusion

In the myth of writing's origin in the postface of the *Shuowen*, the role for yi 意 is notably small. There are no hints of the idea of word-meaning as a mental concept transmitted through script from one human mind to another. Writing's visible features reflect patterns of the cosmos. Kongzi and Zuo Qiuming's method used the old script because it allowed them to obtain yi 意 and explain it. If that yi 意 was an abstract mental concept in the minds of its inventors, its conveyance would not depend on the components of a particular script.

The functions of yi 義 and yi 意 with regard to texts may have encouraged Xu Shen to adopt these terms. Whereas yi 意 was associated with depth in the heartmind, yi 義 was associated with accessibility on the outside (in the contexts of both ethics and texts). In terms of texts as bodies, an yi 意 can be hidden, an yi 義 cannot.

---

37. By "writing," I do not mean the term "*ming* 名," which is not used to mean "graph." See Geaney, "Grounding 'Language' in the Senses," 251–293. See also chapter 2 of *Language as Bodily Practice*, where I discuss the *Xunzi*'s "Zhengming" chapter, which recounts some of the history of *ming* 名 without implying *ming* was invented by the original coiners of writing.

CHAPTER NINE

Yi 義 Justifying with Models

Particularly puzzling uses of *yi* 義 in early Chinese texts often occur in circumstances in which justification or blame is at issue. When we do not understand *yi* 義's function, its presence in such sentences can seem extraneous, tempting us to ignore or replace it with a plausible term. Of the many English translation equivalents that have been taken to apply to such puzzling uses of *yi* 義, it is important to notice "reason," a term that might seem to unify the translations, perhaps because of its own complicated, wide range of uses. If we apply my concept of "model" to passages in which *yi* 義 occurs in answer to the question "Why?" however, we are able to appreciate how *yi* 義 justifies what to do and why things are done without actually being the "reason" or "objective" for those actions or conditions. In other words, *yi* 義 is a model cited for a reason, but it is not functioning to mean "reason."

My exploration of uses of *yi* 義 in this chapter considers examples concerning sayings, texts, and rites in the *Lunheng*, the *Hanshu*, *Yijing* literature, the *Guliangzhuan*, and the *Baihu tong*. The last three are particularly illuminating given their formulaic questions and answers.

Yin, Yang, and *Yi* 義 in the *Baihu tong*

In a certain type of literature, *yi* 義 is invoked in relation to yin-yang. Consider these examples from the first century *Baihu tong*.

火陽、君之象也, 水陰、臣之義也。
Fire is yang, which is the *xiang* 象 of the ruler.
Water is yin, which is the *yi* 義 of the minister.
Baihu tong 白虎通 五行

庶人稱匹夫者, 匹、偶也。

與其妻為偶, 陰陽相成之義也。
Common people are called *pi fu* 匹夫. "*Pi*" is "mate."
With their wives, they are mates.
That is the *yi* 義 of yin-yang mutually completing.
Baihu tong 白虎通 爵

以男生內嚮, 有留家之義;
女生外嚮, 有從夫之義。
此陽不絕, 陰有絕之效也。
A son who is born turns toward the inside, having the *yi* 義 of remaining in the family.
A daughter who is born turns toward the outside, having the *yi* 義 of following the husband.
This is the imitation of yang being unbroken and yin being broken.
Baihu tong 白虎通 封公侯

天道所以左旋, 地道右周何?
以為天地動而不別, 行而不離, 所以左旋。
右周者、猶君臣陰陽, 相對之義。
Why does heaven's dao revolve to the left, while earth's dao circles to the right?
[Answer] Because heaven and earth move but do not divide, proceed ("walk," *xing* 行) but do not separate.
The rightward circling, like lord-subject and yin-yang, has a counterbalancing *yi* 義.
Baihu tong 白虎通 天地

Here we see recurrent uses of *yi* 義 within the patterns involving "yin" and "yang" in a single text. Were we to employ multiple registers to translate *yi* 義 in these instances, the translations would threaten to overshadow the pattern itself.[1] If we were to limit the number of possible translation equivalents, though, we might comfortably choose "duty," the most common translation of *yi* 義, for a variety of cases. In others, however, an ethically neutral, causative term seems more appropriate, with the word "reason" coming readily to mind.[2] Since "reason" can be just

---

1. In his 1949–1952 translation of the *Baihu tong*, Tjan Tjoe Som renders *yi* 義 differently in each case or simply leaves it out.

2. The first *Baihu tong* passage here indicates that *yi* 義 is parallel to *xiang* 象, suggesting yin-yang implications that resonate with later astronomical discourse. Describing a debate about *xiang* 象 and *yi* 儀 (closely related to *yi* 義), Daniel Patrick Morgan cites the *Suishu* 隋書 (seventh century) in which the "two *yi* 儀" are yin and yang, and the distinction between the *xiang* and *yi* is that the *xiang* lacks a sighting tube. Morgan translates *yi* 儀 as "sight" (referring to "graduated sight/range finder pegs of early missile weapons") and *xiang* as "effigy." Morgan, *Astral Sciences*, 65.

another way of saying "because," its flexibility is appealing as a way to tie up the loose threads dangling from the yin-yang polarity. For example, the lines might be translated as "The rightward circling, like lord-subject and yin-yang, has a mutually opposing *rationale*." And "That is the *reason for* yin-yang mutually completing." But if we pause to consider carefully, we might recognize that "reason" is not doing much. Other literary forms, especially proverbs, might also appear to call for translating yi 義 as "reason." Those sayings, to which yi 義 is frequently appended, take the form of justifications, which seem to necessitate invoking a "reason."[3] In what follows, and pursuing a line I have established in previous chapters, I will argue that if yi 義 does in fact provide a reason, it might well be considered a concrete model that justifies.

To return to an example discussed in chapter 6, when confronted with the first chapter of the *Xunzi*'s famous announcement that education's yi 義 begins with the scholar and ends with the sage, a stymied interpreter might reasonably omit the yi 義 as evidently superfluous or settle for a translation like "reason," "purpose," or "objective."[4]

Joseph Needham translates yi as "(armillary) sphere" and xiang as "(celestial) globe." Needham, *Science and Civilisation*, 3:384. For more on connections to xiang 象, see appendix A, note 26.

Yin-yang modeling might seem like "reason" in another case in the *Kongcongzi*. Explaining why a girl must be close to twenty before marrying, Kongzi says:

是陽動而陰應，男唱而女隨之義也。
This is the yi 義 of yang moving and yin responding, the male calling and the female following.
Kongcongzi 孔叢子 卷一《嘉言第一》.

This use of yi 義 is no mere abstract "reason," however, because it depicts a two-part model of response: visible movement as well as audible harmonizing. (According to Martin Kern, the *Kongcongzi* was likely to have been composed in the Eastern Han. Kern, "Speaking of Poetry," 189.)

3. Susanne Günther's conclusions, based on sociolinguistic studies of German and Chinese proverbs, points to the frequent justifying function of proverbs (chengyu 成語), particularly in relation to norms: "The quoting of this 'little genre' functions as backing for the speakers' statements on Chinese norms and ethics." According to Günther, the data on current usage of proverbs generally supports that these "neat packages of concentrated wisdom or guide-lines for proper behaviour are considered to be ready-made and have a strong authoritative character." The repeated sayings of the ancestors are convincing because they imply community consensus. In citing proverbs, the speaker "stands in a relation of 'reduced personal responsibility,' in Goffman's sense (Goffman, 1986: 512) for what she says." Considering yi 義 in light of that, it makes sense that an yi 義 accompanying a proverb is its model rather than its meaning. Günther, "'Language with Taste,'" 399, 413.

4. For example, Knoblock translates yi 義 here as "real purpose." Knoblock, *Xunzi*, 139. Watson has "objective." Watson, *Hsün-Tzu*, 19.

Complicating the situation, the graph yi 意—rather than yi 義—does sometimes function to mean "purpose" (i.e., "intention," as described in chapter 2), and so later usage of yiyi 意義 might foster the impression that uses of the two graphs had always overlapped.

學惡乎始? 惡乎終? 曰: 其數則始乎誦經, 終乎讀禮; 其義則始乎為士, 終乎為聖人。

Where does learning start? Where does it end? It is said, "Its sequence is to begin with reciting the *Shi* and to end with reading aloud the *Li*. Its *yi* 義 is to begin with the scholar and to end with the sage."

Xunzi 荀子 勸學篇第一

The sentence that opens with "Its *yi* 義" parallels that which opens with "Its sequence (*shu* 數)."

But why would the sequence of progressing from one text to another be associated with the *yi* 義 of progressing from (being) one kind of person to (becoming) another? Although it is not incorrect to sense an assertion of purpose in the line, translating *yi* 義 with terms like "reason," "purpose," or "objective" mischaracterizes the features of an *yi* 義. Like the sequence (*shu* 數) it parallels, the *yi* 義 is perceptible; it is, as I have previously shown, an accessible model. As such, its role is to respond to an anticipated question like, "*Why* does its sequence begin with . . ." or "*What* is the goal of having its sequence begin with . . ." In the circumstances set forth in this passage and in other similar situations, the *yi* 義 is the visible model that explains, which is different from saying it is used to *mean* "reason," "purpose," or "objective."

Model Sayings That Authorize

Most sayings do not seem to have an *yi* 義, but often *yi* 義 occurs in reference to well-known didactic sayings by means of which people try to authorize something.[5] For example, an individual might offer an a posteriori justification for a decision by employing an *yi* 義, which might prompt us to think that *yi* 義 is being used to mean "reason." The *Hanshu* describes something that is "not correct but still acceptable" as having the *yi* 義 of a famous saying from the *Gongyangzhuan* (which the *Hanshu* attributes to the *Chunqiu*). The *yi* 義 (model) of this particular saying is to acknowledge that a compromising action has in fact occurred while simultaneously indicating disapproval of it through one's phrasing. The speaker says,

雖不正猶可, 蓋《春秋》實與而文不與之義也。

Although it is not correct, it is still acceptable, which is possibly the *yi* 義 in the *Chunqiu*'s "In action it is given, but in writing it is not given."

Hanshu 漢書 志《五行志第七》

---

5. See note 3.

The *yi* here is a model, rather than a mere reason, but as often happens with famous statements that accommodate such appeals, it is a model that justifies. In another passage citing famous sayings, the *Hanshu* maintains,

> 明有所不見, 聰有所不聞, 舉大德, 赦小過, 無求備於一人之義也。
> The clear-sighted have that which they do not see, the keen of hearing have that to which they do not listen. This is the *yi* 義 of "Raise up those with great virtue, pardon small mistakes," and "Do not seek everything from one person."
> *Hanshu* 漢書 傳 《東方朔傳第三十五》

The *yi* 義 of the two statements—"Raise up those with great virtue, pardon small mistakes" and "Do not seek everything from one person"—supply justification for something like a management tactic. The observation that the senses are limited has no particular ethical implication, and so "duty" would not be an appropriate translation of *yi* 義 in this instance.[6] The observation about sensory limits accords, however, with the same basic model that advocates promoting the virtuous and not relying on a single person: if one well-developed sense faculty cannot do it all, neither can one person.[7]

To interpret *yi* 義 in such uses as the "objective" or "purpose" of the saying amounts to conflating things that are not identical, like duties and management tactics. Instead, justification and blame garner support from the *yi* 義 of certain statements that lend themselves to such appeals.

Justifying in the *Yijing*

Making a case that simultaneously anticipates counterarguments for translating *yi* 義 as a semantic term, like "meaning," and for translating it as a causation-related term, like "reason," is difficult. In this section of the chapter, I will tackle the semantic approach, temporarily suspending a consideration of "reason," which is not normative, as I focus on "model"—in the sense of "exemplar"—which is normative (and therefore appropriate to the texts I will be discussing).

To understand how *yi* 義 functions as a model for justifying in the following examples from *Yijing* literature, one must appreciate its general pattern of *yi* 義 usage.

---

6. In light of such physical language, as I will explain below, I see reasons to resist "principle" as a translation equivalent for *yi* 義.

7. The *yi* 義 of a single saying is often repeatedly invoked—the same line appears in the *Lunheng*, which observes that Kongzi did not act on his own advice with the *yi* 義 of "Do not seek everything from one person." *Lunheng* 論衡 《問孔篇》

In nine cases, the "Tuan" commentary to the *Zhouyi* describes a hexagram using a single syntactically ambiguous phrase that invokes its *yi* 義, as well as its timeliness and greatness ("X之時義大矣哉"). The prominence of timeliness is worth noting because it emphasizes that hexagrams are not atemporal. The phrase also seems to suggest that a hexagram as a whole might possess an *yi* 義 in some way. In every instance, however, the phrase "X之時義大矣哉" concludes the "Tuan" commentary; nothing more is said that would clarify the phrase's obscurity. When the "Xiang" commentary employs *yi* 義 even more frequently, but differently, it might be developing the "Tuan" commentary's (possible) reference to hexagrams having *yi* 義. In any case, the "Xiang" commentary adds what I will refer to as an "*yi*-comment" to the line statements (the statements following each line of the hexagram), as if some sort of additional statement about *yi* 義 is called for. Whereas the "Tuan" commentary's uses of *yi* 義 can be read as stating that the hexagrams serve as models, the "Xiang" commentary's use is more specifically a model that justifies something.

In the "Xiang" commentary, which uses *yi* 義 as a model that provides an ethical supplement, or justification, *yi*-comments occur in distinct formulas. In the half dozen cases where the *yi*-comment reaffirms that there will be good fortune—as well as, in the case of *Sui* (隨), when it reaffirms that there will be bad fortune—the commentary simply tacks the term "*yi* 義" onto a line-statement expression that asserts the prognosis. For example, when a line statement for the Xiao Xu (小畜) says "good fortune" (*ji* 吉), the commentary adds, "Its *yi* 義 is good fortune." (其義吉也). The same terse formula reappears after a line statement in Sui (隨) predicts bad fortune. The line statement says, "In following, there is a catch. The determination is inauspicious" (隨有獲, 貞凶). Again, the "Xiang" commentary's contribution is minimal. It appends this, "In following, there is a catch. Its *yi* 義 is inauspicious" (隨有獲, 其義凶也). Thus the "Xiang" commentary treats *yi* 義 like a small, but somehow necessary, enhancement of a prognosis.

Given that they function exclusively to reaffirm prognoses already asserted in the line statements, these *yi*-comments most certainly operate as normative appendages rather than statements about something like linguistic meaning. In other words, their retrospective character makes it unlikely that they should be read as "Its meaning is X." On the contrary, the *yi*-comments seem to address imagined readers in search of an explanation of the prognosis, by saying, in effect, "Here is the model that justifies it."

Two further examples may be helpful. In these cases, the "Xiang" commentary deploys *yi*-comments to offer an ethical defense of a negative determination. *Yi* 義 is not being used in an ethical sense to mean propriety or duty because the actions that possess *yi* 義 are unethical. At the same time, however (as noted above), "reason" does not suffice because a normative term is required. The two examples of justifying unpropitious predictions occur in relation to line statements for *Lu* ("Traveling" 旅). For the nine in the third line from the bottom, a traveler burns his lodging and loses a servant, which earns him the determination of peril ("losing his young servant: the determination is peril," 喪其童僕, 貞厲). In the "top nine," a traveler loses an ox, which earns him the prognosis of misfortune ("losing an ox at Yi: inauspicious," 喪牛于易, 凶). (Whether the line statements inform each other is an interpretive question that is not pertinent to my present analysis.)

The "Xiang" commentary affirms the justice of both the peril and misfortune predicted in the line statements, but it does so with a method less direct than is typical. That is, it does not merely add *yi* 義 to the determination or the prediction. Were that the case, for nine in the third, it would say, "Its *yi* 義 is peril" (其義厲也), and for the top nine, it would say "Its *yi* 義 is misfortune" (其義凶也). Instead, the commentary identifies two specific actions that justify the bad prognosis and appends its *yi*-comment onto those actions. For the nine in the third line from the bottom, it says, "Its *yi* 義 is the loss [of the servants]" (其義喪也). For the "top nine" it says, "Its *yi* 義 is the burning" (其義焚也)."[8] Thus, for these lines which predict bad fortune, the commentary departs from its usual formula regarding the *yi*-comment. It locates a fault that justifies the unfortunate determination and then places the *yi* 義 in front of that.

Because of the way in which they are phrased, these particular *yi*-comments might give the misleading impression that the loss of a servant or the burning is ethical. In other words, it might seem as if the comments are saying, "Its ethicalness is the loss [of the servants]," or "Its ethicalness is the burning [of the nest]." If we interpret these atypical *yi*-comments in terms of the patterns established in more representative *yi*-comments, however, the commentary merely affirms the justice of the prognosis, not the actions of the subject who fulfilled it. In effect, it says, "The model (for justifying this bad outcome) is this." Thus, the "Xiang" commentary's *yi*-comments offer potentially puzzled readers not the reasons for the dire predictions but the models (*yi* 義) that possibly justify them.

Justifying in the *Guliangzhuan*

The nature of the exchange in the *Guliangzhuan* is formulaic—a dialogue between an easily persuaded questioner, whom I will call the student, and an authority figure with answers about the content of the *Chunqiu*, whom I will refer to as the teacher.[9] Although some of the questions only seek information, others are more

---

8. The immediate reference of "burning" is birds burning their nest in the statement for the top nine, but the next phrase mentions the loss of the ox (其義焚也。喪牛于易). Again, whether this line should be read in light of the prior line about the burnt lodging is an interpretative question.

9. All of my translations of the *Guliangzhuan* (a Western Han text) are indebted to those of Göran Malmqvist. Malmqvist, "Studies," 67–222.

pointed; the answers to the latter often involve yi 義.[10] For example, the *Chunqiu* describes a worthy person being passed over in favor of a rightful ruler, which perplexes the student.

> 衛人者、眾辭也,立者、不宜立者也。晉之名、惡也。其稱人以立之何也? 得眾也。得眾則是賢也,賢則其曰不宜立何也?
> 《春秋》之義, 諸侯與正而不與賢也。
>
> -The phrase "the people of Wei" is an expression denoting a multitude. *Li* 立 (to establish) implies that it was not proper to establish him [as their ruler]. The fact that Jin is referred to by his personal name implies condemnation.
> -[Question] Why does it cite the people (*ren* 人) as the means of establishing him?
> -[Answer] He [Jin] had gained support of the masses.
> -[Question] Since this was so, he must have been worthy. If he was worthy, why does the text state that it was improper to establish him?
> -[Answer] The yi 義 of the *Chunqiu* is: the status of feudal lord was granted to the proper heir and not to the [one whose moral qualifications made him more] worthy.
> *Guliangzhuan* 春秋穀梁傳 隱公《隱公四年》1.4.7

Here, the *Guliangzhuan* justifies something that appears to be an ethical inconsistency: why the *Chunqiu* implies that Jin is virtuous even as it says he is not the right person to be appointed to a particular position of influence. In this context, yi 義 is invoked to justify the inconsistency. Although such an ostensible injustice may puzzle a mere student, an authority like the speaker recognizes the yi 義 in the *Chunqiu*'s writing and makes it available to others. The yi is a model—"the status of feudal lord was granted to the proper heir and not to the [one whose moral qualifications made him more] worthy"—as the authority demonstrates by pointing it out.[11]

In some cases in which the *Guliangzhuan* deploys yi, it seems to be attempting to justify technical aspects of the *Chunqiu* that might undermine its reliability. Doubt about the *Chunqiu*'s trustworthiness seems implied in this question about scrambling the date of a single event.

---

10. In the *Guliangzhuan*, the uses of yi 義 as model seem to be part of the formal technique of the genre employed for resolving apparent tensions.

11. Malmqvist translates yi as "doctrine" here. Malmqvist, "Studies," 79.

鮑卒何為以二日卒之？《春秋》之義，信以傳信，疑以傳疑，陳侯以甲戌之日出，己丑之日得，不知死之日，故舉二日以包也。

-[The Marquis of Chen] Bao's death, why is it on two different days?
-[Answer] The *yi* 義 of the *Chunqiu* is: trustworthy things are transmitted as trustworthy and doubts are transmitted as doubts. The Marquis of Chen went out on the day *jia shu*. He was found [dead] on the day *ji chou*. Since the day of his death was not known, it mentions the two days to cover both.
Guliangzhuan 春秋穀梁傳 桓公 《《桓公五年》》

Assuming this is a challenge about the *Chunqiu*'s inclusion of both dates, then *yi* 義, in the catchy saying to which the *Guliangzhuan* attaches it, is the model of a saying that can be repeated and emulated. Although the *Guliangzhuan* goes on to explain the *Chunqiu*'s clever straddling of a chronological dilemma, the reason it offers for doing so is distinct from the passage's *yi*-comment.

Some of the *yi*-comments in the *Guliangzhuan* are not framed as answers to queries and yet they too seem to vindicate the *Chunqiu* in the face of potential challenges. Diverging from its usual treatment of events that happened on the same day (i.e., not repeating the day's name), the text repeats the day's name in each entry on the date when two events happened. The *Guliangzhuan* provides a normative defense of the stylistic departure, claiming that the *Chunqiu* does so because the day is decisive.

再稱日，決日義也。
Repeating the day's name: the *yi* 義 is the day's decisiveness.
Guliangzhuan 春秋穀梁傳 桓公 《《桓公十二年》》 2. 12. 8

One might interpret the line to be saying that the day's name is repeated to render decisive (*jue* 決) the day's significance.[12] But a more probable assumption would be that day itself, not its significance, is decisive. Moreover, the events of the day are what made the day decisive, not the *Chunqiu*'s treatment of the day. Hence the repeated use of the day's name would not *make* it decisive but would only reinforce its decisiveness. The crucial interpretive clue for understanding the role of *yi* 義 in this passage is that it is brought into play to explain an instance in which the *Chunqiu* seems to be breaking its own rules. The model that justifies the *Chunqiu* is

---

12. This is the gist of Malmqvist's translation.

that it is a decisive day. Again, the *Guliangzhuan* uses *yi* 義 as a model that justifies the *Chunqiu*'s departure from its norm.

In another passage in the *Guliangzhuan*, interpreting *yi* 義 as a model that justifies something helps align an answer with its corresponding question. The *Guliangzhuan* discusses the *Chunqiu*'s report of the arrival of a duke's new wife, Lady Jiang. The *Chunqiu* describes her as "entering," and the *Guliangzhuan* asserts that the use of "enter" signals that the people within did not accept her. In the last line, the *Guliangzhuan* uses *yi* 義 to mean the normative model that insiders used to justify rejecting her.

> 入者、內弗受也。日入，惡入者也。何用不受也？以宗廟弗受也。其以宗廟弗受何也？娶仇人子弟以薦舍於前，其義不可受也。
> -*Ru* ("to enter") indicates that those who were inside did not accept her. It mentions the day of the entering in order to condemn the one who entered.
> -[Question] On what account did they deny acceptance?
> -For the sake of the ancestral temple, they refused to accept her.
> -[Question] Why, for the sake of the ancestral temple, did they refuse to accept her?
> -Marrying the daughter and younger sister of a feud enemy and placing her in front [of the ancestors]: that *yi* 義 could not be accepted.
> *Guliangzhuan* 春秋穀梁傳 莊公 《《莊公二十四年》》 3.24.5

The question requests clarification about the ancestral temple's role in the insiders' rejection of the duke's new wife. The response would not speak to the particular inquiry if it were to be phrased as "The significance [of marrying the enemy's daughter] could not be accepted." The query calls for a reason that accounts for the ancestral temple's role, not "What is the importance of X?" The response would reverse causality if it were to posit "Marrying the enemy's daughter is the significance of her not being accepted." Marrying the enemy's daughter is the probable reason for the rejection, not the significance of it. Placing the enemy's daughter in front of the ancestors is the model. One could say that the ancestral temple could not accept that "*model of* appropriateness," but not that it could not accept that "appropriateness," because the situation describes an impropriety, not a propriety. Hence something like "model" is needed as a translation equivalent to encompass this use of *yi* 義. In short, the "model" (*yi* 義) serves to justify by being the thing to blame.

In the majority of examples I have cited, interpreting *yi* 義 as a model for justifying retains a connection to uses of *yi* 義 as a virtue, which translations like "meaning," "significance," or "reason" would not preserve. Some of the uses of *yi* 義 in the *Guliangzhuan* focus specifically on justifying that which people do not accept.[13] A normative connection is also called for by the *Guliangzhuan*'s commitment to explaining the ethical nature of *Chunqiu*'s every statement.

Justifying in Other Texts

In the *Baihu tong*, *yi* 義 as models used to justify are central to the responses to questions posed. In addition to the fourth example of *yi* 義 with yin-yang listed above, other examples are as follows:

歲再祭[之]何?
春求(穀)[秋][報]之義也。
Why do sacrifices to earth and millet happen twice in a year?
[Answer] The *yi* 義 is: in spring it seeks, and in autumn it gives back.
Baihu tong 白虎通 社稷

所以合子、男從伯者何?
王者受命,改文從質,無虛退人之義,故上就伯也。
[Of the Yin ranks] why were the *zi* and *nan* ranks joined with the *po*?
[Answer] When the ruler, having received the mandate, switched from form (*wen* 文) to following substance (*zhi* 質), there was no *yi* 義 for unsubstantiated rescinding of rank, and therefore [the ranks of *zi* and *nan*] were advanced forward to that of *po*.[14]
Baihu tong 白虎通 爵

---

13. One case that focuses on what cannot be accepted is unfortunately unclear because the identity of a key word is in doubt. The word that seems to require emendation is *ru* 如.

其不言如何也? 其義不可受於京師也。
-Why does the text not say "*ru*"?
-That *yi* 義 surely could be not accepted in the king's capital.
Guliangzhuan 春秋穀梁傳 莊公 《莊公元年》 3.1.3

Malmqvist takes this to be *ru* 入 "entering," because of the *Guliangzhuan*'s association of "entering" with "invading," (莊公 3.24.5 莊公二十四年). Malmqvist, "Studies," 118.

14. The lack (*wu* 無) of an *yi* 義 is also a justification. This example is also important for showing that *yi* 義 is not necessarily normative. If there were such a thing as an *yi* 義 of groundlessly removing someone's rank, then the *yi* 義 is not being used to mean something like an ethical obligation.

所以十月行鄉飲酒之禮何？
所[以]復尊卑長幼之義。
Why is the rite of district feasting in the tenth month?
[Answer] In order to thereby restore the yi 義 between senior and junior, and elder and younger.[15]
Baihu tong 白虎通 鄉射

天子聞諸侯薨，哭之何？
慘怛發中，哀痛之至也。使大夫（吊）[弔]之，追遠重終之義也。
When the Son of Heaven hears of the death of a feudal lord, why does he weep for him?
[Answer] Sadness and suffering develop within, and his pain and sorrow reach their limit. So he has a great officer go to condole [on his behalf], on the yi 義 of pursuing to the distance and giving proper weight to endings.[16]
Baihu tong 白虎通 崩薨

告天何？
示不敢自專〔也〕。
非出辭反面之道也。
與宗廟異義。
還不復告天者，天道質無內外，故不復告也。
Why does [the ruler also] announce his departure to Heaven?
[Answer] [In order] to show that he does not dare to act alone.
This is not the dao of saying parting words, and presenting his face on return.
Regarding the ancestral temple, this is a different yi 義.
On returning he does not again announce to heaven. The heavenly dao's substance has no inner/outer, so he does not announce again.
Baihu tong 白虎通 三軍

In the last illustration, the reference to a ritual with a "different yi 義" indicates that what was just described was the yi 義 of a rite. If announcing, saying parting words, and presenting oneself are features of yi 義 that distinguish one yi 義 from another, then yi 義, again, is more like a normative model than simply a duty or reason.

---

15. Aside from being a justifying model, the phrases "the yi 義 of senior and junior" and "the yi 義 of elder and younger" are themselves *chengyu* (sayings or model forms of speaking).

16. Pursuing to the distance (*jueyuan* 追遠) is also a set phrase.

In another case of manifest behavior, like showing or announcing, consider this instance of the *yi* 義 of courtly ranks as a model that justifies relations with the masses.

爵人於朝者, 示不私人以官, 與眾共之義也。
Ranks for people at court demonstrate (*shi* 示) that they are not offices for personal interests. This is the *yi* 義 of participating together with masses.
Baihu tong 白虎通 爵

In one example, a request for explanation is not forthcoming, but the justification is nonetheless provided.

踰年稱公者, 緣[臣]民之心不可一日無君也。
緣終始之義, 一年不可有二君 (也)。
[After the ruler has died] beyond one year people call the ruler's son "Duke," which follows (*yuan* 緣) the people's heartminds' not allowing that there be a single day without a ruler.
Following (*yuan* 緣) the *yi* 義 of succession, in one year there cannot be two rulers.[17]
Baihu tong 白虎通 爵

A passage from the *Lunheng* concerning ritual behavior describes five different justifications for a rain ceremony that is performed to prevent or end a drought. The occasion for the description is a question from a skeptic, who wonders why anyone would claim that the rain sacrifice is necessarily "fitting" (何以言必當雩也). Because the response entails marshaling reasons, we can infer that what follows is a list of justifications. *Yi* 義 occur in the last two justifications but not the first three. Each justification involves a lengthy paragraph, which I will skip and go straight to the numbered list in which *yi* 義 appear.[18] The fourth justification says,

---

17. *Zhongshi zhi yi* occurs three times in CHANT's Pre-Han and Han Transmitted Texts database.
18. The first explanation is framed in terms of "suitability" (*dang* 當).

得禮無非, 當雩一也。
Achieving the rite cannot be wrong: this is the first suitability of the rain sacrifice.
Lunheng 論衡 《明雩篇》

The second is framed in the same way (當雩二也). The third does not mention *dang* 當 or *yi* 義, and simply describes the justification. The third justification says,

冀復災變之虧, 獲鄧穰之報, 三也。
Wishing to restore the loss caused by the disastrous change, and being rewarded with obtaining an abundant harvest is the third.

禮之心悃愊，樂之意歡忻。悃愊以玉帛效心，歡忻以鍾鼓驗意。
雩祭請祈，人君精誠也。精誠在內，無以效外，故雩祀盡己惶懼，關納精心於雩祀之前，玉帛鍾鼓之義，四也。

The heartmind (xin 心) of ritual action is melancholy and distressed, whereas the intentions (yi 意) of music are happy and delighted. Melancholy and distress use jade and brocade to produce effects on the heartmind (xin 心). Happiness and delight use bells and drums to fulfill the intentions (yi 意).

The sacrifice and worship and the beseeching and praying are the ruler's pure sincerity. [But] his pure sincerity, being on the inside, lacks interaction with the outside, hence the rain sacrifice [serves to] expend the fear and anxiety. Presenting his pure heartmind at the altar of the rain sacrifice—the yi 義 of jewels, brocade, bells, and drums—is the fourth.[19]

In other words, the beautiful sights and sounds represent the ruler's sincere heartmind interacting externally—thereby releasing pent-up feelings that need to be made visible and audible. These public sights and sounds are the fourth model that justifies the sacrifice. The fifth and last yi 義 also focuses on public display:

臣得罪於君，子獲過於父，比自改更，且當謝罪。惶懼於旱，如政治所致，臣子得罪獲過之類也。默改政治，潛易操行，不彰於外，天怒不釋，故必雩祭。惶懼之義，五也。

A minister who commits an offense against his sovereign, and a son who has transgressed against his father, reform when they are punished and moreover apologize for their faults. As for fear and anxiety about droughts, if it is caused by the government, it belongs to the same category as the minister's offense and the son's transgression. If [the offense] is silently corrected and set to order, if hidden transformations are put in practice, and if they do not display these on the outside, then heaven's anger will not be dissipated. Therefore there must be a rain sacrifice. The yi 義 of fear and anxiety is the fifth.
Lunheng 論衡 《明雩篇》

When the government causes people to worry about droughts, heaven becomes angry with it, just as rulers and fathers are enraged by offenses perpetrated by their ministers and sons. Covert corrections are not sufficient. Public reform and apology are required in all cases. This is the fifth model that justifies the rain sacrifice. In addition to beautiful sounds and sights, the rain sacrifice is justified by the need

---

19. My translation of this last line is tentative.

for audible and visible displays of rectifying the sources of fear and anxiety, thus confirming the understanding of yi 義 as a publicly accessible model.

These two justifications for the ritual are enumerated in terms of their fittingness (dang 當) and yi 義. The "meaning of" jewels, brocade, fear, and anxiety is not at issue, nor is yi 義 serving as an ethical norm related to these things. That is, justifications four and five do not say, "The propriety is jewels" or "The ethical norm is fear." Rather, they propound the necessity for public manifestation. The justifications are the models of presenting jewels and drums as well as exhibiting the repair of the causes of fear and anxiety. Modeling such outward displays, then, makes the rain sacrifice fitting.

A passage that supplies a rationale for asking an officer to shoot an arrow presents another use of yi 義 as a justifying model.

> 孔子曰:「士,使之射,不能,則辭以疾。縣弧之義也。」
> Kongzi said, "With an officer, require him to shoot, and if he is not able, he declines on the ground of being ill. Its yi 義 is the Suspended Bow [ritual]."
> Liji 禮記〈郊特牲〉

The suspended bow ritual involves hanging a bow on the left side of an entrance door to mark the birth of a son. Suggesting that the rite constitutes the meaning or propriety of requiring the officer to shoot seems illogical. Nor does meaning or propriety have anything to do with an *inability* to shoot an arrow. The rite, which is performed at a birth, therefore justifies asking the grown male soldier to use his bow, whether or not he is able to comply. The yi 義 of the suspended bow ritual is the model (hanging a bow on a door) that justifies the request that he shoot.

An example from the *Hanshu* illustrates a case in which yi 義 functions as a model that justifies a proposal. A speaker cites a line from the *Shujing*.

> 臣聞廣謀從眾,則合於天心,故《洪範》曰『三人占,則從二人言』,言少從多之義也。
> I have heard that when you broadly solicit plans from the masses, it is in accord with heaven's heartmind (xin 心). Therefore when the Great Plan says, "When three officers are appointed, then follow the [agreed upon] speech of two of them," it is asserting (yan 言) the yi 義 for "the minority [should] follow the majority."
> Hanshu 漢書 志《郊祀志第五》

Although it might appear as if the yi 義 in this passage is glossing or explicating the saying from the Great Plan, the speaker is instead extracting from it support for his position. Rather than explaining what meaning should be taken from "follow the . . . speech of two," he is pointing out the model justifying that "the minority [should] follow the majority." Having already claimed the support of heaven's heartmind, he adds that the line from the Great Plan provides the normative model for believing that the few should follow the many.

Wuxing 五行 in the Baihu tong

Often in connection with the "Five Activities" (*wuxing* 五行), which explain how bodies alter their shape and function, the *Baihu tong* involves itself with what we might call patterns or models. We might think of the Five Activities as five "walkings" (*xing* 行), keeping in mind that they not only elucidate but are themselves bodily motion, albeit not that of human bodies. They and their *yi* 義 are not abstract, and they are not situated outside of space-time; in fact, they require both space and time.

Consider the following passage.

> 五行者、何謂也?
> 謂金、木、水、火、土也。
> 言行者、欲言為天行氣之義也。
> [Question] The Five Activities (*wuxing* 五行), what does that refer to?
> [That is what we] call metal, wood, water, fire, and earth.
> By saying "*xing* 行" (action, walking), we wish to say it is the *yi* 義 of heavenly *xing* 行 (acting) qi.
> *Baihu tong* 白虎通 五行

It is important to point out that the discourse of metal, wood, water, fire, and earth is a discourse about models. Therefore, the placement of *yi* 義 in the passage suggests that its comment about *xing* 行 also involves a model; otherwise the addition of *yi* 義 would be irrelevant. If *yi* 義 were not present, the line would read, "By saying 'walking,' we wish to say, heavenly walking qi." As a gloss, it would be complete. Adding *yi* 義 would be redundant, not to mention out of character with the simple way in which early Chinese texts gloss terms. If, on the other hand, *yi* 義 actually contributes something, then it would say, "By saying 'walking,' we wish to say it is on the *model* of heavenly walking qi."

In the context of discussing the Five Activities, the *Baihu tong* (like other early Chinese texts) uses *yi* 義 and *fa* 法 interchangeably to mean "model." Witness three phrases from the *Baihu tong* concerning bodily cohesion.

> 骨肉無相去離之義也。
> . . . the *yi* 義 of flesh and blood not departing or leaving.

> 地無去 (夫) [天]之義也。
> ... the *yi* 義 of earth not departing from heaven. [This refers to wife and husband, who are said to share a single body.]

> 父子一體而分, 無相離之法。
> ... father and son as portions of one body, lack the *fa* 法 of leaving each other.

Each of these phrases evokes a paradigmatic prohibition against bodily separation, with *yi* 義 and a *fa* 法 each signaling a particular model at play. There does not seem to be much difference between the text's use of *yi* 義 and *fa* 法.

As I noted above, the "Wuxing" (Five Activities) chapter of the *Baihu tong* explains that fire is yang, which is the *xiang* 象 of the ruler. Correspondingly, water is yin, which is the *yi* 義 of the minister (火陽、君之象也, 水陰、臣之義也。). (The difference between a *xiang* 象 and an *yi* 義 is not elucidated.) The chapter's anonymous inquirer raises the troubling inference that in that case, the minister might be able to conquer the ruler since water can douse a fire. The answer is reassuring: only unfit rulers can be deposed. As the answer is elaborated, it moves into a more strictly Five Activities register, noting that water vanquishes by means of metal and earth. But the questioner wants to know: Since wood gives birth to fire, why does fire destroy wood? The response hinges on the *yi* 義 of pregnancy.

> 金勝木, 火欲為木害金, 金者堅強難消, 故母以遜體助火燒金, 此自欲成子之義。
> Metal conquers wood, and fire desires to harm metal for the sake of wood. Metal is hard and strong, difficult to destroy, so the mother (the wood) helps the fire (her child) burn metal by abdicating her own body. This is the *yi* 義 of a spontaneous desire to form a child.
> *Baihu tong* 白虎通 五行

The unity of a mother's body with her child's is, in another chapter, extended to her oneness with her husband. Thus, she may admonish him, but she cannot leave him even if he rejects her admonitions. As implicit justification, the "Jianzheng" 諫諍 passage offers this *yi*-comment: earth cannot depart from heaven.

> 妻得諫夫者, 夫婦[一體], 榮恥共之。《詩》云:「相鼠有體, 人而無禮; 人而無禮, 胡不遄死?」此妻諫夫之詩也。諫不從、不得去之者, 本娶妻非為諫正也。故一與[之]齊, 終身不改, 此地無去 (夫) [天]之義也。
> A wife can remonstrate with her husband because wife and husband are one body so their glory and shame are shared. The *Shijing* says, "Look at the rat that has limbs. A person without the rites! A person

without the rites! How should they not die?" This is an ode where the wife remonstrates with her husband. But if he does not comply with the remonstrance, she cannot depart from him. At root, taking a wife is not about remonstration for correction. So once mated, for the rest of her life the wife does not alter. This is the *yi* 義 of earth not departing from heaven.
Baihu tong 白虎通 諫諍

The passage that immediately follows addresses the case of sons, who are also of one body with their fathers. In this example, the passage discusses *yi* 義 as well as a polar term, *en* 恩, (kindliness). Perhaps for this reason, the *Baihu tong* employs a variation of the formula, replacing *yi* 義 with *fa* 法 except when it pairs with *en* 恩.

子諫父,［父不從］,不［得］去者,父子一體而分,無相離之法,猶火去木而滅也。《論語》:「事父母幾諫。」下言「又敬不違」。
臣之諫君何取法? 法金正木也。子之諫父,法火以楺木也。臣諫君以義,故折正之也。子諫父以恩,故但揉之也,木無毀傷也。
待放去,取法於水火,無金則相離也。

When a son remonstrates with his father, and the father does not comply, the son cannot depart because the father and son are portions of a single body. They lack the *fa* 法 of mutually leaving one another. It is like the way a fire cannot depart from wood without going out. The *Lunyu* says, "When serving one's father and mother on occasion you may remonstrate," [but] next it says, "Increase your respect and do not disobey."

[Question] What *fa* 法 is selected when a minister remonstrates with his ruler?
[Answer] [They use] the *fa* 法 of metal straightening wood. When a son remonstrates with his father, the *fa* 法 is using fire to soften wood. A minister remonstrates with his ruler by means of *yi* 義, thus cutting straightens it. A son remonstrates with his father by means of *en* 恩, thus [he or it] only softens it. The wood is not destroyed or harmed.

By departing after awaiting being released, [the minister] selects the *fa* 法 of water and fire. In the absence of metal, then there is mutual leaving.
Baihu tong 白虎通 諫諍

In the use of *yi* 義 with *en* 恩, as above, the pairing assumes an ethical function. But *fa* 法 functions here in a way that is similar to *yi* 義 in other passages. That is, in the context of material symbols like wood, fire, and metal, *fa* 法, like *yi* 義, serves as a model of flesh not departing.

My translation of the final line of the passage above (from the "Jianzheng" 諫諍 chapter) presumes that the minister is the implied subject who departs because the son, as the first lines announce, has no possibility of leaving. The theme recurs in the "Zhufa" 誅伐 chapter, in which the *Baihu tong* describes a son avenging his father as having a single *yi* 義 with (義一也) an avenging minister. On the surface, this "single" *yi* 義 seems to signal that the son and the minister share an identical duty, but the passage undermines that understanding.

> 子得為父報讎者，臣子[之]於君父，其義一也。忠臣孝子所以不能已，以恩義不可奪也。故曰：「父之讎不與共天下，兄弟之讎不與共國，朋友之讎不與同朝，族人之讎不共鄰。」
>
> A son taking vengeance on an enemy of his father and a minister [doing the same for] his ruler have a single *yi* 義 (其義一也). The reason a loyal minister and a filial son can never give up [avenging] is that kindliness (*en* 恩) and obligation (*yi* 義) cannot be removed.
>
> Thus it is said, "With the enemy of one's father, one cannot share the same world. With the enemy of one's brothers, one cannot share the same state. With the enemy of one's friend, one cannot share the same court. With the enemy of one's clan, one cannot share the same neighborhood."
>
> *Baihu tong* 白虎通 誅伐

While the space a man is able to safely inhabit if he has not avenged his brothers, friend, and clan grows progressively larger, a son who has not yet avenged his father can find refuge nowhere on earth. But although the first half of the passage compares a son's obligations to those of a minister toward his ruler, the second half abandons that analogy. *If we choose to interpret the two parts of the passage as a coherent whole*, however, the single *yi* 義 of sons and ministers cannot be taken to mean that their duties are identical.[20] Even though sons and ministers have a duty to avenge, their duties diverge to the point that they cannot be covered by the singleness of one *yi* (*yiyi* 義一). Whereas a son's duty is constant, no matter where in the world he travels, the minister's duty would apparently dissolve if he were to be dismissed (assuming that how the "Jianzheng" 諫諍 chapter treats such a situation applies here as well).[21]

---

20. The second part's sequence includes friends, but as far as I know that does not fall within the scope of sharing a body.

21. I interpret the line as saying, "By departing after awaiting being released, [the minister] selects the *fa* 法 of water and fire. In the absence of metal, then there is mutual leaving." However, the *Baihu tong* does mention an objection:

> 或曰：天子之臣不得言放，天子以天下為家也。
> Others say: The Son of Heaven's minister cannot to be dismissed, because for the Son of Heaven everything under heaven is home.

Thus, the minister and the son do not share a "single duty," because the scopes of their obligations differ. "Never give up [avenging]" could count as a duty, a principle, or a model, but only "model" is a sufficiently capacious translation equivalent of *yi* 義 to accommodate the son's and minister's differences within sameness.

A final example concerns the allotment of property to blood relations:

受命不封子者, 父子手足無分離異財之義。
至昆弟 (皮) [支]體有分別, 故封之也。

As for [the ruler] receiving the mandate and not enfeoffing his son, [this is] the *yi* 義 of father and son being hand and foot: not [something] to be divided or separated into different properties.
As far as elder and younger brothers, they are branches of the body that are divisible, so he enfeoffs them.
Baihu tong 白虎通 封公侯

Resorting to abstract terms like "reason" and "principle" to account for uses of *yi* 義 in relation to the Five Activities would be to ignore the emphatic embodiment. We visualize father and son as hand and foot and brothers as the branches of a trunk. This is a world in which bodies matter. In its Five Activities terminology, the *Baihu tong* presents its *yi* 義 not as embodied abstractions but as physical models that have extension, mass, and visibility; they are real and they are powerful.

Conclusion

If I am right that the uses of *yi* 義 I have explored have to do with physical modeling, then we might ask the following: Why leave purpose or reason implicit? In other words, what does a material model do that a reason or purpose might not?

When a "reason" is the answer to a question, the reason specifies the cause or purpose for a discrete event's occurrence. When the answer to a question is an *yi* 義, the *yi* 義 involves a broader pattern. The pattern is likely to be repeatable and have wider applications (often explicitly normative). Even when the question concerns a distinct occurrence, the *yi* 義 in the answer provides a potentially larger model than a single instance of a cause.

Models resonate with a discourse centered on observations about the movements of material things (like fire and water) that "walk" as human bodies walk. Moreover, a model can be more commodious than a reason or purpose. A model justifies at the level of a pattern rather than discretely, case by case. And finally, a model extends beyond what is merely observed in the present to offer guidance, instruction, or direction in future, similar circumstances.

CHAPTER TEN

Yi 義 in the *Shuowen Jiezi*

Composing a dictionary of over 10,000 entries (including 1,163 variants) in the first century CE would have required access to the entire imperial library. Earlier lexicographies would have informed the monumental process, and the rich Chinese commentarial tradition would have offered hermeneutic strategies. We can assume that all of the texts we have explored concerning the prior history of *yi* 義 and *yi* 意—*Zhouyi* commentaries, *Chunqiu* commentaries, the "Masters" texts, the *Lunheng*, the *Baihu tong*, etc.—would have been available to Xu Shen, but his dictionary of *graphic* etymology was a first of its kind. Applying semantic metalinguistic terms to dictionary entries' graphs had no clear-cut precedent.[1]

The metalinguistic information presented in the *Shuowen*'s entries for different graphs varies considerably, and so it appears that a good deal of uncertainty surrounded the use of such terminology. Occasionally, when glossing a graph, the *Shuowen* uses *yi* 意 as something like the intended-meaning.[2] The *Shuowen* does not, however, use *yi* 義—the later formal term for word-meaning—in that function. Nonetheless, the *Shuowen* periodically enlists both *yi* 義 and *yi* 意 as supplementary, technical metalinguistic terms. These applications are similarly supplementary but differ in ways that remain unclear. In the chapter that follows, I will offer a possible rationale for why the *Shuowen* adopted these new metalinguistic terms and propose a hypothesis about the significance of their uses in the *Shuowen*.

---

1. For a claim that such uses of *yi* 意 and *yi* 義 can be read back into earlier texts, see Poul Andersen, "Concepts," 172.

2. The *Shuowen* regards graphs as "word" equivalents in the sense of being the items that implicitly serve as the most concise semantic units. While it recognizes some words as names (*ming* 名), it treats graphs as more general and more basic.

The Location of the *Yi*-Function in the *Shuowen Jiezi*

The *Shouwen* entries are comprised of various identifiable features. These features are, however, generally more easily characterized by what they are *not* than by what they are, as their precise function all too often remains obscure.

For my purposes, the entries' constituents (which can be dissected more finely) include the following:[3]

- *The gloss of the head character*: At least one gloss appears immediately following the head character and applies to the graph as a whole. The gloss does not necessarily correspond to the graph's use at the time.[4] It tends to follow some formula along the lines of "X: Y 也," "X: Y, Z 也," or "X: Y 者." In rare cases, it includes "*zhiyi* 之意" (twice) or "*yi ye* 意也 (twelve times)."[5]

- *The sound element*: The sound portion of the graph relates to the sound of other graphs. It does not necessarily correspond to the pronunciation

---

3. Bottéro and Harbsmeier provide a more comprehensive list of constituents. They translate *yi* 意 as "idea," and do not mention *yi* 義. I am very much indebted to their clear analysis of *Shuowen* entries, but I will address things that merit further clarification about using the terms "idea," "semantic," and "meaning" to talk about the *Shuowen*'s entries. Bottéro and Harbsmeier, "*Shuowen Jiezi* Dictionary," 252–253.

4. Bottéro and Harbsmeier contend that the gloss that occupies the beginning of the entry is not a "basic meaning," but they do consider it a "meaning," even though they note that they sometimes need to treat it as "X is (a way of) Y-ing" etc. because they "find it impossible to believe that Xu Shen meant to say that X simply meant Y, in other words, that X and Y were synonymous." Bottéro and Harbsmeier, 263.

5. The metalinguistic use of *yi* 意 in glosses of head characters makes it likely that implied readers would have taken those glosses to mean that graphs had intended meanings (*yi* 意 meanings). As in the *Shuowen*'s postface, however, *yi* 意 might function as a metaphor for intentions that belong to the cosmos rather than human inventors.

In any case, the other formulas in the initial glosses, such as "X, Y 也" can be used for referring. Both intending and referring could account for why the glosses do not always work like synonyms. To borrow one of Bottéro and Harbsmeier's examples, the *Shuowen* glosses breathing as panting, but since breathing is not necessarily panting or even a way of panting, we should consider alternatives to the theory that the glosses are supposed to be synonyms. Instead we might interpret "*xi, chuan ye* 息: 喘也" as saying that the graph "breathe," written in a certain script, at some point in some context, was intended for saying, or referred to, "panting." Doing so would leave the source of those intentions or references unspecified.

In appealing to context and use at some historical moment, however, I part company with Bottéro and Harbsmeier's assertion that the *Shouwen* is <u>entirely</u> concerned with *langue* and not *parole*. Bottéro and Harbsmeier, 251.

of the graph current at the time. It tends to appear at the end of the entry.

- *The cong* 从 *X formula*: This feature generally pertains to the non-sound elements (those that are unrelated to sound) insofar as they relate to other graphs. The *Shuowen* entries do not name these non-sound functions.[6]

- *The yi-function:* This element issues a claim about the *yi* 義 or *yi* 意 of the graph. When it occurs in the entry, it appears at its end, where the sound element is located when present. It supplements the initial gloss.[7] It usually acts to assert some form of similarity.

Although my list poses more questions than it answers, I want to focus on the dissimilarity, insofar as it can be discerned, between *yi* 意 and *yi* 義 in the *yi*-function. Some basic features of the *yi*-function are as follows:

- Entries that contain these special uses of either *yi* 意 or *yi* 義 are quite rare: less than 1 percent of the total.[8]

- The *yi*-function does not indicate the sound-element.

- Whether it relates to the graph as a whole or merely a component is uncertain.

- For the moment, I am assuming that *yi* 意 or *yi* 義 perform the same role in the *yi*-function. My basis for doing so is twofold. As Françoise Bottéro and Christoph Harbsmeier put it, each *Shuowen* entry is like a form, with empty boxes in various locations that need to be filled in.[9] In this form, the *yi*-function's position remains the same whether

---

6. Bottéro and Harbsmeier note that there is no name for the X 从 Y formula, but they sometimes translate it as "semantic constituent." They note that in rare cases it occurs with *sheng* 聲 to indicate a phonetic component. Bottéro and Harbsmeier, 258, 259n19.

7. *Yi* 義 never appears in the first gloss. I take it that *yi* 意 is being used in the *yi*-function when it appears later in the entry—not when it occurs in the gloss that immediately follows the head character, which happens at least a dozen times, and also not when the entry calls the head character *huiyi* 會意, which happens six times. (These calculations are estimates, because it is not always easy to tell when *yi* 意 is being used metalinguistically as opposed to simply being used as "intention," "plan," "guess," or any other common use of *yi* 意.)

8. Again, the *Shuowen* includes 9,353 entries.

9. Bottéro and Harbsmeier do not mention the *yi*-function, but it could fit somewhere in their seven-part scheme. Bottéro and Harbsmeier, "*Shuowen Jiezi* Dictionary," 252, 263.

its box is filled with *yi* 意 or *yi* 義. Moreover, when they appear in that location, *yi* 意 or *yi* 義 almost always serve to make an assertion about the sameness of something.[10] And so, the two terms seem to be performing the same function. We have seen, however, that other texts from Early China use the terms differently, and those differences persist in the *Shuowen*. And those differences continue to matter.

Tong 同, Similarity

Yi 意 and *yi* 義 operate similarly in the *yi*-function insofar as, in this special capacity, both terms join with *tong* 同 (similar, same) to assert similarity. Some examples will be useful. (Readers should be warned that it is difficult to translate the *Shuowen* entries with confidence since the genre deprives the terms of context. My translations are tentative, but in any case my main goal is to draw attention to the entry's structure.)[11] **When not all of the entry is translated, the parts in bold are.**

> 1728 譱: 吉也。从誩从羊[羋]。**此與義美同意**。
> *Shan* 譱: auspicious. . . . This, with *yi* 義 and *mei* 美, has a similar *yi*-function (意).[12]

> 9418 勺: 挹取也。象形，中有實，**與包同意**。凡勺之屬皆从勺。
> *Zhuo* 勺: ladle. . . . With [regard to] *bao* 包, [it] has a similar *yi*-function (意). . . .

In general, in instances such as these, in which *yi* 意 is said to be similar (*tong* 同), the *Shuowen* seems to be explicating the structure of the head character by providing an example of another graph possessing a similar structural element. When the graph *yi* 義 occurs along with *tong* 同 in assertions about similarity, it too seems to involve a similarity of structural elements. For example:

> 5200 卓: 高也。早匕爲阜，匕卪爲卬，**皆同義**。
> *Zhuo* 卓: lofty. 早 and 匕 become 阜 (lofty), 匕 and 卪 become 卬 (raise up). All these have a similar *yi*-function (義). [On my translation of *yi* 義, "All these have/are a similar model."]

---

10. I consider entries that read, "X is Y's *zhiyi* 之意" or "X is Y's *zhiyi* 之義" to be making declarations of some kind of similarity between X and Y.

11. The entries and the numbering system were accessed from Shuowenjiezi.com.

12. The line could also be read taking *yi* 義 as an ethics term: "This, in terms of moral flourishing (*yimei* 義美), has a similar *yi*-function (意)."

Preceded by Zhi 之

The uses of *yi* 意 and *yi* 義 manifest more differences in entries that involve the phrases *zhiyi* 之意 and *zhiyi* 之義 in the position of the *yi*-function. Consider two examples of each, with tentative translations as follows.

3139 益: 饒也。从水、皿。皿, 益之意也。
Yi 益: overflowing. . . . Vessel has/is the *yi*-function (意) for *yi* 益.

4511 㪔: 分離也。从攴从林。林, 分㪔[㪔]之意也。
San 㪔: scatter. . . . Woods and divide has/are the *yi*-functions (意) for *san* 㪔.

6626 奏: 奏進也。从夲[本]从廾[収]从屮。屮, 上進之義。
Zou 奏: advance presents. . . . Sprout has/is the *yi*-function (義) for sending upward (上進). [On my translation of *yi* 義, "Sprout has/is the model of sending upward."]

1750 丞: 翊也。从廾[収]从卩[卩]从山。山高, 奉承之義。
Cheng 丞: to assist/respect. From 廾, from 卩, and from 山. "Advancing upward" (山高) has/is the *yi*-function (義) of "ingratiate" (奉承). [On my translation of *yi* 義, "Advancing upward has/is the model of ingratiate."][13]

I take these four entries to be cases of the *yi*-function because, first, *yi* 義 and *yi* 意 appear in the entry's *yi*-location and, second, their usage indirectly asserts similarity by identifying the *yi* 義 or *yi* 意 that is possessed.

But the latter two examples, which use *zhiyi* 之義, do not as obviously concern graphic structure (insofar as it is preserved in the current graphic form) as do the first two examples, which use *zhiyi* 之意. In the first case of *zhiyi* 之義 above, the thing that possesses the *yi* 義 does not seem to be the head character. And in the second case of *zhiyi* 之義, the line quite simply resists parsing. That entry *might* be using *zhiyi* 之義 to address a matter other than the structure of the graph, as my reading indicates.

The dearth of examples at this point in my argument does not justify concluding anything more than that some differences in the *yi*-functions fulfilled by *yi* 意 and *yi* 義 are worth noting.

---

13. Alternative reading: Mountain 山, lofty 高, and tribute 奉 have/are the *yi*-functions (義) of *cheng* 承. On my translation of *yi* 義, that reads: "Mountain, lofty, and tribute have/are the model of indebted to." The alternative reading is less likely, however, because it is does not contain a term like *jie* 皆 (all) to collect the prior terms before the *zhiyi* 之義.

Yi-Function as Intentions (Yi 意)

The *Shuowen*, it is important to emphasize, privileges yi 意 over yi 義: 1) it sometimes employs yi 意 in its glosses of the graph itself; 2) it focuses on yi 意 in the postface; and 3) it employs yi 意 in the yi-function more frequently and more consistently than it does yi 義.

More than a dozen times in the *Shuowen*, yi 意 appears in the entry's first gloss. Note the following representative examples.

> 5538 歁: 悲意。从欠嗇[嗇]聲。
> Se 歁: yi 意 (intends?) sadness. From 欠, with se 嗇 as sound-element.

> 9409 錗: 側意。从金委聲。
> Wei 錗: yi 意 (intends?) leaning. From 金, with wei 委 as sound-element.

In the most unusual case, six different words in the *Shuowen* have an identical initial gloss that seems to indicate that the graph possesses the yi 意 of "to walk" (*zou* 走).[14] For example:

> 1002 趌: 走意。从走吉聲。讀若髻結之結。
> Jie 趌: *zouyi*. . . .

It is unlikely that all six graphs would involve "intending to walk." Alternatively, if all six graphs "intend" walking, then this choice of metalinguistic term in the head gloss seems tentative and experimental.[15] In any case, these six instances are further evidence of the prevalence of yi 意 relative to yi 義 in the *Shuowen*.

In the *Shuowen*'s postface, too, yi 意 occurs more often than yi 義. Yi 意 appears repeatedly in the postface's analysis of graphic formation. Without getting into the complexities and controversies regarding how to understand the text's "six writings" (*liushu* 六書),[16] those categories frequently deploy the graph yi 意. The "six writings" begin with "pointing to events" (*zhishi* 指事), which makes yi 意 visible upon

---

14. This includes entries 1002–1006, as well as 1031. In every case, the *cong* 从X formula indicates that the graph is derived from *zou* 走.

15. When calculating instances of yi 意-meaning, I did not include these uses of *zouyi*, but perhaps after all—despite the uncharacteristic location—"to walk" is their yi 意-meaning.

16. Bottéro and Harbsmeier make a compelling case that *shu* 書 was not used to mean graphs (whereas *wen* 文 and *zi* 字 were); hence, the six categories should be understood as verbal. They translate this as "six scribal acts." Their point is that the action of writing is what is categorized into six forms. Bottéro and Harbsmeier, "*Shuowen Jiezi* Dictionary," 253.

inspection (*cha er jian yi* 察而見意), while the fourth and fifth highlight "associating *yi* 意" (*huiyi* 會意) and having the same *yi* 意 (*tongyi* 同意), respectively. In addition, as mentioned in chapter 8, the postface notes that the "old script" allows *yi* 意 to be readily obtained and explained (*yi ke de er shou* 意可得而說).

The compound term *tongyi* 同意, which encompasses the most common appearance of *yi* 意 in the *yi*-function, occurs regularly in early Chinese texts, and so readers likely would have recognized the *Shuowen*'s application as an extension of ordinary usage.[17] *Tong* 同 "similar" with *yi* 意 in other early Chinese texts asserts the sameness of *yi* 意, as in music sharing *yi* 意 (intention) with heaven or the sages making shared *yi* 意 (intentions) for the world. In thirty-two cases, the *Shuowen* entries use *tongyi* 同意 to say that one or more graphs have an *yi*-function similar to a component of the head character in question. Since the phrasing of *yi* 意 as *yi*-function in these entries does not differ from how it is used in other texts, the *Shuowen*'s implied readers would probably have understood it to signify "similar intention," that is, that the graphs shared an intended construction or an intention in the form of a structural constituent.

Yi-Function as Models (*Yi* 義)

Without presupposing that word-meanings are necessarily abstract entities, the *Shuowen*'s uses of *yi* 義 in the *yi*-function should be considered in light of the resources available to Xu Shen for thinking metalinguistically, specifically the earlier conceptions I have presented regarding how *yi* 義 applies to texts, sayings, figures, and writing.

The number of disparities in the *Shuowen*'s uses of *yi* 義 to assert similarity contrasts dramatically with the consistency of its use of *yi* 意 in the case of *tongyi* 同意. As I have stated, I am considering *yi* 義 to resemble *yi* 意 in this function because they occupy the same place in the entry and because they both assert a similarity. But *yi* 義 is employed in that way much less frequently, and when it is, the form of the assertion varies almost every time.[18] In the eight uses of *yi* 義 in the *yi*-function that identify a sameness between graphs, the *Shuowen* couches that assertion in six different constructs, as follows.[19]

---

17. Other forms include *yi* 意 by itself, *zhiyi* 之意, *yi ye* 意也, and *huiyi* 會意.
18. Again, as in the case of *yi* 意, I do not feel confident asserting an exact number. It is sometimes not clear whether *yi* 義 is being used as an ethical term or a metalinguistic term.
19. In addition to these assertions about sameness, there are a few other cases in the *Shuowen* entries that simply mention an unspecified similarity (*tong* 同) to something else, but stop without naming the element that is similar as either *yi* 義 or *yi* 意. *Shuowen* 4285, 6664, and 2219.

2499 and **8367** *yi dang yong* 義當用	[Its] *yi* in current use . . .²⁰
2727 *kao qi yi, dang zuo* 考其義, 當作	Check its *yi*, which is currently acting as . . .²¹
5200 *jie tong yi* 皆同義	. . . all [these have] similar *yi*.
6626 and **1750** *zhiyi* 之義	. . . has X's *yi*.
7752 *yi dang tong yong* 義當通用	[Its] *yi* currently interfaces with uses of . . .²²
8064 *yi yi tong* 義亦同	[Its] *yi* is also similar.

Of these differently phrased uses of *yi* 義, three are of particular interest. *Dangyong* 當用, *dangtongyong* 當通用, and *dangzuo* 當作—do not occur with *yi* 意 in the *Shuowen*. Nor do they appear with either *yi* 義 or *yi* 意 in the CHANT database for texts from the Pre-Han and Han periods. Because *dang* 當 and *yi* 義 both can be employed as normative terms, all three examples could be explained by taking *yi* 義 as something like "appropriate" or "should"—in other words, not a metalinguistic term at all.

If, however, *yi* 義 has a semantic use in these entries that deviates from the common patterns of phrasing, then the deviation is noteworthy because, as we have just seen, the *Shuowen*'s uses of 意 are technical even though the compounds of which they are constituent elements do not depart from the norm. The unusual locutions involving *yi* 義 associate it with "using" (*yong* 用) and "treating" (*zuo* 作). Thus, they imply that graphs are things that are employed. Of course, speculating on the basis of such a limited data set is unwise; still, these atypical occurrences of *yi* 義 do not seem to indicate a similarity of constituent structure (as cases of *yi* 意 tend to). For example,

> **2499** 玈: 黑色也。从玄, 旅[旂]省聲。義當用䰄。
> *Lu*: the color black. . . . Its *yi* in current use is *lu* 䰄.²³

---

20. Alternative reading: [Its] *yi* should be used as/for . . .

21. Alternative reading: Check its *yi*, which should act as . . .

22. Alternative reading: [Its] *yi* should interface with uses of . . .

23. Alternative Readings: "Its *yi* 義 should be used for *lu* 䰄" or "Its appropriate current use is *lu* 䰄."

Lu 㳚 and *lu* 鱸 do not have any obvious structural similarity, and the entry mentions "use" (*yong* 用). Hence, rather than affirming the presence of a shared structural constituent, the locution seems to assert that two graphs are being used similarly. Before jumping to the conclusion that "*yi* 義-meaning is use," however, we should keep in mind that these occurrences of *yi* 義 are extremely rare, and some instances of *yi* 義 in the *yi*-function do not depart from focusing on graphic structure (see, e.g., 5200 above). Perhaps the *Shuowen* is exploring options with its use of *yi* 義. Perhaps the variation in its use of *yi* 義 signals an attempt to say something new about a graph. In any case, the *Shuowen* uses *yi* 義 as the *yi*-function more erratically than it does *yi* 意.

Deficient *Yi*-Function

We have few clues for interpreting uses of *yi* 義 in the *yi*-function. One lone entry in the *Shuowen* depicts an *yi* 義 in negative terms.

> 1085 些: 語辭也。見《楚辭》。从此从二。其義未詳。
> Xie: a conversational term. See the *Chuci*. From 此 and from 二. Its *yi* 義 is not comprehensive (fully detailed, fully specified).

In the *Chuci*, the term *xie* 些 is an expressive word or an interjection like "O!" which often occurs at the end of a line—what is technically called a non-lexical conversation sound. How the *Shuowen* characterizes it—*yiweixiang* 義未詳—is germane.[24] The phrase "*weixiang* 未詳" appears in thirteen entries. Only two specify precisely *what* is not "fully detailed" (*xiang* 詳): in one entry, *yi* 義 (*yiweixiang* 義未詳), and in the other, *yiyi* 意義 (*weixiangyiyi* 未詳意義). Before turning to these instances, we must consider the most frequent use of *weixiang* 未詳.

In ten entries, *weixiang* 未詳 is located within the 从X formula (two non-sound structural components of the graph).[25] Normally, that formula involves at least two items, but in the "*weixiang* 未詳" cases, one item of the 从X formula is missing. Thus, "*weixiang* 未詳" indicates that one element is unspecified. By contrast, in appending *yi* 義 to *weixiang* 未詳, the *Shouwen* explicitly identifies that which is not fully known—the *yi* 義. Therefore, *yiweixiang* 義未詳 is not operating as a constituent of the 从X formula.

---

24. The Chinese grammatical terminology for "empty term" did not yet exist.

25. In one case, *weixiang* 未詳 appears at the end of the entry by itself, making it difficult to discern its function or even guess about the constituent to which it refers.

What, then, is the deficient *yi* 義—the *yi* 義 that is "not comprehensive (fully detailed or specified)"? Again, the line reads:

1085 些: 語辭也。見《楚辭》。从此从二。其義未詳。
Xie: a conversational term. See the *Chuci*. From 此 and from 二. Its *yi* 義 is not comprehensive (fully detailed, fully specified).

The term *weixiang* 未詳 can be interpreted as "unknown," and that is how it is sometimes understood, but it implies, more precisely, that something requiring details to make up a comprehensive picture (in this case, an *yi* 義) is incomplete.

The *Shuowen* entry for *xiang* 詳 glosses it as "careful consideration" (*shenyi* 審議). It also glosses *xi* 悉 (detailed, full, or entire), using *xiang* 詳, as "comprehensively complete" (詳盡也). Thus, although the outcome of comprehensiveness is knowledge, *weixiang* 未詳 "not comprehensive" is not identical to "not known"—*weizhi* (未知) or *wuzhi* (無知).[26] So it is best to read *yiweixiang* 義未詳 as saying that the *yi* 義 of something lacks some kind of completion.

With comprehensiveness in mind, the *xie* 些 entry is particularly helpful to my discussion because everything about the entry seems to be complete. That is, it contains the gloss of the whole graph; hence, we can infer that the gloss is not the thing that lacks comprehensiveness. And the sound element is also present, so that is not what is lacking. Moreover, the 从X formula also seems complete, since it includes two parts that comprise the whole of the head character (此 and 二). Having ruled out the gloss of the whole graph, the sound element, and the structural constituents that are not sound related, we can conclude that the deficient *yi* 義 can be understood as some sort of additional feature.

In light of uses of *yi* 義 in contemporaneous texts, this *yi* 義 likely functions as some kind of detailed model pertaining to the graph. To clarify my reasoning, let's compare the deficiency of the *yi* 義 of *xie* 些 to the deficiency of an expression like "O!" In saying (or writing) "O!" we might, for instance, finish off a line with emphatic expression or just supply a pause that indicates an ending. The use and effect of such expressions is highly dependent on context. Moreover, they are neither random nor devoid of intended meaning, since they often pack an emotional resonance that divulges the speaker's state of mind. How might we describe the difference between such verbalizations and ordinary words? We might be tempted to suggest that the missing element in expressions like "O!" is a "signified" (or "sense") insofar as we expect words to possess it. But before we credit Xu Shen with creating an entirely new type of linguistic ontological commitment for Early China, we should examine his phrasing and terminology.

---

26. *Weizhi* (未知) only occurs in commentaries. *Wuzhi* (無知) occurs once, when *wa* 聉 is glossed as without knowing its *yi* 意—7777聉: 無知意也.

Xu Shen's precise phrasing suggests that the model is specifically a model for how to use a graph. Two observations support this conclusion: first, the entry does not say that *xie* 些 has no *yi* 義 at all, and second, it deploys the word "comprehensive." Let's closely examine those observations. The entry does not say that *xie* 些 has no *yi* 義 at all. If the claim had been that *xie* 些 possessed no *yi* 義, it might seem like *xie* are "meaningless" as words. But we have seen that expressions are not "meaningless," in the sense of lacking intention (which would be *yi* 意). Do they, then, lack a signified? We must remember, however, that the entry does not say that *xie* 些 has no *yi* 義 at all. Instead, it says that the *yi* 義 of *xie* 些 is not complete or comprehensive (*weixiang* 未詳). Adding a signified to an expression is not the same as making it "comprehensive." Evaluating words on a scale of comprehensiveness seems like a different sort of exercise entirely. Rather than treating words according to the polarity of sense/nonsense, "comprehensiveness" is arguably a more fitting way to depict the difference between expressive words and ordinary words—a difference that is not very clear-cut. In the gloss of *xie* 些, the distinction that is apparently being drawn is between ordinary words with highly controlled norms for use and expressions that have less tightly bounded options for use.

The *xie* 些 gloss is a single case, but if we treat it as exemplary, it reveals more about what might be implied in the idea of a graph's *yi* 義. We might recall some of the examples of *yi* 義 serving as "model" mentioned in prior chapters: a sundial shows how to plot the movement of the sun; a hexagram tells the lord of a state how to govern; a famous saying justifies certain actions. So, too, perhaps the model of a graph tells us *how it was used or how to use it*. A model for a graph has the ontological status of these other models. Like the *yi* 義 of a year traveling across the sky, it is not static. Graphs are based on models for use and the model for *xie* 些 has yet to be fully fleshed out.

The point gains clarity if we compare the *Shouwen*'s single use of *yiweixiang* 義未詳 with its single use of *weixiangyiyi* 未詳意義. Here, too, *yi* 義 is lacking but *yi* 意 is lacking as well.

3837 梵: 出自西域釋書, 未詳意義。

Fan: Comes from Buddhist texts from the western region, [it has] unspecified *yiyi* 意義.[27]

Because, as we have seen, a deficiency in a graph might pertain to its *yi* 義 alone, and because this one is deficient in both *yi* 意 and *yi* 義, we can infer that metalinguistic uses of *yi* 意 and *yi* 義 are not synonymous. Thus, *xie* lacks pre-arranged

---

27. Daniel Boucher maintains that *fan* 梵, in many contexts means the *brahmi* script. He argues that, by contrast, *hu* 胡 "appears to have been used with the technical sense of *kharosthi* script in records on Indian source texts underlying early Chinese translations." Boucher, "*Hu* and *Fan*," 23.

models (yi 義) for use, but the intent (yi 意) of its users is sufficiently specified. By contrast, the paired terms yi 意 and yi 義 as applied to fan 梵 asserts that neither the graph's intentions nor its models are completely understood. We might illustrate the difference in the Shouwen's use of yiweixiang 義未詳 and weixiangyiyi 未詳意義 as akin to the difference between comprehending, on the one hand, a recognized expressive term and on the other, a bit of unknown script. In short, the intentions of expressive terms in a familiar language generally do not pose an interpretive problem. By contrast, a foreign script is completely unfamiliar.

In the case of fan 梵, the Chinese readers who first saw samples of the Buddhist script would lack any intentions (yi 意) associated with the script. Additionally, they would lack models for understanding not only the script but also its usage in practice. In these two rare but telling entries, the Shouwen reveals that it sometimes treats the meaning of a graph as a combination of intention and models for use.

Conclusion

Yi 義, as we know in retrospect, eventually became the scholarly term for meanings in a dictionary. On the whole, philosophers of language in "the West" have treated such word-meanings as abstract entities.[28] In Early China, however, word-meanings were not likely to have been thought of as abstract entities—indeed, no more so than they were in India at the time.[29] As I have argued in prior chapters, in Early China, yi 義—which was used as an ethical term as well as interchanged with the ceremonial term yi 儀 (deportment, instrument)—was understood as a public standard that was based on the metaphor of a material model. By contrast, yi 意 often referred to intentions. Whereas intentions were understood to originate in the inner depths of the heartmind (although sufficiently material to be perceived), yi 義 was associated with models visible in the larger framework of the cosmos.[30]

The Shuowen registers an ambivalence about yi 意 and uncertainty about yi 義. At this point in Chinese history, the prospect of retrieving the yi 意 of texts seemed to pose a serious difficulty, and reducing written language to a series of individual

---

28. Ganeri, Artha, 5.
29. Regarding the view of word-meanings in classical India, see Ganeri's Artha.
30. Fung Yu-Lan briefly mentions this contrast in A History of Chinese Philosophy. Fung points out an instance in which yi 義 and yi 意 appear to be the same, but he also notes a contrast between them insofar as Wang Bi (226–249) equates yi 義 with li 理, whereas he presents yi 意 as something more mental. Fung, History of Chinese Philosophy, 2:186. Steven Van Zoeren makes a case for a significant distinction between yi 意 and yi 義 in the eleventh and twelfth centuries, which he thinks formed the foundation for debates about hermeneutic strategies. Van Zoeren, Poetry and Personality, 151–217.

graphs would understandably have exacerbated that perceived challenge. Whereas the heartmind's yi 意 is conveyed in speech and writing, the yi 意 of a single graph does not offer a correspondingly appropriate level of expressive potential. By a process of elimination, then, yi 義 had certain attributes to offer that yi 意 did not.

The ways in which yi 意 and yi 義 operate metalinguistically in the *Shuowen* help illustrate the push-pull that in due course eventuated in a resolution. When what I have referred to as the yi-function involves yi 意, it generally posits that the items involved shared intentions, which encourages the impression that understanding graphs (or their constituents) is a matter of delving down into the heartminds that produced them. But whose heartminds? The sages who originated writing? Non-human entities that are conceived of as having heartminds and yi 意? Or people (of some period) who codified intentions? If, for example, the founding sages' intentions are at issue, other questions can be posed: Are the sages propounding a general statement about all graphs or are they imbuing each graph with its own, singular intention? It is possible that such unresolved ambiguities advanced the quest for a more coherent terminology.

With yi 義 in the yi-function, on the other hand, a level of specificity could be achieved within an overarching generality. If a graph is said to have an yi 義, it has a model. Models represent and present. They represent material bodies or elements in the physical world, and they present themselves as standards to be emulated. As noted above, in occurrences with *tong* 同, the yi 義 seems to supply an example of another graph with a similar structural element, which certainly seems to suggest that graphs are based on material models that reflect the physical world, like markings on the earth, not an abstract entity, like a "signified" or "sense."

Moreover, because models mimic patterns of observable behavior as exhibited by physical bodies (whether the *wuxing* 五行 "walkings" or ritual action), models also encompass the ways in which people use graphs in writing. Affirmations of similar yi 義 might assert, then, either congruence with a certain usage of the graph, the current usage of the graph, or the appropriate usage of the graph. All told, the metalinguistic uses of yi 義 and yi 意 in the *Shuowen* emphasize both how graphs are used and the intentions "behind" or "in" them.

Conclusion

聆聽前世, 清視在下, 鑑莫近於斯矣。
Attentively listen to previous generations,
Clearly look at what came next.
Mirrors do not get any closer than this.
Fayan 法言 五百卷第八

Even though we can no longer "listen" to the past, attending to it and noting how it affects the present is important. Now, as tactile media, like books, seem to be receding in the face of the internet, our present, which will become the past of future generations, seems as if it may be reduced to a vast digital database. The subject of this book spans a period of transition from an oral *and* visual culture to a writing-centered visual culture, as writing's visible graphs gained dominance by the first century CE to replace the former focus on names.

Whereas in the aural/oral *and* visual culture, names as sounds pointed to referents, actual bodies in the world, one might be tempted to think that the referents of sinographs were either abstractions or mental images. But when the *Shuowen* uses *yi* 義 as the *yi*-function of the graph, it is emphasizing the modeling potential of inscriptions. By contrast, when it uses *yi* 意 as an *yi*-function, it underscores intentions in a way that personifies graphs.

Why does the *Shuowen* use both *yi* 義 and *yi* 意, at times separately and at others together, in certain of its entries? As we have seen in discussions of interpreting texts, *yi* 意 and *yi* 義 are not mutually exclusive; indeed, they seem to complement each other in instances entailing both breadth and depth. Looking back at earlier and contemporaneous texts, we can find precedents for using *yi* 意 to label elements of writing, as well as for talking about the *yi* 義 of texts as their models.

Looking beyond the *Shuowen* to metalinguistic terms later Chinese Buddhist texts, the options for such usage expand but remain within the same range. In addition to *yi* 義, the terms Xu Shen could have adopted involve a different pair of metaphors based on human activity: pointing (*zhi* 指, *zhi* 旨) and intending (*yi* 意). As we have seen, early Chinese texts use *yi* 意 regularly to convey the ways in which humans express themselves with speech and phrases. As we have also seen, "pointing" or "the point" (*zhi* 指, *zhi* 旨) is a metaphor derived from a human being referring to something outside themselves. While both metaphors appear in discussions of textual interpretation, the application of a pointing metaphor is less developed in relation to written works.

When the *Shuowen* chose to name an *yi*-function with *yi* 意, it adopted a term that made sense in the context of speakers, writers, and editors but perhaps less so for graphs. Arguably, the *Shouwen* aims to unearth the hidden structure—and even the heartmind—of the head character by means of the seal script and the 从 X formula, which make its structural constituents visible. But it is difficult to extend the metaphor because although a text can be said to have a heartmind, nothing is really buried, so to speak, in a single graph. That is, aside from the structure, there is nothing that could rise to the surface upon closer inspection. Applying the intention metaphor to graphs has limited utility. More important, since the inaccessibility of intentions had caused some concerns (because, as the *Lunheng* puts it, one has to be present with a person to know them), positing graphic intentions might have seemed even less attractive. Indeed, the *Shouwen* does not appear to be entirely comfortable with espousing the view that the sages harbored specific intentions for each graph given that its own retelling of the origins of writing is silent on the matter. Moreover, as discussed in chapter 8, the choice of script for the head characters does not necessarily foreground the ancients' intentions.

Yi 義 is exceptional in that it is more distant from the human body than intending or pointing, although *yi* 義 is sometimes conjoined with *zhi* 指 or *zhi* 旨 (both used to mean "to point"), reinforcing the understanding that *yi* 義 is external, outside the personal sphere. Hence, by also naming the *yi*-function a "model," the *Shuowen* takes a suggestive step away from human metaphors. According to this paradigm, the model is borrowed from heaven and earth; it is not an attribute of the graph's users or creators. In the past, the cosmos inspired sages with its traces of birds' feet and animal hooves, and those models are still visible now—whether in the cosmos or in the graph. The models upon which the graphs are based preexisted the intentions of their founders. The ancients merely noticed the presence of their models and drew them forth.

Xu Shen might have recognized the advantages of using *yi* 義 as a metalinguistic term. In comparison to using *yi* 意, when interpretation is a matter of *yi* 義, one's standards will be more accessible. A focus on *yi* 義 produces something quite different from a focus on an agent's heartmind (whether intentions or aims). With *yi* 義, agency shifts away from the confines of intersubjective communication to something widely and easily observable. The complexities of interpreting heaven and texts could be minimized because one could turn to visible models and forego the painstaking process of dredging up something submerged. Furthermore, the association of *yi* 義 with the outside is suitable for describing graphs insofar as they are visible. The association of *yi* 義 with the earth and with externality also comports with myths of graphic origin. Unlike intentions (*yi* 意), models (*yi* 義) provide a public foundation for explanation.

One important aspect of models being "outside" is that the inside is necessarily linked to it. And so, humans need only find a way to discern the external order that informs everything. (Or, in the case of rulers, in making ritual calendars, they must "grant" the timing so that it fits the order that is already present.) "Meaning," then, is always available. What might the effect be if we were to put models at the center of our thinking?

Appendix A
Why Translate Yi 義 as "Model"?

Many scholars have explored translations of *yi* 義 serving as an ethical term, but few have discussed the challenges that emerge when translating its early Chinese metalinguistic uses—variously rendered in English as: meaning, significance, principle, rightness, reason, purpose, objective, and motive. Here I describe several scholars' explanations for their metalinguistic translations, and subsequently present my own.

Standard Translation Equivalents for Metalinguistic Yi 義

In texts from Early China, *yi* 義 is closely connected with two graphs—*yi* 儀 (ceremony) and *yi* 宜 (appropriateness)—both of which factored in the process by which *yi* 義 would accrete a metalinguistic usage.[1] Explanations for this development of *yi* 義 emphasize its obvious association with *yi* 宜 (appropriateness).[2] Peter Boodberg

---

1. David Hall and Roger Ames credit the role of *yi* 儀 (ceremony, demeanor) in the Confucian conception of exemplary humans, but do not comment on *yi* 義's subsequent metalinguistic development. After noting that people associated with *yi* 義 possess high status (as a result of self-realization), they add, "This [exalted status] would, of course, account for the cognate of *yi* 義, *yi* 儀, as an exemplary model by virtue of proper demeanor and comportment." Hall and Ames, *Thinking Through Confucius*, 93.

2. For example, *yi* 義 is fully identified with *yi* 宜 in this passage from the *Hanfeizi*.

義者,君臣上下之事,父子貴賤之差也,知交朋友之接也,
親疎內外之分也。臣事君宜,下懷上[宜],子事父宜,(眾)[賤]敬貴宜,知交友朋之相助也
宜,親者內而疎者外宜。義者,謂其宜也,宜而為之。

Yi 義 pertains to service between above and below and rulers and ministers;
disparities between superiors and inferior and fathers and sons;
connections of those one knows and interacts with as acquaintances and friends;
separations between close and distant and internal and external.
It is appropriate (*yi* 宜) for the minister to serve the ruler;

observes that semantic meaning connoted appropriateness for language as well as ethos, and William Boltz argues similarly: "[yi 義] means 'meaning' in the linguistic sense, i.e., what is the proper inherent sense of a given vocable, the semantic 'fit' of a word."³ For evidence, Boltz points to the ideas of Xu Kai (920–974) and, even earlier, the use of yi 宜 (appropriate) in glosses of yi 義 and yi 儀 in the Shiming 釋名, which he attributes to Liu Xi (ca. 200 CE).⁴ Following Boodberg's coinage of "compropriety," Boltz suggests a translation of yi 義 that combines "appropriate" and "propriety" as "appropriety."⁵ Thus, Boodberg and Boltz argue that metalinguistic yi 義 means "meaning" because, like yi 宜, meaning is suitable.

Henry Rosemont and Roger Ames reverse the explanation: yi 義 means "meaning" because appropriateness (yi 宜) is meaningful. Rosemont and Ames broadly construe "meaning" to encompass a variety of spheres (aesthetic, ethical, religious, etc.) and contend that the kind of appropriateness that characterizes yi 義 is "contextually inclusive," i.e., responsive to its circumstance. As they put it, yi 義 is the "sense of appropriateness that enables one to act in a proper and fitting manner given the specifics of a situation." "By extension," they assert, "yi is also a recognition of 'meaning' as it is expressed and comes to reside in personal excellence and conduct."⁶ As I interpret this claim, yi 義's use as "meaning" proceeds from a

---

> It is appropriate (yi 宜) for those below to cherish those above;
> It is appropriate (yi 宜) for sons to serve fathers;
> It is appropriate (yi 宜) for inferiors to respect superiors;
> It is appropriate (yi 宜) for acquaintances and good friends to mutually assist each other;
> And it is appropriate (yi 宜) for the close to be treated as insiders and the distant treated as outsiders.
> Yi 義 is what is called appropriate (yi 宜). It is appropriate (yi 宜), so it is done.
> Hanfeizi 韓非子 解老第二十

3. Boodberg, "Chinese Script," 118; Boltz, *Origin and Early Development*, 175. Boltz does not spell out *how* semantic fit could serve as the equivalent to semantic meaning.

Expanding on Boodberg's observation on the similarities of yi < *zngraj-s 誼 and yi < *zngraj-s 義, Boltz also proposes a slight contrast: yi 誼 as suitable in an everyday sense, and the more formal, yi 義 as "the moral and ethical aspects of one's personal social responsibility." Boltz, "Why So Many *Laozi-s*?" 16n20.

4. I do not agree with Boltz that the *Shiming*'s entry of yi 義 "is clearly the linguistic sense," because there is nothing linguistic about the gloss "to divide and regulate to make things accord" (裁制事物). That gloss comes closer to ethics-related uses of yi 義, which are also far more common and therefore likely to be included in the *Shiming*. Boltz, *Origin and Early Development*, 175.

5. Boltz, *Origin and Early Development*, 175. For Boodberg's coinage of "compropriety," reflecting his view that *wo* 我 was a semantic component of the graph, see Boodberg, "Semasiology," 330–331.

6. Rosemont and Ames, *Chinese Classic*, 90. In an earlier exploration of yi 義 as "meaning," David Hall and Roger Ames devote a section of *Thinking Through Confucius* to uniting these "two halves of an idea." To do so, they suggest, "A person, like a word, achieves meaning in the

connection to yi 宜 *because* appropriate behavior generates the idea of meaningful human conduct.⁷

The connection to yi 宜 reinforces yi 義's ethical uses, enhancing the merit of metalinguistic translations that do not entirely distance yi 義 from normativity.⁸ The interchanges and glosses with yi 宜, however, weaken normative translations that sound absolute or precise, such as "rightness" and "principle." As many scholars have noted, the type of normativity associated with yi 宜 is not an independent standard.

Ming Dong Gu takes an approach to translating metalinguistic uses of yi 義 that is not reliant on similarities of yi 義 and yi 宜 (appropriateness) in his analysis of Wang Bi's (226–249 CE) "General Remarks on the *Zhou Yi*."⁹ Gu contends that Wang Bi employs yi 義 to mean "significance" as it pertains to readers, in contrast to yi 意, meaning "ideas in the mind of the author." Thus, yi 義 arises from reading, whereas yi 意 is involved in creation. Gu describes Wang Bi's distinction between the author's yi and reader's yi as comparable to E. D. Hirsh's distinction between meaning and significance.¹⁰ According to Hirsh, meaning is the "whole verbal meaning," but it originates with authorial intention. By contrast, the whole meaning's relation to the world beyond the text is its "significance."¹¹ In Gu's comparison, then, Wang Bi uses yi 意 to mean the text's "whole verbal meaning" (author), and yi 義 to mean its "significance" in a larger context (reader, world).

---

interplay between bestowing its own accumulated significance and appropriating meaning from its context." Hall and Ames, *Thinking Through Confucius*, 90, 95. They point to a tradition's ritual forms of propriety, which are available to those who perform them, observing that "[yi 義] is also the meaning invested by a cumulative tradition in the forms of ritual propriety that define it. This import can be appropriated by a person in the performance of these roles and rituals." Ames and Hall, *Focusing the Familiar*, 84.

7. Huaiyu Wang is right to caution us against assuming yi 義 functions to mean "the meaning of human life or human existence," as he notes in a comment on David Hall and Roger Ames's *Thinking Through Confucius*. Wang, "Way of the Heart," 352.

8. Early Chinese texts often note a normative dimension of speech, as well as an obligation to speak and name according to norms. References to "straightening names" (*zhengming* 正名), however, do not pertain to the development of yi 義 as a metalinguistic term for word-meaning. Names were thought of as referring directly to things without any intervening meaning. The minimal units to which metalinguistic yi 義 apply are graphs/words (*wen* 文 and *zi* 字), and only rarely to a specific way of naming people. (See chapter 7.) *Ming* 名 (names) and *zi* 字 ("graphs/words") were not two sides of a coin. (See Geaney, "Grounding 'Language' in the Senses.").

9. Wang Bi 王弼's contrast of yi 意 and yi 義 occurs in the "*Ming Xiang* 明象" chapter of the "General Remarks on the *Zhou Yi*" (*Zhouyi lueli* 周易略例).

10. Gu writes, "This passage [from "*Ming Xiang* 明象"] confirms not only Wang Bi's distinction but also his conception of the difference between the author's yi and the reader's yi. His distinction is incredibly modern and its value may be duly appreciated when we compare it with E. D. Hirsh's distinction between 'meaning' and 'significance.'" Gu, *Chinese Theories*, 134.

11. Gu, 134.

The third-century writings of Wang Bi are outside the time frame of my research, but Gu's appeal to Hirsch's terminology is nonetheless of interest.¹² Hirsch's hermeneutic method proposes to constitute historical knowledge because it posits a "fixed" event of authorial intention originating the text's "meaning"—which Gu associates with *yi* 意. By contrast, Hirsch's "significance," which Gu equates with *yi* 義, draws upon that historically grounded original meaning to apply it to some context.¹³ If correct, Chinese hermeneutics must have changed appreciably from sources that predate Wang Bi, wherein a text's *yi* 意 is not equivalent to *authorial intention*, and the text's *yi* 義 consists of qualities within the text itself.¹⁴

Advantages of Translating *Yi* 義 as "Model"

We cannot be satisfied with simply translating *yi* 義 as "meaning" because, as this book's introduction contends, meaning itself is need of explanation.¹⁵ Furthermore, doing so would not account for rules that seem to influence phenomena to which early Chinese texts ascribe *yi* 義. For instance, specific relationships (e.g., ruler/minister, father/son), sayings, and natural patterns often possess an *yi* 義.¹⁶ Yet the *Chunqiu* is practically the only text endowed with an *yi* 義, and few human beings are so honored.¹⁷

In his study of translating the early Chinese metaphor of "norm," Lukas Zadrapa briefly remarks on a resemblance to Greek etymologies linking "justice" to "model." He notes a possible resemblance to the way *yi* 義 relates to *yi* 儀, cit-

---

12. The pairing of *yi* 意 and *yi* 義 seems to overlap with certain uses of "purport" and "import," but *yi* 義 is not something that metaphorically "enters" like an "import" (in trade). Insofar as *yi* 義 is characteristically "external" (see chapter 4), it remains outside.

13. Hirsch, "Meaning and Significance," 204.

14. On the subject of "authorship," see chapter 8, note 12.

    Explaining eleventh-century *yi* 義 and *yi* 意 contrasts, Steven Van Zoeren takes the use of *wenyi* 文義 to mean "literal significance," which he identifies as the meanings of the words (graphs) as distinct from the context and author's intent. Although Van Zoeren selects "significance" to characterize the *yi* 義 of a text, his definition of "significance" emphasizes ethics: "the understanding of texts most consequential for character and moral behavior." Van Zoeren, *Poetry and Personality*, 165, 197.

15. In terms of Early China, as Huaiyu Wang observes, "The connection between the sense of 'signification and meaning of texts' and other senses such as 'dignity of the self, right, just, appropriate, norm and principle' is a complicated matter in need of separate study." Wang, "Way of the Heart," 352.

16. For examples of the possessive use of *yi* 義 (*zhiyi* 之義): see chapter 6 for hexagrams, chapter 7 for figurative language, and chapter 9 for proverbs that justify.

17. Database searches for *zhiyi* 之義 reveal that the *yi* 義 of Yanzi 晏子 (a famous official) is most common: appearing in the *Yanzi Chunqiu*, the *Shuoyuan*, and the *Lüshi Chunqiu*. The *yi* 義 of a few others occur, albeit rarely: including Yao 堯 (a sage), Bo Yi 伯夷 (a loyal minister), and Zhongni 仲尼 (Kongzi's courtesy name).

ing "model" as one possible translation of yi 儀.¹⁸ My argument takes yi 儀's use as "model" one step further in order to explain the emergence of metalinguistic uses of yi 義.¹⁹ I attribute this selection specifically to the materiality, dyadic structure, and instructional functions of models.

Materiality of Yi 義

By describing yi 義 as "material," I mean perceptible to the senses, involved in causality, and located in space and time.²⁰ The yi 義 of a ruler, for example, might seem like the abstract property of dutifulness, but we cannot justify inferring that early Chinese texts employ a substance-property ontology when no discussion of it occurs.²¹ Yi 義 is something paradigmatically accessible. This seems true whether the yi 義 in question pertains to a ruler or the *Chunqiu*. Just as we might conceive of dutifulness as appropriate actions and speech, we can readily understand yi 義 as normative behavior or textual models.²²

Setting aside the *Chunqiu*, queries for "its yi" (*zhiyi* 之義) or "great yi" (*dayi* 大義) that attribute yi 義 to texts suggest more frequent occurrences beginning around the first century BCE. For instances of *Chunqiu zhiyi* 春秋之義 versus 春秋之意 see chapter 8, note 5.

18. Zadrapa writes, "the Greek etymological connection between justice and a model might be quite interestingly mirrored in the Chinese pair yi 儀 *ŋ(r)aj 'standard, model' and yi 義 *ŋ(r)aj-s 'social propriety, righteousness,' itself probably derived from yi 宜 *ŋ(r)aj "appropriate, deserved,' that is, if the words are related." Zadrapa, "Structural Metaphor, 31."

19. Although this dual aspect might apply to some conceptions of signs, the emphasis on materiality and illustration is more obvious with "model." At the same time, the dual aspect might also suggest Pierce's "diagram," with its skeletal relations. Stjernfelt, "Diagrams as Centerpiece," 357–384.

20. For an overview of ontology and language in Early China, see Chris Fraser's response to Chad Hansen's theory of mereological nominalism. Fraser, "Language and Ontology," 420–456.

21. Often translated as "properties," li 理 are patterns and shapes that are visible and divisible. Geaney, "Binaries in Early Chinese Texts," 280–282. Resemblance nominalism or trope nominalism might be apt if mereological nominalism is not.

22. Although yi 義 is not particularly associated with qi coming out of the mouth (as is yi 意), it is interesting to note the compound, *yiqi* 義氣, which is cold and austere.

> 天地嚴凝之氣，始於西南，而盛於西北，此天地之尊嚴氣也，此天地之義氣也。
> Heaven and earth's severe icy qi 氣 begins in the south-west and is abundant in the north-west. This is heaven and earth's severe venerable qi, which is heaven and earth's yi qi 義氣.
> *Liji* 禮記 〈鄉飲酒義〉 46.3

Yiqi 義氣 is also timely and expansive.

> 信氣中易，義氣時舒。
> The trusting qi is centered and easy, the yi qi is timely and expansive.
> *Yi Zhou Shu* 逸周書 〈〈官人解〉〉

Dyadic *Yi* 義 versus Triadic Signs

The triadic structures of modern semiotics are evident in Charles Sanders Peirce's formulations of *icon*, *index*, and *symbol*; *qualisign*, *sinsign*, and *legisign*; and *rheme*, *dicisign*, and *argument*.[23] Ferdinand Saussure's model of a sign, although seemingly dyadic, is also triadic in structure. Along with signifier and signified, Saussure's sign includes a referent, which he leaves unanalyzed and bracketed in order to enable a "science" of signifiers/signifieds.

Unlike those triadic signs, *yi* 義 participates in the dyadic natural patterns so pervasive in texts from Early China.[24] *Yi* 義 relates directly to the thing of/for which it is an *yi* 義. It does not mediate or stand in for something other than itself. Thus, for instance, when an *yi* 義 pertains to rulers and ministers (*junchen zhiyi* 君臣之義), the *yi* 義 is the observable model that rulers and ministers emulate. *Yi* 義 remains dyadic even in more complex cases, such as this claim in the *Baihu tong*: "Fire is yang, which is the *xiang* 象 (emblem) of the ruler; water is yin, which is the *yi* 義 of the minister;" (火陽、君之象也, 水陰、臣之義也).[25] In this water-fire, yin-yang, and minister-ruler series, *yi* 義 and *xiang* 象 terminate a list of behaviors or processes in the ordinary world to which they, too, belong in an uncomplicated way.[26] The pairing suggests *yi* 義 has the same metaphysical status as *xiang* 象.[27]

---

23. Peirce's definition of sign is as follows: ". . . a sign is something, A, which brings something, B, its *interpretant* sign determined or created by it, into the same sort of correspondence with something, C, its *object*, as that in which itself stands to C." Peirce, *New Elements of Mathematics*, 4:20–21. Frege's *Sinn* is also in a "third realm."

24. To establish ontological status absent an explicit discussion in the texts, one can investigate whether terms were used in connection to the heartmind or its activities (*si* 思, *nian* 念, *guan* 觀, *lü* 慮, or *xiang* 想), as well as used in conjunction with terms for things located outside of the person (*zhi* 指, *zhi* 旨, or *shi* 實). On this basis, I argue throughout this book that both *yi* 意 and *yi* 義 are concrete entities: whether deeply buried and hard to unearth, in the case of *yi* 意; or preferably large, but sometimes disappointingly small, in the case of *yi* 義. Hence, neither term had much promise for becoming an entirely abstract entity.

25. The line could also be read as "Fire and yang are the ruler's *xiang* 象; water and yin are the minister's *yi* 義." (火陽、君之象也, 水陰、臣之義也). *Baihu tong* 白虎通 五行.

26. The specific yin-yang alignment might depend less on *yi* 義 and *xiang* 象 themselves than on the activity, entity, or location in question. For instance, the *Hanshu*'s instructions for sacrificial orientation connect *yi* 義 with yang and *xiang* 象 with yin.

> 祭天於南郊, 就陽之義也; 瘞地於北郊, 即陰之象也。
> To sacrifice to heaven in the southern suburb is the *yi* 義 of yang.
> To sacrifice to the earth in the northern suburb is the *xiang* 象 of yin.
> *Hanshu* 漢書 志 《郊祀志第五》

27. Tsaiyi Wu describes *xiang* 象 as an early Chinese "literary device where the material qualities of a thing, while creatively interpreted for human meanings, remain ontologically a strong physical presence." Wu, "Chinese Thing-Metaphor," 523.

Using Yi 義 for Illustration, Emulation, and Instruction

A dual aspect distinguishes models from things like meaning and significance. Models are both physical representations *and* things to be emulated.[28] Clifford Geertz's definition of religion as a "system of symbols" illustrates how models operate.[29] Models, Geertz explains, are "sets of symbols whose relations to one another 'model' relations among entities." Thus the "model" entails two processes, which he calls "models of" and "models for." Models "parallel" the structure of things and also give "objective conceptual form" to social and psychological reality.

Similarly, yi 義 both replicates and shapes the world.[30] Its association with modeling is most striking in the closely related term, yi 儀, a late Han armillary sphere that demonstrates celestial movements and translates as a "sight."[31] In earlier contexts, yi 儀 and yi 義 operate, not merely as "etiquette" or "comportment," but as awe-inspiring ritual behavior, markings of the cosmos, and the figures of *Zhouyi* hexagrams.[32] Evidence of yi 義 by itself functioning as model is most clear in relation to writing, hexagrams, and texts. By the fifth century, the six yi 義 are scripts of different sorts.[33] But as early as the Han, it can be understood as a genre or

---

28. In this sense yi 義 is like the related term, fa 法 (standard, method, model). Fraser, "Mohism."

    Yi 義 and fa 法 are sometimes used in similar ways. For instance, along with "the *dao* of the *Chunqiu* 《春秋》之道," the phrase, "the *fa* of the *Chunqiu* 《春秋》之法" occurs many times in the *Chunqiu Fanlu* and once in the *Yantie Lun*. (See also chapter 9.) As distinct from fa 法, yi 義 is associated more often and explicitly with ethics, as well as with things that are specifically visible. Yi 義 is also not used for "method." In early translations of Buddhist terminology, fa 法 is one of the terms later used for *dharma*, whereas yi 義 is adopted for *artha*.

29. Whereas Geertz uses the idea of a model to explain symbols, I am using it to explain what I mean by "model." Geertz, *Interpretation of Cultures*, 93–94.

30. See example from the *Shuijing Zhu* in chapter 7.

31. Daniel P. Morgan writes, "The term yi 儀 ('sight') derives from the graduated sight/range-finder pegs of early military weapons, which extended to the armillary sphere, came to stand for sighting pegs, graduated rings and the instrument itself." According to Morgan, in modern terminology it "refers to an observational or demonstrational armillary sphere" as distinct from a celestial globe (*xiang* 象), but the imperial sources used the terms inconsistently. Morgan, *Astral Sciences*, 65–66. Morgan translates yi 儀 as 'sight' because it allows one *to see the stars*, like a finder in archery (which is called a "sight"), through pegs or pins that guide the eyes to the target.

32. See chapter 4, note 7. The "externality" of yi 義 is consistent with the close relation to yi 儀 (awe-inspiring behavior), well described in Jia and Kwok "Clan Manners," 33–42.

33. See chapter 7.

a "style," and, in the *Qianfu Lun*, as an allegory.[34] A modeling "instrument" of a linguistic sort, an *yi* 義 instructs and facilitates understanding.[35]

In certain ways, *yi* 義 is very much like *fa* 法, which is also used to mean "model," as well as "standard" and "method."[36] Although the differences might seem slight, these words have discernably different uses. As "duty," *yi* 義 is more explicitly a term of ethics and it is not used for "method."[37] An *yi* 義 is not merely a standard—or even just a visible standard—an *yi* 義 is a display, like scale model or a pictographic model. Thus, the accessible, external spectacle of *yi* 義 resolves the puzzle of why it was adopted for what is now called "word-meaning." By the same token, however, when the *Shuowen Jiezi* employs *yi* 義 as a metalinguistic term, the translation "word-meaning" is not quite apt. Perhaps we are really seeing the first known instance of an unfamiliar concept: a visible "word-model."

---

34. In reference to the genres of *fu* 賦 and *shi* 詩 in the *Hanshu*'s "Yi Wen Zhi" chapter, Lee Hur-li translates *yi* 義 in this context as "style" 漢書 志 《藝文志第十》. Lee, *Intellectual Activism in Knowledge Organization*.

35. The *Qianfu Lun* introduces an illustrative story by labeling it an "empty *yi*" (*xuyi* 虛義), arguably something like an allegory. The speaker, Wang Fu (ca. 78–163), explains,

> 吾傷世之不察貞偽之情也，故設虛義以喻其心。
> I am hurt by the way people do not check the circumstances of true and false,
> so I set up a *xuyi* to illustrate their mindset (*xin* 心).
> *Qianfu Lun* 潛夫論 《賢難第五》

36. See note 28. "The *fa* of the *Chunqiu*" (春秋之法) also appears once in the *Yantie Lun*.
37. See note 28.

Appendix B

Yi 義's Externality in Dispute: The *Mengzi* and the *Mo Bian*

As I demonstrate in chapters 4 and 5, the majority of early Chinese texts that reference the externality of yi 義 seem to do so reflexively, without any apparent attention to competing ways of thinking.[1] Occasionally, however, claims concerning the externality of yi appear in texts generally viewed as expressing carefully considered philosophical positions. Such is the case with the *Mo Bian* and, more famously, the *Mengzi*, both of which dispute the externality of yi 義.

Here I employ an unusual method that highlights the ways in which the arguments in the *Mengzi* and the *Mo Bian* are at cross-purposes with or misunderstand other ideas about the externality of yi 義.

The *Mengzi* on Yi 義 as External

<u>A Justification for My Unusual Approach</u>.—Mengzi's position in his debates with Gaozi has generated numerous interpretations. Given my present focus, I am not able to do justice to the finely nuanced differences among them; however, with one exception (noted below), my presentation of Mengzi's argument does not veer far from a traditional view.[2] The aspect of my interpretation that is unusual pertains to Gaozi as well as to the person who speaks on his behalf in the second debate.

---

1. Arthur Waley notices this automatic response, although he mistakenly equates externality with objectivity. Waley writes, "[Yi 義] for example meant something entirely 'external' and objective, and it had been applied to acts concordant with the circumstances, to behavior such as tradition taught people to demand and expect. But now the Confucians insisted that it was something that existed inside one, a sort of extra 'sense' built up and nourished by particular sorts of behavior." Waley, *The Way and Its Power*, 66.

2. Alan Chan presents an interesting interpretation of the Mengzi-Gaozi debate, arguing that, for Mengzi, yi 義 does not motivate people through the appeal of maximizing profit for the world. Instead, people's very own xin impels them to prefer yi 義 in the way we like certain foods. In the debate with Gaozi, it is important that people are fond (hao 好) of yi 義, because "liking" consists of qi from the xin, which makes yi 義 "internal." Chan, "Harmony as a Contested Metaphor," 60–61.

Here, I depart from the more familiar approach of seeking to consolidate the ideas of the figure of Gaozi in the *Mengzi*, even though the text briefly asserts that his various statements are related.[3] Instead, I create a heuristic, a fictive "Gaozi" (distinguished from the *Mengzi*'s Gaozi by the name's appearance within quotation marks) who represents persistent assumptions, spanning a corpus of early Chinese texts across hundreds of years, about the externality of *yi*, assumptions such as those I have been tracing and exemplifying in previous chapters. I then place these two Gaozis in conversation with one another. In fact, Gaozi and "Gaozi" are not radically different in the views they express. Rather, by way of analogy, they are positioned at either end of a "telephone" or "whisper" game. "Gaozi" speaks first, and the message is clear; then, along the line, as intermediaries successively misinterpret the original message, it becomes distorted, resulting in the fragmented version that Gaozi utters. My point, I want to stress, is not that the *Mengzi* deliberately misrepresents Gaozi but, rather that, given the vagaries of textual transmission, it gets him only half right.[4] In short, whereas the traditional approach to the *Mengzi* is to interpret it with an eye toward textual consistency, my tactic is to posit a historical consistency in the character of "Gaozi" against which the text's debates about the externality of *yi* 義 may be interpreted.

"Gaozi" takes it for granted that *yi* is external. *Yi* is specifically geared for dealing with people with whom one is not closely associated. It is in tension with *ren*, which characterizes the relationship most people have with family members (most of the time). *Yi* establishes necessary distinctions and creates clear boundaries and hierarchies that people who are not intimate can readily understand and observe. *Yi* is a relatively stern virtue concerned with recognizing patterns and using them to establish order. Even though "Gaozi" sees *ren* and *yi* as pertaining to separable spheres, he recognizes that *yi* is sometimes useful within the family and that, in certain circumstances, someone who is not family can be treated with *ren*.

Mengzi and "Gaozi" do not disagree merely about the externality of *yi*; they also have different understandings of what is at stake. For Mengzi, the issue is whether *yi* is within one's own heartmind and therefore something that everyone possesses (and for which each individual can be held responsible). Thus, for Mengzi the question about *yi* pertains specifically to the location being inside or outside *the person*. Other questions about whether *yi* applies to the sphere outside the family,

---

3. Moreover, I treat the people who appear in the text as literary constructions. Little is known about the historical figures who appear in the *Mengzi*, and I do not presume to make any claims about them.

4. Dialogues in early Chinese texts are not likely to be a direct report of a conversation with historical figures. Given the nature of textual construction, misunderstanding, exaggeration, and other "unfair" presentations of ideas (even in one's own tradition) is not unusual, but it is beyond the scope of this project to speculate on reasons for any particular misrepresentation.

the neighborhood, or the state do not feature in Mengzi's comments. By contrast, "Gaozi" presumes that *yi* is deeply involved in orderly categorizing and normative ritual standards that are discriminating, clear, and publicly accessible. What is at stake for "Gaozi" is the nature of *yi*, not whether it is inside or outside a person.

If we acknowledge these conflicting agendas and presumptions in the debates, we see that the participants ostensibly in "conversation" are actually talking past one another. Such might be the case, because in many parts of the debates, the opponents' answers do not seem to respond to the questions being posed. In light of the text's unresolved interpretive problems, adding my unusual perspective on *ren-yi* as an internal-external binary to the long list of the text's potential analyses seems justified.

<u>My Interpretation of the Mengzi Debates.</u>—The first exchange in *Mengzi* 6A4 begins and ends with the reader suspecting that Gaozi's position may not have been well represented. The passage opens with a report that Gaozi has said that food and sex are features of the *xing* 性, but neither sex nor the *xing* reappear in what follows, so I will not try to wedge them into the argument.[5] Where I depart from the conventional wisdom about Mengzi is that I think he demonstrates from the outset an indifference to Gaozi's reasons for viewing *yi* as external, even though he solicits Gaozi's explanations. Gaozi says,

> 「彼長而我長之，非有長於我也；
> 猶彼白而我白之，從其白於外也，故謂之外也。」
> Someone is older, so I treat him as older. It is not that there is [something] older in me. It is like the case of something being white, so I treat it as white. [I] follow (*cong* 從) its whiteness, which is from outside. Therefore I call it [*yi*] external.
> *Mengzi* 6A4, 11.4 孟子《告子上》

Gaozi explains *yi* in terms of what, in early Chinese texts, functions as a paradigmatically visual example: seeing the color white.

Mengzi promptly dismisses the analogy without asking why it was offered. Instead, he questions whether Gaozi recognizes any distinction between a horse and

---

5. There are several options here. One is that this statement about *xing* 性 has nothing to do with the discussion of the externality of *yi* 義, and it just happens to have been something Gaozi said that the writers of the *Mengzi* thought might be relevant. Another is that the general view, presumably also shared by Gaozi, is that the *xing* is internal. Alan Chan makes that case by noting evidence that likes and dislikes are matters of *xing* and by showing how Mengzi's argument links the issue of the heartmind's preferences to *yi* 義. Chan, "Harmony as a Contested Metaphor," 54–60. Yet another option, defended by Dan Robins, is that Gaozi considers the *xing* to be neither internal nor external. Robins, "The Debate over Human Nature," 117–125.

a person being older than he. Thus, a difference of opinion about the nature of *yi* has already emerged. For "Gaozi," it has something to do with being observant of external, visible things, which includes the age of an elder person.[6] For Mengzi, *yi* belongs to the category of virtues, specifically human virtues, and has nothing in particular to do with visible things.

Mengzi goes on to ask whether Gaozi is calling the older person *yi* or calling the one who treats someone as older *yi*.[7] Gaozi responds,

>「吾弟則愛之，秦人之弟則不愛也，是以我為悅者也，故謂之內。
>長楚人之長，亦長吾之長，是以長為悅者也，故謂之外也。」
>
>If it's my brother, I love him. It it's the brother of some guy from Qin, I don't love him. This takes me as the concern.[8] Thus I call it internal. I treat as elder an elder from Chu. And I treat as elder my own elder. This takes elderliness as the concern. Thus I call it external.
>
>*Mengzi* 孟子《告子上》

Gaozi's reply both supplements his initial comment, by offering an example of what he means by internal, and clarifies what he means by "following" (*cong* 從) by providing additional information about his process of making a determination. Furthermore, he treats the idea of *yi* in regard to foreigners from Qin and Chu.

But for all his words, Gaozi has not answered either of Mengzi's questions. He does not comment on the difference between a horse and a person being older. And he does not say whether *yi* refers to the agent of the act or its recipient. But if we remember the figure of "Gaozi," we can understand why the *Mengzi* might depict its character Gaozi as ignoring Mengzi's questions. "Gaozi" could answer Mengzi's question about the horse with even more discussion of *yi* being like visual things, but Mengzi already peremptorily dismissed his example about white. Concerning Mengzi's point about agent and recipient, "Gaozi" would claim that *yi* is neither. *Yi* is located on a spectrum from near to far, depending on the situation; it does not reside within either agent or recipient. Gaozi brings up people from Qin and Chu, thereby emphasizing the importance of taking distance into consideration. Indeed, the distance between things is a relevant factor when determining whether something is *yi*. Generally, *yi* applies to distant relations, but context determines what counts as distance. Such are the points that "Gaozi" would have made or would have been understood to be making, but Gaozi leaves them unspoken in the first exchange.

---

6. The topic of whiteness might echo debates about white horses, but the fact that elderliness is in many cases visible in white hair also fits the statement's context.

7. The line says, "Do we refer to as *yi* the old man or the one who 'olds' him?" 謂長者義乎？長之者義乎？

8. The term *yue* 悅, which is sometimes emended, is used to mean "pleasure," but here it seems more like "concern."

Mengzi has the last word. He cites an example that the *Mengzi*'s authors/editors presumably find compelling but that hardly settles the two interlocutors' differences of opinion. Mengzi counters Gaozi's reference to an elder from Chu with an analogy. There is no distinction, he claims, between our liking for our own roasted meat and meat roasted by people from Qin. The implied conclusion is that, no matter the cook, the taste is in oneself. Thus, Mengzi reasons, if other people do not determine his taste for food, then they also are not responsible for whether or not he treats someone as an elder. In both cases, the agent is the deciding factor. With his analogy to cooking, Mengzi assumes that he has sealed his argument because Gaozi would hardly be able to maintain that tastes are externally determined.[9]

But "Gaozi" would insist that a crucial difference between the sense of sight and the sense of taste invalidates Mengzi's analogy. The sense of sight pertains to the external sphere, where things have form. This is also the sphere of ritual action, which one employs to manage affairs with people outside of one's family: that is, affairs requiring *yi*. By contrast, tastes and sounds are inchoate. In their fuzzy, indeterminate state, they belong to the purview of the intimate and *ren*. In terms of a bodily analysis, tastes and sounds are not as easily differentiated as visible forms. Thus, they would be a weak foundation upon which to build relations with those who are outsiders. In short, "Gaozi" would reject Mengzi's analogy insofar as it belongs to the internal sphere of *ren* rather than the external sphere of *yi*. Since *yi* and *ren* are a polar relation, an example of *ren* could not weaken a claim about *yi*. To "Gaozi" at least, Mengzi's coup de grâce is, to mix metaphors, a red herring.

The second part of the debate, where go-betweens do the talking, is a variation on the same clash of unspoken presuppositions. The Gaozi spokesperson, Meng Jizi, asks why the Mengzi spokesperson thinks *yi* is internal. The Mengzi proxy, Gongduzi, replies that he considers *yi* internal because it enacts his own respect.

「行吾敬，故謂之內也。」
I do my respect,[10] therefore I call it (*yi*) internal.

---

9. This might account for the writers of the *Mengzi* beginning the segment with Gaozi's comment relating food to *xing* 性 (spontaneous character), but again, there are other possibilities, including that Mengzi simply believes most people would agree with him.

10. The use of *xing* 行 (act/walk) followed by "my" makes the line difficult to translate without implying an appearance/reality contrast between "merely" acting and "really" being.

See above, where respect applies to the inside, in contrast to *yi*. The "Wenyan" (文言) commentary to the *Zhouyi* says,

君子敬以直內，義以方外。
The *junzi* uses respect to align the inside, and *yi* to square the outside.
"Wenyan" 文言 *Zhouyi* 周易 《坤第二》

The *Xunzi* 13.7 and the *Hanshiwaizhuan* 6.8 both characterize a person of *ren* as someone who respects (*jing* 敬) others. This is not to deny that respect is characteristically associated with *yi*, but apparently it can also be associated with *ren* and internality.

Gongduzi assumes that doing respectful things renders something *yi*, but for Meng Jizi doing respectful things can be either *ren* or *yi*, depending on the context. To clarify the relationship between *yi* and respect, Meng Jizi poses a situation requiring discrimination: In a ritual context, who does the respectful individual serve first, one's older brother or an even older villager? Gongduzi, the Mengzi proxy, responds that he respects his brother more but is likely to serve the village elder first. The Gaozi-like counter, as delivered by Meng Jizi, follows.

> 「所敬在此, 所長在彼, 果在外, 非由內也。」
> That which you respect is this/here. That which you [treat as] elder is that/there. After all, [*yi*] is external, [it] does not come from inside.

Again, the Gaozi position is not framed in the terms Mengzi favors; specifically, the agent and the recipient of the action (as when Mengzi asks Gaozi whether he is calling the old person *yi* or calling the person who treats someone as old *yi*). If Gaozi's answer were framed in those terms, it would speak of *jing* (respect) and *suojing* (that which/who you respect). Instead, it focuses on two *different* issues: "that which you *respect*" and "that which you treat as *elder*." In doing so, it not only rejects Mengzi's approach to identifying what counts as *yi* 義 but also introduces two new terms "this/here" (*ci* 此) and "that/there" (*bi* 彼), which locate the "respect" nearby and the "treat as elder" at a distance. The statement concludes by reaffirming that externality is the decisive factor in cases of *yi*.

After Gongduzi loses the debate, Mengzi tells his proxy how to trap Meng Jizi when the argument resumes. In the hypothetical dialogue Mengzi constructs, Meng Jizi will ask, "Who deserves more respect: an uncle or a younger brother standing in for a dead ancestor?" Presuming that the answer is the younger brother, Mengzi implies that circumstantial, ritual positions determine who is served first, but *yi* is internal because the internal respect for the uncle is unaffected by those circumstances. Thus, Mengzi challenges the Gaozi proxy to acknowledge that different contexts affect how people act but not necessarily whom they respect, which is important because Mengzi considers *yi* to include respect.

The Gaozi proxy's response, upon hearing Mengzi's new question, addresses the matter of circumstances but reverses the implication concerning *yi*. The nature of *yi* is in dispute, because the very things that Mengzi views as mere circumstance exemplify *yi*—the appropriateness of a visible respectful rite of serving wine. When circumstance calls for a particular action, the action counts as respect. As Meng Jizi, the Gaozi proxy, states,

> 「敬叔父則敬, 敬弟則敬, 果在外, 非由內也。」
> [When] I respect my uncle, then that is respect. [When] I respect my younger brother, then that is respect. After all, [*yi*] is external, [it] does not come from inside.

The statement's "if/then" structure, I believe, conveys a sense of timeliness. Respecting is indexed to an occasion when something should be done.

Timeliness and circumstances are also at issue in the reply's final line, issued by the Mengzi proxy. Although the grammatical pattern is replicated, the remark reaffirms Mengzi's opinion that circumstances are trivial.

> 「冬日則飲湯，夏日則飲水，然則飲食亦在外也？」
> When it is a winter day, then we drink soup. When it is a summer day, then we drink water. In that case, [are you saying] eating and drinking are external?

This drinking example might seem no different from the taste example in the closing line of the first exchange, but it improves upon its predecessor. In this second round of the debates, the closing line seems to acknowledge the concerns that make a "Gaozi" view *yi* as external. It evokes the patterns, elaborately laid out in the *Liji*, according to which, eating and drinking respond to seasonal differences and other factors.[11] But the example does not supply enough information for our fictional "Gaozi" to entertain the question seriously. Whether an act of eating and drinking counts as external depends on various contextual factors. In a ritual context of serving wine, as we just saw, drinking might count as external and *yi*. But this concluding example supplies no context other than weather: no elders, no one from foreign places, not even a little brother. The resulting impression is that the interlocutors in the *Mengzi* debates are talking past one another.

The *Mo Bian* on *Yi* 義 as External

The *Mo Bian*'s criticism of the argument for *yi*'s externality involves no dialogue partner and is considerably more obscure than the *Mengzi*'s, but the *Mo Bian* pas-

---

11. In the passage, which I discuss in chapter 5, the *Liji* says:

    > 天高地下，萬物散殊，而禮制行矣。流而不息，合同而化，而樂興焉。春作夏長，仁也；秋斂冬藏，義也。仁近於樂，義近於禮。樂者敦和，率神而從天，禮者別宜，居鬼而從地。故聖人作樂以應天，制禮以配地。
    > Heaven is above and earth below. The ten thousand things scatter apart, and ritual regulations move (*xing* 行) them. In flow without ceasing, there is uniting and transforming, and music arises within it. In the spring there is creation and in the summer there is growth. This is *ren*. In the autumn there is holding back and in winter there is storing. This is *yi*. *Ren is close to music. Yi is close to ritual action.* Music is kindly and harmonious. It leads spirit-souls and follows heaven. Ritual action is differentiating and appropriate. It stores ghost-souls and follows the earth. Therefore the sage creates music in response to heaven, and establishes rites in accompaniment with earth. *Liji* 禮記 〈樂記〉

sage (*Mozi* B76) does seem at least vaguely familiar with some of the concerns of "Gaozi." Like most aspects of the *Mo Bian*, a technical text that was lost for most of Chinese history and then reconstructed, *Mozi* B76 is hard to interpret. But it articulates, and then refutes, what it takes to be the argument for *yi*'s externality. The passage does not mention Gaozi or Mengzi, and of course it might not have anything to do with them.

> *Mozi* B76 仁義之為外內也, (內) 詩, 說在仵顏
> (仁)。仁愛也, 義利也。愛利此也, 所愛所利彼也。愛利不相為內外, 所愛利亦不相為內外。其為仁內也義外也, 舉愛與所利也。是狂舉也。若左目出, 右目入。
> *Ren* and *yi* as external-internal—this is contrary. Explained by: matching the face.
> *Ren* is love. *Yi* is profit. "Love" and "profit" are this/here. "The loved" and "the profited" are that/there. "Love" and "profit" do not mutually constitute inside and outside. "The loved" and "the profited" also do not mutually constitute inside and outside. This deeming *ren* internal and *yi* external picks out "love" and "the profited" [for its claim]. This is random picking. It is like the left eye exiting and the right eye entering.[12]
> *Mozi* 墨子卷十 10.2 《〈經下第四十一〉》

The gloss of *ren* as love is in line with the various *ren-yi* contrasts outlined in chapters 4 and 5, but the gloss of *yi* as profit (*li* 利) is unusual.[13]

In many ways, *yi* and profit are at odds in early Chinese texts. References to the problem of people seeing profit (*jianli* 見利) and forgetting *yi* are widespread.[14] A comment in the *Zuozhuan* suggests, however, that the source of the problem is not profit (*li* 利) per se but the use of force to acquire it as well as the unbridled desire to accumulate it.

---

12. An alternative reading: going out the left eye and going in the right eye.

13. The critical tone sometimes attached to uses of the word "profit" characterizes uses of *li* 利 in early Chinese texts as well, so "profit" (rather than "benefit") is a good translation. Whether translating *li* as "profit" instead of "benefit" sounds like a disparagement of the idea depends on what kind of profit is at issue (i.e., profiting the whole world is not morally suspect, but profiting oneself might be). For discussions of puzzling uses of *li* 利 see Carine Defoort, "Profit That Does Not Profit," 153–188. See also Roel Sterckx, "Economics of Religion," 839–880.

14. The *Lunyu* 14.12 articulates the noble goal: "see profit and think of *yi*" (見利思義). The general opposition between *li* 利 and *yi* 義 is noted in the *Liji*, the *Lüshi Chunqiu*, the *Xunzi*, the *Guanzi*, the *Huainanzi*, the *Mengzi*, the *Mozi*, and the *Shangjun Shu*, among other places.

凡有血氣, 皆有爭心, 故利不可強, 思義為愈。
義、利之本也。(蘊) [薀]利生孽。
Those who have blood and *qi* all have contending heartminds.
Therefore, *li* 利 (profit) cannot be about forcing.
Thinking about *yi* 義 creates betterment.
Yi 義 is the root of *li* 利 (profit). [But] accumulating *li* 利 generates disaster.
Zuozhuan 春秋左傳 昭公 B10.10 《昭公十年傳》

The *Shangjun Shu* considers *yi* and profit in similar terms.

> 吾所謂利者, 義之本也。而世所謂義者, 暴之道也。
> What I call profit is the root of *yi*. But what the world calls *yi*, is a *dao* of violation.
> *Shangjun Shu* 商君書 開塞

One can treat *yi* as the source of innumerable profits, in which case *yi* and profit are not inherently in conflict.[15] The *li* 利 of earth (its "profits") are the benefits of the earth's resources.[16] The "Wenyan" commentary on the *Zhouyi* glosses *li* as *yi*.

> 《利》者、義之和也,
> Profit is the harmony of *yi*.
> "Wenyan" 文言 *Zhouyi* 周易 《乾第一》

Sometimes "taking" (*qu* 取) such profits is not objectionable; it is in the nature of the taking that *yi* becomes involved.[17] That is, *yi*'s association with profit depends

---

15. Of the ancient kings, the *Lüshi Chunqiu* says,

> 故義者百事之始也, 萬利之本也。
> *Yi* was the beginning of a hundred matters and the root of ten-thousand profits.
> *Lüshi Chunqiu* 呂氏春秋 慎行論第二 《無義》

16. See the *Yantie Lun* 鹽鐵論卷一 《力耕第二》 passage in chapter 5, which refers to earth's resources (地財 *dicai*) in contrast to heaven.

17. The terms *qu* "take/pick" and *li* (profit) often appear together. This is one example from the *Huainanzi*:

> 蓋聞君子不棄義以取利。
> I have heard that the *junzi* does not abandon *yi* to take profits.
> *Huainanzi* 淮南子 人間訓

on who is doing the taking, who profits, and how that profit is obtained.[18] If one profits the whole world, then one's *yi* will be seen from afar.[19] This is why it is possible to take *yi* as one's profit.[20] According to a "ten triads" chapter of the *Mozi* ("Against War I"), *yi* is not contrary to profit as long as one's profit does not harm someone else.[21] The *Mozi* assumes that *yi* is what profits the world. Thus, while it might seem odd to see *yi* simply glossed as profit—as if the idea were not controversial—the gloss is not without justification.

In declaring that it is a random "picking" to claim that *yi* is external, the *Mo Bian* employs the terms "that which" (*suo* 所), "this/here" (*ci* 此), and "that/there" (*bi* 彼). These words are associated with *yi*'s externality in no other early Chinese text except the *Mengzi* passages discussed above.[22] It is possible, then, that the *Mo*

---

18. The *Lüshi Chunqiu* says,

    非其義，不受其利。
    If it is against *yi*, do not accept its profits.
    Lüshi Chunqiu 呂氏春秋 離俗覽第七 《離俗》

19. The *Guanzi* says,

    舉一而為天下長利者，謂之舉長。舉長則被其利者眾，而德義之所見遠。
    If you initiate one thing and the whole world profits, this is called long-lasting initiating. If you initiate long-lastingly then the masses profit and your *de* (virtue/potencies) *yi* will be seen from afar.
    Guanzi 管子卷第二十 形勢解第六十四

    According to Rickett, the "Xingshi jie" (形勢解) cannot be assigned a date before the first century BCE. Rickett, *Guanzi*, 1:62.

20. The *Liji* explains the scenario and concludes:

    此謂國不以利為利，以義為利也。
    This is called, "In a state, do not treat profit as profit, [instead] treat *yi* as profit."
    Liji 禮記 〈大學〉

21. The *Mozi* chapter implies this when explaining why one should not steal someone else's peaches.

    以虧人自利也。
    This is diminishing others to profit yourself.
    Mozi 墨子卷五 5. 1 《非攻上第十七》 The dates of the "ten triads" chapters are uncertain, but see chapter 3, note 13.

22. Even the association of *yi* with *li* 利 might refer to the *Mengzi*, if Alan Chan is correct that Mengzi rejected the association of *yi* with *li* in favor of the idea that people naturally preferred *yi*. Chan, "Harmony as a Contested Metaphor," 54–55.

Bian is referencing the *Mengzi*'s version of the debate with Gaozi.[23] The *Mo Bian* interprets the use of *suo* in relation to the externality of *yi* as a way to mark a distinction between agent and acted-upon, on the assumption that the inner-outer distinction of *ren* and *yi* is based on that. This resembles what Mengzi asks Gaozi: "Are you calling the older person *yi* or are you calling the one who treats someone as older *yi*?" Hence, *Mo Bian*'s use of "that which" (*suo* 所), "this/here" (*ci* 此), and "that/there" (*bi* 彼) echoes the position of Mengzi, who thinks of *yi* in terms of agent and acted-upon. But the use of "that which" (*suo* 所), "this/here" (*ci* 此), and "that/there" (*bi* 彼) in the *Mengzi* actually occurs in a line that Gaozi's proxy directs at his opponent: "That which you respect is this/here. That which you [treat as] elder is that/there" 所敬在此, 所長在彼. In other words, this line is not a Gaozi-like defense of the externality of *yi* (as presented in the *Mengzi*), but a criticism that the Gaozi proxy uses against Mengzi's position. Hence, the *Mo Bian* argues against a version of "*yi* is external" that only seems to be employing similar terms to Gaozi in the *Mengzi*: it uses the specialized vocabulary the *Mengzi* attributes to Gaozi, but it does not use the terms as the *Mengzi* shows Gaozi using them.

At the same time, certain details in the *Mo Bian*'s account seem to suggest an awareness of some aspects of other early Chinese texts' internal-external contrasts of *ren* and *yi*. The reference to a face (*yan* 顏), for example, is arguably relevant because faces are one of the paradigmatically visible features of a person. As noted in chapter 5, the *Heguanzi* contrasts *ren* to *yi* on just this point.

> 同和者、仁也, 相容者、義也。
> Similarity in harmony is *ren*.
> Likeness in visual appearance (countenance) is *yi*.
> *Heguanzi* 鶡冠子 泰鴻第十

Moreover, the face is the location of the bodily features that determine the contrast of *ren-yi* as internal and external. That is, the type of things that enter the eyes, as distinct from the ears, accounts for the general conception whereby visible things are *yi*, in contrast to taste/sound being *ren*. *Yi* is external because it pertains to the visual sphere in which things have shape, which rites form into patterns. By contrast, *ren* is internal because it is like the indistinctness and inchoateness of sounds and tastes, which are ill-suited to be applied as public standards. Thus, what might seem like bizarre references to entering and exiting orifices is perhaps not that far off base. In a sense, one could say the conception of *ren* as internal and *yi* as external has to do with matching the parts of the face.

---

23. This is not to say that there was any other version, but there could be. It is also possible that the *Mo Bian* arrived at this version on its own.

Conclusion

A broad view of the ways in which early Chinese texts construct *yi* 義 as external helps clarify exchanges on that subject in the *Mengzi* and the *Mo Bian*. Both texts demonstrate at least a minimal awareness of the larger context in which *yi*'s externality is discussed. We could speculate about why the *Mengzi* and the *Mo Bian* depart from those established habits of thinking, but I have resisted the impulse to impose coherence since to do so would imply that early Chinese texts were invested in accurate representation. From the look of it, the authors/editors of the *Mengzi* and the *Mo Bian* might not be interested enough in Gaozi's position to characterize it fairly. Such a posture accords with a general tendency in early Chinese texts to borrow bits and pieces with no special regard for how they were embedded in the "original" context of speech or text.

Thus, in both the *Mengzi* and the *Mozi* passages, the opponents' arguments probably presume what most of the references to the externality of *yi* introduced in chapters 4 and 5 also presume: *yi* pertains to the outside insofar as it differs from things pertaining to the inside. Taken together, passages that involve *yi* in various internal-external binaries reinforce one another. The *Mengzi* and the *Mo Bian* cases notwithstanding, *yi* is linked to externality in so many different passages and contexts that externality is part of the expectation that most writers and intended readers ordinarily brought to uses of the term.

Appendix C
Glossary of Terms with Aural or Visual Associations

Nine terms in *The Emergence of Word-Meaning in Early China* whose aural or visual associations will benefit from further explication are listed here in alphabetical order. The glossary supports and continues, with additional examples, the argument I have developed in the text. For each term I indicate whether it is paradigmatically aural or visual, and in some cases I provide counterexamples that constitute exceptions—either a change in usage over time or just an irregularity. An asterisk next to a word's first mention in each entry indicates that it, too, appears on the list.

Cha 察 (*mainly visual*): examine, discern, discerning

Cha 察, when it appears alone, is often aligned with seeing. For example,

1.6 明足以察秋毫之末，而不見輿薪。
My eyesight is clear enough to *cha* 察 (examine) the tip of an autumn hair, but I do not see a wagon of firewood.
Mengzi 孟子 《梁惠王上》

While *cha* 察 can involve other senses, including that of hearing, when hearing and seeing are explicitly contrasted, "*cha* 察" is always allied with the eyes, as in the following.

夫聽聲有術，則察色有數矣。
Listening to sounds has a method,
and *cha* 察 (examining) colors has a calculation.
Lunheng 論衡 《實知篇》

離婁之明，不能察帷薄之內；師曠之聰，不能聞百里之外。
The clear-sightedness of Li Lou cannot *cha* 察 (examine) inside a screen; the acute hearing of Shi Kuang cannot listen beyond a hundred *li*.
Lunheng 論衡 《書虛篇》

聞審謂之聰 . . . 見察謂之明。
Hearing and investigating is called perspicacious . . .
Seeing and *cha* 察 (examining) is called clear-sighted.
Guanzi 管子卷第四 宙合第十一

夫目察秋毫之末者, 耳不聞雷霆之聲 。
Now with eyes that *cha* 察 (discern) the tip of an autumn hair,
the ears do not hear the sound of thunder.
Wenzi 文子 九守 (also *Huainanzi* 淮南子 俶真訓)

故唯耶 (聖) 人能察无刑 (形), 能聽无聲。
Therefore only the sage is able to *cha* 察 (examine) that which is without
shape (*xing* 形) and able to listen (*ting* 聽) to that which is without sound.
Mawangdui "Yuan Dao" 老子乙本卷前古佚書 馬王堆漢墓帛書・老子乙本
卷前古佚書-道原

必審名察刑 (形) 。
It is necessary to scrutinize the name/fame (*ming* 名*) and *cha* 察 (examine) the shape (*xing* 形).
Mawangdui "Shun Dao" 老子乙本卷前古佚書 馬王堆漢墓帛書・老子乙本
卷前古佚書-十六經 順道

In a few instances, when no direct contrast between hearing and seeing is involved, the ears can also be described as *cha*, as the next two examples show.

夫目之察度也, 不過步武尺寸之閒; 其察色也, 不過墨丈尋常之閒。耳之察和也, 在清濁之閒; 其察清濁也, 不過一人之所勝。
Now the eyes' *cha* 察 (discernment) of measurements does not exceed the area of several feet. And their *cha* 察 (discernment) of colors does not exceed the area of a few dozen feet.
The ears' *cha* 察 (discernment) of harmony lies in the sphere of clear and turbid sounds. Their *cha* 察 (discernment) of clear and turbid does not exceed the limits of one person.
Guoyu 周語 《單穆公諫景王鑄大鍾》

This is also evident in the *Chunqiu Fanlu*.[1]

---

1. Sarah Queen and John Major ascribe this chapter to Dong Zhongshu. Queen and Major, *Luxuriant Gems*, 27.

雖有察耳，不吹六律，不能定五音 。
Even with *cha* 察 (discerning) ears, if you do not blow the six pitch pipes, you cannot hear the five tones.
Chunqiu Fanlu 春秋繁露卷一《楚莊王第一》

Ci 辭; also *ci* 詞 (mainly aural): phrases, phrasing

To some extent, the term "*ci* 辭" (also *ci* 詞, which is interchangeable with *ci* 辭) is used similarly to *yan* 言* (speech), but in part *ci* 辭 differs from *yan* 言 insofar as it is also used to mean well phrased.[2]

We can see that *ci* represents something that comes from the mouth in this passage from Yang Xiong's *Fayan*.

君子事之為尚。事勝辭則伉，辭勝事則賦，事、辭稱則經。足言足容，德之藻矣！
What the *junzi* esteems is service/deeds (*shi* 事*). When the service/deed (*shi* 事) wins out over the *ci* 辭 (phrasing), there is bluntness. When the *ci* 辭 (phrasing) wins out over the service/deed (*shi* 事), it is like the *fu* (the name of a literary genre that Yang Xiong dislikes). When the service/deeds (*shi* 事) and the *ci* 辭 (phrasing) are balanced, it is a standard. Having enough *yan* 言 (speech) and enough looks (*rong* 容): that is the embellishment of *de* (power/virtue).[3]
Fayan 法言 吾子卷第二

Just as speech (*yan* 言) balances with something visible (countenance, looks, *rong* 容), so does *ci* 辭 balance with something visual, service/deeds (*shi* 事). Therefore, balancing *ci* 辭 and *shi* 事 creates parity between something aural and something visual. Like speaking, *ci* 辭 also implicitly contrasts with *shi* 實* (fruit, action, deeds) in this set of two pairs of aural-visual reversals concerning a story of someone who wants a house built but who out-talks the carpenter who tries to explain to him, correctly, that the house will collapse.[4]

---

2. One exception to the idea that *ci* 辭 is well-formulated speech appears to be an anomalous use of *ci* involving what we might want to call one word in the *Lunheng*.

故「毋」、「必」二辭，聖人審之。
Thus, as for "not" and "must," these two *ci* 辭, the sage examines them.
Lunheng 論衡《譴告篇》

See a discussion of the idea of a single unit of language in chapter 1.

3. Michael Nylan translates *shi* 事 here as "substance," but she notes that *shi* 事 could also be interpreted as deeds (事功), as in Wang Rongbao, *Fayan yishu* 法言義疏 [Meaning and Subcommentary on Model Sayings] (Beijing: Zhonghua shuju, 1987). Nylan, *Exemplary Figures*, 29.

4. See Major et al., *Huainanzi*, 729.

或直於辭而不（害）[周]於事者，
或詘於耳忤於心而合於實者。

Some people (the homeowner) are direct in their *ci* 辭 (phrasing) but not thorough about matters/deeds (*shi* 事).
Some people (the carpenter) are deficient in tone (literally ear 耳) and stubborn of mind but in accord with outcomes (*shi* 實).
Huainanzi 淮南子 人間訓

The homeowner, a smooth talker (whose phrasing is impressive), does not understand construction, whereas the builder, a bumbling speaker, has difficulty conveying his opinions to others' ears or heartminds, but his judgments are borne out when the house the homeowner has instructed him to build collapses.

Ci 辭 is often described in ways that suggest it is used to mean well-formed speech. In the next case, it is contrasted to sincere speech.

懇言則辭淺而不入，深言則逆耳而失指。

With earnest speech (*yan* 言), there is shallow *ci* 辭 (phrasing), and it does not penetrate.
With deep speech (*yan* 言), there is grating on the ear and it loses the point.
Yantie Lun 鹽鐵論 卷六《箴石第三十一》

Another passage in the *Lunheng* contrasts the admirable distinguishing of the heartmind to the facile distinguishing of the mouth, which suggests that *ci* 辭 is sometimes used to mean unreliably stylized phrasing:

心辯則言醜而不違，口辯則辭好而無成。

When the heartmind distinguishes, the speaking (*yan* 言) is ugly, but it does not violate; when the mouth distinguishes, the *ci* 辭 (phrasing) is pleasant but it does not come to completion.
Lunheng 論衡《定賢篇》

Both *ci* 辭 and *yan* 言 (speech) are used to mean that which proclaims the *yi* 意 (what is on the heartmind). The *Lüshi Chunqiu* treats *ci* 辭 and *yan* 言 as having the same purpose in relation to *yi* 意, that is, to reveal it.

言者，以諭意也。
夫辭者，意之表也。

Speech (*yan* 言) is for proclaiming what is on the heartmind (*yi* 意).
Ci 辭 (phrasings) are exterior signs of what is on the heartmind (*yi* 意).
Lüshi Chunqiu 呂氏春秋 審應覽第六《離謂》

Glossing the graph *ci* 詞, which is interchangeable with *ci* 辭, the *Shouwen Jiezi* (a first-century dictionary of graphic etymology) says that it is *yi* 意 (what is on the heartmind) on the inside and speech on the outside.

> 詞: 意內而言外也。
> *Ci* 詞: "What is on the heartmind" (*yi* 意) on the inside, and speech (*yan* 言) on the outside.
> *Shouwen Jiezi* 《說文解字》

Ci 辭 (phrases) proclaim the *yi* 意 in the *Xunzi*'s version of what I call the "tripartite division of argument."[5]

> 名也者、所以期累實也。辭也者、兼異實之名以（論）〔諭〕一意也。辨說也者, 不異實名以喻動靜之道也。
> Names or naming (*ming* 名*) is that by which one arranges[?][6] accumulated[7] (*shi* 實) actions/things.
> With *ci* (phrases or phrasing): Compound the names of different *shi* (actions/things) in order to proclaim one *yi* 意 (what is on the heartmind).
> With distinguishing explanations (*bianshuo* 辨說): Do not[8] differentiate actions/things (*shi* 實) from names (*ming* 名) in order to elucidate the dao of movement and stillness.
> *Xunzi* 荀子 正名篇第二十二

In another example, where *ci* 辭 is used to mean well-formed speaking, the *Lunheng* distinguishes it from, while also comparing it to, the formation of inscriptions on rocks:

> 刻為文, 言為辭, 辭之與文, 一實也。民刻文, 氣發言。
> Carvings make inscriptions.
> Speaking (*yan* 言) makes *ci* 辭 (phrasing).
> *Ci* 辭 (phrasing) and carvings are one action/thing (*shi* 實).
> People carve inscriptions. *Qi* 氣 expresses (*fa* 發) speech.
> *Lunheng* 論衡 《紀妖篇》

---

5. *Ming* 名 differ from *yan* 言 insofar as they do not express or proclaim the *yi* 意. This is an argument from absence, the point being that *ming* are not used in close connection to *yi*. See chapter 2, where I consider the rare, possible counterexamples.

6. The term *qi* 期 is used frequently and obscurely in the "Zhengming" chapter.

7. It is possible that this graph should be *yi* 異, meaning "different things, actions"; hence, the translation is uncertain.

8. The graph for "not" here is arguably extraneous.

Thus, this is an aural-visual parallel in which *ci* 辭 are embellished forms of speech comparable to inscriptions that are decorative forms of carving.⁹

In later texts, *ci* 辭 (phrasing) might also be used to discuss written words. In the *Taixuan Jing*, for instance, readers observe the *ci* 辭 of a text with the expectation that the phrases will exhibit its motivations, which in this case is likely to mean looking at graphs because the reader performs a series of visual acts.

> 不沈則其意不見。是故文以見乎質，辭以睹乎情，觀其施辭，則其心之所欲者見矣。
> Were it [the *Taixuan Jing* itself] not deep, its intentions (*yi* 意) would not reveal anything.
> For this reason, pattern is used to see (*jian* 見) into the simple;
> and *ci* 辭 (phrasing) to look into (*du* 睹) the manifestations.
> If we take a close look (*guan* 觀) at the *ci* 辭 (phrases) it lays out, then surely its heartmind's desires will be revealed.¹⁰
> *Taixuan Jing* 太玄經 87 〈太玄瑩〉

Guan 觀 (*mostly visual*): observe

Guan 觀 is a term that can be used more generally as "observe," but the following cases show a specific tendency to use the term for visual entities:

> 5.10 始吾於人也，聽其言而信其行；今吾於人也，聽其言而觀其行。
> In the beginning, with other people, I listened to their speech (*yan* 言*) and trusted their actions (*xing* 行*). Nowadays, with other people, I listen to their speech (*yan* 言) and *guan* 觀 (observe) their actions.
> *Lunyu* 論語 〈公冶長〉第五

> 今聽言觀行 。
> Now, listen to the speech (*yan* 言) and *guan* 觀 (observe) the action (*xing* 行).
> *Hanfeizi* 韓非子 問辯第四十一

> 明主聽其言必責其用，觀其行必求其功。
> An astute ruler, when listening to their speech (*yan* 言), must make it responsible to its uses; when *guan* 觀 (observing) their action (*xing* 行), must seek their results.
> *Hanfeizi* 韓非子 六反第四十六

---

9. It is worth noting that the source of speech here is *qi*, not the heartmind.
10. Michael Nylan translation modified. Nylan, *Canon of Supreme Mystery*, 436.

2.28 發而安中者言也，久而可觀者行也。
What is expressed and pacifies the center/interior is speech (*yan* 言).
What endures and can be *guan* 觀 (observed) is action (*xing* 行).
Hanshiwaizhuan 韓詩外傳卷第二

17.58 聾者不謌, 無以自樂; 盲者不觀, 無以接物。
The deaf do not sing. They lack that which automates music.
The blind do not observe (*guan* 觀). They lack that which connects to things (*wu* 物).
Huainanzi 淮南子 說林訓 說林訓 (also *Wenzi* 上德)

聖人矢口而成言, 肆筆而成書, 言可聞而不可殫, 書可觀而不可盡。
Sages [shoot] arrows from their mouths and thereby bring their *yan* 言 to completion.
They let loose their brushes and thereby bring their writings to completion.
Their speech (*yan* 言) can be heard and cannot be depleted.
Their writings can be *guan* 觀 (discerned) and cannot be exhausted.
Fayan 法言 五百卷第八

Thus, *guan* 觀 is used to mean paradigmatically visual observation.[11]

---

11. In support of my contention, the *Mo Bian* uses the same phrase twice to describe *qin* 親 (up close or in person) with *guan* (身觀焉, 親也). First, it lists three kinds of knowing: hearing, explaining, and *qin* (in person, up close).

10.1.62 知、（聞）〔聞〕、說、親。
Knowing: Hearing, explaining, up-close (in person).
Mozi 墨子卷十 10.1 《《經上第四十》》

It is possible that this means that up-close (*qin* 親) knowing is either hearing or seeing. But if that were the case, why would hearing be listed as its own form of knowing, whereas seeing is not? Given that the first two kinds of knowing are both related to sound, it seems likely that at least one form of knowing would focus on sight. The Explanation seems to make that assertion by saying the body's knowing is observing (*guan* 觀) "up-close" (*qin* 親).

10.3.76 知。傳受之, 聞也。方不廪, 說也。身觀焉, 親也。
Knowing:
Receiving it by transmission: is hearing.
Square does not (unknown graph, possibly *zhang* 廪): is explaining.
The body/person *guan* 觀 (observes) it: is up close (*qin* 親).
Mozi 墨子卷十 10.3 《《經說上第四十二》》

Because *guan* 觀 is generally used with vision, this could imply that up-close knowing is visual observation in particular. The only example the *Mo Bian* uses for *qin* 親 "up-close knowing"

Ming 名 (*audible*): generally personal names, titles, naming

In texts from Early China, *ming* 名 is not used to signify a written graph (although there are two rare exceptions that, as I have argued, reflect attempts on the part of early Chinese authors and scribes to select a standard term to mean "graph").[12] The evidence that *ming* 名 is not used for "graph" derives mainly from the constant contrasts of *ming* 名 to something visual.

Texts from Early China typically use the term *ming* 名 to mean personal names as well as titles. The *Liji* includes "*ming* 名" in a list of certain kinds of names to denote a personal name given in childhood:

---

involves seeing. Someone outside a room has "up-close knowing" of a color, in contrast to having explanatory knowing of a color that is inside the room.

> 10.4.69 外,親智也。室中,說智也。
> The outside is up-close (in-person, *qin* 親) knowing. Inside the room is knowing by explaining.
> *Mozi* 墨子卷十 10.4 《經說下第四十三》

In another case, in what appears to be a contrast to secondhand information, the *Mo Bian* describes knowing "in person" as the body/person observing.

> 10.3.78 聞。或告之,傳也。身觀焉,親也。
> Hearing:
> Someone telling it: is by transmission.
> The body/person *guan* 觀 (observes) it: is up close (*qin* 親).
> *Mozi* 墨子卷十 10.3 《經說上第四十二》

On the other hand, the hypothesis that *guan* 觀 is thus aligned with seeing is complicated by the fact that the *Mo Bian*, repeating the same phrase, also presents *qin* 親 as one of two kinds of hearing.

> 10.1.65 聞、(博)〔傳〕、親。
> Hearing: Transmitted, up close (*qin* 親).
> *Mozi* 墨子卷十10.1 《經上第四十》

Moreover, Graham mentions a case from the *Mozi* (not the *Mo Bian*) of hearing the sound of something up close. Graham, *Later Mohist Logic*, 329. The use of *qinwen* 親聞 that he refers to is its only occurrence in pre-Qin texts, however, and seeing up close (*qinjian* 親見) is significantly more common in other early texts. In sum, *guan* is generally used to mean observing, and there is a strong suggestion that observing is more likely to be understood as using the eyes than the ears.

12. For an explanation for the rare exceptions, see Geaney, "Grounding 'Language' in the Senses," 251–293.

幼名, 冠字, 五十以伯仲, 死諡, 周道也。
Youth *ming* 名 (name), the capping name (*zi* 字), "elder uncle" or "younger uncle" at fifty years, and honorary titles after death (*shi* 諡): these were the way of the Zhou.
Liji 禮記 〈檀弓上〉

While *ming* 名 are personal names, their vocal descriptions attest that they are not graphs assigned at birth. The *Baihu tong* notes that *ming* 名 permit people to cough up (*tu* 吐) their *qing* 情.[13]

人必有名何? 所以吐情自紀, 尊事人者也。
Why must people have *ming* 名 (names)? To spew forth one's *qing* 情 for the reverential service of others.
Baihu tong 白虎通 姓名

Babies are sometimes born with *ming* 名 written on their hands, but the writing itself is not *ming* 名. In every such case in the *Zuozhuan*, the text refers to the writing as *wen* 文 (visible pattern/writing).[14] When a baby is named, the vocal articulation of that name constitutes its *ming*. The ruler names the child by means of some kind of sound.

12. 46 適子庶子見於外寢, 撫其首, 咳而名之。
A [second] son or any other son by the wife proper was presented in the outer chamber, when [the ruler] laid his hand on its head, and with gentle voice named (*ming* 名) it.[15]
Liji 禮記 〈內則〉

Ming 名, which are audible, pair with visible things. The *Guoyu* notes that the ears are for names:

夫目以處義, 足以踐德, 口以庇信, 耳以聽名者也。
Now the eyes are for dwelling in duty. The feet are for treading virtue. The mouth is for guarding trustworthiness. The ears are for listening to/obeying *ming* 名 (titles/decrees).
Guoyu 周語 《〈單襄公論晉將有亂〉》; also, *Jiayi Xinshu* 卷十 10.2 禮容語下

---

13. On *qing* 情, see chapter 3, note 8.
14. See chapter 昭公 B 10.32.4., chapter 閔公 B 4.2.4., and chapter 昭公 B 10.1.12.
15. James Legge translation. Legge, *Li Ki*, 3:474–475.

The *Xin Shu* says,

> 視遠（曰）〔日〕絕其義。。。 聽淫（曰）〔日〕離其名。
> To look into the distance is called cutting short one's duty. . . . Listening to looseness (*yin* 淫) is called departing from one's *ming* 名 (name, title).
> *Xin Shu* 新書 賈誼新書卷十 《禮容語下》

We hear names because we hear reputations. The *Kongzi Jiayu* pairs hearing Kongzi's name with what amounts to seeing his form.

> 聞子之名, 不覩子之形, 久矣!
> For a long time, I have heard your *ming* 名 (name), but have not observed your shape (*xing* 形)!
> *Kongzi Jiayu* 孔子家語 本姓解第三十九

> 名不可得而聞, 身不可得而見, 其惟江上之丈人乎?
> He whose *ming* 名 (name/fame) cannot be gotten (*de* 得) and heard, and whose body/person (*shen* 身) cannot be gotten and seen: this could only be the old man on the banks of the Yangzi.
> *Lüshi Chunqiu* 呂氏春秋 孟冬紀第十 《異寶》

Although part or all of the following passage might date to a later time, it is instructive in that it explicitly shows names to be oral/aural (echoes) in relation to things that are visible (shadows).

> 言美則響美, 言惡則響惡; 身長則影長, 身短則影短。
> 名也者、響也,（身）[行]也者、影也。
> If the speech (*yan* 言*) is good, then the echo is good. If the speech (*yan* 言) is bad, then the echo is bad. If the body/person (*shen* 身) is long, then the shadow is long, if the body/person (*shen* 身) is short, then the shadow is short. *Ming* 名 (name) are echoes. Bodies-persons (*shen* 身) [or, as emended in the CHANT database, *xing* 行*] are shadows.
> *Liezi* 列子 說符第八

Names paired with visual items align with speech paired with various things that can be seen.

> 夫以實（告）[害]我者, 秦也, 以名救我者, 楚也。
> 聽楚之虛言
> 而輕（誣）強秦之實禍,
> 則危國之本也。

[The state of] Qin is harassing us in deed (*shi* 實*) while Chu is rescuing us in *ming* 名 (name). If we listen to the empty speech (*yan* 言) of Chu and make light of forceful Qin's fulfilled (*shi* 實) calamity, that is the root of endangering the state.
Hanfeizi 韓非子 十過第十

故視而可見者, 形與色也; 聽而可聞者, 名與聲也。
Thus, that which can be seen from looking is shape (*xing* 形) and color. That which can be heard by listening is *ming* 名 (name/fame) and sound.
Zhuangzi 莊子 天道第十三

道也者, 視之不見, 聽之不聞。。。不可為形, 不可為名。
Regarding the Dao, we look for it, but do not see [it], and we listen for it, but do not hear [it]. . . . it cannot be given shape (*xing* 形), it cannot be given a *ming* 名 (name).
Lüshi Chunqiu 呂氏春秋 仲夏紀第五 《大樂》

名不可得而聞, 身不可得而見。
. . . [his] *ming* 名 (name/fame) could not be heard,
[his] body/person (*shen* 身) could not be seen.
Lüshi Chunqiu 呂氏春秋 孟冬紀第十 《異寶》

When the *Mo Bian* says that the name of something mates with its *shi*, the pairing signifies that audible naming is matched with a visible action/thing that it names.

10.3.77 所以謂, 名也。所謂, 實也。名實耦, 合也。
That by which something is called is the *ming* 名 (name).
What is called is the action (*shi* 實). The mating of *ming* 名 (name) and
shi 實 (fruit, action, deed) is uniting.
Mozi 墨子 墨子卷十 10.3 《經說上第四十二》

Thus, early Chinese texts consistently use *ming* 名 as something that is audible.

My rebuttal to the assumption that early Chinese texts use *ming* 名 to mean "word" is two-pronged: first, *ming* 名 is certainly used to signify "name," which is not the same as "word," and second, word-types are not obvious categories.[16] A name appears to be a relatively obvious category: a tag for a person or thing. Words, on the other hand, are theoretical abstractions. Even definitions of a word are contested. Those definitions might, broadly speaking, contrast "words" to "names" in two ways: 1) those that distinguish names from words by highlighting the grammatical

---

16. See chapter 1.

or semantic functions of words, and 2) those that stress the idea that a word is a unit of language, perhaps a minimally meaningful one. Both of these approaches, however, presume theorizing about language in ways that are not characteristic of early Chinese texts, which do not postulate the idea of grammar or analyze the nature of semantic meaning as such. Moreover, as noted in the introduction, prior to the first century, early Chinese texts exhibit no investment in positing uniform terms for specific units of what we call "language." "One *ming* 名" for instance, is sometimes the same as, and at other times different from, "one *yan* 言." If "*ming* 名" were being used to mean "word" and "*yan* 言" to mean "language," then "one *yan* 言" would mean "one language"; it would not be used to refer to the same thing as "one *ming* 名." In part, establishing standards for such units is what characterizes the abstraction "language."

Another significant difference between uses of "*ming* 名" (name) and "*yan* 言" (speech) should dissuade us from thinking about *ming* as word-types. Rather than stressing grammar, semantic features, or unit-hood, early Chinese texts subtly distinguish *ming* 名 from *yan* 言 on the basis of the area from which they proceed. As explained in chapter 2, *yan* 言 emerge from inside the person: from the mouth and the heart. By contrast, *ming* 名 are typically heard outside and imposed from outside (sometimes by a ruler as a title or command). In other words, *yan* 言 has an expressive function, but *ming* 名 does not.

Shi 事 (*visual*): service, deeds, affairs, matters

Shi 事 (service, deeds, affairs, matters) is interchangeable with *shi* 實* (action, thing) and is used for things that are visible.

The visibility of *shi* 事 and its interchangeability with *shi* 實 are evident in the passage cited above from the *Huainanzi* (淮南子 人間訓) concerning a man who persuades a carpenter to build a house. The phrasing (*ci* 辭*) represents audible skills; the matter at hand (the house) and the deed (building it) are in the visual realm. Lacking aural skills (defective with regard to the ears) and lacking action (*shi* 事 and *shi* 實), in this case the building of a house, form a pair.

The "Heng Xian" uses *shi* 事 (deeds/service) as the visible pair term for audible names (*ming* 名*). Note in particular that, if these are aural-visual parallels in the first and last two lines, they might suggest that *ming* and *shi* 事 might stand in for the more familiar pair of *ming* and *shi* 實:[17]

名出於言，事出於名。。 。言非言，無謂言。名非名，無謂名。事非事，無謂事。

Names (*ming* 名) emerge from speech (*yan* 言*).

---

17. William Baxter and Laurent Sagart's reconstructions are *shi* 事 (*[m-s-]rəəʔ-s) and *shi* 實 (*məə.li[t]). Baxter and Sagart, *Old Chinese: A New Reconstruction*, 100.

Shi 事 (deeds/service) emerge from names (*ming* 名).
. . . If speech (*yan* 言) is not speech, it is not called speech.
If names (*ming* 名) are not names, they are not called names.
If *shi* 事 (deeds/service) is not *shi* 事, it is not called *shi* 事.[18]
"Heng Xian" 楚竹書十二 《〈恒先〉》四

Shi 事 contrasts to *ming* in the following examples, suggesting aural-visual pairs like *ming* 名 and *shi* 實 (action, thing) or *ming* 名 and *xing* 形 (shape):

使名自命，令事自定。
Make names (*ming* 名) ordered of themselves.
Make *shi* 事 (service) settled of itself.
Hanfeizi 韓非子 揚權第八 and 韓非子 主道第五

有言者自為名，有事者自為形。
Those who possess *yan* (speech) make themselves a name (*ming* 名).
Those who possess serving *shi* 事 (service) make themselves a shape (*xing* 形).
Hanfeizi 韓非子 主道第五

臣任力，同其忠而無爭其利，不失其事而無有其名。
In the ministers' bearing of their power, they are the same in their loyalty and do not contend about profit, they do not lose the *shi* 事 (service), and do not have the name (*ming* 名).
Guanzi 管子 管子卷第四 宙合第十一

A potentially later passage included in the *Chunqiu Fanlu* is unusual insofar as it associates *shi* 事 with hearing.[19]

王者貌曰恭，恭者、敬也。
言曰從，從者可從。視曰明，明者知賢不肖者，分明黑白也。
聽曰聰，聰者能聞事而審其意也。
The king's expression (*mao* 貌) is said to be respectful. The respectful are reverent.

---

18. The translation is tentative. See Goldin, "*Heng Xian* and the Problem of Studying Looted Artifacts," 153–160; and Brindley, Goldin, and Klein, "Philosophical Translation of the *Heng Xian*," 145–151.

19. Sarah Queen and John Major ascribe this chapter to Dong Zhongshu's immediate circle ca. 130–100 BCE. Queen and Major, *Luxuriant Gems*, 27–28.

His speech (*yan* 言) is said to be compliant. The compliant should be followed.
His sight is said to be clear. The clear know the distinction between the virtuous person and the unworthy, and separate clearly black and white.
His listening is said to be perspicacious. The perspicacious can listen to an event (*shi* 事) and examine its intent (*yi* 意).
Chunqiu Fanlu 春秋繁露 春秋繁露卷十四 《《五行五事第六十四》》[20]

The assumption that a *shi* 事 is the thing about which people speak might account for such an alignment of *shi* 事 with hearing:

聽言之道 必以其事觀之
The way of listening to speech (*yan* 言) is certainly using its *shi* 事 (service/deeds) to observe (*guan* 觀*) it.
Dadai Liji 大戴禮記 大戴禮記卷第二 《《禮察第四十六》》

Shi 實 (*visual*): fruit, action, deeds

This entry expands on my discussion of the visual associations of *shi* 實 in chapter 2 of *Language as Bodily Practice*. A *shi* is a fruit or grain. Patterns in early Chinese texts show *shi* 實 to be something seen by the eyes, in parallel to names being heard by the ears. Like fruit and grain, a *shi* 實 fills space by growing and expanding its contours, making it visible. We can see the assumption that *shi* is paradigmatically visible when certain passages interchange names and actions (*ming* 名* and *xing* 行*) for names and *shi* 實, and when they use the terms speech (*yan* 言*) and *shi* 實 instead of speech and action (*xing*). More directly, there are passages such as these that mention seeing *shi* 實.

有華言矣, 未見其實也。
[This] is having flowery speech but not yet seeing its *shi* 實 (fruits).
Yantie Lun 鹽鐵論 鹽鐵論卷五 《《相刺第二十》》

嬰聞察實者不留聲, 觀行者不譏辭。
I, Ying, have heard that one who examines (*cha* 察*) the *shi* 實 (action/thing) does not pay attention to sound.
One who observes the enacting (*xing* 行) does not criticize the phrasing.
Lüshi Chunqiu 呂氏春秋 先識覽第四 《《觀世》》

---

20. Modified from a translation by Queen and Major, *Luxuriant Gems of the Spring and Autumn*, 488.

Some examples in which *shi* 實 pertains to a human being contrast hearsay to seeing *shi* 實 "in the flesh."

> 臣聞古人有辭天下而無恨色者, 臣聞其聲, 於王而見其實。
> I, your minister, have heard of people of old who gave up the world with no regret on their faces. I have heard the sound [of such people] and in you I see its *shi* 實.
> *Lüshi Chunqiu* 呂氏春秋 貴直論第三 《過理》 (see also *Xin Xu* 新序 雜事第五)

A different sense of seeing someone's *shi* 實 occurs in the context of a question about whether a person had died.

> 少君之死, 臨尸者雖非太史公, 足以見其實矣。
> When Li Shao Jun died, although the Grand Annalist was not among those approached the corpse, he was close enough to see its *shi* 實.
> *Lunheng* 論衡 《道虛篇》

Even if this use of *shi* 實 is interpreted as "its reality," rather than the dead person's visible form, it still indicates that a *shi* 實 is something that is seen.

Wu 物 (*generally both aural and visual, but sometimes specifically visual*): a thing in general

On the one hand, *wu* 物 (thing) is used to mean a thing in general. As such, it has both aural and visual aspects. For example, when the *Zhuangzi* considers whether something (either life or the dao) should be characterized by *shi* (fullness) or emptiness, it treats having a name (*ming* 名*) and an action/thing (*shi* 實*) as what constitutes being a located *wu* 物 (thing):

> 有名有實, 是物之居。是物之居; 无名无實, 在物之虛。
> It has a name (*ming* 名) and it has an action/thing (*shi* 實), this is residence of a *wu* 物.
> Not having a name and not having an action/thing, this is in the emptiness of a *wu* 物.
> *Zhuangzi* 莊子 則陽第二十五

On the other hand, the "Xing Zi Ming Chu" aligns *wu* 物 with vision in particular by characterizing a *wu* as anything that is visible:

> 凡見者之謂物。
> Anything that can be seen is called a *wu* 物.

"Xing Zi Ming Chu" 《性自命出》一 (see also "Xingqing Lun" 《性情論》七)

This passage in the *Guoyu* also implies a specific association with visual things.

> 聲一無聽, 物一無文, 味一無果, 物一不講。
> If sounds are all one, there is no listening.
> If *wu* 物 are all one, there is no ornamentation (*wen* 文).
> If tastes are all one, there is no fruit.
> If *wu* 物 are all one, there is no thoroughness.
> *Guoyu* 國語 鄭語 《史伯為桓公論興衰》

Although the last line seems to use *wu* 物 to mean anything, the second connects it to visible patterns. The *Huainanzi* contains a visual use.

> 17.58 聾者不謌, 無以自樂; 盲者不觀, 無以接物。
> The deaf do not sing. They lack that which automates music.
> The blind do not observe (*guan* 觀*). They lack that which connects to *wu* 物 (things).
> *Huainanzi* 淮南子 說林訓 (The same line occurs in the *Wenzi* 文子 上德.)

In two parallel passages about the officers in charge of hearing and those in charge of seeing, the *Zuozhuan* aligns *wu* 物 with vision. The officers of hearing are addressed first:

> B10.9.5 「女為君耳, 將司聰也。辰在子、卯, 謂之疾日, 君徹宴樂, 學人舍業, 為疾故也。君之卿佐, 是謂股肱。股肱或虧, 何痛如之? 女弗聞而樂, 是不聰也。」
> "You are the ruler's ears, and in command of the management of keen-hearing. The cyclical day of Zimao is called a baneful day. Because of the banefulness, the ruler does not have feasts or music, and learners give up their business of studying. The ruler's officers and assistants are his limbs. If one of his limbs is damaged, how will the pain be? You did not hear and are making music. That is not keen-hearing."
> *Zuozhuan* 春秋左傳 昭公 B10.9 《昭公九年傳》

Next, the officers of vision are held to account:

> B10.9.5 「女為君目, 將司明也。服以旌禮, 禮以行事, 事有其物, 物有其容。今君之容, 非其物也; 而女不見, 是不明也。」

「女為君目，將司明也。服以旌禮，禮以行事，事有其物，物有其容。今君之容，非其物也; 而女不見，是不明也。」

"You are the ruler's eyes, and in command of the management of clear seeing. Clothes are for manifesting *li*, and *li* is for enacting tasks (*xing shi* 行事). Serving (*shi* 事) involves *wu* 物 (things), and *wu* 物 (things) have their visible features (*rong* 容). Now the ruler's visible features (*rong* 容) are contrary to the matter (*wu* 物). You did not see. That is not clear-sighted."

A more tentative connection of *wu* 物 to vision is implied in two passages below.

物有同狀而異所者，有異狀而同所者，可別也。狀同而為異所者，雖可合，謂之二實。狀變而實無別而為異者，謂之化。有化而無別，謂之一實。

Things (*wu* 物) include those of the same look (*zhuang* 狀) and different locations and those of a different look in the same location, which can be separated (*bie* 別). If the look is the same but the location is deemed different, although they can be united, call them two *shi* 實 (fruit/action/deeds). If the look changes but the *shi* 實 (fruit, action, deed) has no separation (*bie* 別), although it is deemed different, call it transformed. If it is transformed but there is no separation (*bie* 別), call it one *shi* 實 (fruit/action/deeds).

Xunzi 荀子 正名篇第二十二

If we keep in mind that *shi* 實 (action/thing) is paradigmatically visible, that *zhuang* 狀 (one's look) is visible appearance, and that locations tend to be perceived through the eyes, then *wu* 物 falls within the visible range.

In the following passage, the *wu* 物 seems more directly related to the shape (*xing* 形) than it is to the name (*ming* 名).

物固有形，形固有名 。

Wu firmly possess shapes (*xing* 形). Shapes (*xing* 形) firmly possess *ming* 名 (name, fame).

Guanzi 管子 管子卷第十三 心術上第三十六

In short, a *wu* 物 seems to signal primarily visual things, and perhaps its extension to mean all things implies that things are paradigmatically visible.

Xing 行 (*visual*): walk, act

This entry expands on my discussion of the visual associations of *xing* 行 in chapter 7 of *Language as Bodily Practice*. The term *xing* 行, which is typically visual, is used to mean to "walk" or to "act."

> 然後聖人聽其言,迹其行。。。
> The sages listened to their speech, retraced their *xing* . . .
> *Mozi* 墨子卷二 2.2 《尚賢中第九》

While nonhumans are also able to *xing* 行, when the term is used in relation to humans in particular, it can also be translated as "conduct" or the more general "behavior." For the purposes of my argument, however, those translations are misleading, for both "conduct" and "behavior" can be taken to mean what people say as well as what they do. Or perhaps more to the point, from the perspective of performative language, "saying" can be taken to mean "doing." Because, as I argue, texts from Early China consistently demonstrate a parallelism (often in the form of a contrast) between saying and doing, translations that potentially conflate the two obscure a crucial feature of early Chinese ideas about "language." Translating *xing* as "action" does not entirely evade that problem, but it seems to be the best way to signal a difference between the sounds that people make and their (visible) bodily actions.[21]

Yan 言 (aural): speech

To fully appreciate the difference between uses of the terms *yan* 言 (speech) and "language," it is important to note that people's character and intentions are reflected in their *yan* 言.

> 言、身之文也。
> *Yan* 言 (speech) is the embellishment of the body/person (*shen* 身).
> *Zuozhuan* 春秋左傳 僖公 B5.24 《僖公二十四年傳》

The link between *yan* 言 and the body/person is even more apparent when *yan* emerges from the mouth.

> 惡言出於口。
> Bad *yan* 言 (speech) comes out from the mouth.
> *Guanzi* 管子卷第十一 小稱第三十二

> 4.70 其言吶吶然如不出諸其口。
> His *yan* 言 (speech) was like stuttering, as if he could not get it out of his mouth.
> *Liji* 禮記 〈檀弓下〉

---

21. See also Geaney, *Epistemology of the Senses*, 50–84.

23.36 壹出言而不敢忘父母, 是故惡言不出於口, 忿言不反於身。
In emitting (chu 出) one yan 言 (speech), he should not forget his parents, and thus bad yan 言 would not issue from his mouth, and angry yan 言 would not reflect on his body/person (shen 身).
Liji 禮記 〈祭義〉

氣發言。
Qi expresses (fa 發) yan 言.
Lunheng 論衡 《紀妖篇》

The verbs describe yan 言 as being "emitted" (chu 出) or "issued" (fa 發). We do not say that "language" emerges from the body; hence, either the abstraction "language" is not an appropriate translation term or, conversely, its use for yan in early Chinese texts requires us to reconceive what we mean by language.

2.28 發而安中者言也, 久而可觀者行也。
Yan 言 is what is issued (fa 發) and pacifies the middle.
Actions (xing 行*) are what endures and can be observed (guan 觀*).
Hanshi Waizhuan 韓詩外傳 韓詩外傳卷第二

11.1 子貢曰:「出言陳辭, 身之得失, 國之安危也。」
Emitting (chu 出) yan 言 and arranging phrases (ci 辭*) is the person's gain or loss and the state's peace or danger.
Shouyuan 說苑 善說

7.24 先生何為出此言也?
Master, why do you emit (chu 出) such yan 言?
Mengzi 孟子 《離婁上》

In accordance with being something that comes out of the mouth, yan 言 is sound, which parallels between hearing and seeing make apparent.

12.20 察言而觀色
[A person of achievement (da 達)] examines people's yan 言 and observes (guan 觀) their countenances.
Lunyu 論語 〈顏淵〉第十二

孝子言為可聞, 行為可見。
Filial children's yan 言 is what is possible to hear, and their actions (xing 行) are what is possible to see.
Xunzi 荀子 大略篇第二十七

5.10 今吾於人也, 聽其言而觀其行。
Nowadays, in my dealings with others, upon listening to their *yan* 言, I observe (*guan* 觀) their action (*xing* 行).
Lunyu 論語 〈公冶長〉第五

2.18 多聞闕疑, 慎言其餘, 則寡尤;
多見闕殆, 慎行其餘, 則寡悔。
If you listen (*wen* 聞) broadly, set aside the doubtful, and cautiously *yan* 言 on the rest, you will make few errors.
If you look (*jian* 見) broadly, set aside what is perilous, and cautiously act (*xing* 行) on the rest, you will have few regrets.
Lunyu 論語 〈為政〉第二

然後聖人聽其言, 迹其行, 察其所能。
Afterward, the sages listened to their *yan* 言, retraced their action (*xing* 行), and examined (*cha* 察) their capabilities.
Mozi 墨子 墨子卷二 2.2 《尚賢中第九》

辯士〔之〕言可聽也, 其所以言不可形也。
Discerning scholars' *yan* 言 can be heard, but what makes them *yan* 言 cannot be given form (*xing* 形).
Huainanzi 淮南子 齊俗訓

13.16 及其聞一善言, 見一善行, 若決江河, 沛然莫之能禦也。
When he heard a single good *yan* 言, or saw a single good action (*xing* 行), he was like the bursting of a stream or a river, so overwhelming that none could withstand it.
Mengzi 孟子 《盡心上》

7.15 聽其言也, 觀其眸子, 人焉廋哉?
Listen to a person's *yan* 言 and look at his/her pupils: how can the person be concealed?
Mengzi 孟子 《離婁上》

聽言之道 必以其事觀之
The way of listening to *yan* 言 is certainly using its service/deeds (*shi* 事) to observe (*guan* 觀) it.
Dadai Liji 大戴禮記 大戴禮記卷第二 《禮察第四十六》

References to writing in later texts continue to align *yan* 言 (speech) with sound.

言、心聲也，書、心畫也。
Yan is the sound of the heartmind (*xin* 心), and writing is the paintings of the heartmind.
Fayan 法言 問神卷第五

聖人矢口而成言，肆筆而成書，言可聞而不可殫，書可觀而不可盡。
Sages [shoot] arrows from their mouths and thereby bring their *yan* 言 to completion.
They let loose their brushes and thereby bring their writings to completion.
Their *yan* 言 can be heard and cannot be depleted.
Their writings can be observed (*guan* 觀) and cannot be exhausted.
Fayan 法言 五百卷第八

To expand on my discussion of the association of *yan* 言 and *yi* 意 in chapters 2 and 3 as something that issues from, emerges from, proclaims, or expresses something about a person, *yan* 言 is a source for getting *yi* 意 (what is on the heartmind).

意出於性，言出於意。
Yi 意 emerges from spontaneous disposition (*xing* 性).
Yan 言 emerges from *yi* 意.[22]
"Heng Xian" 楚竹書十二《恒先》四

The *Zhuangzi* asserts that the purpose of speech lies in the *yi* 意 (what is on the heartmind).

言者所以在意，得意而忘言。
The purpose of *yan* 言 is in the *yi* 意.
[We/I] get the *yi* 意 and forget the *yan* 言.

Zhuangzi 莊子 外物第二十六

The *Lüshi Chunqiu* features a similar claim that extends the assertion about speech to one about phrases (*ci* 辭).

---

22. The translation is tentative. See Goldin, "*Heng Xian* and the Problem of Studying Looted Artifacts," 153–160; and Brindley, Goldin, and Klein, "A Philosophical Translation of the *Heng Xian*," 145–151.

言者，以諭意也.
夫辭者，意之表也。
鑒其表而棄其意、悖。故古之人，得其意則舍其言矣。聽言者以言觀意也。
聽言而意不可知，其與橋言無擇。

Yan 言 is for proclaiming yi 意.
Phrasings (ci 辭) are exterior signs of yi 意.
To reflect on the sign but discard the yi 意 is unruliness.
Thus, people of old discarded the yan 言 when they obtained the yi 意.
Listening to yan 言 is for observing (guan 觀) yi 意.
If you listen to the yan 言 and the yi 意 cannot be known, there is no way to pick that out from crazy yan 言.
Lüshi Chunqiu 呂氏春秋 審應覽第六 《離謂》

The purpose of speech, according to the following passage from the *Lüshi Chunqiu*, is for proclaiming the mind.

言不欺心，則近之矣。凡言者，以諭心也。
When yan 言 does not cheat the heartmind (xin 心), that comes close to it.
Now, yan 言 is for proclaiming the heartmind (xin 心).
Lüshi Chunqiu 呂氏春秋 審應覽第六 《淫辭》

People can reveal what is in their heartminds either by actions (which are visible) or by speech (which is audible).

中心懷而不諭，(其)〔故〕疾趨卑拜而明之;
實心愛而不知，故好言繁辭以信之。
When one's inner heartmind (xin 心) harbors something but has not proclaimed it, [one] quickly hastens and bows low to show it.
When one's full (shi 實*) heartmind (xin 心) loves something but has not made it known, then [one uses] good yan 言 and complex phrasing (ci 辭) to accredit it.
Hanfeizi 韓非子 解老第二十

Yan 言 is the source for getting things related to the heartmind, because yan 言 is not an abstraction but, rather, something like speech or utterances that emerge from the person. The *Shiming* (potentially as late as the second century) describes speech as something that speaks one's yi.

又曰言, 言其意也。
It is also said, *yan* 言 is *yan* 言-ing one's *yi* 意.
Shiming 釋名 《釋名第六卷》釋書契第十九

The *Lunheng* characterizes good *yan* 言 as emerging from the *yi* 意. It also describes a "shared root" with actions that come from the heartmind.

人君有[善言]善行, 善行動於心, 善言出於意, 同由共本, 一氣不異。
When noble people act (*xing* 行) well, their good actions move from their heartminds (*xin* 心), and their good *yan* 言 emerge from their *yi* 意. Together, they come from a shared root, and are one qi without differentiation.
Lunheng 論衡 《變虛篇》

The shared root could be the *yi* 意 and the heartmind insofar as *yi* 意 is understood as being near the location of the heartmind. The *yi* 意 and the heartmind also have or share a single (or unified) bit of qi.

The following example implies that speech is the source (although not an exhaustive source) of *yi* 意, while writing is the source (also not an exhaustive source) of speech.

書不盡言, 言不盡意
Writing does not exhaust *yan* 言, and *yan* 言 does not exhaust *yi* 意.
Zhouyi 周易 《繫辭上》

A passage in the *Hanshu* (first century) advocates speaking directly to exhaust one's *yi* 意 and not to assume any taboos on names.

直言盡意, 無有所諱。
Directly *yan* 言 and exhaust one's *yi* 意, without having anything be unmentionable (tabooed).
Hanshu 漢書 本紀 《元帝紀第九》

Speech, while not as close to the heartmind as *yi* 意, is closer than shapes, ponderings, and knowledge.

心之中又有心。意以先言, 意然後刑, 刑然后思, 思然后知。

> Within the heartmind there is another heartmind. The *yi* 意 comes before *yan* 言. After *yi* 意, there are shapes. After shapes, there is pondering. After pondering, there is knowing.[23]
>
> *Guanzi* 管子卷第十三 心術下第三十七

Yi 意 is something that can be gotten from listening, presumably to speech.[24]

> 10.1.82 聞、耳之聰也。
> 10.1.84 循所聞而得其意, 心(也)[之]察也。
> Hearing is the keenness of the ear.
> Following what you hear and getting its *yi* 意: that is the heartmind's examining.
>
> *Mozi* 墨子卷十 10.1 《《經上第四十》》

With speaking, the *yi* 意 becomes visible ("gets seen").

> 10.1.86 言、口之利也。
> 10.1.88 執所言而意得見, 心之辯也。
> *Yan* 言 is the fluency of the mouth.
> Grasping what is *yan* 言-ed, and the *yi* 意 getting visibility: that is the heartmind's discriminating.
>
> *Mozi* 墨子卷十 10.1 《《經上第四十》》

---

23. A second example might be corrupted because *yan* appears in more than one location in the sequence. Still, the passage affirms a link between speech and *yi* (or tones, *yin* 音, depending on how the graph is read).

> 心之中又有心(馬)[焉]。彼心之心, (音)[意]以先言。(音)[意]然后形, 形然后言。言然后使, 使然后治。
> Within the mind there is another mind. Within that mind's mind, the *yi/yin* (tone) comes before *yan*. After the *yi/yin* (tone), there are shapes. After shapes, there is *yan*. After *yan*, there is serving, after serving there is order.
>
> *Guanzi* 管子卷第十六 內業四十九

24. See also the discussion of the Mo Bian 10.1.82 in Geaney, *Language as Bodily Practice*, chapter 6.

Bibliography

Chinese Classical Works

Unless otherwise noted, all references are to Chinese Ancient Texts (CHANT) database.

Baihu tong 白虎通
Cai Zhonglang Ji 蔡中郎集
Chuci 楚辭
Chunqiu Fanlu 春秋繁露
Chunqiu Gongyangzhuan 春秋公羊傳
Chunqiu Guliangzhuan 春秋穀梁傳
Chunqiu Zuozhuan 春秋左傳
Dadai Liji 大戴禮記
"Dao Yuan" 《道原》
Dengxizi 鄧析子
Dongguan Hanji 東觀漢記
Erya 爾雅
Fangyan 方言
Fayan 法言
Fengsu tongyi 風俗通義
Gongsun Longzi 公孫龍子
Guanzi 管子
Guoyu 國語
Hanfeizi 韓非子
Hanshi waizhuan 韓詩外傳
Hanshu 漢書
Heguanzi 鶡冠子
"Heng Xian" 《恒先》
Hou Hanshu 後漢書
Huainanzi 淮南子
Huangdi Neijing 黃帝內經
Kongcongzi 孔叢子
Kongzi Jiayu 孔子家語
Laozi 老子
Lienu zhuan

Liezi 列子
Liji 禮記
"Liude" 《六德》
Lunheng 論衡
Lunyu 論語
Lüshi Chunqiu 呂氏春秋
Maoshi 毛詩
Mengzi 孟子
"Min Zhi Fumu" 《民之父母》
Mozi 墨子
"Mu He" 《繆和》 See Shaughnessy, *I Ching*
Qianfu Lun 潛夫論
Qian Hanji 前漢紀
Simafa 司馬法
Shangjun Shu 商君書
Shangshu 尚書
Shangshu Dazhuan 尚書大傳
Shanhai Jing 山海經
Shiji 史記
"Shiliu Jing" 《十六經》
Shiming 釋名
Shizi 尸子
Shuijing Zhu 水經注
"Shun Dao" 《順道》
"Shuo Gua" 《說卦》
Shuowen Jiezi 說文解字 Chinese Text Project, edited by Donald Sturgeon, http://ctext.org/
Shuowen Jiezi Zhu 說文解字注 Searchable online text maintained by Alain Lucas and Jean-Louis Schott at the École française d'Extrême-Orient
Shuoyuan 說苑
Taiping Jing 太平經
Taixuan Jing 太玄經
"Tang Yu Zhi Dao" 《唐虞之道》
"Tuan" 《彖》
Weilaozi 尉繚子
Wenxin Diaolong 總術第四十四《文心雕龍》《卷九》《總術》 Chinese Text Project, https://ctext.org.
"Wenyan" 《文言》
Wenzi 文子
"Wuxing" 《五行》
Wu Yue Chunqiu 吳越春秋
"Xiang" 《象》
Xiaojing 孝經
"Xici" 《繫辭》
"Xingqing Lun" 《性情論》
"Xing Zi Ming Chu" 《性自命出》

Xinshu 新書
Xinyu 新語
Xunzi 荀子
Yantie Lun 鹽鐵論
Yanzi Chunqiu 晏子春秋
Yili 儀禮
"Yi Zhi Yi" 《易之義》. See Shaughnessy, *I Ching*
Yi Zhou Shu 逸周書
"Yuan Dao" 《道原》
"Yucong Yi" 《語叢一》
Yuejue Shu 越絕書
Zhanguo ce 戰國策
"Zhao Li" 《昭力》 See Shaughnessy, *I Ching*
Zhonglun 中論
Zhoubi Suanjing 周髀算經
Zhouli 周禮
Zhouyi 周易
Zhuangzi 莊子
"Ziyi" 《緇衣》

Secondary Sources

Allen, Joseph R. "The Babel Fallacy: When Translation Does Not Matter." *Culture Critique* 102 (2019): 117–150.

———. "I Will Speak, Therefore, of a Graph: A Chinese Metalanguage." *Language in Society* 21 (1992): 189–206.

Ames, Roger T. *Confucian Role Ethics: A Vocabulary*. Honolulu: University of Hawai'i Press, 2016.

———. "Meaning as Imaging: Prolegomena to a Confucian Epistemology." In *Culture and Modernity: East-West Philosophic Perspectives*, edited by Eliot Deutsch, 227–244. Honolulu: University of Hawai'i Press, 1991.

———. "The Meaning of the Body in Classical Chinese Philosophy." In *Self as Body in Asian Theory and Practice*, edited by Thomas P. Kasulis, Roger T. Ames, and Wimal Dissanayake, 157–177. Albany: State University of New York Press, 1993.

———. "Putting the Te Back into Taoism." In *Nature in Asian Traditions of Thought: Essays in Environmental Philosophy*, edited by J. Baird Callicott and Roger T. Ames, 113–144. Albany: State University of New York Press, 1989.

———. *Sun-tzu: The Art of Warfare: The First English Translation Incorporating the Recently Discovered Yin-ch'üeh-shan Texts*. New York: Ballantine Books, 1993.

———. "Were the Early Confucians Virtuous?" In *Ethics in Early China: An Anthology*, edited by Chris Fraser, Dan Robins, and Timothy O'Leary, 17–39. Hong Kong: Hong Kong University Press, 2011.

Ames, Roger T., and David L. Hall. *Focusing the Familiar: A Translation and Philosophical Interpretation of the "Zhongyong."* Honolulu: University of Hawai'i Press, 2001.

Ames, Roger T., and Henry Rosemont, trans. *The Analects of Confucius: A Philosophical Translation*. New York: Ballantine Books, 1999.
Andersen, Poul. "Concepts of Meaning in Chinese Ritual." *Cahiers D'Extrême-Asie* 12, no. 1 (2001): 155–183. doi:10.3406/asie.2001.1169.
Andresen, Julie Tetel. *Linguistics and Evolution: A Developmental Approach*. Cambridge: Cambridge University Press, 2013.
Angle, Stephen C., and John A. Gordon. "'Dao' as a Nickname." *Asian Philosophy* 13, no. 1 (2003): 15–27. doi:10.1080/09552360301666.
Arditi, Jorge. "Role as a Cultural Concept." *Theory and Society* 16, no. 4 (1987): 565–591.
Asad, Talal. *Genealogies of Religion: Discipline and Reasons of Power in Christianity and Islam*. Baltimore: Johns Hopkins University Press, 1993.
Bal, Mieke. *Travelling Concepts in the Humanities: A Rough Guide*. Toronto: University of Toronto Press, 2002.
Bao, Zhiming. "Abstraction, *Ming-Shi* and Problems of Translation." *Journal of Chinese Philosophy* 14, no. 4 (1987): 419–444. doi:10.1111/j.1540-6253.1987.tb00352.x.
———. "Language and World View in Ancient China." *Philosophy East and West* 40, no. 2 (1990): 195–219. doi:10.2307/1399228.
Baratin, M., B. Cassin, I. Rosier-Catach, F. Ildefonse, J. Lallot, and J. Léon. "Word." In *Dictionary of Untranslatables*, edited by B. Cassin, E. Apter, J. Lezra, and M. Wood. Princeton, NJ: Princeton University Press, 2013.
Barreto, Cristiano Mahaut de Barros. "Translation and Metalanguage in *Laozi*: A Perspectivist Approach." PhD diss., Pontificia Universidade Catolica, 2015.
Baxter, William Hubbard, and Laurent Sagart. *Old Chinese: A New Reconstruction*. Oxford: Oxford University Press, 2014. http://ocbaxtersagart.lsait.lsa.umich.edu/BaxterSagartOCbyMandarinMC2014-09-20.pdf.
Behr, Wolfgang. "Language Change in Premodern China: Notes on Its Perception and Impact on the Idea of a 'Constant Way.'" In *Historical Truth, Historical Criticism, and Ideology: Chinese Historiography and Historical Culture from a New Comparative Perspective*, edited by Helwig Schmidt-Glintzer, Achim Mittag, and Jörn Rüsen, 13–51. Leiden: Brill, 2005.
———. "Role of Language in Early Chinese Constructions of Ethnic Identity." *Journal of Chinese Philosophy* 37, no. 4 (2010): 567–587. doi:10.1111/j.1540-6253.2010.01605.x.
———. "'To Translate' Is 'To Exchange' 譯者言易也—Linguistic Diversity and the Terms for Translation in Ancient China." In *Mapping Meanings: The Field of New Learning in Late Qing China*, edited by Michael Lackner and Natscha Vittinghoff, 173–209. Leiden: Brill, 2004.
Berg, R. M. van den. *Context: Ancient Theories of Language and Naming*. Leiden: Brill, 2008.
Berger, Douglas. "Did Buddhism Ever Go East? The Westernization of Buddhism in Chad Hansen's Daoist Historiography." *Philosophy East and West* 61, no. 1 (2011): 38–55.
Berkson, Mark. "Language: The Guest of Reality—Zhuangzi and Derrida on Language, Reality, and Skillfulness." In *Essays on Skepticism, Relativism and Ethics in the Zhuangzi*, edited by Paul Kjellberg and P. J. Ivanhoe, 97–126. Albany: State University of New York Press, 1996.
Billeter, Jean François. "Stopping, Seeing and Language: An Interpretation of Zhuangzi's *Qi Wulun*." Translated by Mark Elvin. *East Asian History* 15/16 (1998): 1–32.

Blakeley, Barry B. "'On the Authenticity and Nature of the *Zuo Zhuan*' Revisited." *Early China* 29 (2004): 217–267.
Boltz, William. "Composite Nature of Early Chinese Texts." In *Text and Ritual in Early China*, edited by Martin Kern, 50–78. Seattle: University of Washington Press, 2011.
———. "*Hsiao Ching* 孝經." In *Early Chinese Texts: A Bibliographical Guide*, edited by Michael Loewe, 141–153. Berkeley: Society for the Study of Early China; Institute of East Asian Studies, University of California, 1993.
———. *The Origin and Early Development of the Chinese Writing System*. New Haven, CT: American Oriental Society, 1994.
———. "Where Have All the Prefixes Gone?" *Asiatische Studien* 3–4 (2007): 755–773.
———. "Why So Many *Laozi*-s?" In *Studies in Chinese Manuscripts: From the Warring States Period to the 20th Century*, edited by Imre Galambos, 1–32. Budapest: Institute of East Asian Studies, Eötvös Loránd University, 2013.
Boodberg, Peter A. "The Chinese Script: An Essay on Nomenclature (the First Hecaton)." *Bulletin of the Institute of History and Philology, Academia Sinica* 29 (1957): 113–120.
———. "Semasiology of Some Primary Confucian Concepts." *Philosophy East and West* 2, no. 4 (1953): 317–332.
Bottéro, Françoise. "Revisiting the *wen* 文 and the *zi* 字: The Great Chinese Characters Hoax." *Bulletin of the Museum of Far Eastern Antiquities* 74 (2002): 14–33.
Bottéro, Françoise, and Christoph Harbsmeier. "The *Shuowen Jiezi* Dictionary and the Human Sciences in China." *Asia Major* 21, no. 1 (2008): 249–271.
Boucher, Daniel. "Gāndhārī and the Early Chinese Buddhist Translations Reconsidered: The Case of the Saddharmapuṇḍarīkasūtra." *Journal of the American Oriental Society* 118, no. 4 (1998): 471–506. doi:10.2307/604783.
———. "On *Hu* and *Fan* Again: The Transmission of 'Barbarian' Manuscripts to China." *Journal of the International Association of Buddhist Studies* 23, no. 1 (2000): 7–28.
Boudeinjnse, Barbara. "The Conceptualization of Ritual: A History of Its Problematic Aspects." *Jaarboek voor Literugieonderzoek* 11 (1995): 31–56.
Branner, David Prager. "On Early Chinese Morphology and Its Intellectual History." *Journal of the Royal Asiatic Society JRAS* 13, no. 1 (2003): 45–76. doi:10.1017/s1356186302003000.
———. "Phonology in the Chinese Script and Its Relationship to Early Chinese Literacy." In *Writing and Literacy in Early China: Studies from the Columbia Early China Seminar*, edited by Li Feng and David Prager Branner, 85–137. Seattle: University of Washington Press, 2011.
Brashier, Kenneth. *Public Memory in Early China*. Cambridge: Harvard University Press, 2014.
Bremmer, Jan N. "Religion, Ritual, and the Opposition of Sacred and Profane." In *Ansichten Griecher Rituale. Geburtstags-Symposium für Walter Burkert*, edited by F. Graf, 9–32. Stuttgart: B. G. Teubner, 1998.
Brindley, Erica F. *Music, Cosmology, and the Politics of Harmony in Early China*. Albany: State University of New York Press, 2012.
Brindley, Erica F., Paul R. Goldin, and Esther S. Klein, trans. "A Philosophical Translation of the *Heng Xian*." *Dao: A Journal of Comparative Philosophy* 12, no. 2 (2013): 145–151. doi:10.1007/s11712-013-9322-5.

Brooks, E. Bruce, and A. Taeko Brooks. *The Original Analects: Sayings of Confucius and His Successors*. New York: Columbia University Press, 1998.

Brown, Miranda, and Uffe Bergeton. "'Seeing' Like a Sage: Three Takes on Identity and Perception in Early China." *Journal of Chinese Philosophy* 35, no. 4 (2008): 641–662. doi:10.1111/j.1540-6253.2008.00509.x.

Bruya, Brian. Review of *Text and Ritual in Early China*, edited by Martin Kern. *China Review International* 14, no. 2 (2007): 338–354.

Bullock, Jeffrey S., trans. *Fayan*. Chinese Text Project. Edited by Donald Sturgeon. http://ctext.org/

Cai, Zong-qi. *A Chinese Literary Mind: Culture, Creativity and Rhetoric in "Wenxin Diaolong."* Stanford, CA: Stanford University Press, 2001.

———. "The Early Philosophical Discourse on Language and Reality and Lu Ji's and Liu Xie's Theories of Literary Creation." *Frontiers of Literary Studies in China* 5, no. 4 (2011): 477–510. doi:10.1007/s11702-011-0139-5.

———. "The Richness of Ambiguity: A Mencian Statement and Interpretive Theory and Practice in Premodern China," *Journal of Chinese Literature and Culture* 1, no. 1–2 (2014): 262–288.

———. "Toward an Innovative Poetics: Wang Changling on *Yi* 意 and Literary Creation," *Journal of Chinese Literature and Culture* 4, no. 1 (2017): 180–207.

Cao, Feng 曹峰. 《老子》首章与"名"相关问题的重新审视——以北大汉简《老子》的问世为契机 "'Laozi' shou zhang yu 'ming' xiangguan wenti de chongxin shenshi—yi bei dahan jian 'Laozi' de wenshi wei qiji." 《哲学研究》 *Zhe xue yan jiu* 4 (2011): 58–67.

———. "A New Approach to Pre-Qin Discourse on Name," *Frontiers of Philosophy in China* 3, no. 2 (2008): 220, 224–225.

———. 《荀子·正名》篇新论 "Xunzi 'Zhengming' pian xin lun." 《儒林》 *Ru Lin* 4 (2008): 268–282.

———. 《尹文子》所见名思想的研究 "'Yin Wenzi' suo jian ming sixiang yanjiu." 《新哲学》 *Xin zhe xue* 7 (2008): 144–162.

Carr, Michael. "The *Shi* 'Corpse/Personator' Ceremony in Early China." In *Reflections on the Dawn of Consciousness: Julian Jaynes's Bicameral Mind Theory Revisited*, edited by Marcel Kuijsten, 343–416. Henderson, NV: Julian Jaynes Society, 2006.

Chan, Alan Kam-leung. "Harmony as a Contested Metaphor." In *How Should One Live? Comparing Ethics in Ancient China and Greco-Roman Antiquity*, edited by R. A. H. King and Dennis Schilling, 37–62. Berlin: De Gruyter, 2011.

———, ed. *Mencius: Contexts and Interpretations*. Honolulu: University of Hawai'i Press, 2002.

Chang, I-jen, William Boltz, and Michael Loewe. "*Kuo yü* 國語." In *Early Chinese Texts: A Bibliographical Guide*, edited by Michael Loewe, 263–268. Berkeley: Society for the Study of Early China; Institute of East Asian Studies, University of California, 1993.

Chang, Wonsuk. "Reflections on Time and Related Ideas in the *Yijing*." *Philosophy East and West* 59, no. 2 (2009): 216–229. doi:10.1353/pew.0.0047.

Chao, Y. R. *A Grammar of Spoken Chinese*. Berkeley: University of California Press, 1968.

Chemla, Karine. "Shedding Some Light on a Possible Origin of a Concept of Fractions in China: Division as a Link between the Newly Discovered Manuscripts and 'The Gnomon of the Zhou [Dynasty].'" *Sudhoffs Archiv* 97, no. 2 (2013): 174–198.

Chen, Guying 陳鼓應. *Zhouyi zhuyi yu yanjiu* 周易注譯與研究 [Commentary and research on the *Zhouyi*]. Taibei: Taiwan Shangwu yinshuguan, 1999.

Cheung, Martha P. Y. *An Anthology of Chinese Discourse on Translation*. Kinderhoek, NY: St. Jerome Publishing, 2006.

Chien, Chi-Hui. "'Theft's Way' A Comparative Study of Chuang Tzu's Tao and Derridean Trace." *Journal of Chinese Philosophy* 17, no. 1 (1990): 31–49. doi:10.1111/j.1540-6253.1990.tb00031.x.

Chow, Rey. "How (the) Inscrutable Chinese Led to Globalized Theory." *PMLA* 116, no. 1 (January 2001): 69–74.

Coblin, W. South. "*Erh ya* 爾雅." In *Early Chinese Texts: A Bibliographical Guide*, edited by Michael Loewe, 94–99. Berkeley: Society for the Study of Early China; Institute of East Asian Studies, University of California, 1993.

Connery, Christopher Leigh. *The Empire of the Text: Writing and Authority in Early Imperial China*. Lanham, MD: Rowman & Littlefield, 1998.

Cook, Scott. "Xunzi on Ritual and Music." *Monumenta Serica* 45 (1997): 1–38.

Course, Magnus. "The Birth of the Word: Language, Force, and Mapuche Ritual Authority." *Journal of Ethnographic Theory* 2, no. 1 (2012): 1–26.

Crump, J. I., trans. *Chan-kuo Ts'e*. Oxford: Clarendon, 1970.

Csikszentmihalyi, Mark. *Material Virtue: Ethics and the Body in Early China*. Leiden: Brill, 2004.

Cua, Antonio. "Virtues of *Junzi*." In *Confucian Ethics in Retrospect and Prospect*, edited by Qingsong Shen and Kwong-loi Shun, 7–26. Washington, DC: Council for Research in Values and Philosophy, 2008.

Cullen, Christopher. "*Chou pi suan ching* 周髀算經." In *Early Chinese Texts: A Bibliographical Guide*, edited by Michael Loewe, 33–38. Berkeley: Society for the Study of Early China; Institute of East Asian Studies, University of California, 1993.

———. *The Suan shu shu* 筭數書 *"Writings on Reckoning": A Translation of a Chinese Mathematical Collection of the Second Century BC, with Explanatory Commentary*. Cambridge, UK: Needham Research Institute, 2004.

Dang, Shengyuan, and John Makeham, trans. *Balanced Discourses: A Bilingual Edition*. Beijing: Foreign Languages Press, 2004.

Daston, Lorraine, and Peter Galison. *Objectivity*. New York: Zone Books, 2007.

Davidson, Donald. *Inquiries into Truth and Interpretation*. Oxford: Clarendon, 1984.

———. "A Nice Derangement of Epitaphs." In *Philosophical Grounds of Rationality: Intentions, Categories, Ends*, edited by Richard Grandy and Richard Warner. Oxford: Oxford University Press, 1986.

———. "On the Very Idea of a Conceptual Scheme." *Proceedings and Addresses of the American Philosophical Association* 47 (1974): 5–20.

Defoort, Carine. "Excavated Manuscripts and Political Thought: Cao Feng on Early Chinese Texts." *Contemporary Chinese Thought* 44 (2013): 3–9.

———. "Instruction Dialogues in the *Zhuangzi*: An 'Anthropological' Reading." *Dao: A Journal of Comparative Philosophy* 11, no. 4 (2012): 459–478. doi:10.1007/s11712-012-9294-x.

———. *The Pheasant Cap Master (He Guan Zi): A Rhetorical Reading*. Albany: State University of New York Press, 1997.

———. "The Profit That Does Not Profit: Paradoxes with *Li* in Early Chinese Texts." *Asia Major* 21, no. 1 (2008): 153–188.

———. "Ruling the World with Words: The Idea of *Zhengming* in the *Shizi*." *Bulletin of the Museum of Far Eastern Antiquities* 1 (2001): 217–242.

DeFrancis, John. *The Chinese Language: Fact and Fantasy.* Honolulu: University of Hawai'i Press, 1984.

———. *Visible Speech: The Diverse Oneness of Writing Systems.* Honolulu: University of Hawai'i Press, 1989.

DeFrancis, John, and J. Marshall Unger. "Rejoinder to Geoffrey Sampson, 'Chinese Script and the Diversity of Writing Systems.'" *Linguistics* 32, no. 3 (1994): 549–554. doi:10.1515/ling.1994.32.3.549.

De Grazia, Margreta. "Words as Things." *Shakespeare Studies* 28 (2000): 231–235.

Derrida, Jacques. *Of Grammatology.* Baltimore: Johns Hopkins University Press, 1976.

Descombes, Vincent. "The Quandaries of the Referent." In *The Limits of Theory*, edited by Thomas M. Kavanagh, 51–75. Stanford, CA: Stanford University Press, 1989.

DeWoskin, Kenneth J. *A Song for One or Two: Music and the Concept of Art in Early China.* Ann Arbor: Center for Chinese Studies, University of Michigan, 1982.

Dixon, Robert M. W., and Alexandra Aikhenvald. *Word: A Cross-Linguistic Typology.* Cambridge: Cambridge University Press, 2002.

Dubs, Homer. *Hsuntze: The Moulder of Ancient Confucianism.* London: Probsthain, 1927.

Durrant, Stephen. "*Yen tzu ch'un ch'iu* 晏子春秋." In *Early Chinese Texts: A Bibliographical Guide*, edited by Michael Loewe, 483–489. Berkeley: Society for the Study of Early China; Institute of East Asian Studies, University of California, 1993.

Durrant, Stephen, Wai-yee Li, and David Schaberg, trans. *Zuo Tradition/"Zuozhuan": Commentary on the "Spring and Autumn Annals."* Seattle: University of Washington Press, 2016.

Duyvendak, J. J. L. *The Book of Lord Shang: A Classic of the School of Law.* London: Probsthain, 1928.

Ekstroem, M. S. "Illusion, Lie, and Metaphor: The Paradox of Divergence in Early Chinese Poetics." *Poetics Today* 23, no. 2 (2002): 251–289. doi:10.1215/03335372-23-2-251.

Els, Paul Van. "The Philosophy of Proto-*Wenzi*." In *Dao Companion to Daoist Philosophy*, edited by Xiaogan Liu, 325–340. New York: Springer, 2015.

Eno, Robert. *The Confucian Creation of Heaven.* Albany: State University of New York Press, 1990.

Erbaugh, Mary S. *Difficult Characters: Interdisciplinary Studies of Chinese and Japanese Writing.* Columbus, OH: National East Asian Languages Resource Center, Ohio State University, 2002.

Fech, Andre. "Auditory Perception and Cultivation: The *Wenzi* 文子." In *Cultivating a Good Life in Early Chinese and Ancient Greek Philosophy: Perspectives and Reverberations*, edited by Karyn Lai, Rick Benitez, and Hyun Jin Kim, 208–220. London: Bloomsbury Academic 2019.

Fehr, Johannes, and Petr Kouba, eds. *Dynamic Structure: Language as an Open System.* Prague: Litteraria Pragensia, 2007.

Fingarette, Herbert. *Confucius: The Secular as Sacred.* New York: Harper & Row, 1972.

Forke, Alfred, trans. *Lun-Heng: Philosophical Essays of Wang Ch'ung*. 2 vols. London: Leipzig, 1907.

Fraser, Chris. "Language and Logic in the *Xunzi*." In *Dao Companion to the Philosophy of Xunzi*, edited by Eric L. Hutton, 291–321. New York: Springer, 2016.

———. "Language and Ontology in Early Chinese Thought." *Philosophy East and West* 57, no. 4 (2007): 420–456. doi:10.1353/pew.2007.0045.

———. "The Limitations of Ritual Propriety: Ritual and Language in *Xúnzǐ* and *Zhuāngzǐ*." *Sophia* 51, no. 12 (2012): 257–282.

———. "Mohism." In *Stanford Encyclopedia of Philosophy*. Winter 2020. https://plato.stanford.edu/archives/win2020/entries/mohism/.

———. "Mohist Canons." In *Stanford Encyclopedia of Philosophy*. September 13, 2005. http://plato.stanford.edu/archives/fall2013/entries/mohist-canons/.

———. "School of Names." In *Stanford Encyclopedia of Philosophy*. Winter 2015. http://plato.stanford.edu/archives/win2015/entries/school-names/.

Fraser, Chris, Dan Robins, and Timothy O'Leary, eds. *Ethics in Early China: An Anthology*. Hong Kong: Hong Kong University Press, 2011.

Fung, Yu-lan. *A History of Chinese Philosophy*. Vol. 2. Translated by Derk Bodde. Princeton, NJ: Princeton University Press, 1983.

Furniss, Ingred. "Unearthing China's Informal Musicians: An Archaeological and Textual Study of the Shang to Tang Periods." *Yearbook for Traditional Music* 41 (2009): 23–41.

Galambos, Imre. "The Myth of the Qin Unification of Writing in Han Sources." *Acta Orientalia* 57, no. 2 (2004): 181–203. doi:10.1556/aorient.57.2004.2.2.

———. *Orthography of Early Chinese Writing: Evidence from Newly Excavated Manuscripts*. Budapest: Department of East Asian Studies, Eötvös Loránd University, 2006.

Galvany, Albert. "Debates on Mutilation: Bodily Preservation and Ideology in Early China." *Asiatische Studien* 64, no. 1 (2009): 67–91.

Ganeri, Jonardon. *Artha: Meaning*. Oxford: Oxford University Press, 2006.

Geaney, Jane. "Aural and Visual Hierarchies in Texts from Early China: Beyond *Epistemology of the Senses*." In *Mapping China's Modern Sensorium*, edited by Wu Shengqing and Huang Xuelei. Philadelphia: Routledge Press, forthcoming.

———. "Binaries in Early Chinese Texts: Locating Entities on Continuums." *International Communication of Chinese Culture* 3, no. 2 (2016): 275–292.

———. "Critique of A. C. Graham's Reconstruction of the Neo-Mohist Canons." *Journal of the American Oriental Society* 119 (1999): 1–11.

———. "Grounding 'Language' in the Senses: What the Eyes and Ears Reveal about Ming 名 (Names) in Early Chinese Texts." *Philosophy East and West* 60, no. 2 (2010): 251–293. doi:10.1353/pew.0.0097.

———. *Language as Bodily Practice in Early China: A Chinese Grammatology*. Albany: State University of New York Press, 2018.

———. "*Míng* (名) as 'Names' Rather than 'Words': Disabled Bodies Speaking without Acting in Early Chinese Texts." In *Having a Word with Angus Graham: On the First Quarter Century of His Immortality*, edited by Carine Defoort and Roger T. Ames. Albany: State University of New York Press, 2018.

———. "Movement and Míng 名": A Response to "Incongruent Names: A Theme in the History of Chinese Philosophy." *Dao: A Journal of Comparative Philosophy* 19 (2020): 635–644. doi:10.1007/s11712-020-09751-y.

———. *On the Epistemology of the Senses in Early Chinese Thought*. Honolulu: University of Hawai'i Press, 2002.

———. "Self as Container: Metaphors We Lose By in Understanding Early Chinese Texts." *Antiquorum Philosophia* 5 (2011): 11–30.

———. "The Sounds of Zhèngmíng (正名): Setting Names Straight in Early Chinese Texts." In *Ethics in Early China: An Anthology*, edited by Chris Fraser, Dan Robins, and Timothy O'Leary, 107–118. Hong Kong: Hong Kong University Press, 2011.

———. "What Is Míng 名? 'Name' Not 'Word'" In *Dao: A Companion to Chinese Philosophy of Logic*, edited by Yiu-ming Fung, 15–32. New York: Springer, 2020.

Geertz, Clifford. *The Interpretation of Cultures: Selected Essays*. New York: Basic Books, 1973.

Goffman, Erving. *Frame Analysis: An Essay on the Organization of Experience*. York, PA: Northeastern University Press, 1986.

Goldin, Paul Rakita. "*Heng Xian* and the Problem of Studying Looted Artifacts." *Dao: A Journal of Comparative Philosophy* 12 (2013): 153–160.

———. "Personal Names in Early China: A Research Note." *Journal of the American Oriental Society* 120, no. 1 (2000): 77–81. doi:10.2307/604887.

———. "Xunzi in the Light of the Guodian Manuscripts." *Early China* 25 (2000): 113–146.

Goody, Jack. "Against 'Ritual': Loosely Structured Thoughts on a Loosely Structured Topic." In *Secular Ritual*, edited by Sally Falk Moore and Barbara G. Myerhoff, 25–35. Amsterdam: Van Gorcum, 1977.

———. *The Interface between the Written and the Oral*. Cambridge: Cambridge University Press, 1987.

Gou, Dongfeng 苟东锋. 《孔子正名思想探源》 [Exploring the source of Confucius' idea of Zhengming]. 《湖南大学学报》 *Hunan daxue xuebao* 29, no. 5 (2015): 45–52.

———. 《儒家之'名'的三重内涵》 [Three connotations of Confucian Ming]. 《哲学研究》 *Zhe xue yan jiu*, 8 (2013): 42–48.

Grafflin, Dennis. "The Onomastics of Medieval South China: Patterned Naming in the Lang-Yeh and T'ai-Yüan Wang." *Journal of the American Oriental Society* 103, no. 2 (1983): 383–398. doi:10.2307/601460.

Graham, A. C. "The Background of the Mencian Theory of Human Nature." *Tsing Hua Journal of Chinese Studies* 6 (1967): 215–274.

———, trans. *Chuang-tzǔ: The Inner Chapters*. Indianapolis: Hackett, 2001.

———. *Disputers of the Tao: Philosophical Argument in Ancient China*. La Salle, IL: Open Court, 1989.

———. *Later Mohist Logic, Ethics, and Science*. Hong Kong: Chinese University Press, 1978.

———. *Studies in Chinese Philosophy and Philosophical Literature*. Albany: State University of New York Press, 1990.

———. *Yin-Yang and the Nature of Correlative Thinking*. Occasional Paper and Monograph Series no. 6. Singapore: Institute of East Asian Philosophies, 1986.

Grandy, Richard. "Reference, Meaning, and Belief." *Journal of Philosophy* 70, no. 14 (1973): 439–452. doi:10.2307/2025108.

Gu, Ming Dong. *Chinese Theories of Reading and Writing: A Route to Hermeneutics and Open Poetics*. Albany: State University of New York Press, 2005.

Günther, Susanne. "'A Language with Taste': Uses of Proverbial Sayings in Intercultural Communication." *Text & Talk: An Interdisciplinary Journal of Language, Discourse & Communication Studies* 11, no. 3 (1991): 339–418.

Hacking, Ian. *Why Does Language Matter to Philosophy?* Cambridge: Cambridge University Press, 1975.

Hall, David L., and Roger T. Ames. *Thinking from the Han: Self, Truth, and Transcendence in Chinese and Western Culture*. Albany: State University of New York Press, 1998.

———. *Thinking Through Confucius*. Albany: State University of New York Press, 1987.

Halliday, Michael A. K. *The Collected Works*. Edited by Jonathan Webster. London: Continuum, 2003.

Hanks, William F. *Language and Communicative Practices*. Boulder, CO: Westview Press, 1996.

Hansen, Chad. "Chinese Ideographs and Western Ideas." *Journal of Asian Studies* 52, no. 2 (1993): 373–399. doi:10.2307/2059652.

———. "Dao as a Naturalistic Focus." In *Ethics in Early China: An Anthology*, edited by Chris Fraser, Dan Robins, and Timothy O'Leary, 267–297. Hong Kong: University of Hong Kong Press, 2011.

———. *A Daoist Theory of Chinese Thought: A Philosophical Interpretation*. New York: Oxford University Press, 1992.

———. *Language and Logic in Ancient China*. Ann Arbor: University of Michigan Press, 1983.

———. "Language in the Heart-mind." In *Understanding the Chinese Mind: The Philosophical Roots*, edited by Robert E. Allinson, 75–124. Hong Kong: Oxford University Press, 1989.

———. "Metaphysics of Dao." In *Comparative Approaches to Chinese Philosophy*, edited by Bo Mou, 205–224. Aldershot, UK: Ashgate, 2003.

———. "Principle of Humanity vs. Principle of Charity." In *Moral Relativism and Chinese Philosophy: David Wong and His Critics*, edited by Yang Xiao and Yong Huang, 71–101. Albany: State University of New York Press, 2014.

———. "Why Chinese Thought Is Not Individualistic: Answer 1 of n." In *The Moral Status of Persons: Perspectives on Bioethics*, edited by Gerhold K. Becker, 79–94. Amsterdam: Rodopi, 2000.

Harbsmeier, Christoph. "On the Very Notion of Language and of the Chinese Language." *Histoire Épistémologie Langage* 31, no. 11 (2009): 143–161.

———. "A Reading of the Guōdiàn 郭店 Manuscript Yǒcóng 語叢 1 as a Masterpiece of Early Chinese Analytic Philosophy and Conceptual Analysis." *Studies in Logic* 4, no. 3 (2011): 3–56.

———. *Science and Civilisation in China*. Vol. 7, part 1, *Language and Logic*. Cambridge: Cambridge University Press, 1998.

Harper, Donald. "A Chinese Demonography of the Third Century B.C." *Harvard Journal of Asiatic Studies* 45, no. 2 (1985): 459–498.

———. "Communication by Design: Two Silk Manuscripts of Diagrams (*Tu*) from Mawangdui Tomb Three." In *Graphics and Text in the Production of Technical Knowledge in China: The Warp and the Weft*, edited by Francesca Bray, Vera Dorofeeva-Lichtmann, and Georges Métailié, 169–190. Leiden: Brill, 2007.

Harris, Roy. *Language, Saussure, and Wittgenstein: How to Play Games with Words*. London: Routledge, 1988.
———. *The Origin of Writing*. London: G. Duckworth, 1986.
———. *Rethinking Writing*. Bloomington: Indiana University Press, 2000.
———. *Signs of Writing*. London: Routledge, 1995.
Hawkes, David. *The Songs of the South: An Ancient Chinese Anthology of Poems by Qu Yuan and Other Poets*. London: Penguin Books, 1985.
Hayot, Eric, Haun Saussy, and Steven G. Yao. *Sinographies: Writing China*. Minneapolis: University of Minnesota Press, 2008.
He, Tian 何恬. "此山之外——20世纪70年代以来的英美孔子研究" [The study of Confucius in UK and USA since 1970s]. 《孔子研究》 *Confucius Studies* 2 (2009): 112–121.
Hendrichke, Barbara. "Dialogue Forms in the *Taiping jing* (Scripture of Great Peace)." *Journal of the American Oriental Society* 137, no. 4 (2017): 719–736.
Heng, Jiuan. "Understanding Words and Knowing Men." In *Mencius: Contexts and Interpretations*, edited by Alan Kam-leung Chan, 151–168. Honolulu: University of Hawai'i Press, 2002.
Henricks, Robert G., trans. *Lao-Tzu: Te-Tao Ching: A New Translation Based on the Recently Discovered Ma-Wang-Tui Texts*. New York: Ballantine Books, 1989.
Hightower, James Robert, trans. *Han Shi Wai Chuan: Han Ying's Illustrations of the Didactic Application of the Classic of Songs*. Cambridge, MA: Harvard University Press, 1952.
Hintikka, Jaakko. *Lingua Universalis vs. Calculus Ratiocinator: An Ultimate Presupposition of Twentieth-Century Philosophy*. Dordrecht: Springer Science and Business Media, 2013.
Hirsch, E. D., Jr. "Meaning and Significance Reinterpreted." *Critical Inquiry* 11, no. 2 (1984): 202–225.
Hogan, John T. "The ξίωσις (Greek) of Words at Thucydides 3.82.4." *Greek, Roman, and Byzantine Studies* 21 (1980): 139–149.
Hopkins, L. C., trans. *The Six Scripts; Or, the Principles of Chinese Writing by Tai Tung. A Translation by L. C. Hopkins, with a Memoir of the Translator by W. Perceval Yetts*. Cambridge: Cambridge University Press, 1954.
Hsu, Wen. "The First Step toward Phonological Analysis in Chinese: *Fanqie*." *Journal of Chinese Linguistics* 23 (1995): 137–158.
Huang, Cheng-teh James, and Yen-hui Audrey Li, eds. *New Horizons in Chinese Linguistics*. Dordrecht: Kluwer Academic, 1996.
Hunter, Michael, and Martin Kern, eds. *Confucius and the Analects Revisited: New Perspectives on Composition, Dating, and Authorship*. Leiden: Brill, 2018.
Ihde, Don. *Listening and Voice: Phenomenologies of Sound*. Albany: State University of New York Press, 2007.
Im, Manyul. "Horse-parts, White-parts, and Naming: Semantics, Ontology, and Compound Terms in the White Horse Dialogue." *Dao: A Journal of Comparative Philosophy* 6, no. 2 (2007): 167–185. doi:10.1007/s11712-007-9010-4.
———. "Rectification of Names (*zhengming* 正名)." *Manyul Im's Chinese Philosophy Blog*. http://manyulim.wordpress.com/2008/01/28/rectification-of-names-zhengming.
Ing, Michael David Kaulana. *The Dysfunction of Ritual in Early Confucianism*. New York: Oxford University Press, 2012.

Ivanhoe, P. J., and David S. Nivison. *Chinese Language, Thought, and Culture: Nivison and His Critics*. Chicago: Open Court, 1996.
Jackendoff, Ray. *Patterns in the Mind: Language and Human Nature*. New York: Basic Books, 2008.
Jameson, Fredric. *The Prison-House of Language: A Critical Account of Structuralism and Russian Formalism*. Princeton, NJ: Princeton University Press, 1972.
Jay, Martin. *Downcast Eyes: The Denigration of Vision in Twentieth-Century French Thought*. Berkeley: University of California Press, 1993.
Jia, Jinhua, and Kwok Pang-Fei. "From Clan Manners to Ethical Obligation and Righteousness: A New Interpretation of the Term *Yi* 義." *Journal of the Royal Asiatic Society* 17, no. 1 (2007): 33–42.
Johnston, Ian, trans. *The Mozi: A Complete Translation*. New York: Columbia University Press, 2010.
Jullien, Francois. *Detour and Access: Strategies of Meaning in China and Greece*. Translated by Sophie Hawkes. New York: Zone Books, 2000.
Kahrs, Eivind. *Indian Semantic Analysis: The Nirvacana Tradition*. Cambridge: Cambridge University Press, 1998.
Kaplan, David. "Comments and Criticism: Words on Words." *Journal of Philosophy* 108, no. 9 (2011): 504–529.
———. "Words." *Aristotelian Society Supplementary Volume* 64, no. 1 (1990): 93–120.
Keightley, David N. "Art, Ancestors, and the Origins of Writing in China." *Representations* 56 (1996): 68–95. doi:10.2307/2928708.
———. *These Bones Shall Rise Again: Selected Writings on Early China*. Edited by Henry Rosemont. Albany: State University of New York Press, 2014.
Keliher, Macabe. "The Manchu Transformation of Li: Ritual, Politics, and Law in the Making of Qing China, 1631–1690." PhD diss., Harvard University, 2015. ProQuest (3738854).
Kern, Martin. "Early Chinese Literature, Beginnings through Western Han." In *The Cambridge History of Chinese Literature*, edited by Kang-i Sun Chang and Stephen Owen, vol. 1, 1–115. Cambridge: Cambridge University Press, 2010. doi:10.1017/CHOL9780521855587.003.
———. "Early Chinese Poetics in the Light of Recently Excavated Manuscripts." In *Recarving the Dragon: Understanding Chinese Poetics*, edited by Olga Lomová, 27–72. Prague: Charles University–Karolinum Press, 2003.
———. "Kongzi as Author in the Han." In *Confucius and the Analects Revisited: New Perspectives on Composition, Dating, and Authorship*, edited by Michael Hunter and Martin Kern, 268–307. Leiden: Brill, 2018.
———. "The Performance of Writing in Western Zhou China." In *The Poetics of Grammar and Metaphysics of Sound and Sign*, edited by Sergio La Porta and David Shulman, 109–176. Leiden: Brill, 2007.
———. "The Poetry of Han Historiography." *Early Medieval China* 10–11, no. 1 (2004): 23–65.
———. "Speaking of Poetry: Pattern and Argument in the *Kongzi Shilun*." In *Literary Forms of Argument in Early China*, edited by Joachim Gentz and Dirk Meyer, 175–200. Leiden: Brill, 2015.
———. *Text and Ritual in Early China*. Seattle: University of Washington Press, 2005.

Kinney, Anne. *The Art of the Han Essay: Wang Fu's "Ch'ien-fu lun."* Tempe, AZ: Center for Asian Studies, Arizona State University, 1990.

Klein, Esther S. "Constancy and the Changes: A Comparative Reading of *Heng Xian*." *Dao: A Journal of Comparative Philosophy* 12, no. 2 (2013): 207–224. doi:10.1007/s11712-013-9316-3.

———. *Reading Sima Qian from Han to Song: The Father of History in Pre-Modern China.* Leiden: Brill, 2019.

———. "Were There 'Inner Chapters' in the Warring States? A New Examination of Evidence about the *Zhuangzi*." *T'oung Pao* 96, no. 4–5 (2010): 299–369.

Knoblock, John, trans. *Xunzi: A Translation and Study of the Complete Works.* 3 vols. Stanford, CA: Stanford University Press, 1988–1994.

Knoblock, John, and Jeffrey K. Riegel, trans. *The Annals of Lü Buwei: A Complete Translation and Study.* Stanford, CA: Stanford University Press, 2000.

Kober, Michael. *Deepening Our Understanding of Wittgenstein.* Amsterdam: Rodopi, 2006.

Kohn, Livia, and Michael LaFargue, eds. *Lao-tzu and the Tao-te-ching.* Albany: State University of New York Press, 1998.

Kreinath, Jens, Jan Snock, and Michael Stausberg, eds. "Ritual Studies, Ritual Theory, Theorizing Rituals—An Introductory Essay." In *Theorizing Rituals: Issues, Topics, Approaches, Concepts.* Leiden: Brill, 2006.

Krijgsman, Rens. "Traveling Sayings as Carriers of Philosophical Debate." *Asiatic Studien* 68, no. 1 (2014): 83–116.

Kristeva, Julia. *Language—The Unknown: An Initiation into Linguistics.* New York: Columbia University Press, 1989.

Ku, Mei-kao, trans. *A Chinese Mirror for Magistrates: The Hsin-yü of Lu Chia.* Faculty of Asian Studies Monographs 11. Canberra: Australian National University, 1988.

Küng, Guido. "Ingarden on Language and Ontology." In *The Later Husserl and the Idea of Phenomenology*, edited by Anna-Teresa Tymieniecka, 204–217. New York: Springer, 1972. doi:10.1007/978-94-010-2882-0_17.

Lacan, Jacques. *Ecrit: The First Complete Edition in English.* Translated by Bruce Fink. New York: W. W. Norton, 2007.

Lagerwey, John. "Wu Yüeh ch'un ch'iu 吳越春秋." In *Early Chinese Texts: A Bibliographical Guide*, edited by Michael Loewe, 473–476. Berkeley: Society for the Study of Early China; Institute of East Asian Studies, University of California, 1993.

Lam, Sandy. "詞不達意" *Ci bu da yi* [Inaccurate words]. Spotify, 2006. https://open.spotify.com/track/4arcrPMPxXrUEPqn8oFXbr.

Latour, Bruno. "How to Talk About the Body? The Normative Dimension of Science Studies." *Body & Society* 10, no. 2–3 (2004): 205–229. doi:10.1177/1357034x04042943.

———. *Politics of Nature.* Cambridge, MA: Harvard University Press, 2004.

Lau, D. C., trans. *Mencius.* New York: Penguin Books, 1970.

Lau, D. C., and Roger T. Ames, trans. *Yuan Dao: Tracing Dao to Its Source.* New York: Ballantine Books, 1998.

Lee, Benjamin. *Talking Heads: Language, Metalanguage, and the Semiotics of Subjectivity.* Durham, NC: Duke University Press, 1997.

Lee. Hur-li. *Intellectual Activism in Knowledge Organization: A Hermeneutic Study of the Seven Epitomes*. Taipei: National Taiwan University Press, 2016.

Lefevere, Andre. "Chinese and Western Thinking on Translation." In *Constructing Cultures: Essays On Literary Translation*, edited by Andre Lefevere and Susan Bassnett, 12–25. Clevedon, UK: Multilingual Matters, 1998.

Legge, James, trans. *The Ch'un Ts'ew with the Tso Chuen*. Vol. 5 of *The Chinese Classics*. London: Trübner, 1861.

———, trans. *The Li Ki*. Vol. 3 of *The Sacred Books of China: The Texts of Confucianism*. Oxford: Clarendon, 1875.

———, trans. *The She King or The Book of Ancient Poetry*. Vol. 4 of *The Chinese Classics*. London: Trübner, 1871.

Levi, Jean. "*Han fei tzu* 韓非子." In *Early Chinese Texts: A Bibliographical Guide*, edited by Michael Loewe, 115–124. Berkeley: Society for the Study of Early China; Institute of East Asian Studies, University of California, 1993.

Lewis, Mark Edward. "Ritual Origins of Warring States." *Bulletin De L'Ecole Française D'Extrême-Orient* 84, no. 1 (1997): 73–98. doi:10.3406/befeo.1997.2473.

———. *Writing and Authority in Early China*. Albany: State University of New York Press, 1999.

Li, Chenyang. "*Li* as Cultural Grammar: On the Relation between *Li* and *Ren* in Confucius' *Analects*," *Philosophy East and West* 57, no. 3 (2007): 311–329.

Li, Wai-yee. "Concepts of Authorship." In *The Oxford Handbook of Classical Chinese Literature*, edited by Wiebke Denecke, Wai-Yee Li, and Xiaofei Tian, 360–376. Oxford: Oxford University Press, 2017.

Li, Zehou. *The Chinese Aesthetic Tradition*. Translated by Maija Bell Samei. Honolulu: University of Hawai'i Press, 2010.

Liao, W. K., trans. *The Complete Works of Han Fei Tzŭ: A Classic of Chinese Legalism*. 2 vols. London: Probsthain, 1939.

Lin, Yushan. *Hanyu Yufa Xueshi* 漢語語法學史 [History of Chinese grammar studies]. Changsha: Hunanjiaoyu Chubanshi, 1983.

Link, Arthur E. "The Earliest Chinese Account of the Compilation of the Tripitaka (II)." *Journal of the American Oriental Society* 81, no. 3 (1961): 281–299.

Liu Baonan 劉寶楠. *Lunyu zhengyi* 論語正義 [*Analects* correctly explained]. Vol. 3. Taibei: Taiwan Commercial Press, 1968.

Liu, James J. Y. *Language—Paradox—Poetics: A Chinese Perspective*. Princeton, NJ: Princeton University Press, 1988.

Liu, Joanna. "Music [Yue] in Classical Confucianism." In *Confucian Ethics in Retrospect and Prospect*, edited by Vincent Shen and Kwong-loi Shun, 61–77. Washington, DC: Council for Research in Values and Philosophy, 2008.

Liu, Yucai, and Luke Habberstad. "The Life of a Text: A Brief History of the *Liji* 禮記 (Rites Records) and Its Transmission." *Journal of Chinese Literature and Culture* 1, no. 1–2 (2014): 289–308. doi: https://doi.org/10.1215/23290048-2749455.

Loy, Hui-Chieh. "*Analects* 13.3 and the Doctrine of Correcting Names." In *Confucius Now: Contemporary Encounters with the Analects*, edited by David Jones, 223–242. LaSalle, IL: Open Court, 2015.

———. "The Word and the Way in Mozi." *Philosophy Compass* 6, no. 10 (2011): 652–662. doi:10.1111/j.1747-9991.2011.00426.x.

Lung, Rachel. "Perceptions of Translating/Interpreting in First-Century China." In *Interpreting Chinese, Interpreting China*, edited by Robin Setton, 11–28. Amsterdam: John Benjamins, 2011.

Lurie, David. "Language, Writing, and Disciplinarity in the Critique of the 'Ideographic Myth': Some Proleptical Remarks." *Language and Communication* 26 (2006): 250–269.

Lynn, Richard John, trans. *The Classic of Changes: A New Translation of the I Ching as Interpreted by Wang Bi*. New York: Columbia University Press, 1994.

———. "Truth and Imagination in China: Opposition and Conciliation in the Tradition." In *Imagination: Cross-Cultural Philosophical Analyses*, edited by Hans-Georg Moeller and Andrew K. Whitehead, 13–28. New York: Bloomsbury Academic, 2019.

Mair, Victor. "What Is a Chinese 'Dialect/Topolect'? Reflections on Some Key Sino-English Linguistic Terms." *Sino-Platonic Papers* 29 (1991): 1–51.

Major, John S., Sarah Queen, Andrew Meyer, and Harold D. Roth, trans. *The Huainanzi: A Guide to the Theory and Practice of Government in Early Han China, by Liu An, King of Huainan*. New York: Columbia University Press, 2010.

Makeham, John. *Name and Actuality in Early Chinese Thought*. Albany: State University of New York Press, 1994.

Malmqvist, Göran. "Studies on the Gongyang and Guliang commentaries." *Bulletin of the Museum of Far Eastern Antiquities* 43 (1971): 67–222.

Martens, Lorna. *Shadow Lines: Austrian Literature from Freud to Kafka*. Lincoln: University of Nebraska, 1996.

Mattice, Sarah. "On 'Rectifying' Rectification: Reconsidering *Zhengming* in Light of Confucian Role Ethics." *Asian Philosophy* 20, no. 3 (2010) 247–260.

McKeon, Richard, ed. *The Basic Works of Aristotle*. New York: Random House, 1941.

McNeal, Robin. *Conquer and Govern: Early Chinese Military Texts from the Yi Zhou Shu*. Honolulu: University of Hawai'i Press, 2012

Mei, Y. P. *The Ethical and Political Works of Motse*. London: Probsthain, 1929.

Meighoo, Sean. "Derrida's Chinese Prejudice." *Cultural Critique* 68, no. 1 (2008): 163–209. doi:10.1353/cul.2008.0010.

Milburn, Olivia. "The Five Types of Name: A New Methodology for Interpreting Zhou Dynasty Naming Practices." *Chinese Studies* 24, no. 2 (2006): 397–423.

———, trans. *The Glory of Yue: An Annotated Translation of the Yuejue Shu*. Leiden: Brill, 2010.

Miller, Roy Andrew. "Shih Ming 釋名." In *Early Chinese Texts: A Bibliographical Guide*, edited by Michael Loewe, 424–428. Berkeley: Society for the Study of Early China; Institute of East Asian Studies, University of California, 1993.

Moeller, Hans Georg. "Chinese Language Philosophy and Correlativism," *Bulletin of the Museum of Far Eastern Antiquities* 72 (2000): 91–109.

———. "Chinese Theory of Forms and Names and Its Relation to a 'Philosophy of Signs.'" *Journal of Chinese Philosophy* 24, no. 2 (1997): 179–190.

———. "Zhuangzi's Fishnet Allegory: A Text-Critical Analysis." *Journal of Chinese Philosophy* 27, no. 4 (2000): 489–502. doi:10.1111/0301-8121.00028.

Mol, Annemarie. "I Eat an Apple. On Theorizing Subjectivities." *Subjectivity* 22, no. 1 (2008): 28–37. doi:10.1057/sub.2008.2.

Morgan, Daniel P. *Astral Sciences in Early Imperial China: Observation, Sagehood and Society*. Cambridge: Cambridge University Press, 2017.

Mou, Bo, ed. *Comparative Approaches to Chinese Philosophy*. Aldershot, UK: Ashgate, 2003.

———, ed. *Davidson's Philosophy and Chinese Philosophy: Constructive Engagement*. Leiden: Brill, 2006.

Munro, Donald J. *The Concept of Man in Early China*. Stanford, CA: Stanford University Press, 1969.

Nattier, Jan. *A Guide to Early Chinese Buddhist Translations: Texts from the Eastern Han* 東漢 *and Three Kingdoms* 三國 *Periods*. Tokyo: International Research Institute for Advanced Buddhology, Soka University, 2008.

Needham, Joseph. *Science and Civilisation in China*. Vol. 3. *Mathematics and the Sciences of the Heavens and the Earth*. Cambridge: Cambridge University Press, 1959.

Nivison, David S. *The Ways of Confucianism: Investigations in Chinese Philosophy*. Edited by Bryan Van Norden. Chicago: Open Court, 1996.

Nulty, Timothy J. "A Critical Response to Zhang Longxi." *Asian Philosophy* 12, no. 2 (2002): 141–146. doi:10.1080/0955236022000043874.

Nylan, Michael. "Baihu tong 白虎通." In *Encyclopedia of Confucianism*, edited by Xinzhong Yao, vol. 1, 23–24. Philadelphia: Routledge, 2013.

———, trans. *The Canon of Supreme Mystery by Yang Hsiung: A Translation with Commentary of the T'ai Hsuan Ching*. Albany: State University of New York Press, 1993.

———, trans. *Exemplary Figures: Fayan*. Seattle: University of Washington Press, 2013.

———. *The Five "Confucian" Classics*. New Haven, CT: Yale University Press, 2001.

———. "Hsin shu 新書." In *Early Chinese Texts: A Bibliographical Guide*, edited by Michael Loewe, 161–170. Berkeley: Society for the Study of Early China; Institute of East Asian Studies, University of California, 1993.

———. "Textual Authority in Pre-Han and Han." *Early China* 25 (2000): 205–258.

———. *Yang Xiong and the Pleasures of Reading and Classical Learning in China*. New Haven, CT: American Oriental Society, 2011.

Olberding, Amy. "Ascending the Hall: Demeanor and Moral Improvement in the Analects." *Philosophy East and West* 59, no. 4 (2009): 503–522.

———. "Confucius' Complaints and the Analects' Account of the Good Life." *Dao: A Journal of Comparative Philosophy* 12, no. 4 (2013): 417–440.

———. "Dreaming of the Duke of Zhou: Exemplarism and the Analects." *Journal of Chinese Philosophy* 35, no. 4 (2008): 625–639.

———. "The Educative Function of Personal Style in the Analects." *Philosophy East and West* 57, no. 3 (2007): 357–374.

Olson, David R. *The World on Paper: The Conceptual and Cognitive Implications of Writing and Reading*. Cambridge: Cambridge University Press, 1994.

O'Neill, Timothy. "Xu Shen's Scholarly Agenda: A New Interpretation of the Postface of the *Shuowen Jiezi*." *Journal of the American Oriental Society* 133, no. 3 (2013): 413–440. doi:10.7817/jameroriesoci.133.3.0413.

Owen, Stephen. "Liu Xie and the Discourse Machine." In *A Chinese Literary Mind: Culture, Creativity and Rhetoric in Wenxin Diaolong*, edited by Zong-qi Cai, 175–191. Stanford, CA: Stanford University Press, 2001.

Ownes, Wayne D. "Tao and Differance: The Existential Implications." *Journal of Chinese Philosophy* 20, no. 3 (1993): 261–277. doi:10.1111/j.1540-6253.1993.tb00175.x.

Park, So Jeong. "Musical Thought in the *Zhuangzi*: A Criticism of the Confucian Discourse on Ritual and Music." *Dao: A Journal of Comparative Philosophy* 12, no. 3 (2013): 331–350.

Peirce, Charles Sanders. *The New Elements of Mathematics by Charles S. Peirce*. Edited by Carolyn Eisele. 4 vols. The Hague: Mouton, 1976.

Peterson, Willard J. "Making Connections: 'Commentary on the Attached Verbalizations' of the *Book of Change*." *Harvard Journal of Asiatic Studies* 42, no. 1 (1982): 67–116.

Peyraube, Alain. "Recent Issues in Chinese Historical Syntax." In *New Horizons in Chinese Linguistics*, edited by James C. T. Huang and Yen-hui Audrey Li, 161–214. Dordrecht: Kluwer Academic, 1996.

Picken, Laurence. "The Shapes of the *Shi Jing* Song-texts and their Musical Implications." *Musica Asiatica* 1 (1977): 85–109.

Pines, Yuri. "Dating of a Pre-imperial Text: The Case Study of the Book of Lord Shang." *Early China* 39 (2016): 145–184. doi:10.1017/eac.2016.3.

———. "Disputers of the *Li*: Breakthroughs in the Concept of Ritual in Preimperial China." *Asia Major* 13, no. 1 (2000): 1–41.

———. "Lexical Changes in Zhanguo Texts." *Journal of the American Oriental Society* 122, no. 4 (2002): 691–705. doi:10.2307/3217610.

Plaks, Andrew. "Before the Emergence of Desire." In *Keywords in Chinese Culture: Thought and Literature*, edited by Wai-yee Li and Yuri Pines, 317–334. Hong Kong: Chinese University of Hong Kong Press, 2019.

Platvoet, Jan. "Ritual: Religious and Secular." In *Theorizing Rituals: Issues, Topics, Approaches, Concepts*, edited by Jens Kreinath, Jan Snock, and Michael Stausberg, 161–205. Leiden: Brill, 2006.

Powers, Martin. *Pattern and Person: Ornament, Society, and Self in Classical China*. Cambridge, MA: Harvard University Asia Center, 2006.

Queen, Sarah, and John S. Major, eds. *Luxuriant Gems of the Spring and Autumn: Attributed to Dong Zhongshu*. New York: Columbia University Press, 2016.

Raphals, Lisa Ann. *Knowing Words: Wisdom and Cunning in the Classical Traditions of China and Greece*. Ithaca, NY: Cornell University Press, 1992.

———. *Sharing the Light: Representations of Women and Virtue in Early China*. Albany: State University of New York Press, 1998.

Reddy, Michael. "The Conduit Metaphor—A Case of Frame Conflict in Our Language about Language." In *Metaphor and Thought*, edited by Andrew Ortney, 284–310. Cambridge: Cambridge University Press, 1979.

Richey, Jeffrey. "Ascetics and Aesthetics in the Analects." *Numen* 47, no. 2 (2000): 161–174.

Richter, Matthias L. *The Embodied Text: Establishing Textual Identity in Early Chinese Manuscripts*. Leiden: Brill, 2013.

———. "Suggestions Concerning the Transcription of Chinese Manuscript Texts—A Research Note." *International Research on Bamboo and Silk Documents: Newsletter* 國

際簡帛研究通訊 3, no. 1 (March 2003): 1–12. http://www.bamboosilk.org/admin3/html/Matthias%20Richter01.htm

Rickett, W. Allyn. *Guanzi: Political, Economic, and Philosophical Essays from Early China: A Study and Translation*. 2 vols. Princeton, NJ: Princeton University Press, 1985–1997.

Riegel, Jeffrey. "*Li chi* 禮記." In *Early Chinese Texts: A Bibliographical Guide*, edited by Michael Loewe. 293–307. Berkeley: Society for the Study of Early China; Institute of East Asian Studies, University of California, 1993.

———. "*Ta Tai Li chi* 大戴禮記." In *Early Chinese Texts: A Bibliographical Guide*, edited by Michael Loewe. 456–459. Berkeley: Society for the Study of Early China; Institute of East Asian Studies, University of California, 1993.

Robinet, Isabelle. "Later Commentaries: Textual Polysemy and Syncretistic Interpretations." In *Lao-tzu and the Tao-te-ching*, edited by Livia Kohn and Michael LaFargue, 119–142. Albany: State University of New York Press, 1998.

Robins, Dan. "The Debate over Human Nature in Warring States China." PhD diss., University of Hong Kong, 2001.

———. "The Later Mohists and Logic," *History and Philosophy of Logic* 31, no. 3 (2010): 247–285.

———. "Names, Cranes, and the Later Moists." *Journal of Chinese Philosophy* 39, no. 3 (2012): 369–385. doi:10.1111/j.1540-6253.2012.01728.x.

———. "The Warring States Concept of 'Xing." *Dao: A Journal of Comparative Philosophy* 10, no. 1 (2011): 31–51. doi:10.1007/s11712-010-9197-7.

———. "Xunzi." In *Stanford Encyclopedia of Philosophy*, edited by Edward N. Zalta. Spring 2014 ed. https://plato.stanford.edu/archives/spr2014/entries/xunzi/.

Rosemont, Henry, and Roger T. Ames. *The Chinese Classic of Family Reverence: A Philosophical Translation of the "Xiaojing."* Honolulu: University of Hawai'i Press, 2009.

———. "Were the Early Confucians Virtuous?" In *Ethics in Early China: An Anthology*, edited by Chris Fraser, Dan Robins, and Timothy O'Leary, 17–39. Hong Kong: University of Hong Kong Press, 2011.

Rošker, Jana S. *Searching for the Way: Theory of Knowledge in Premodern and Modern China*. Hong Kong: Chinese University Press, 2008.

———. *The Yields of Transition: Literature, Art, and Philosophy in Early Medieval China*. Newcastle upon Tyne, UK: Cambridge Scholars, 2011.

Roth, Harold David. "*Chuang tzu* 莊子." In *Early Chinese Texts: A Bibliographical Guide*, edited by Michael Loewe, 56–57. Berkeley: Society for the Study of Early China; Institute of East Asian Studies, University of California, 1993.

Roth, Harold David, and A. C. Graham. *A Companion to Angus C. Graham's Chuang Tzu: The Inner Chapters*. Honolulu: University of Hawai'i Press, 2003.

Sagart, Laurent. *The Roots of Old Chinese*. Amsterdam: John Benjamins, 1999.

Sanft, Charles Theodore. "Rule: A Study of Jia Yi's *Xin shu*." PhD diss., University of Münster (Westphalia), 2005.

Sato, Masayuki. *The Confucian Quest for Order: The Origin and Formation of the Political Thought of Xunzi*. Leiden: Brill, 2003.

Saussure, Ferdinand de. *Course in General Linguistics*. Translated by Wade Baskin. London: Fontana Collins, 1974.

Saussy, Haun. *Great Walls of Discourse and Other Adventures in Cultural China*. Cambridge, MA: Harvard University Asia Center, 2001.

———. "The Prestige of Writing: *Wen*, Letter, Picture, Image, Ideography." *Sino-Platonic Papers* 75 (1997): 1–40.

———. *The Problem of a Chinese Aesthetic*. Stanford, CA: Stanford University Press, 1993.

Sawyer, Ralph D., and Mei-chün Sawyer, trans. *The Seven Military Classics of Ancient China*. Boulder, CO: Westview Press, 1993.

Schaberg, David. "*Classics (jing* 經)." In *The Oxford Handbook of Classical Chinese Literature*, edited by Wiebke Denecke, Wai-Yee Li, and Xiaofei Tian, 170–183. Oxford: Oxford University Press, 2017.

———. *Patterned Past: Form and Thought in Early Chinese Historiography*. Cambridge, MA: Harvard University Asia Center, 2001.

———. "Song and the Historical Imagination in Early China." *Harvard Journal of Asiatic Studies* 59, no. 2 (1999): 305–361. doi:10.2307/2652717.

Scharf, Peter. "Early Indian Grammarians on Speaker's Intention." *JAOS* 115, no. 1 (1995): 66–76.

Schuessler, Axel. *ABC Etymological Dictionary of Old Chinese*. Honolulu: University of Hawai'i Press, 2007.

Schuessler, Alex, and Michael Loewe. "*Yueh Jueh Shu* 越絕書." In *Early Chinese Texts: A Bibliographical Guide*, edited by Michael Loewe, 490–493. Berkeley: Society for the Study of Early China; Institute of East Asian Studies, University of California, 1993.

Schwartz, Benjamin I. *The World of Thought in Ancient China*. Cambridge, MA: Belknap Press of Harvard University Press, 1985.

Schwermann, Christian, and Raji C. Steineck, eds. *That Wonderful Composite Called Author: Authorship in East Asian Literatures from the Beginnings to the Seventeenth Century*. Leiden: Brill, 2014.

Schwitzgebel, Eric. "Zhuangzi's Attitude Toward Language." In *Essays on Skepticism, Relativism and Ethics in the Zhuangzi*, edited by Paul Kjellberg and P. J. Ivanhoe, 68–96. Albany: State University of New York Press, 1996.

Seargeant, Philip. "The Historical Ontology of Language." *Language Sciences* 32 (2010): 1–13.

Severi, Carlo. "Language." In *Theorizing Rituals: Issues, Topics, Approaches, Concepts*, edited by Jens Kreinath, Jan Snoek and Michael Stausberg, 583–593. Leiden: Brill, 2006.

Shankman, Steven, and Stephen W. Durrant. *Early China/Ancient Greece: Thinking through Comparisons*. Albany: State University of New York Press, 2002.

Shaughnessy, Edward L. *I Ching: The Classic of Changes*. New York: Ballantine Books, 1997.

———. *Unearthing the Changes: Recently Discovered Manuscripts of the "Yi Jing" ("I Ching") and Related Texts*. New York: Columbia University Press, 2014.

———. "The Writing of the *Xici Zhuan* and the Making of the *Yijing*." In *Measuring Historical Heat: Event, Performance, and Impact in China and the West*. Heidelberg: Symposium in Honour of Rudolf G. Wagner on His 60th Birthday, 2001. http://www.sino.uni-heidelberg.de/conf/symposium2.pdf.

Shepherd, Robert J. "Perpetual Unease or Being at Ease?—Derrida, Daoism, and the 'Metaphysics of Presence.'" *Philosophy East and West* 57, no. 2 (2007): 227–243. doi:10.1353/pew.2007.0025.

Shun, Kwong-Loi. *Mencius and Early Chinese Thought*. Stanford, CA: Stanford University Press, 1997.
Simon, G., J. Cléro, S. Wolfson, B. Cassin, S. Laugier, A. Libera, and G. Spinosa. "Sense/Meaning." In *Dictionary of Untranslatables*, edited by B. Cassin, E. Apter, J. Lezra, and M. Wood, 949–966. Princeton, NJ: Princeton University Press, 2013.
Skorupski, John. *Symbol and Theory: A Philosophical Study of Theories of Religion in Social Anthropology*. Cambridge: Cambridge University Press, 1976.
Slingerland, Edward Gilman. *Confucius Analects: With Selections from Traditional Commentaries*. Indianapolis: Hackett, 2003.
Staal, Fritz. "The Meaninglessness of Ritual." *Numen* 26 (1979): 2–22.
Stampe, Dennis. "Toward a Grammar of Meaning." *Philosophical Review* 77, no. 2 (1968): 137–174.
Sterckx, Roel. *The Animal and the Daemon*. Albany: State University of New York Press, 2002.
———. "The Economics of Religion in Warring States and Early Imperial China." In *Early Chinese Religion: Part One: Shang through Han (1250 BC–220 AD)*, edited by John Lagerwey and Mark Kalinowski, 839–880. Leiden: Brill, 2009.
———. "Transforming the Beasts: Animal and Music in Early China." *T'oung Pao* 86, Fasc. 1/3 (2000): 1–46.
Stjernfelt, Frederik. "Diagrams as Centerpiece of a Peircean Epistemology." *Transactions of the Charles S. Peirce Society* 36, no. 3 (2000): 57–384.
Stout, Jeffrey. "What Is the Meaning of a Text?" *New Literary History* 14 (1982): 1–12.
Svensson Ekstrom, Martin. "Illusion, Lie, and Metaphor: The Paradox of Divergence in Early Chinese Poetics." *Poetics Today* 23, no. 2 (2002): 251–289. doi:10.1215/03335372-23-2-251.
Syrotinski, Michael. "Idea." In *Dictionary of Untranslatables*, edited by B. Cassin, E. Apter, J. Lezra, and M. Wood. Princeton, NJ: Princeton University Press, 2013.
Tang, Junyi. *Zhongguo Zhexue Yuanlun* 中國哲學原論: *Yuandao Pian Juan 1* 原道篇卷一 [On the origins of Chinese philosophy: The origin of the Dao, vol. 1]. Taipei: Xuesheng Shuju, 1986.
Tang, Zaixi. "Metaphors of Translation." *Perspectives: Studies in Translatology* 14, no. 1 (2006): 40–54.
Tavor, Ori. "Xunzi's Theory of Ritual Revisited: Reading Ritual as Corporal Technology." *Dao: A Journal of Comparative Philosophy* 12 (2013): 313–330.
Teboul, Michel. "The Enumeration Structure of 爾雅 *Erya*'s Semantic Lists." In *Texts, Textual Acts, and the History of Science*, edited by Karine Chemla and Jacques Virbel, 267–278. Cham, Switzerland: Springer, 2015.
Tjan, Tjoe Som. *Bo Hu Tong: The Comprehensive Discussions in the White Tiger Hall*. 2 vols. Leiden: Brill, 1949–1952.
Tsien, Tsuen-hsuin. "*Chan kuo ts'e* 戰國策." In *Early Chinese Texts: A Bibliographical Guide*, edited by Michael Loewe, 1–11. Berkeley: Society for the Study of Early China and Institute of East Asian Studies, University of California, 1993.
Turner, Victor. *The Forest of Symbols: Aspects of Ndembu Ritual*. Ithaca, NY: Cornell University Press, 1967.

van Gulik, R. H. *Siddham: An Essay on the History of Sanskrit Studies in China and Japan.* Sarasvati-Vihara Series, vol. 36. Nagpur: International Academy of Indian Culture, 1956.

Van Norden, Bryan. *Confucius and the Analects: New Essays.* Oxford: Oxford University Press, 2002.

———. *Virtue Ethics and Consequentialism in Early Chinese Philosophy.* New York: Cambridge University Press, 2007.

Van Zoeren, Steven. *Poetry and Personality: Reading, Exegesis, and Hermeneutics in Traditional China.* Stanford, CA: Stanford University Press, 1991.

Vankeerberghen, Griet. "Rulership and Kinship: The *Shangshu dazhuan*'s Discourse on Lords." *Oriens Extremus* 46 (2007): 84–100.

Vermeer, Hans. *Skizzen Zu Einer Geschichte Der Translation.* Frankfurt: Iko-Verlag für Interkulturelle Kommunikation, 1992.

Vervoorn, Aat. "Music and the Rise of Literary Theory in Ancient China." *Journal of Oriental Studies* 43, no. 1 (1996): 50–69.

Volosinov, V. N. *Marxism and the Philosophy of Language.* Translated by Ladislav Matejka and I. R. Titunik. Cambridge, MA: Harvard University Press, 1986.

Von Rosthorn, A. "The *Erh-ya* and Other Synonymicons." *Journal of the Chinese Language Teachers Association* 10, no. 3 (1975): 137–145.

Wagner, Rudolf G. *A Chinese Reading of the "Daodejing": Wang Bi's Commentary on the "Laozi" with Critical Text and Translation.* Albany: State University of New York Press, 2003.

———. *The Craft of a Chinese Commentator: Wang Bi on the "Laozi."* Albany: State University of New York Press, 2000.

———. *Language, Ontology, and Political Philosophy in China: Wang Bi's Scholarly Exploration of the Dark (Xuanxue).* Albany: State University of New York Press, 2003.

Waley, Arthur, trans. *The Book of Songs.* New York: Grove Press, 1996.

———. *The Way and Its Power.* Boston: Houghton, 1935.

Walton, Kendall. "Listening with Imagination: Is Music Representational?" In *Musical Worlds: New Directions in the Philosophy of Music*, edited by Philip Alperson, 47–62. University Park: Pennsylvania State University Press, 1998.

Wang, Aihe. *Cosmology and Political Culture in Early China.* Cambridge: Cambridge University Press, 2000.

Wang, Huaiyu. "The Way of the Heart: Mencius' Understanding of Justice." *Philosophy East and West* 59, no. 3 (2009): 317–363.

Wang, Rongbao. *Fayan yishu* 法言義疏 [Meaning and subcommentary on the *Fayan*]. Beijing: Zhonghua shuju, 1987.

Wang Tingxian (王廷賢). *Wenyan xiuci xinlun* 文言修辞新论 [A new discussion of rhetoric in literary Chinese]. Gansu: Gansu Renmin Chubanshe, 2005.

Wang, William S.-Y., and Chaofen Sun. *The Oxford Handbook of Chinese Linguistics.* Oxford: Oxford University Press, 2015.

Wang, Youru. *Linguistic Strategies in Daoist Zhuangzi and Chan Buddhism: The Other Way of Speaking.* London: RoutledgeCurzon, 2003.

Wang, Youxuan. *Buddhism and Deconstruction.* Richmond, UK: Curzon, 2001.

Watson, Burton, trans. *Hsün Tzu: Basic Writings.* New York: Columbia University Press, 1963.

Weingarten, Oliver. "The Sage as Teacher and Source of Knowledge: Editorial Strategies and Formulaic Utterances in Confucius Dialogues." *Asiatische Studien* 68, no. 4 (2014): 1175–1223.

Wertsch, James V. *Mind as Action*. New York: Oxford University Press, 1998.

———. *Voices of the Mind: A Sociocultural Approach to Mediated Action*. Cambridge, MA: Harvard University Press, 1991.

———. *Vygotsky and the Social Formation of Mind*. Cambridge, MA: Harvard University Press, 1985.

Wheatley, Jon. "Names." *Analysis* 25 (1965): 73–85. doi:10.2307/3326720.

Wilhelm, Richard, and Cary F. Baynes. *The I Ching; Or, Book of Changes*. Princeton, NJ: Princeton University Press, 1967.

Wilkinson, Endymion Porter. *Chinese History: A Manual*. Cambridge, MA: Harvard University Asia Center for the Harvard-Yenching Institute, 1998.

Wilson, John. "'The Customary Meanings of Words Were Changed,' or Were They?" *The Classical Quarterly* 2, no. 1 (1982): 18–20.

Wong, David. "Response to Hansen." In *Moral Relativism and Chinese Philosophy: David Wong and His Critics*, edited by Yang Xiao and Yong Huang, 215–240. Albany: State University of New York Press, 2014.

———. "Review of *A Daoist Theory of Chinese Thought: A Philosophical Interpretation*, by Chad Hansen." *Journal of Asian Studies* 57, no. 3 (1998): 824–825.

Wong, Peter Yih-Jiun. "The Music of Ritual Practice—An Interpretation." *Sophia* 51 (2012): 243–255.

Wu, Tsaiyi. "Chinese Thing-Metaphor: Translating Material Qualities to Spiritual Ideals." *Philosophy East and West* 70, no. 2 (2020): 522–542.

Xiao, Yang. "How Confucius Does Things with Words: Two Hermeneutic Paradigms in the Analects and Its Exegeses." *Journal of Asian Studies* 66, no. 2 (2007): 497–532. doi:10.1017/s0021911807000897.

———. "The Pragmatic Turn Articulating Communicative Practice in the *Analects*." *Oriens Extremus* 45 (2005/6): 236–254.

———. "Reading the *Analects* with Donald Davidson: Mood, Force, and Communicative Practice in Early China." In *Davidson's Philosophy and Chinese Philosophy: Constructive Engagement*, edited by Bo Mou, 247–268. Leiden: Brill, 2006.

Xiao, Yang, and Yong Huang, eds. *Moral Relativism and Chinese Philosophy: David Wong and His Critics*. Albany: State University of New York Press, 2014.

Yates, Robin D. S. *Five Lost Classics: Tao, Huang-Lao, and Yin-Yang in Han China*. New York: Ballantine Books, 1997.

———. "The Yin-Yang Texts from Yinqueshan," *Early China* 19 (1994): 75–144.

Yau, Shun-chiu. "Temporal Order in the Composition of Archaic Chinese Ideograms." *Journal of Chinese Linguistics* 11, no. 2 (1983): 187–213.

Yearley, Lee. "Daoist Presentation and Persuasion: Wandering among Zhuangzi's Kinds of Language." *Journal of Religious Ethics* 3, no. 3 (2005): 503–535.

Yeh, Michelle. "The Deconstructive Way: A Comparative Study of Derrida and Chuang Tzu." *Journal of Chinese Philosophy* 10, no. 2 (1983): 95–126. doi:10.1111/j.1540-6253.1983.tb00276.x.

Zadrapa, Lukas. "Structural Metaphor at the Heart of Untranslatability in Ancient Chinese and Ancient Chinese Texts: A Preliminary Study of the Case of the Lexical Field of 'Norm.'" *Acta Universitatis Carolinae Philologica* 4 (2017): 11–50.

Zhang, Hanmo. *Authorship and Text-Making in Early China*. Boston: De Gruyter, 2018.

Zhang, Longxi. *The Tao and the Logos: Literary Hermeneutics, East and West*. Durham, NC: Duke University Press, 1992.

Index

Page numbers in bold refer to Appendix C: A Glossary of Terms.

accessibility/inaccessibility
  of *yi* 義, 137, 148–154, 196, 203, 206
  of *yi* 意, 52, 110, 123, 137, 143, 144, 196
  See also externality; externality of *yi* 義; visibility
actants, 17
actions/acting. See *shi* 實; *xing* 行
affairs. See *shi* 事
Aikhenvald, Alexandra Y., 23n7
aims. See *zhi* 志
Allen, Joseph R., 6n22
Ames, Roger, 199n1, 200
appropriateness. See *yi* 宜
archaizing scripts, 158–159
artha (word-meaning), 156–157
aspiration. See *zhi* 志
audient ones. See *sheng* 聖人
authors/writers, 142, 145–146, 152

Baihu tong 白虎通 (Ban Gu)
  ming 名 in, 227
  on style-names, 133n18
  yan 言 in, 29
  yi 義 associated with death/dying, 85n3
  yi 義 as different in, 130–131
  yi 義 vs. *en* 恩 in, 77
  yi 義 as model for justifying in, 171–173
  yi 義 as one in, 130
  yi 義 as physical models in, 175–180
  yi 義 of X formula in, 107n4, 108
  yi 義 and yin-yang in, 161–164
Ban Biao, 150
Ban Gu. See *Baihu tong* 白虎通; *Hanshu* 漢書
Ban Zhao. See *Hanshu* 漢書

Bao Zhiming, 11n42
benzhi 本旨, 153n24
bi 彼, 212, 216–217
binaries
  externality of *yi* 義 and, 88–100
  hearing-seeing, 98–99, 219–220
  heaven-earth, 89–92, 93, 95, 96, 113–114
  inside-outside, 145–146
  same-different, 127–131
  soft-hard, 89–92
  sound-vision, 92–100
  yin-yang, 88–89, 92, 94–95, 113–114, 161–164, 204
Boltz, William, 5n17, 7n27, 15, 96n29, 200
Boodberg, Peter, 70n7, 199–200
Bottéro, Françoise, 4n12, 158n34, 182–183nn3–6, 183, 186n16
Boucher, Daniel, 6n25, 155, 191n27
Buddhist texts, 6, 155–157, 195
burial times, 149

Cai Yong. See *Zhonglang Ji* 蔡中郎集
Cai Zongqi, 47n3, 70n5
calculations. See *shu* 數
Cang Jie, 157–158
ceremonies. See *yi* 儀
cha 察, 152–153, **219–221**
Chan, Alan, 36n10, 69n3, 207n2, 208n5, 216n22
change. See *qing* 情
Chao, Yuan Ren, 7
Chen, Guying, 123n6
Chinese language
  as bodily phenomena, 33
  Buddhist influences on, 155, 157

Chinese language (*continued*)
  immersed language model and, 11–15
  language conception in, 2–3
  puns to explain meaning of two different terms in, 13, 15
  stylistic patterns in, 17
Chinese scripts, 158–159
Chuci 楚辭, 59–60, 189–190
Chunqiu Fanlu 春秋繁露
  cha 察 in, 221
  fa 法 in, 205n28
  shi 事 in, 231–232
  yan 言 in, 29–30
Chunqiu Gongyangzhuan 春秋公羊傳
  shi 實 in, 32n36
  yi 義 vs. *ren* 仁 in, 79, 85n3
  on *yi* 義 in *Yili* 儀禮, 138n2
Chunqiu Guliangzhuan 春秋穀梁傳
  yi 義 as model for justifying in, 168–171
  yi 義 vs. *ren* 仁 in, 74, 76–77
  yi 義 of X formula in, 107
  yiyi 意義 in, 139–141
Chunqiu Zuozhuan 春秋左傳, 140–141. See also *Zuozhuan* 春秋左傳
ci 此, 140–141, 212, 216–217
ci 詞, 221, 223. See also *ci* 辭
ci 辭, **221–224**
  externality of, 39
  linguistic measurements and, 13, 27–28, 31
  ming 名 and, 44
  shi 事 and, 221–222
  yan 言 and, 222–223
  yi 意 and, 39, 44, 48–49, 61n33
close-up/intimacy. See *qin* 親
compass. See *yi* 意
comprehensiveness. See *weixiang* 未詳
conduct/behavior. See *xing* 行
cong 從 X formula, 183, 189, 190, 196
conjecture. See *yi* 意
counting. See *shu* 數

da 達, 23–24, 138n3, 148, 151n20, 237
Dadai Liji 大戴禮記
  shi 事 in, 232
  yan 言 in, 238
  yan 言 and *ming* 名 in, 36–37

dang 當, 173n18, 175, 188
dayi 大義, 148–149, 153–154, 203n17
de 德, 97, 132–135
deeds. See *shi* 事; *shi* 實
deliberate/consider. See *lü* 慮
depth
  of *yi* 義, 149–150
  of *yi* 意, 143–144
Dharmaraksa, 155–156
diagramming, 115–116, 119
dictionaries
  in general, 3, 4
  in China, 3n12, 5–6 (see also *Erya Yinyi* 爾雅音義; *Fangyan* 方言; *Shuowen Jiezi* 說文解字)
  in Mesopotamia, 4
ding 定, 36
discerning. See *cha* 察
disposition. See *xing* 性
Dixon, R. M. W., 23n7
Dongguan Hanji 東觀漢記, 154n25
dredging. See *shu* 抒
duties. See *yi* 義
dyadic structures, 204

ears
  cha 察 and, 220–221
  si 思 and *lü* 慮 and, 53–55, 65
  yi 意 and, 33, 58, 60, 65
en 恩, 74–75, 77, 178
Erya Yinyi 爾雅音義 (Sun Yan), 1n1, 5
examining. See *cha* 察
explaining/explanations. See *shuo* 說
externality
  of *ci* 辭, 39
  of *ming* 名, 33–35, 37–39, 46
  objectivity and, 207n1
  of *ren* 仁, 70
  of *yan* 言, 39
  of *yi* 義 (see externality of *yi* 義)
  See also internality
externality of *yi* 義, 69–81, 83–101
  in general, 67, 69–70, 80–81, 83, 100–101, 150, 202n12
  binaries and, 88–100
  external standards vs. internal equalizing, 78–80
  family intimacy and, 75–78

Mengzi 孟子 on, 207–213
Mozi 墨子 on, 213–217
pervasiveness of, 70–78
in self-cultivation and politics, 83–88
territory and, 71–73
traveling and, 73–75
See also accessibility/inaccessibility
eyes
cha 察 and, 220
pupils of, 152–153
si 思 and lü 慮 and, 53–55, 65
yi 意 and, 58, 60, 65

fa 法
in general, 113
translations equivalents of, 51n12
yi 義's interchangeability with, 176–178, 205n28, 206
See also fayi 法儀/法義
faces. See yan 顏
family intimacy, externality of yi 義 and, 75–78
fan 梵, 191–192
Fangyan 方言 (Yang Xiong), 5–6
Fayan yishu 法言義疏 (Wang Rongbao), 221n3
Fayan 法言 (Yang Xiong)
"body of a text" metaphor in, 151n20
ci 辭 in, 221
guan 觀 in, 225
"listen" to the past in, 195
ren 仁-yi 義 as soft-hard in, 90
yan 言 in, 8n31, 239
yi 意 in, 143
fayi 法儀/法義, 110
"figurative" language, 125–127
"Five Activities," 176–180
fix/fixing. See ding 定
focusing attention. See si 思
fruits. See shi 實
function words, use of ming 名 and, 24–25
Fung Yu-Lan, 192n30

Ganeri, Jonardon, 156
Gaozi (spokesperson in Mengzi 孟子), 69n3, 207–213, 217
Geertz, Clifford, 205
gender, yin-yang binary and, 89n11, 92n24

glosses, in Shuowen Jiezi, 182–193
Gongduzi (spokesperson in Mengzi 孟子), 211–212, 217
Grafflin, Dennis, 14n52
Graham, A. C., 16, 25n15, 47n2, 61n33, 66nn42–44
graphs
models and, 193
pronunciation of, 4, 26, 31
as word equivalents, 181n2
See also zi 字
grouping. See lei 類
Gu, Ming Dong, 201–202
gua 卦, 115–116, 119. See also hexagrams
guan 官, 2, 53n17
guan 觀, **224–225**
Guanzi 管子
on audient ones, 100n40
cha 察 in, 220
externality of yi 義 in, 84–87
lü 慮 and xin 心 in, 55n24
on naming, 32
ren 仁-yi 義 as heaven-earth in, 95
shi 事 in, 231
wu 物 in, 235
yan 言 in, 236
yi 義's externality in, 71, 72
yi 義, profitable to pursue, 216n19
yi 義 vs. ren 仁 in, 83–87
yi 意 and yan 言 in, 38–39, 242
yi 意/yin 音 in, 242n23
Günther, Susanne, 163n3
Guoyu 國語
cha 察 in, 220
ming 名 in, 227
wu 物 in, 234
yan 言 and ming 名 in, 35
yi 義 in, 96–97

Habberstad, Luke, 42n26
Hall, David, 199n1, 200–201n6
Hanfei. See Hanfeizi 韓非子
Hanfeizi 韓非子 (Hanfei)
on audient ones, 100n40
guan 觀 in, 224
ming 名 in, 34, 228–229
shi 事 in, 231
yan 言 and xin 心 in, 240

Hanfeizi 韓非子 (Hanfei) *(continued)*
  yi 義 and *li* 禮 in, 97
  yi 義 and *yi* 宜 in, 199–200n2
  yi 意 in, 142
  yi 意 and *xiang* 想 and *xiang* 象 in, 61, 63, 64–65
  yu 語 in, 31n33
Hansen, Chad, 10n37, 28n24, 40n23, 48n4
Hanshi Waizhuan 韓詩外傳
  guan 觀 in, 225
  yan 言 in, 237
  yi 義 vs. *ren* 仁 in, 80
Hanshu 漢書 (Ban Gu)
  on the *Tai* 泰, 126–127
  wen 文 in, 26
  wenyi 文義 in, 150n18
  yi 義 in, 164–165
  yi 義 as model for justifying in, 175–176
  yi 義 vs. *ren* 仁 in, 77, 98n34
  yi 義 as yang in, 204
  yi 意 in, 61n33
  yi 意 and *yan* 言 in, 241
Harbsmeier, Christoph, 11n42, 13n47, 158n34, 182–183nn3–6, 183, 186n16
harmony. See *he* 和
hating, 79–80
he 和, 91n21, 98
hearing-seeing binary, 98–99, 219–220
heartmind. See *xin* 心
heaven-earth binary, 89–90, 93, 95, 96, 113–114
Heguanzi 鶡冠子
  yi 義 as model in, 111–112
  yi 義 vs. *ren* 仁 in, 79, 97–98, 217
  yi 意 and *shu* 抒 in, 50
Hendrichke, Barbara, 138n4
"Heng Xian" 《恒先》, 37, 230–231, 239
hexagrams, 112, 114–116, 117–119, 126–127, 157–158, 166, 205
hidden *yi* 意, 141–148. See also visibility
Hirsh, E. D., 201
A History of Chinese Philosophy (Fung), 192n30
Hsu Wen, 1n1
Huainanzi, *zhi* 知 and *lü* 慮 in, 53
Huainanzi 淮南子
  ci 辭 and *shi* 事 in, 222
  ci 辭 and *shu* 抒 in, 50
  guan 觀 in, 225
  interchangeability of *shi* 事 with *shi* 實 in, 230
  ming 名 in, 25
  qu 取 in, 215n17
  shu 抒 in, 49
  wu 物 in, 234
  yan 言 in, 238
  yi 義 as one in, 128–129
  yi 義 as two in, 131
  on *yi* 義 in *Zhouyi*, 106–107, 114
  yi 意 in, 57n28, 142
  zhi 知 and *lü* 慮 in, 53
human body
  coherence of, 176–178
  cultivation of, 84–87

I. See *wo* 我; *yu* 予
ideas, concept of, 47–48
Ihde, Don, 4
indexicals, 23
inside-outside binary, 145–146
intentions. See *yi* 意
interchangeability
  of *shi* 事 with *shi* 實, 230
  of *yi* 義 with *fa* 法, 176–178, 205n28, 206
  of *yi* 義 with *yi* 儀, 110
  of *yi* 義 with *yi* 意, 137–139
interlocking parallel style (IPS), 17n62
internality
  of *ren* 仁, 84–85, 91
  of *yan* 言, 33–35, 46
  of *yi* 意, 48–50
  See also externality
intimacy/close-up. See *qin* 親
Iyer, Subramania, 156n31

Jia, Jinhua, 70n7
Jia Yi. See *Xin Shu* 新書

Kahrs, Eivind, 156n31
Kern, Martin, 145n12
killing, 79–80, 85n3
kindness. See *en* 恩; *ren* 仁
"knowers," 98–99

knowing. See *zhi* 智; *zhi* 知
Kongcongzi 孔叢子, 163n2
Kongzi
  on speech, 122
  on writing, 123
  writing of, 145, 146
  on *yan* 言, 28
  on *yi* 意, 57–58
Kongzi Jiayu 孔子家語, 228
Ku Mei-kao, 95n27
Kwok Pang-Fei, 70n7

language models
  abstract, 10–11
  engaged, 9–10, 11–12
  immersed, 9–10, 11–15
language(s)
  Chinese. *See* Chinese language
  conception, 2–3
  "figurative," 125–127
  models. *See* language models
  reality and, 12
  Sanskrit, 155n28, 156–157
  Sumer/Akkad, 4–5
leaving. See *qu* 去
lei 類, 23–24, 132, 133
Li Daoyuan. *See Shuijing Zhu* 水經注
li 利, 214–216
li 禮
  women and, 131
  xin 心 of, 174
  yi 義 and, 72, 75, 93, 95n27, 96, 97, 211, 213n11
  See also *liyi* 禮義
Liezi 列子, 228
life. See *sheng* 生
Liji 禮記
  ming 名 in, 226–227
  on naming taboos, 14n52
  ren 仁-*yi* 義 as sound-vision in, 93–94, 213n11
  si 思 in, 52n16
  xiang 象 in, 6n24, 63
  yan 言 in, 236–237
  yi 義's externality in, 72
  yi 義 in, large vs. small, 149
  yi 義 as model for justifying in, 175

yi 義 as one in, 129, 130
yi 義, profitable to pursue, 216n20
yi 義 vs. *ren* 仁 in, 74–75
yi 義 of X formula in, 108n5
yi 意 vs. *zhi* 知, 65
zhiyi 志義 in, 41–42
Lin Yushan, 12n45
linguistic measurements
  ci 辭 and, 13, 27–28, 31
  ming 名 and, 13
  wen 文 and, 26, 30
  yan 言 and, 8, 13, 28–31
  zi 字 and, 26, 30
Liu Xi, 200
Liu Xiang. *See Shuoyuan* 說苑
Liu Xie, 47n3
Liu Yi 六義 (Six Writing Models), 124
Liu Yucai, 42n26
"Liude" 《六德》, 74, 75
liushu 六書 ("six writings"), 186–187
liyi 禮義, 76, 97
Loewe, Michael, 88n8
longing/yearning. See *si* 思
Lu Ji, 47n3
lü 慮, 52–56, 65
lu 旅, 188–189
lu 鑢, 188–189
lun 論, 30, 49
Lunheng 論衡 (Wang Chung)
  cha 察 in, 219
  ci 辭 in, 31, 221n2, 222, 223
  "figurative" phrases in, 125–126
  length and style of, 151–152
  shi 實 in, 233
  wenzi 文字 in, 27
  xiang 象 in, 63, 64
  yan 言 in, 8n32, 30, 237
  yi 義 in, 165n7
  yi 義, accessible, in, 148–154
  yi 義 as model for justifying in, 173–175
  yi 義 of names in, 131–134
  yi 義 and *qian* 淺 in, 150
  yi 義 as two in, 128n10
  yi 意 associated with foreknowledge in, 60
  yi 意 associated with senses in, 52

Lunheng 論衡 (Wang Chung) *(continued)*
   yi 意, hidden, in, 144–148
   yi 意 and *yan* 言 in, 241
   on *zhangju* 章句, 154n25
   zhiyi 志義 in, 42
Lunyu 論語
   guan 觀 in, 224
   ming 名 and *yan* 言 in, 38
   yan 言 in, 27–28, 237, 238
   yi 意 and *xin* 心 in, 57
Lüshi Chunqiu 呂氏春秋
   ci 辭 and *yan* 言 in, 222
   ming 名 in, 33–34, 228, 229
   qi 氣 and *zhi* 志 in, 49n5
   shi 實 in, 232–233
   yan 言 and *xin* 心 in, 240
   yi 義's externality in, 73
   yi 義, profitable to pursue, 216n18
   yi 意 and *ci* 辭 in, 39
   yi 意 as conjecture in, 59
   yi 意, hidden, in, 142
   yi 意 vs. knowing in, 65
   yi 意 and *xiang* 想 in, 62
   yi 意 and *yan* 言 in, 39, 239–240

Mao Heng, 124n8
Mao Shi 毛詩. See *Shijing* 詩經
materiality, 17, 203–204
matters. See *shi* 事
meaning
   in general, 11
   use of term, 1–2
   See also word-meaning; *yi* 義
measurement, linguistic. See linguistic measurements
Mengzi 孟子
   cha 察 in, 219
   si 思 and *xin* 心 in, 53, 55
   yan 言 in, 237, 238
   on *yi* 義 as external, 207–213
   yi 義 as one in, 129
   yi 義 vs. *ren* 仁 in, 73–74
mental activity
   of *si* 思 and *lü* 慮, 52–56
   of *yi* 意, 56–60
Mesopotamia, 4
min meng 民萌, 40

ming 名, **226–230**
   in general, 3, 5, 7–8, 21
   actions and, 26
   applications of, 32
   ci 辭 and, 44
   externality of, 33–35, 37–39, 46
   lexical terms, function words, grammar and, 24–26
   linguistic measurements and, 13
   particulars vs. groups and, 23–24
   puns involving, 15
   shi 實 and, 12–13, 32n36, 44–45
   as sociological word, 9
   suoyi 所以 and, 45
   taboos in speaking and, 14
   yan 言 and, 32–38, 230
   yi 意 and, 39–45
   Zheng Xuan on, 9n34, 32
   See also *mingci* 名辭
ming 鳴, 15
mingci 名辭, 43
Mo Bian 墨辯 (Mohist Canons)
   in general, 23n9
   ming 名 in, 23–24, 229
   qin 親 in, 225n11
   tripartite division of argument in, 40n23, 43, 49
   on *yi* 義 as external, 213–217
   yi 意 in, 51
   yi 意 and *ci* 辭 in, 45, 49
   yi 意 vs. knowing in, 66
   yi 意 and *ming* 名 in, 40n23, 43
   yi 意 and *shu* 抒 in, 50
   See also *Mozi* 墨子
models
   graphs and, 193
   six writing, 124
   use of term, 109, 110
   yi 義 as. See *yi* 義 as model
   yi 儀 as, 111, 112–113
   See also *fa* 法; language models
morality. See *yi* 義
Morgan, Daniel Patrick, 162n2, 205n31
movements. See *xing* 行
Mozi 墨子
   books 40–45 of. See *Mo Bian* 墨辯
   qin 親 in, 225n11

silü 思慮 in, 53–54
xing 行 in, 236
yan 言 in, 238
yi 義, profitable to pursue, 216n21
yi 義, single, in, 138–139n4
yi 儀 as model in, 111
yi 意 and yan 言 in, 242
"Mu He" 〈〈繆和〉〉, 78, 115, 119
Munro, Donald, 15
music, ren 仁 and, 93–94, 95n27

names/naming
  in general, 32
  differences between words and, 21–23
  nouns and, 25
  taboos in speaking, 14
  use of term, 23
  See also ming 名; shi 謚
Nattier, Jan, 155n26, 155n28
nature. See xing 性
Needham, Joseph, 163n2
non-glottal writing, 7, 121–123
nouns
  words and, 25
  See also ming 名
Nylan, Michael, 6n21, 17n63, 145n12, 221n3

objectives. See yi 義
objectivity, externality and, 207n1
observe. See guan 觀

peace. See he 和
Peirce, Charles Sanders, 204
phrasing/phrases. See ci 詞; ci 辭
point/pointing. See zhi 指; zhi 旨
posthumous titles. See shi 謚
potency. See de 德
Powers, Martin, 51n12
power/virtue. See de 德
predictions, 59–60, 167
procedure. See fa 法
proclaiming. See yu 語
profit. See li 利; yi 義
pronunciation, of graphs, 4, 26, 31
properties. See yi 義

proverbs
  functions of, 163n3
  on yi 意, 136–137
puns, to explain meaning of two different terms, 13, 15
purpose. See yi 意; yi 義

qi 氣, 13, 49n5
Qianfu Lun 潛夫論 (Wang Fu), 206
qin 親, 75, 225–226n11
qing 情, 49–50, 56n26, 80, 86, 144, 145, 227
qu 去, 87
qu 取, 132, 215

reaching. See da 達
reality, language and, 12
reasons. See yi 義
reference. See shi 實; yi 義; zhi 指
ren 仁
  death/dying and, 79–80, 85n3
  externality of, 70
  internality of, 84–85, 91
  music and, 93–94, 95n27
  vs. yi 義, 73–80, 83–85, 214, 217
  vs. yi 義, as soft-hard, 89–92
  vs. yi 義, as sound-vision, 92–100
reputations, 86. See also ming 名
ritual actions/rites. See li 禮
Rosemont, Henry, 200
ru 如, 171n13

Saddharmapundarikasutra, 155
sages, 58, 64–65, 98–99, 123, 147, 158, 193, 196
  See also sheng 聖人
same-different binary, 127–131
sameness of yi 義. See tongyi 同義
Saṅghabhadra, 157n31
Sanskrit, 155n28, 156–157
Saussure, Ferdinand de, 10n38, 204
Scharf, Peter, 156n31
Schuessler, Alex, 88n8
scripts, Chinese, 158–159
senses. See guan 官
services. See shi 事

Index / 273

Shangjun Shu 商君書
   on audient ones, 100n40
   yi 義 in, 215
Shangshu Dazhuan 尚書大傳, 149n16
sheng 生, 62, 86
sheng 聖人, 58n31, 98–100
sheng 聲, 86
shi 事, **226–230**
   ci 辭 and, 221–222
   shi 實's interchangeability with, 230
shi 實, **232–233**
   ming 名 and, 12–13, 32n36, 44–45
   shi 事's interchangeability with, 230
   translations equivalents of, 26n17
   wen 文 and, 32n36
   yan 言 and, 32n36
   zi 字 and, 32n36
shi 謎, 29, 30, 227
Shiji 史記
   lü 慮 and *xin* 心 in, 54
   si 思 and *yi* 意 in, 53n16
   yan 言 in, 29
   yi 義 in, 153
   yi 意 in, 143
Shijing 詩經
   Baihu tong 白虎通 on, 177–178
   Hanshu 漢書 on, 126
   Huainanzi 淮南子 on, 107, 114
   Lunheng 論衡 on, 125
   Lunyu 論語 on, 28
   on six writing models, 124
Shiming 釋名
   in general, 2
   yi 義 in, 200
   yi 意 and *yan* 言 in, 240–241
shu 抒, 49–50, 61n33
shu 書, 32n36, 186n16
shu 舒, 49n6
shu 術, 60
shu 數, 60, 149, 164
Shuijing Zhu 水經注 (Li Daoyuan), 124
Shujing 書經
   Baihu tong 白虎通 on, 107n4
   Hanshu 漢書 on, 175
   Huainanzi 淮南子 on, 107, 114
   Lunheng 論衡 on, 125
"Shun Dao" 〈〈順道〉〉, 220

"Shuo Gua" 說卦, 89n11
shuo 說, 45, 49, 143
Shuowen Jiezi 說文解字 (Xu Shen)
   in general, 1, 2–3
   archaizing script in, 158–159
   Buddhist influences on, 155, 157
   ci 詞 and *yan* 言 in, 223
   compiling of, 181
   fan 梵 in, 191–192
   myth about origin of writing in, 157–159
   pronunciation of graphs in, 4, 26, 31
   structure of glosses in, 182–183
   tong 同 and *yi* 義 in, 184
   tong 同 and *yi* 意 in, 184
   word-meaning and, 159, 181, 206
   xie 些 in, 189–191
   yi 義 in, 137, 157–159, 181, 183–184, 187–193
   yi 意 in, 137, 157–159, 181, 182, 183–184, 186–187, 192–193
   yi-function in glosses in, 182–193
   zhiyi 之義 in, 185
   zhiyi 之意 in, 185
Shuoyuan 說苑 (Liu Xiang), 49–50, 57–58, 237
si 思, 52–56, 65
sight. See *yi* 儀
significance. See *yi* 義
Simafa 司馬法, 78
similarities. See *tong* 同
Six Writing Models (*Liu Yi* 六義), 124
"six writings" (*liushu* 六書), 186–187
skills. See *shu* 術
sociological words, 7–8
soft-hard binary, 89–92
sorting. See *lun* 論
sound element, in *Shuowen Jiezi* glosses, 182–183
sound-vision binary, 92–100
speculation. See *yi* 意
speech. See *yan* 言
Stampe, Dennis, 11n41
standards. See *fa* 法
Stout, Jeffrey, 1–2
style-names, 133–134
Suishu 隋書, 162n2
suitability. See *dang* 當

Sumer/Akkad language, 4–5
Sun Yan. See *Erya Yinyi* 爾雅音義
suo 所, 45, 216–217
suoyi 所以, 45
synonymicons, 5
Syrotinski, Michael, 48n4

taboos, in speaking names, 14
Tai 泰, 117, 126–127
Taiping Jing 太平經, 138–139n4, 139n6
Taixuan Jing 太玄經 (Yang Xiong), 26, 143–144, 224
taking. See *qu* 取
"Tang Yu Zhi Dao" 〈〈唐虞之道〉〉, 76
Taniguchi, Hiroshi, 145n12
Teboul, Michel, 5n19
techniques. See *shu* 術
territory, externality of *yi* 義 and, 71–73
texts
  analysis of, 16–17 (see also *zhangju* 章句)
  body of, 150–152
  Buddhist, 6, 155–157, 195
that by which. See *suoyi* 所以
that which. See *suo* 所
that/there. See *bi* 彼
things. See *wu* 物
think/thinking. See *xiang* 想
this/here. See *ci* 此
titles. See *ming* 名
tones. See *yin* 音
tong 同, 184
tongyi 同義, 125–126, 133, 134, 184, 188
tongyi 同意, 184, 187
translation equivalents of *yi* 意
  compass and, 51
  conjecture, 58–59
  dredging and, 61n33
  intentions, 186–187
  purpose, 163n4
  speculation/guessing, 58n29
translation equivalents of *yi* 義
  in general, 199–202
  meaning of human existence, 201n7
  model (see *yi* 義 as model)
  morality, 69n1
  reason/objective, 161, 162–164

  significance, 117–118, 201
  word-meaning, 1, 134–135, 200
translations
  of Buddhist texts, 6, 155–157, 195
  of *yi* 義 (see translation equivalents of *yi* 義)
  of *yi* 意 (see translation equivalents of *yi* 意)
traveling, externality of *yi* 義 and, 73–75
triadic structures, 204
"Tuan" 〈〈彖〉〉, 92n24, 166

Van Zoeren, Steven, 202n14
Vashubhandu II, 157n31
violence, 79–80, 85n3
visibility
  in myth about origin of writing, 158
  of *shi* 事, 230
  of *yan* 言, 123n6
  of *yi* 義, 107–108, 111, 121–123
  See also accessibility/inaccessibility; hidden *yi* 意

Wagner, Rudolf, 17n62
Waley, Arthur, 207n1
walk/walking. See *xing* 行
Wang Bi, 192n30, 201–202
Wang Chung. See *Lunheng* 論衡
Wang Fu, *Qianfu Lun* 潛夫論
Wang Rongbao, 221n3
Wang Youxuan, 156–157n31
weixiang 未詳, 189–190, 191
weixiangyiyi 未詳意義, 191–192
wen 文
  linguistic measurements and, 26, 30
  shi 實 and, 32n36
  yi 義 and (see *wenyi* 文義)
Wenxin Diaolong 文心雕龍, 9n33
"Wenyan" 文言, 72, 211n10, 215
wenyi 文義, 150
Wenzi 文子, 58n31, 98–99, 220
wenzi 文字, 27
wo 我, 134–135
women, 89n11, 131
word-meaning
  in general, 3–6, 17, 23n7, 193
  in Buddhist traditions, 156–157

word-meaning (continued)
  Shuowen Jiezi and, 159, 181, 206
  yi 義 as, 1, 134–135, 200 (see also yi 義)
  yisi 意思 and, 47
word-pattern analysis, 16–17
words
  differences between names and, 21–23
  sociological, 7–9
  use of term, 2–3, 23
  See also ming 名; zi 字
writers/authors, 142, 145–146, 152
writing(s)
  body of, 150–152
  conceptions on, 7
  hexagrams and, 157–159
  myth about origin of, 157–159
  speech and, 151–152
  "Xici" 《繫辭》 on, 121–122
  yi 義 of, 148, 152–153
  yi 意 and, 144–148
Wu, Tsaiyi, 204n27
Wu Yue Chunqiu 吳越春秋, 130
wu 物, 24n11, **233–235**
"Wuxing" 《五行》, 90, 91n19, 98
wuxing 五行, 176–180

xiang 想, 61–62
xiang 詳, 189–190
"Xiang" 《象》, 166–167
xiang 象
  in Liji 禮記, 6n24
  sounds and, 63–64
  translations equivalents of, 61n34
  xiang 想 and, 62
  yi 義 and, 122–123, 162–163n2, 204
  yi 儀 and, 162n2
  yi 意 and, 60–65
Xiaojing 孝經, 96
"Xici Shang" 《繫辭上》, 38
"Xici" 《繫辭》
  on speech, 122–123
  on writing, 121–122
  yi 儀 as model in, 112–114
xie 些, 189–191
Xin Shu 新書 (Jia Yi), 40–41, 228
xin 心
  as earthly ruler, 91–92

of li 禮, 174
si 思 and lü 慮 with, 52–56
yan 言 and, 35, 240
vs. yi 義, 78
yi 意 and, 38, 52, 56–60, 139n4, 143–145
"Xing Zi Ming Chu" 《性自命出》
  wu 物 in, 233–234
  yi 義 in, 80
  yi 義 vs. ren 仁 in, 79
xing 行, 26, 93, 99, 176, 211n10, **235–236**
xing 性, 37, 85n3, 209, 211n9
Xinyu 新語
  ren 仁-yi 義 as yin-yang in, 95
  yi 義 and li 禮 in, 95n27
  yi 義 vs. ren 仁 in, 76
Xu Gan. See Zhonglun 中論
Xu Kai, 200
Xu Shen. See Shuowen Jiezi 說文解字
Xun Kuang. See Xunzi 荀子
Xunzi 荀子 (Xun Kuang)
  ci 辭 in, 223
  liyi 禮義 and de 德 in, 97
  lü 慮 and xin 心 in, 55–56
  on names, 14–15
  tripartite division of argument in, 43–44, 223
  wu 物 in, 234–235
  xiang 象 in, 64
  on xin 心, 91–92
  yan 言 in, 237
  yi 義 in, 106, 129, 163–164
  yi 義 vs. ren 仁 in, 74, 79
  yi 意 in, 56
  yi 意 and ci 辭 in, 48–49
  yi 意 and ming 名 in, 41, 43–44

yan 言, **236–242**
  ci 辭 and, 222–223
  externality of, 39
  guan 觀 and, 224–225
  internality of, 33–35
  linguistic measurements and, 8, 13, 28–31
  ming 名 and, 32–38, 230
  physiological trajectory of, 34–38
  shi 實 and, 32n36

shi 諡 and, 29
as sociological word, 7–9
visibility of, 123n6
writing and, 151–152
"Xici" 〈〈繫辭〉〉 on, 122–123
xin 心 and, 35, 240
yi 義 and, 29–30
yi 意 and, 33, 35, 37, 38–39, 239–241
zhi 志 and, 122
yan 顏, 217
Yang Xiong. See *Fangyan* 方言; *Fayan* 法言; *Taixuan Jing* 太玄經
Yantie Lun 鹽鐵論
 ci 辭 in, 222
 on sages and heaven, 99
 shi 實 in, 232
 yi 義 as one in, 130
 yi 義 vs. *ren* 仁 in, 74
Yanzi Chunqiu 晏子春秋, 72
yi yan 一言, 2
"Yi Zhi Yi" 〈〈易之義〉〉
 on *ren* 仁-*yi* 義, 89–91
 on *yi* 義, 106, 113–115
Yi Zhou Shu 逸周書
 he 和-*yi* 義 as soft-hard in, 91n21
 yi 義 as earth in, 96
 yi 義's externality in, 71
 yiqi 義氣 in, 203n22
Yi 易, 106, 107n4, 113, 115–116
yi 宜, 30, 69n1, 122, 199–201
yi 枍, 27
yi 義
 in general, 1, 2
 accessibility of, 137, 148–154, 196, 203, 206
 binaries and, 88–100 (see also yin-yang binary (below))
 de 德 and, 132–135
 death/dying and, 85n3
 depth and, 149–150
 as diagrammed, 115–116, 119
 empty, 206n35
 vs. *en* 恩, 74–75, 77, 178
 externality of (see externality of *yi* 義)
 fa 法 and (see *fayi* 法儀/法義)
 fa 法's interchangeability with, 176–178, 205n28, 206
 great (*dayi* 大義), 148–149, 153–154, 203n17
 heaven and, 125–126
 li 禮 and, 72, 75, 93, 95n27, 96, 97, 211, 214n11 (see also *liyi* 禮義)
 materiality of, 17, 203–204
 as model (see *yi* 義 as model)
 normativity of, 17, 69, 105–106, 115, 201
 patterning and, 79–80
 for/of people, 117–119
 profitable to pursue, 214–216
 qian 淺 and (see *yiqian* 義淺)
 vs. *ren* 仁, 73–80, 83–85, 214, 217
 vs. *ren* 仁, as soft-hard, 89–92
 vs. *ren* 仁, as sound-vision, 92–100
 sameness of, 125–127
 in *Shuowen Jiezi*, 137, 157–159, 181, 183–184, 187–193, 195, 196–197
 single, 130, 138–139n4, 179
 six writing models and, 124
 small, 148–149
 of texts/writing, 148, 152–154
 tong 同 and (see *tongyi* 同義)
 translation of (see translation equivalents of *yi* 義)
 visibility of, 107–108, 111, 121–123
 wen 文 and (see *wenyi* 文義)
 wuxing 五行 and, 176–180
 of X formula (see *yi* 義 of X formula)
 xiang 象 and, 122–123, 162–163n2, 204
 vs. *xin* 心, 78
 yan 言 and, 29–30
 yi 儀 and, 199–200, 202–203
 yi 儀's interchangeability with, 110
 yi 意 and, 42–43 (see also *yiyi* 意義)
 yi 意 and, differences between, 154, 202
 yi 意's interchangeability with, 137–139
 yin-yang binary and, 89, 92n24, 161–164, 204
 zhi 之 and (see *zhiyi* 之義)
 zhi 志 and (see *zhiyi* 志義)
yi 義 as model
 in general, 202–203
 binaries and, 112–115
 diagramming and, 115–116
 dyadic structures and, 204

yi 義 as model (continued)
  for explaining, 161–164
  "figurative" phrases and, 125–127
  instructional function of, 205–206
  for justifying, 164–176
  as material model, 109–112
  of names, 131–135
  non-glottal writing and, 121–123
  of/for people and, 117–119
  physical, 175–180
  of same, different or one, 127–131, 138–139n4
  for types of writing, 124, 153
  yi-function and, 187–189
yi 義 of X formula, 105–112
  in general, 105–109
  common translation of yi 義 in, 105
  as model, 109–112
yi 儀
  fa 法 and (see fayi 法儀/法義)
  as model, 111, 112–113
  as sight, 205
  xiang 象 and, 162n2
  yi 義 and, 199–200, 202–203
  yi 義's interchangeability with, 110
yi 意
  in general, 48
  archaizing script and, 159
  ci 辭 and, 39, 44, 48–49, 61n33
  creativity and, 47–48
  depth and, 143–144
  ears and, 33, 58, 60
  eyes and, 58, 60
  hidden, in general, 123, 141–144
  hidden, in Lunheng 論衡, 141–148
  inaccessibility of, 52, 110, 123, 137, 143, 144, 196
  internality of, 48–50
  knowing, in absence of, 56–60
  ming 名 and, 39–45
  as perceptible, 50–52
  predictions and, 59–60
  proverb on, 136–137
  shu 抒 and, 50
  in Shuowen Jiezi, 137, 157–159, 181, 182, 183–184, 186–187, 192–193
  of texts, 143, 144–147, 154
  tong 同 and (see tongyi 同意)
  translation of (see translation equivalents of yi 意)
  xiang 想 and, 61–62
  xiang 象 and, 60–65
  xin 心 and, 38, 52, 56–60, 139n4, 143–145
  yan 言 and, 33, 35, 37, 38–39, 239–241
  yi 義 and, 42–43 (see also yiyi 意義)
  yi 義 and, differences between, 154, 202
  yi 義's interchangeability with, 137–139
  zhi 之 and (see zhiyi 之意)
  zhi 志 and, 51–52, 67 (see also zhiyi 志意)
  vs. zhi 知, 65–67
  zhi 致 and, 57
yi-function in Shuowen Jiezi, 183–192
  in general, 183–184
  similarity/sameness and, 184, 187–189
  tongyi 同意/tongyi 同義 in, 184, 187
  yi 義 in, 181, 183–184, 187–189, 193, 195
  yi 義 in, deficient, 189–192
  yi 義 in, as model and, 187–189, 196–197
  yi 意 in, 181, 182, 183–184, 192–193
  yi 意 in, as intentions, 186–187
  zhiyi 之意/zhiyi 之義 in, 185
Yijing literature, 112, 165–176
Yili 儀禮, 9n34, 136–137
yin 音, 242n23
yin-yang binary, 88–89, 92, 94–95, 113–114, 161–164, 204
"The Yin-Yang Texts from Yinqueshan," 89n11
yiqi 義氣, 203n22
yiqian 義淺, 150
yiran 義然, 107–108
yiweixiang 義未詳, 189–190, 192
yiyi 意義, 67, 137–141
yizhi 義旨, 150
yizhi 義指, 150
Yu Yue, 95n27
yu 予, 134–135
yu 語, 31n33
yu 諭, 49
"Yuan Dao" 〈〈道原〉〉, 220

"Yucong Yi" 《語叢一》, 73, 76
Yuejue Shu 越絕書, 73, 87–88

Zadrapa, Lukas, 202–203
zhangju 章句, 153–154nn24–25
"Zhao Li" 《昭力》, 117–118, 125
Zheng Xuan, 9, 32
zhi 旨, 195–196. See also *benzhi* 本旨; *yizhi* 義旨
zhi 志
  as aspiration, 36n10
  Lüshi Chunqiu 呂氏春秋 on, 49n5
  yan 言 and, 122
  yi 意 and, 51–52, 67 (see also *Hanshu* 漢書)
zhi 知
  lü 慮 and, 53–54
  vs. *yi* 意, 65–67
  (See also *zhizhe* 知者)
zhi 指, 146, 195–196. See also *yizhi* 義指
zhi 致, 57
zhi 智, 59n31, 66
zhiyi 之義, 184, 202–203nn16–17
zhiyi 之意, 184
zhiyi 志義, 41–43
zhiyi 志意, 43
zhizhe 知者, 59n31
Zhonglang Ji 蔡中郎集, 153n24
Zhonglun 中論 (Xu Gan), 154n25
Zhoubi Suanjing 周髀算經, 99
Zhouyi 周易
  commentaries on (see "Mu He" 《繆和》; "Tuan" 《彖》; "Wenyan" 文言; "Xiang" 《象》; "Xici Shang" 《繫辭上》; "Xici" 《繫辭》; "Yi Zhi Yi" 《易之義》; "Zhao Li" 《昭力》)

xin 心 vs. *yi* 義 in, 78
yan 言 in, 241
yan 言 and *yi* 意 in, 38
yi 義 as diagrammed in, 115–116
yi 義 as model in, 113–115
yi 義 for/of people in, 117–118
yi 義 of X formula in, 106–107, 108–109
yi 儀 as model in, 112–113
yin-yang binary in, 92n24
Zhuangzi 莊子
  ming 名 in, 229
  silü 思慮 in, 54, 55n25
  wu 物 in, 233
  yi 義 vs. *ren* 仁 in, 75
  yi 意 and *xin* 心 in, 56–57
  yi 意 and *yan* 言 in, 39, 239
  yiran 義然 in, 107–108
zi 字
  in general, 3–4
  as graph, 8
  linguistic measurements and, 26, 30
  ming 名 or, 9
  shi 實 and, 32n36
  as source of style-names, 133
Zuo Qiuming, 143, 158. See also *Zuozhuan* 春秋左傳
Zuozhuan 春秋左傳 (Zuo Qiuming)
  li 利 in, 214–215
  li 禮 and *yi* 義 in, 96
  on naming taboos, 14n52
  on speech's limitations, 122
  wu 物 in, 234
  yan 言 in, 236
  yan 言 and *ming* 名 in, 36
  yi 義 of names in, 132
  yin-yang binary in, 89n11

www.ingramcontent.com/pod-product-compliance
Ingram Content Group UK Ltd.
Pitfield, Milton Keynes, MK11 3LW, UK
UKHW050540150426
5217IPUK00026B/2005